Lead, Kindly Light

What we now need to discover in the social realm is the moral equivalent of war: something heroic that will speak to men as universally as war does, and yet will be as compatible with their spiritual selves as war has proved itself to be incompatible.

WILLIAM JAMES: *The Varieties of Religious Experience*, Lecture XV

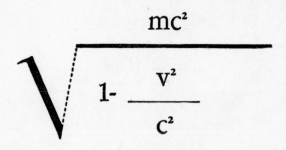

$$\sqrt{1-\dfrac{mc^2}{\dfrac{v^2}{c^2}}}$$

EINSTEIN: *Relativity*

Hast any philosophy in thee, shepherd?
As You Like It, III, ii

Lead, Kindly Light

VINCENT SHEEAN

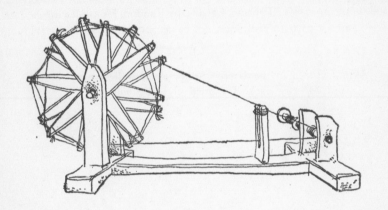

RANDOM HOUSE

New York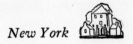

First Printing

Manufactured in the United States of America by H. Wolff, New York. Designed by Marshall Lee.

Note and Acknowledgment

The title of this book derives from that of Mahatma Gandhi's favorite Christian hymn.

Sanskrit words, where they must be used, are spelled phonetically, without diacritical marks. Gandhi is occasionally called Gandhiji or Mahatmaji, in Indian fashion; the suffix "ji" is perhaps a little more respectful than the English "Mr." English rough-and-ready usage, as adopted in the nineteenth century, spells one important word "Brahmin" when it refers to human beings of the highest caste, or the name of that caste; the same word becomes "Brahman" when it refers to the essence of godhead. The difference does not exist in Sanskrit but as a convenience for Western readers it is now established. "Muslim" is the way in which the word Moslem is both spelled and pronounced in India, although nowhere else in the world, and "Muslim" it therefore is in this book.

Quotations from Plato are in the Jowett translation; from the Upanishads (in general) from the Yeats-Purohit translation; from the *Isha Upanishad*, in Aurobindo's translation.

For those who wish to go farther in the unfamiliar regions of Hinduism which lie behind the life work of Gandhi, additional material is provided under the name of "Another Part of the Forest," under the general headings of *Caste, Karma and Darshan, The Gita and the Gandhi-Gita* and *The Forerunners of Gandhi*. These sections give details which, on a subject which to many readers must be wholly new, might only confuse and impede the main text of the book.

The author acknowledges with thanks the permission from Shri Aurobindo to quote freely from his works; also the aid of

vii

Professor S. Radhakrishnan of All Souls, Oxford, who has contributed not only from his published work but also in private correspondence to clear up some questions. Acknowledgment is also made to Professor A. N. Whitehead and his publishers, The Macmillan Co., for permission to quote from *Science and the Modern World*, Copyright, 1925, by The Macmillan Co.; and to Mrs. W. B. Yeats, Shree Purohit Swami and Faber and Faber for permission to quote from *The Ten Principal Upanishads*, Copyright, 1937, by Shree Purohit Swami and W. B. Yeats. Used by permission of The Macmillan Co.

Contents

I

On Setting Forth

.... *"Volgi gli occhi in giue:*
buon ti sarà, per tranquillar la via,
veder lo letto delle piante tue."

(Virgil speaks to Dante, halfway up the hill of Pur-
gatory: "Turn your eyes downward; it will be good for
you, to tranquilize your way, to see the imprint of your
own footsteps.")
Purgatorio, XII, *13*

On Setting Forth

The life of the Western world has given each of its children a sense of external power which is in many respects delusive. For not only is such power beyond the capacity of most men to use wisely, but it has a way of slipping from the grasp when it is most needed. Above all, even when it can be used, its most resplendent successes fail to satisfy an inner requirement of which mankind has been conscious through all the ages, that which demands of life in at least some of its aspects and some of its moments that it be true, that it be good and that it be beautiful. When we survey the ruin we have made of half the world, we cannot feel peace within, and, as we look to the path before us, we are chilled by the thought that there may be no peace ahead. Behind us there are long vistas of struggle and aspiration, with occasional attainments we shall not soon forget, but in order to "tranquilize our way," as the poet says, we must look far back. The recent past does not encourage peace of mind.

Our society and the nation-states which express it now appear to be divided into two inimical or at least opposing groups, in which the material organization of men's efforts is taken to be the

determinant of destiny—all we know and all we need to know.
For a good many years I have doubted this view of life; I now
reject it altogether. How long it would have taken me to do so if
I had not gone to India in the winter of '47-'48 is a question I cannot
answer, but in point of fact it makes no difference: I did go and
I did, I think, learn something. In this book I am attempting to
state, in a manner which is necessarily compounded partly of explanation and partly of narrative, what it was I think I learned.
It was a decisive journey and would have been decisive even without those events which made it for me supremely memorable. For
I had come to the end of my tether in the West: after long years
of a struggle against the tribal ideas bound up in the word Fascism
—first as a writer and then in the army, but as some kind of com-
batant throughout—it seemed to me that the result was likely to
be still another disaster: withered were the garlands of the war.
In India, and specifically in Mahatma Gandhi, I hoped to find
some clue to a different view of reality, something in which the
relentless opposition of material forces need not endlessly and
forever lead to ruin.

This journey had been, so to speak, impending, had been hanging over my head, for quite a while. I had been afraid of India
for some years and more particularly afraid of Gandhi. It seemed
to me that I had already discerned, in my one short visit there in
1944, and even before that by means of reading, some hint of a
power which it was in my nature to distrust. I had relied upon
reason and evidence too much, unwilling to see that much that
happens in life is extremely unreasonable; and I had thought
myself soundly grounded in a rationalistic view from which I
could never depart. According to this scheme of thought and
action those things for which I could not find ready explanation in the sciences were to be explained at some later date by
further advances in science. In other words, life was the sum of its
conditions plus—perhaps—some other element or elements which
science would eventually analyze and describe when men grew
wiser. At some periods during the past twenty years I have been
quite near to the illusion of Condorcet, under which the perfectibility of mankind is seen to be without end, and progress
consists in learning more and ever more to that purpose. Most
important of all the arrangements of life, as it seemed under this

view—and as it still seems for a large area of experience—was the social and economic system. I do not believe that I ever thought the social and economic system was the end-all and be-all; but certainly it weighed heavily on my mind in the twenties and thirties. An inclination toward speculative inquiry kept me from going overboard in that respect, as it preserved me from orthodoxies in general; as the years passed I read more philosophy and (conceivably) understood it better; but the armature of a child of the century, born in a materialist society in the age of scientific supremacy, was not easily penetrated. We absorb the assumptions of the time and place almost without knowing it, and find ourselves equipped with weapons we have never bought. It takes years to learn how to throw them all away and go, defenseless and undefending, toward whatever the truth may be.

In the relations of war and peace, a conclusive failure had been that of the United Nations. I had gone to San Francisco in the spring of 1945, like hundreds of other people, in high hope, and had been almost immediately soaked in the cold shower of disillusionment. The opening days of the conference which brought the United Nations into being were themselves a key to all that was to follow. Then, as the ensuing two years and a half brought every weakness into the open and emphasized it anew, the fact appeared to be that this attempt to regulate the dangerous interaction of rivalries between nation-states was either insincere (i.e., not intended to succeed) or hopelessly inept, or possibly a combination of both: it was a clamorous reverberant stage for the exaggeration of differences, not for their settlement. And the ghost that stalked the corridors was, through all this time, atomic energy: the triumph of mathematics or of the Upanishads (it matters little which you say) but in any case not of the humane instincts which forever try to mitigate the devastation brought by strife.

This was the general situation from which I was, in a very real sense, a fugitive when I went to India. In the head-on collision of the materialist societies there seemed little to be foreseen except destruction. This could not (so an obstinate instinct asserts in all of us) be the only sense or meaning of existence. There must be something else. In the world we know, only one culture remains even today outside the main currents of materialism and preserves within itself the living current of a more ancient belief: that is the culture of India. In spite of poverty, disease and illiteracy, material conditions as bad as any to be found anywhere, and an unhappiness that almost exudes from the people, there was some force in India which contradicted the overbearing assumptions of our technological societies. This I knew from 1944. I knew very little else—it was a matter of instinct or intuition more than of knowledge—and it startles me now to reflect how little I had read of India's past even a year ago: but there was enough to suggest that I might seek and find, not solutions, of course (who would be so bold in 1948?), but a hint, a clue, an indication. What specific hope I had in this regard centered about the figure of Mahatma Gandhi, in whose long, rectilinear life, compact with discipline and logic, I felt the manifestation of an older force than that of electromagnetics.

It seems to me that by the interweaving of events, the power of Gandhi's personality and some influences which are part of the intellectual climate of India, I did receive some such hint. To make it plain what that was, I shall have to take the reader with me on the same kind of journey I have experienced—not only, that is, in space, to another country with a very different set of tools for living, but also in time, to older notions than those which obtain among us. This has required considerable help, in my own case, from reading: experience alone might have been (at times was) inexplicable, and only by search through the books was it possible to set the events which took place under my eyes in their correct relations. Gandhi himself, for example, was not an isolated phenomenon; he did not spring fully armed from the head of Jove. Centuries of Hinduism produced him. In innumerable ways he showed, both in his writing and his talk, the profundity of his Hinduism, and to understand him at all demands at least an acquaintance with those systems, ideas and aspirations which created and used him. History and scripture, the structure of Hindu society—all this must needs come into it, far more, actually, than the details of a purely temporary relation between India and the British Empire: the political struggle was, in my view, almost incidental, even though it did lead to the liberation of India. What counts most of all for us of the West is what hold Gandhi (and India) had of the truth or of a truth, how much of this can help us in our extremity, and what possible alternative may be offered to the sterile and self-destructive rush of our materialism. If we do not expect specific maps and diagrams, which have never been anything but delusive for an inquiring mind, I think we can come somewhere near to a concept of reality more stable and more durable than those to which most of us have adhered.

2

It is hard to strike a balance on such a subject as this: to some it is familiar, has been familiar for years, and to others it is wholly strange. I can only confess my own unfamiliarity with it up to a year ago, and attempt to describe my discoveries (with the aid of the authorities when necessary) as they occurred. It will thus be seen that this is no scholarly work. It is for my own kind to read: those who have watched and wondered. The fact is that I know no Sanskrit and no other Oriental language. Where Sanskrit names or words must be used I intend to spell them phonetically, since the signs and symbols of scholarship are only a mystification to most of us. (Thus I say "Shri Krishna" instead of "Sri Krsna," and Sanskrit rather than Samskrt.) I have consulted authorities most sedulously, and propose to list them in a bibliography at the end, but only those who wish to pursue the subject further will be tempted to investigate them. For the truth is that the whole subject of Hinduism has been almost monopolized by, on the one hand, Sanskrit scholars and philosophers of the most rarefied academic quality, and, on the other, theosophists and "new thought" addicts and other specialized devotees who are very much on the fringe of the citizenry. I draw only from the first group, since scholarship (however remote from ordinary life) always acknowledges its obligations and therefore, even in error, cannot greatly mislead. The second group does not engage much of my sympathy and will not be considered hereafter. I have—to paraphrase a German Orientalist of the last century—concluded that theosophy bears the kind of relationship to Hinduism that the Book of Mormon does to the Old Testament. It is, to put it mildly, distant, and cannot help us.

The journey we undertake leads at times far back into the forest of antiquity. The way is strewn with unfamiliar relics and inscriptions, the signals across the centuries of those who have been here before. There may be difficulties, but I think there are also rewards. Through the green ceiling of the Vedic forest may be seen, as over the cities of our moment in their steel and stone, the same punctual and invariant stars. Some view of life that remains, like them, unchanged by the vicissitudes of human fortune, neither in pity nor indifference but in pure beauty outriding all, might serve its turn again in the need that has come upon us. I do not say that we can find it, or that it will be the same for any number of us at a time if we do, but we are still permitted to seek.

II

What Is the Blessing?

---

*Know that effluences flow from all things that have
come into being.*
EMPEDOCLES (*Fragment 89*)

What Is the Blessing?

*B*efore I went to India the ordinary varieties of crowd formation and behavior had been well known to me, or so I thought. In the West crowds form out of curiosity, respect, anxiety and a number of other motives which may be mixed or modified, but are for the most part known and easily named by observers of the phenomenon. In India I found another reason for the will of the individual to join in an immensity of his fellows; it was a reason so new and strange to me that the exploration of its meaning may be a task without end, but of its reality and power I can have no doubt. This reason is expressed in the common Hindustani word *darshan*. The word is currently used in all other Indian tongues as well as Hindustani; it occurs constantly in the English of the newspapers, periodicals and books published in India; it is never explained. When the bewildered newcomer asks its meaning he may get as many definitions as he has acquaintances. I was running across the word a dozen times a day before I beheld the thing itself; but having beheld it, and in the truest sense experienced it, during a mighty moment of time, I propose to work out its meaning as best I can. In such matters neither philology nor history nor philosophy itself can take the place of direct perception. And once the perception has occurred, however dimly, the prospect of an increase of light by further pursuing the investigation quickens all that most lives in us to a renewal of the desire to live. We are entombed and digging ourselves out; that glimmer which grows stronger promises the light of day.

2

Darshan[1] is blessing, or benediction, or a beneficent spiritual influence, according to most of those who trouble to find English words for it. Poorly indeed are the equations made by which a word in one language, echoing with associations from far antiquity, is matched to a word in another. As I went on with the inquiry in India I came to the conclusion that nobody had a very precise notion of the significance of the word because it was much too deeply rooted in the general consciousness. It had long since reached the stage of being taken for granted, and the poorest Hindu peasant was neither more nor less able to trace out its causes and effects, its philosophical reach, than the most bookish intellectual. Indians—like other inhabitants of the planet —are accustomed to their own fundamental assumptions; some questions never arise. Only a stranger from the ends of the earth would apply to darshan, as I did, the blank and puzzled "Why?" which so often leads into unmarked fields and dimnesses of time. This case is no exception.

Darshan, in the first place, is certainly not blessing or benediction in the ordinary Christian and ecclesiastical sense of the terms. It is not bestowed or conferred; it is not even necessary for the source of the darshan to be aware of the occurrence. (I saw this too often to doubt it.) Any person, place or thing concerned with the higher reaches of the Indian consciousness, its aspiration toward spirit, its memory-dream of the Himalayan gods or its mere symbolizations of power and beauty beyond the life of the individual, can and does create the glow of happiness which I believe to be inseparable from the concept of darshan as it dwells without words in the Indian mind. Darshan is neither

[1] Sanskrit, *darshana*, (lit.) cognition or even sight.

given nor received: it occurs. The poor peasant who has walked five hundred miles for his first sight of the river Ganges experiences darshan when he sees it, and again when its sacred waters touch his skin. At the Temple of the Master of the World, in Benares—as in innumerable temples throughout India, of course, to a lesser degree—the mere act of being present, without the sacrifice of so much as one marigold, creates darshan. There is darshan in the vision which greets the wayfarer when, after the long journey up through the green forests of the foothills, he comes to an open space and the snowy Himalayan peak of Shiva's Trident rises before him, shimmering down the incalculable centuries from a time behind time.

"Bathing in sacred rivers," says the *Mahabharata*, "or visiting temples with idols of clay and stone may purify you after a long time, but the saints purify you at sight." [2] The word translated as "sight" in this verse is darshan.

All this, perhaps, might be comprehended by analogies to examples more familiar in the West. Pilgrimage is a well-established practice in highly organized churches. Lourdes in France, Kiev in Russia, not to speak of Rome and Jerusalem, are officially sanctified places which authorize either a hope for future benefits or a forgiveness of past sins to the pilgrim. But I have never seen the glow of happiness, the darshan glow, on any face which has come under my observation in Rome or Jerusalem at the times of pilgrimage. I believe the specific purposes for which pilgrimages are undertaken in Christendom may limit the pilgrim's capacity for joy. In any case, darshan is not the reward of pilgrimage, nor is there anywhere a precise list of persons, places or things in India in which darshan inheres or from which darshan may be obtained. There is no Hindu "church" and there is no Hindu dogma; as has often been remarked, one could believe almost anything in the spiritual dilemma and still be a Hindu. The sources of darshan, then, must be designated by the consciousness of the people, either through tradition—the lessons learned in childhood; the environment itself—or by some power of instinct which ever and again finds a new source and goes to it irresistibly, without fear or doubt.

This becomes much clearer when we consider the phenome-

[2] Professor Radhakrishnan in a letter to the author.

non in which darshan plays its most distinctively Hindu part in contemporary India, which is the formation of crowds. If we speak of temples, rivers, mountains or holy places, the purely Hindu nature of darshan—its particularity as a form of happiness—disappears under the false analogy with Western religious customs and ecclesiastical practices. But if we observe, instead, the purely human (or, in the end, the purely political) mass movements which are determined by the desire for darshan, we come much nearer to a comprehension of its essential nature and the reason for its power.

The largest crowds assembled in modern times, perhaps in all times, gather in India. At Allahabad, at the confluence of the sacred rivers, when the ashes of Mahatma Gandhi were consigned to the water on February 12, 1948, there were four million people gathered. As many as three million assembled some months earlier in Calcutta to listen to a political address by the Prime Minister of India, Pandit Jawaharlal Nehru. In both cases the overwhelming mass of those present came—sometimes from great distances and with great difficulty—to experience darshan.

Here we have the essence of the matter, the specifically Hindu mystery. It is a mystery to Westerners because of our habit of classification, of separating and stowing away in discrete, impermeable vaults those various elements of our one life which science (or the scientific method) has taught us to discern. Thus, the nineteenth-century error, philosophically immense, of the isolation of religion from politics; thus, the imbecile notion, current for decades in the United States, that "foreign policy" and "domestic policy" are strangers to one another; thus, the concept of politics as profession and of politicians as specialized functionaries distinct from the body of which they are a part.

In the Western mind, when it accepts the idea of darshan at all, classification has its way. Darshan, it says, is a religious manifestation, dangerously near to superstition, and works most powerfully among the ignorant masses of the Hindu people because they have a long, lamentable history of reverence for "holy men."

The implications of this pigeonholing are, first that religion has nothing to do with the rest of life and consequently darshan cannot be experienced except in special surroundings and atmosphere; second, that educated persons are incapable of experiencing darshan. Both these implications are resoundingly false, but so is the original classificatory pettiness which must cram an immense reality into schoolroom definitions. Darshan is not to be understood, even in the most superficial sense, by any grammarian's apparatus which would separate it from the whole of Indian life. It is itself the most impressive proof, among the masses and from the masses, that the entire teaching of Hindu philosophy and religion has come to be as natural as the air or the earth to all those millions who—with or without the arts of reading and writing—have inherited it in their souls.

If this is understood, then it need occasion no surprise that darshan could assemble millions of people at the moment of the immersion of Mahatma Gandhi's ashes—a manifestly sacred moment to all India for ever—and could assemble other millions for a political address by Mr. Nehru. The one does not exclude the other; no Hindu would imagine that it did. Mr. Nehru is not a "holy man," and nobody in India thinks he is. However, he is a great man, the undisputed national leader, hero of a long struggle for freedom, center of innumerable stories and dear to the people. Thus, a glimpse of him, some sound (however distant) of his voice, the mere act of being present where he was also present, creates darshan.

We approach the necessity for a working definition of darshan. (I hope to sustain and amplify later on, but we cannot get much further without a general concept, owing nothing to grammar or dictionary, of what I believe darshan to be.) It is not "religious" in the Western sense—that is, it is not limited to certain special strands of the consciousness—and it is not the result of a definite act, such as benediction; this much I think we have seen. It can and does occur on purely secular, indeed purely political, occasions, in which the Western mind would see not the slightest element of what it calls "religious" significance. In the case of Rabindranath Tagore it occurred on an enormous scale for many years without either "religious" or "political" implications. There may some day be—almost certainly will be—a scientist or engineer whose devotion to the Indian people will cause them to go to him as a source of darshan. How are we to catch this in words? Let me try.

Darshan in practice is a form of happiness induced among Hindus by being in the presence of some great manifestation of their collective consciousness. It may be person, place or thing, and represent past, present or future, so long as it sets up the definite recognizable glow of suprapersonal happiness.

We have thus avoided the trap of Western religious terminology, which is inapplicable to the case and would lead us into many errors; but obviously there are at least two terms used in this definition—"collective consciousness" and "glow of suprapersonal happiness"—which involve great complexities, including religion as well as the other forces of life. Some examples from observation may make it easier to move on to that much larger area of Hindu truth which I believe to be expressed in darshan.

On January 29, 1948, I accompanied Mr. Nehru on a tour of the frontier districts between India and Pakistan, on the East Punjab side. This was a flying visit and a number of small places, frontier stations and the like had to be visited, as well as the great refugee camp near Amritsar and, finally, a great mass meeting in the public park at Amritsar itself. The mass meeting brought together some four hundred thousand people, the largest crowd I had ever seen until that time, but my friends were quick to tell me that such a tremendous upsurge of the populace was not rare in India—that the crowd was, in fact, no more than must be expected on a Nehru tour. I was lost in its immensity, like a vagrant spar in a high sea, and found myself swept far away from where I had originally intended to take my place. There, as we sat upon the ground like uncountable insects, the eye beheld human beings in an unimaginable mass covering all the earth, perched in the trees, hanging from the branches, alive with happiness. The impression of happiness is not common in India—sadness is the daily fare, or so it always seems to a stranger—but in such a crowd it was impossible not to feel the stir of common joy. And then, as was almost inevitable in such an open space where every wire is at the mercy of a hundred thousand feet, the loud-speaker apparatus failed and not a word of Mr. Nehru's speech could be heard.

I do not know just what I expected the crowd to do. In the West, certainly, it would have begun to drift away when nothing could be heard. I knew that this was a darshan crowd (any crowd of such magnitude is essentially there for darshan) but I had not realized that they would sit there blissfully on the ground, squashed almost into physical oneness, until the whole of the Prime Minister's prepared address had been delivered. It was a speech of great political importance and had to be delivered, if only for the sake of the press and national public. It was the first time any member of the Government of India had openly attacked the Hindu reactionary or proto-Fascist organizations by name—those organizations which were, within twenty-four hours, to take the life of Mahatma Gandhi. Mr. Nehru kept on because he had to keep on, and also because he was never quite sure how well or ill the loud-speaker was functioning; but for the whole time (more than an hour) the immense audience sat there happily, hearing nothing.

Nor did they need to hear; and for most of them hearing or not hearing was the same. This I had already perceived during the morning. We had stopped in villages where every man, woman or child had turned out, had indeed been waiting for hours for Mr. Nehru's arrival. I had seen one withered crone, straight out of *Macbeth*, sitting with a look of rapture on her face throughout the Prime Minister's brief speech. She had been seated on the ground for a long time before we got there. When he reached the platform she raised her two infinitely wrinkled old hands before her face, joined together in the fashion which —once an attitude of prayer, as it still is in the West—now con- stitutes the usual greeting between Hindus. I was much struck by this ancient-of-days because those who were with her were quite unable to make her hear or pay attention to them. She was completely concentrated upon Mr. Nehru, and the look of bliss on her face would be difficult to forget. She had felt darshan.

Again, in those village crowds, I saw small babies held up by their parents so as to catch a glimpse of the Prime Minister. Darshan, I learned, has nothing to do with the surface or self- conscious part of the consciousness. Neither the small babies nor Mr. Nehru knew, but the children received darshan just the same, in the opinion of their parents. It was to receive some shadow of the real darshan that these infants were exposed to the view of their great leader. I saw it again on a very considerable scale in the afternoon (there were thousands of small children at the mass meeting) and could have no doubt in the matter.

In short, what Mr. Nehru said or did made no difference to most of the many thousands who saw him that day. He could have recited a multiplication table and most of them would neither have known nor cared. The words *"Jai Hind!"* (Victory to India!), with which all his speeches end, were perhaps the only ones fully understood by the larger number of those present. I was still, at that time, puzzling out my own interpretation of the darshan concept, and it was on that day that I came to the conclusion that it was a form of communication—that the happiness I saw come into being on faces at the darshan moment was set alight by a peculiar awareness. This awareness between great and small is the secret.

At Pondichéry, on the southeast coast of India, there lives the great sage, philosopher and mystic named Shri Aurobindo Ghose, who retired from the world in 1910. Since then he has emerged from his hermitage three times a year (and latterly four). On each of these occasions, the dates of which are well known throughout India, several thousands of people come from all over the sub-continent to catch a glimpse of him or even to be present in the place where he comes out. He can hardly be visible to half a million people at once; they can certainly not hear his voice; but they receive darshan and are willing to travel immense distances, very often on foot, to get it. Shri Aurobindo, a learned man whose knowledge of Western science and philosophy would appear, from his published writing, to be as ample as his knowledge of the Hindu scriptures, does not disdain this manifestation. From his works (such as I have read in them) I am emboldened to say that he does not disdain it because he really understands it.

Mahatma Gandhi understood it too, although in his own published work he complains of it. Darshan was a great inconvenience to him because it surrounded him and, in a sense, impeded his footsteps, for many long years. Somewhere in his autobiography he describes how difficult it was for him to get from the door to the platform in a hall where he was to make a public speech. Wherever he went, whatever he did, the crowds gathered for darshan and made it difficult for him to move. For

at least thirty-five years—nobody seems to know just how long
—the appellation *Mahatma*, Great Soul, had been attached to his
name by the instinct and will of the people, although he never
at any time accepted it and was at pains to say that he rejected
the notion of *Maha* and *Alpa*, great and small, between souls.
He was helpless against darshan because in the mind of his
people his was the greatest, the mightiest darshan of all. Everybody who came near him experienced darshan and most people
came for that purpose; what is more, in his case they externalized the concept more distinctly than in any other, and it was
quite usual for men or women to greet him and to take their
leave of him in an attitude of prayer. In life he dwelt in darshan
as the fish dwells in the sea, and after his death, up to the moment
of the immersion of his ashes in the river, it was more powerful
than ever. To a man who was first of all a teacher and reformer,
anxious to convey his lesson to his people for their own good,
it must have been an endless vexation of spirit to realize (as he
clearly did) that darshan got in the way. Too often too many of
his people listened to him for the sound of his voice and looked
at him with love, experiencing darshan but caring not at all for
the meaning of his words. This, I think, is the explanation of the
impatience which the Mahatma manifested here and there in
print for the whole idea (which he called a "craze") of darshan.
It was a "craze" because it interfered with his work. If it had
not centered so overwhelmingly upon himself, creating endless
special problems for his life's mission, he would never have had
a word of criticism for it: he was profoundly Hindu.

Among the many instances of externalized darshan which I
observed with the Mahatma there are two which might be mentioned here as cases in point. (As I shall explain later, my experience of him was brief but intense, at the very end of his life, and
from the beginning until the end when his ashes went into the
river it was all darshan.) One evening in January I was standing
at the back of the small crowd which gathered daily in the
garden of Birla House for the prayer meeting. The chanting
of the Gita was going on and the moment was approaching
when the Mahatma was accustomed to speak. He was seated, as
usual, under the central arch of Mr. Birla's summer-house, with
the girls (his relatives) and other members of his circle seated

on the steps at his feet. From where I was standing he looked
very withdrawn indeed, wrapped in shawls and with his eyes
closed.

I became aware of a vigorous pushing and shoving just behind me. I turned to see a bearded Hindu of middle height, who
looked like a hill man (perhaps a Dogra), thrusting his way re-
lentlessly forward. There was a grim look on his face, and his
beard seemed made of black wire which had a threatening aspect
like the quills of an angry porcupine. This man was not going
to take no for an answer. I slipped aside as well as I could in
the crowd which, although small, was packed tightly together.
The man stationed himself, at the end of his masterful penetration, directly in front of me, turning his fierce frown over the
heads of the seated congregation toward the arches at the end.

Then I saw the darshan phenomenon as only rarely it is to be
seen. This man, I thought, remembering the terrible massacres
of the autumn and early winter, might have just come from
murdering his fellow-citizens: he looked capable of every extreme of cruelty or fanaticism. I watched his face because I
wondered what such a cut-throat, such an obvious cut-throat,
was doing at the evening prayers of the gentle Gandhi. As I
watched, the face before me changed in a second. He had seen
Gandhi. His eyelids trembled and a look of unabashed tenderness (the look of a mother for her child) came into his whole
face. (I could hardly believe what I saw even though he was a
few inches away from me; I was pressed against him by the
neighbors.) His lips parted in a half-smile that altered the appearance even of that black wire beard, and three times he repeated, under his breath, "Mahatma! Mahatma! Mahatma!" The
expression was almost one of ecstasy; it seemed downright in-
decent to be looking at it so closely. I edged my way out and
around to the other side of the crowd to avoid scrutinizing him
any more.

Another case of the kind was provided on the first evening
when the Mahatma attended evening prayers after his last fast
of January 13-18, 1948. He was then extremely weak and abstracted—seemed, indeed, unaware of his surroundings except
when he had to arouse himself to speak. As he was carried out
of the place of prayer and down the walk toward the house I

saw a woman and her child prostrate themselves flat on the grass beside his path. They arose from that supine position a few moments later with the look of happiness in both faces, although so far as I could tell the Mahatma had not even seen them; perhaps in prayer, perhaps in deep abstraction, he had been carried past them unnoticing, with closed eyes; but to them it made no difference, darshan had occurred just the same.

I have said that the awareness between great and small is the secret of darshan. This was the conclusion to which I came after considerable reading in Hindu philosophy and religion, including some of the epic stories which are familiar to every peasant in India from childhood. I did not reach the conclusion all at once, and was frequently put off the track by well-meaning Indian friends of the upper classes who told me not to attach too much importance to these practices.

"Darshan is merely a custom among the people," they would say. "Don't take it too seriously."

In saying this they ignored the all-important circumstance that "customs among the people" reveal more of a nation's mind and heart than any other thing—more than many volumes of history, philosophy and anthropology. Educated Hindus, particularly if they come from South India with its excess of religiosity and multitude of gods, tend to be a little self-conscious or apologetic about the customs of the poor and are unwilling to attribute to them anything more than a gross, crude representationalism which has no meaning (they infer) on higher planes. I feel sure, on the contrary, that the villager's crudest representationalism is the end product—or, let us say, the residue —under the conditions of his life, surrounded as he is by threatening elements, adverse forces of economy and social structure, of the highest normative concepts in Hindu thought. It is clear to me that the multiform life which greets the Hindu at birth, which is perhaps even more multiform in India than elsewhere, resolves itself into an essential oneness early in his experience, and that this unity beneath the forms is universally understood in the Hindu world as being the essential truth. This is what every great teacher from the beginning of recorded time has instilled into the mind of India, and although the illiterate peasant may not have heard of Shankara or Ramanuja, he is cognizant in innumerable ways (by temple sculpture, dancing and singing; by the wandering minstrels; by the lessons learned from the mother; by stories told and retold) of the main truth his race has always held to be supreme. This truth not only gives a soul to each human being (a "divine spark," as Gandhi Anglicized it) but makes that soul a part of the spirit of the universe, which contains all things and is contained in them. The universal spirit, as most Hindus understand it, wears the present world as a garment: all persons and things are manifestations, forms taken by that spirit. The individual comes and goes as a form, but his shred or strand of the spirit goes on into other forms until, in the end of its pilgrimage, it is united with the supreme.

How much of this does the villager understand?

In my ignorance of Indian languages I am unable to answer the question. But if I am to depend upon the evidence of authority, I find that there is no doubt expressed: all Indians do know the concepts of Soul and Oversoul, as Tagore usually called them, and all Indians know intimately, from earliest childhood, the concept of the cycle of rebirths, even though a good many modern westernized Hindus no longer take it to be literally true. It is not necessary to be able to read books in order to understand these sovereign ideas of India's whole existence. They are expressed in many ways throughout the life of any Hindu, and he can hardly get through a single day without being reminded of them in the details of life, to whatever caste or region he may belong. A large number of the religious practices and ceremonials to which the devout pay careful attention are designed precisely for the purpose of reminding the Hindu of these main philosophical tenets.

It seems to me that even if I had not the warrant of good authority for saying so, I should have known by direct observation that these central beliefs were common to all Hindus. I should have known it by darshan, if by nothing else. For what is this awareness of which I have spoken? What is this communication between great and small? It is nothing less than the recognition of a community of spirit in which the poorest and humblest of Hindus, belonging to the lowest caste or to no caste at all, can recognize in a Gandhi or a Nehru that which his own *karma* has not permitted him to achieve, but which in some other life he may achieve, the great utterance and embodiment of the aspiration common to all. The Mahatma or the Great Soul is one which has risen above the mass but is still of it, not in any external sense based upon social and economic concepts but in the essence of its being. The one spirit in which all are participants has here thrust nobly upward a visible sign of its perfectibility in nature, thus rejoicing the hearts of the poor earthbound toilers who are, and know themselves to be, far behind on the way.

In the very beginning of his treatise *On the Soul* Aristotle remarks, with his customary bright sobriety, that "to attain any assured knowledge about the soul is one of the most difficult things in the world." Nothing daunted by this difficulty, he goes on to discover its "formulable essence," its "whatness," in the distinctive quality it possesses in a natural body. Thus, if the eye were an animal, *sight* would be its soul. And after examples from the forms of life in actuality and potentiality, he reaches the general conclusion that "soul is an actuality or formulable essence of something that possesses a potentiality of being besouled." He does not deny that potentiality to plants or animals as well as men, and gives all of the besouled a desire to "partake in the eternal and divine." In fact, he says, "that is the goal toward which all things strive, that for the sake of which they do whatsoever their nature renders possible." And however astringent he may make his rationalism, however it may bristle with the mathematics and physics of his time, on this subject Aristotle is not far from the concepts which were being expressed in quite other language in the India contemporary with him; how much nearer to them, therefore, must be Socrates and Plato! It is as we might suppose, and Plato, read again after some slight experience of India, proves to be the poet and artist *in excelsis* of those very perceptions which form the common consciousness of all Hindus.

It may be said, of course, that philosophy through the centuries has familiarized mankind with these notions. The flux of Heraclitus and the atoms of Democritus, conceived as opposing statements of the reality beneath the forms, had a kind of bold absolute which in itself is heaven-storming and world-making, and therefore not materialist. The Greeks in general, for all their careful inquiry and their love of geometry, were inconceivably distant from the materialism of the nineteenth century, that brief nightmare which is now over. Socrates says to Theaetetus: "By the uninitiated I mean the people who believe in nothing but what they can grasp in their hands, and who will not allow that action or generation or anything invisible can have real existence."

If we add to the Greek and German secular philosophers the numerous Christian, Islamic and Judaic mystics who flourished from the time of Plotinus onward, we can see that a marked and continuous tendency of Western thought throughout its history has been in the direction of a reality which transcends the forms or appearances of earth-living. But the point is that these were the thoughts of philosophers or the inner experiences of mystics; their power was felt in the one case in universities and in the other through religious orders or special followings; there has never been a time in the West when the broad mass of the people instinctively or even traditionally held to transcendental beliefs. Christianity itself, Islam itself and Judaism itself do not impose them, and if they did they would not be obeyed because the whole instinct of the European-American complex of peoples is otherwise formed and made concrete in the struggle for existence. In every case we can think of—as with Emerson and his circle in nineteenth-century America—the transcendentalists have been small, esoteric groups regarded as more than a little cracked by their neighbors. In Catholic Europe the mystics were called saints and their teachings thereafter disregarded; sometimes they were turned into the pretext for revels of an exactly opposite nature, as when St. Catherine of Siena became the excuse for an annual outburst of pagan athleticism and pageantry in the city of her vision.

What is distinctive in the broad mass of the Hindu people, as compared to all other great divisions of humanity, is the unquestioning (and largely unthinking) acceptance of transcendental reality in the common consciousness. The Hindu is perhaps born co-conscious with his contemporaries; it sometimes seems as if this may be so; but whether it is or not, he acquires the common consciousness with the growth of his mind and body, so that long before he has learned to formulate his beliefs they are deep in him, ineradicable by subsequent surface processes such as the scientific knowledge taught in colleges. The universality of the spirit, the participation of each person in it, the transmigration of souls, the ultimate "realization of God" (in the mystical sense) as a possibility for every man born—all these ideas, which are philosophical or religious in the West, are part of the most intimate mind of the most ordinary Hindu. It has been proved to me that even illiterate persons in India know and adhere to the larger concepts which underlie and inform all the luxuriant overgrowths of Hinduism, just as the village stone-mason engaged in making an effigy of Hanuman or Ganesh (the monkey-god and the elephant-god) is well aware that these are aspects of the divine without being explicitly God. Some complex philosophical notions, such as the *gunas* (the three strands of reality), are also known to many millions of people who can neither read nor write. There are other millions who wear around their necks or waists the Sacred Thread of the high castes; all these (many of them poor and unlettered) are aware of its trinitarian meanings, Desire, Cognition and Action being the first taught. The great symbols of the Himalaya and the sacred rivers that flow from it, the life-force (the *Shiva-linga*) and the waters and flowers of sacrifice, the Mother, both tender and terrible (Kali), along with hundreds of other personifications and abstractions of good and evil, are familiar from an early age to all born into Hinduism and seem to come without teaching, as an exhalation of the whole environment. We may discern various layers in the cosmogony, as, for example, the earliest deifications (in the Vedic dawn) of the forces of nature, followed by heroic anthropomorphism in the epic period, to be followed in turn by philosophical purification, by Shankara and Ramanuja, but it is all very ancient and has long since become one in the consciousness of India. The Lord Buddha lived and taught five centuries before Christ, but he was a late phenomenon in Indian religion. Ramanuja, who supplied the philosophical basis for almost all the subsequent development of Hinduism, including the worship of Vishnu in a number of incarnations (Krishna being one), was a modern, distinctly a modern, when the whole sweep of the Indian story is considered; he lived and taught in the early part of the twelfth century. And yet from the earliest Hindu scriptures—for which no date can securely be assigned; they may be four thousand years old, but scholars range widely on both sides of that guess—down to Ramanuja, and on to the teachers and masters of the present day, although the variety of the forms is almost infinite and comprehends deifications by the million, the essential Hindu truth has never varied. It is this truth which animates the multitudes who come together to receive darshan, a minimum of spiritual happiness, from the greater expressions or embodiments of their oneness.

3

It has been necessary to refer to metempsychosis, *karma* and caste, all of which are deeply embedded in the whole life of India. They are of religious origin, of course, but their influence permeates every part of the collective existence and cannot be separated from society, politics, literature or thought in general. It is because religious or philosophical concepts long ago took social form that Hindu life differs so sharply from any known in the West—or, for that matter, in the East outside of India. With the seas on three sides and the towering Himalaya on the other, India has been cut off through the ages from the rest of the world, and the extraordinary continuity and independence of the Hindu mindstream inevitably resulted. The relatively modern Islamic invasion set up a contradiction to Hinduism and eventually created—largely through refugees from the caste system—a population within India which was opposed to most of the ideas I have been attempting to indicate here. Those ideas, the essence of Hinduism, did not succumb, and the contemporary Hindu mind dwells within them even when its practical, daily occupations are of a nature which—like laboratory science or engineering—would appear to Europeans inharmonious with their meaning. (The disharmony is only apparent to Westerners and is in no sense real, as I shall hope to show later.)

Since it is given that everything in the world is essentially divine,[3] that God is in everything everywhere,[4] and that in this creation man has the special capacity for manifesting the divinity within him and to unite with the higher form,[5] there must be at

---

[3] *Chhandogya Upanishad III, 14, 1.*   [4] *Isha Upanishad 1.*
[5] *Mundaka Upanishad III, 2, 9.*

the base of the whole Hindu world a much more comprehensive soul-dominion than in any other. At some time in the prehistoric twilight, the sages of old perceived, or thought they perceived, a continuity of the spirit from life to life and evolved the doctrine of re-incarnation or rebirth. The Lord Shri Krishna says to the hero Arjuna, "O Arjuna, both you and I have had many births before this, but I know them all, while you do not." [6] He has earlier declared, "Birth is inevitably followed by death and death by rebirth." [7] From the earliest period known to us this has been the firm conviction of Hinduism, to which almost every characteristic of the Hindu race, society and polity in general owes its origin.

The rebirths are indefinite in number, depending upon the actions performed by the soul's garment (i.e., the embodied life) on earth. This world is *karmabhumi*, the land of action, and what we do here constitutes our karma, the burden of deeds upon our souls. If our karma contains goodness and wisdom, our spirit is then reborn in a higher state of consciousness, nearer perfection and more harmonious with the divine. This process goes on until the soul at last—at whatever period that may be—attains perfection and is united with the supreme and infinite existence. The *Atman* (soul, spirit, divine element) abandons the worn-out body and, after a period of hovering in the upper world, passes into a new body as many times as may be necessary for the process of the rising terms of being to become complete. Nothing we can do in this earthly life can possibly exempt us from the pains or pleasures which are our legacy from preceding lives, although we can, in this life, so build our karma ("acquire merit," as the Christians say) that the next life will be a step higher. We may also conduct ourselves in such a way that the next life will be a recession rather than an advance toward perfection.

Karma—deeds or action—governs the Hindu's terrestrial activity to a considerable extent, and is directly responsible for the caste system. We are born into a certain caste because our karma has so determined. We improve our karma by fulfilling the duties of that caste, whatever it may be, without attempting to escape them or mitigate their rigors, paying due respect to our ancestors, honoring the gods and fulfilling the ceremonies of traditional

[6] *Gita IV, 5.*   [7] *Gita II, 27.*

religion. Thus, if I am born the son of a leather-worker—which happens to be one of the outcast social groups known as "untouchables"—I must, in the strict caste system, limit myself to being a leather-worker to the end of my days. If I am born a Bania (a subdivision of the merchant group of castes) then I must be a Bania as long as I live. An exception is made for those who are called, or think themselves called, to a life of asceticism, devotion and sacrifice: these, the yogi or "holy men," who have always been extremely numerous in India, have at all times been considered to be outside the caste system and in a sense above all ordinary society.

The complication of the system is immense. There are seven or eight hundred main castes in the whole of India, and up until quite recently new ones were being formed by subdivision. All of them are supposed to fall within the great four-fold division of function made in Vedic times: the Brahmin (the priestly caste at the time of the Vedas), the Kshatriya (warriors and rulers), the Vaishya (originally agricultural and industrial, later on also the commercial classes) and the Shudra (working people, identified by most scholars on the evidence of the *Rig Veda* as having been the original inhabitants of India before the Aryans came in).

These functional subdivisions no longer govern function. A Brahmin, for example, can do any sort of work he chooses so long as it is not unclean. There are a great many domestic servants in India who are Brahmins; they will not, of course, wash clothes, and there are certain domestic tasks which must always be given to lower castes or (in the dirtiest jobs) to untouchables, but cooks, butlers and the like are quite often Brahmins. The Vaishya group has been subdivided so much that it includes an enormous number of castes which do almost any sort of work in contemporary times. The professions which rely upon a thick superstructure of westernized education, such as medicine, the law and teaching in higher institutions of learning, draw their recruits from all the castes. All of this tends to break down the age-old rigidity of the system, quite aside from the efforts of reformers for the past hundred years to make over Hindu society from within. The fact remains that there are innumerable customs about diet, water-drinking, association with others, marriage and sexual activity which are based upon the caste system and still have absolute power over the majority of Hindus. Marriage between the castes is still discouraged by orthodox Hinduism in spite of all the reformers; and "pollution," which means the imagined degradation sustained by a person of high caste when a person of low caste touches him or even casts a shadow over him, has by no means disappeared from the consciousness; rites are prescribed, and still scrupulously carried out by the greater number, to overcome it. (In the life of a great city like Calcutta "pollution" must occur hundreds of times every day, whatever precautions are taken against it, so the life of a scrupulous, orthodox Brahmin must be one long series of purificatory ceremonies.)

Much of the system revolts the Western conscience; it seems unjust in the extreme, besides entailing an unnecessary amount of complication in the ordinary business of getting through a day. Supposing even that we belong to a high caste, and thus have all the privileges, still, if we have to accept water only from a person of one caste, and milk only from another, and drink at certain hours and sit at table only with persons prescribed by caste, our day is cluttered up with preoccupations which seem almost senseless. They have, however, their meaning and purpose, and they have for many centuries given Hindu society a stability it could never have attained by its secular organization or political structure, which was seldom good. The caste system differentiated Hindu society from all others and in fact maintained it through long ages of political chaos when a lapse into barbarism would otherwise have been inevitable. *Dharma*, the Sanskrit word which is used indiscriminately for religion, duty and essential nature—very much what Aristotle means by "formulable essence"—is the framework of all life. It comes from the Sanskrit root *dhri* (to hold), and is therefore that to which we hold, as well as that which holds us or sustains our existence. In its sense as duty it imposes the caste system, which thus becomes integral with every other aspect of the life of a Hindu and inseparable from his political or social existence.

The Hindu reformers in modern times have never felt at all easy about the caste system, and most have in fact attempted to alter it or break it down. Efforts were made, with small success, throughout the nineteenth century, and Mahatma Gandhi, although too devoutly Hindu to attack the system as a whole, spent forty years chipping away at it, advocating marriage between castes, education for all castes, and above all defending at every turn those who have no caste at all, the millions who are called "untouchable." Mr. Gandhi held that the four-fold division of function was in itself good if understood as duty, not as privilege, but he never admitted that there was anything right about the exclusion of millions of unfortunates from the framework of Hindu society. Untouchability he regarded as an excrescence upon Hinduism, without ancient authority or modern worth, and he struggled all his life against it by precept and example. He did, nevertheless, submit to birth as the determinant of caste, because not to do so would have been in most Hindu eyes to throw doubt upon karma, and he could never question karma for two excellent reasons: first, because he believed in it himself, and second, because he was, like Socrates, deeply and almost fatefully [8] aware of his primary historic mission, which was to set his people free. Even the appearance of any attack upon karma—if he had wished to undertake such a thing—would have interfered with his mission. (I shall explain later that in my view this mission was the greatest example known to history of karma-yoga, or the way to God through action in the world; it therefore dominated everything else up to the end.)

There are now and have been for a hundred years or more, in all parts of India, sages and teachers who would mitigate or reform the caste system if they could. (Keshab Chander Sen, Ramakrishna, Vivekananda and Dayananda Sarasvati were all alike in this.) At the present time a venerable teacher whose scholarship, sanity and serenity especially appeal to me is Bhagavan Das, the author of *The Essential Unity of All Religions*, now retired from his work as professor in the Hindu University of Benares: he would like to see the caste system transformed by means of vocational selection and training, along lines which he has understood to be followed in the Soviet Union. For many years the idea of the four-fold division of function in society could still remain, but the immense social injustice of classification at birth would disappear, karma would work itself out in

---

[8] "I suppose that these things may be regarded as fated—and I think that they are well." Plato: *Apology*.

other ways in man's life, and a healthier society would result. His exposition of the idea of the caste system, as distinct from its social and economic institutionalization, is succinct and persuasive. "The book governs the sword," he said to me. "The sword protects the purse. The purse nourishes the plough. The plough nourishes and supports all in turn." This is an almost Platonic statement of the Vedic *varnas*. When Bhagavan Das wished to make this statement even more specific, he said: "Teach, guard, feed, serve."

These, then, are the duties of the Brahmin, Kshatriya, Vaishya and Shudra, ideally considered. However, the automatic relegation of a child at birth to some definite sub-caste involving an occupation, an economic standard and an intellectual limit, which is what these things mean in objective reality, seems to Bhagavan Das very wrong. It was one of the points on which he disagreed with Mahatma Gandhi. He holds, furthermore, that no such minute and rigid subdivision as now exists—and as has existed for centuries—was intended by the sages of old who evolved the system. In his view, not only untouchability, but the economics of caste society and its integration into the whole Hindu view of life, are themselves degenerative error and should be corrected.

When all this is said, and when it is further admitted that the caste system is the greatest stumbling block in the way of those Westerners who wish to understand and love the Indian people, it is still necessary to reiterate, against the obstinacy of Western prejudice, that caste stabilized Hindu society and saved the civilization of India. Without it barbarism and chaos would have had their way long ago with what used to be a fourth, and is still a fifth of all humanity.

This people preserved its greatness by means of the caste system, and when that goes, as go it must, the hope is that enough of its "formulable essence" will remain in their consciousness to enable them to withstand the onslaught of turbulence which always pours over the fallen ramparts of the past.

4

To all of the foregoing on metempsychosis, karma and caste, at least in the idea as distinct from the social enactment, we may readily think of Western analogies or parallels. Plato deals with the first two in the *Phaedo* and to some extent in the *Phaedrus;* what he proposes in *The Republic* is a species of caste system with society divided into three parts rather than into four. Quite independently, in various parts of the world, men have arrived at similar concepts, but nowhere else have these ideas permeated the whole extent of a vast polity and made its consciousness one. Only in India has an absolutely transcendental philosophy been diffused throughout the lowest as well as the highest reaches of a social structure. We are entitled to ask, first, why? And we may subsequently be tempted to ask, has there never been any dissenting view of truth?

My own present conclusion is that the natural phenomena of the Indian sub-continent, taken all together would encourage a meditative inclination in almost anybody. I find in the towering Himalaya and in the life-giving rivers which flow from it not only symbols of universal significance at the present day, but convincing indications of the way in which Indian thought was influenced to take the direction it did in the most decisive moment, that of its awakening to wonder in the germinal twilight that preceded the dawn of history. "Wonder is the feeling of a philosopher," says Socrates to Theaetetus, "and philosophy begins in wonder." What must have been the wonder of the thinking men among the Aryan tribes when they first beheld the Himalaya from the plain below? The storm, the wind, the sun, the round of the seasons, the beneficence of water and all the panoply of good and evil in nature have, in those regions, even greater impressive power than elsewhere. Man in his struggle seems to be played upon by superior forces to which in time he relates the form and meaning of his own life, but the desire to do so must have had greater urgency among the newcomers to India than in more moderate climes.

For I have little doubt that the Aryans were newcomers.

Western scholars in general seem convinced of this, and for my part I cannot examine the *Rig Veda* without thinking so. (I am aware that a good many Indian scholars disagree, but it is better not to digress into that argument.) Whoever the Aryans were and whencesoever they came, they must have arrived in the Punjab plain from Iran or by way of Iran, or must have maintained a long and intimate connection with Iran, because the oldest Hindu scripture, the *Rig Veda*, shows overwhelming philological evidence to that effect. A large number of the words used for religious meanings, such as supreme spirit, god or demon, sacrifice, offering, priest and worship (to name a few from a parallel table) are almost exactly the same [9] in the Veda and in the Avesta. (This is not to imply that the Veda and Avesta are contemporary; the *Rig Veda* is probably much older.) Aryan would thus seem to mean Indo-Iranian, since the word is the same in the oldest scriptures known on both sides of the Hindu Kush.

The newcomers to India found a darker-skinned population already in possession. The dark people, the Dasyu, are called in the *Rig Veda* "phallus worshippers," and evil, superstitious practices are ascribed to them. The hymns in the *Rig Veda* constitute evidence that a war of conquest took place, and continued perhaps for a long time, between the Arya and the Dasyu, identified by Western scholars with the Aryan and Dravidian elements in the population of modern India, the Dasyu retreating in time to the south with their own religion modified (and through the centuries to be still more changed) by that of the conquerors.

In the war, in the terror of new conditions and the wonder of a vast new country with its awe-inspiring contrasts of climate and natural configuration, the priests who accompanied the warriors very early reached the apprehension or perception of what was to be the permanent, sovereign teaching of Indian thought under all its forms thereafter. The very first line of the first verse of the *Isha Upanishad* declares that the whole world is the garment of the Lord, the mantle of his appearance. Even after thousands of years, after Aryan and Dravidian had long been merged into one, not only in race but in religion and society, the first verse of the *Isha Upanishad* remains like a fundament to

[9] H. D. Griswold: *The Religion of the Rig Veda*, p. 21.

the Indian universe. No less modern a spirit than Mahatma Gandhi told me, three days before his death, that he considered it to express the sum of human wisdom.

I do not think that the transcendental inclination on the part of Aryan tribes coming in to India and beset alike by danger and by wonder is difficult to understand. The plain of the Punjab was at that time thickly forested, and Tagore, in his lectures at Harvard University—published in 1913 under the title *Sadhana*—ascribed the impulse toward "interpenetration of our being into all objects" to unwalled and frontierless forest-dwelling, the original physical environment of Indian thought, just as he ascribed the character of Western religions to their birth in walled cities. This may indeed be so, and certainly the "sages of the forest" contributed an expression with precise meaning in India: withdrawal from the world can still be expressed as "going to the forest" even when there is no forest. But this historical condition was complicated by some special social and economic circumstances. The Dasyu, the dark-skinned aboriginal inhabitants who had to be conquered by the Arya, could not at once, when conquered, be taken into the Aryan clans. They became a servile class distinguished by their complexions, occupations and social segregation, and the word Shudra (the lowest, or laboring section in the four divisions of society) is already used in the *Rig Veda* as being a synonym for Dasyu.

We have here, it seems to me, the origin of the caste system. Some Indian scholars deny this, too, but it is difficult to see why. The Sanskrit word for caste and the word for color are the same: *varna*. Color-consciousness is rampant in the *Rig Veda*, and if it has disappeared in modern India that is no reason for re-interpreting these extremely ancient texts. It would appear that the incoming Aryans, who already had well-marked functional divisions for warriors and priests, enslaved the Dravidians and caged them into a rigid caste, much as has been done in the Southern states of the United States to the Negroes of African origin. Thus the Aryan peoples for the first time seem to have met with a dark race six or seven thousand years ago and behaved in a way which has been characteristic of them ever since. Amalgamation of the two races through the centuries has left behind it a caste system which no longer shows much evidence of differences in color, but color in the beginning was its visible sign and partial justification.

5

The case to which the perception of the masses most powerfully directed its desire for darshan was, of course, that of Mahatma Gandhi. It pursued him in life and after death. I asked some of his oldest friends and associates when he had first been called "Mahatma." (I had an impression derived from something I had read in America, that Tagore called him by the name in a telegram along about 1918 and thus helped to establish it.) None could remember. Mr. Nehru said: "I met him first in 1916 and he was already Mahatma then." Mrs. Sarojini Naidu said: "I met him in 1914 and he was already Mahatma then." The appellation was apparently given during his years of struggle for the Indians in South Africa, and undoubtedly Indians at home were calling him Mahatma long before he knew about it. It was probably a matter of growth over the years, perhaps from 1902-1905 to 1910-1914. It would not take more than a few years for such a distinctive appellation to get itself firmly attached, if the instinct of the people welcomed it. There are a number of honorifics in use among the Indian masses: the late *Lokamanya* (Friend of the People) Tilak, for example. Mahatma is by no means unique as an appellation. However, the word has such significance in a population where the idea of the immanent spirit dominates— where Plato and Kant would be, you may say, instinctively understood by millions who never heard of either of them—that only men of rare quality have had the name applied to them. It is my guess that it will not be used again in India.

The overtones of the word are the overtones of darshan. The appellation arises from the people as a form of darshan, and from the Mahatma there flows out to the people another form of darshan. "Verily he who has seen, heard, comprehended and known the Self, by him is this entire universe known," says the Upanishad.[10] And the Great Soul is a great expression of that Self. Professor Deussen, paraphrasing or epitomizing the Veda,

[10] *Brihadaranyaka Upanishad*, 2, 4, 5b.

says: "Thy neighbor is in truth thy very self, and what separates
thee from his is mere illusion." [11] This is a language common to
the Upanishads, Plato, Kant and Schopenhauer; in the case we
are examining no other will do. It is the language of the spirit
of India.

Mr. Gandhi, understanding as he did both West and East, was
aware of the incomprehension that divides them in many respects. Having been called "a naked fakir" by such an authority
as Mr. Winston Churchill, he also knew that he was himself
viewed very differently in different parts of the world. His
course was clearly marked out for him, and, like Socrates, he
had an "inner voice." But at the same time he did not want
Westerners and foreigners in general to think of India as a mere
yoga-land, a realm of mystics and superstitious hordes; he valued
sanity and reason above all things in the social relationship; and
for his personal life, that of the entity called Mohandas Karamchand Gandhi, he was far too humble and gentle to think it entitled to the worship of the masses. These were some of the reasons why he disliked being called Mahatma and made efforts for
a good many years to ignore the appellation. He knew, only too
well, since he was Hindu to the depths of his being, all that it
implied. It put upon him a tremendous obligation which was to
be discharged only at the moment of his death. He belonged,
body and soul, to his people; but by calling him Mahatma they
made it too clear. When he spoke of "the craze for darshan,"
when he exhibited a dislike for visible signs of the people's adoration, when he was reluctant to give ostensible "blessings" or
otherwise comport himself in the manner of an official saint, he
was exhibiting the disquiet which overcame him at the pantheistic envelope surrounding India's (and his own) theism. I
think he was, in his heart, probably dismayed at the thought that
he might be deified after death; having been a demigod for forty
years, and knowing the ease with which deification can occur in
India, the possibility could not have escaped him. He might trust
the Government of India to do its best to prevent any such
thing, as it has done; but the processes are beyond legislation.
The installation of Mr. Gandhi in the pantheon of the people's
consciousness has already taken place, and representations of

[11] Deussen: *The Philosophy of the Upanishads*, p. 49.

him are not uncommon in temples. If they must have concrete embodiments to represent aspects of the divine, then it can certainly be said that Mr. Gandhi's life and teaching are better for the purpose than some which already command the people's devotion.

The progress of the funeral train containing his ashes from Delhi to Allahabad, where the three sacred rivers flow together, was a solemn evocation of the instinct for darshan. In the hour before dawn at the Delhi station people had already assembled to watch the train depart. At each stop on the way other crowds appeared to file past the coach containing the urn, which stood on a platform covered with flowers and fully lighted. Between stops there were no crowds, but only the peasants working in their fields, standing at attention as the train passed. At Cawnpore, the largest city on the way, several hundred thousand people had waited all day long for the train, and when it pulled out of the station after two and a half hours many of them had not yet had an opportunity to pass before it. For all the miles into and out of the city the people lined the tracks, sitting on roofs, in trees and on the ground. Their welling, tremendous cheer, in death as in life, was "*Mahatma Gandhi ki-jai!*" (Victory to Mahatma Gandhi!) This was the cheer that had accompanied him on every journey he made in India during the thirty-odd years of his struggle. The people's cry was, under the system of truth which contains their whole consciousness, profoundly right. The great cheer of victory was occasionally varied with another, "*Mahatma Gandhi amar hai!*" (Mahatma Gandhi will never die!) In these expressions, so strangely moving to the hearer, the people told their own story of the deathless spirit, the refusal to recognize death as anything more than an interruption, and the sense of darshan for their own best and bravest. What, then, is to be said of the scene at the confluence of the rivers? There an uncountable mass had gathered and waited for days to see the ashes of the father consigned to the water. Some of them, some thousands of them went into the Ganges at the same time, washing away the dross of the earthbound existence in waters made holier by the presence of his ashes for a little while, there where the rivers meet on their way from the far Himalaya to the no less distant sea. On that day, I think, as I passed over the great expanse of water into the blue Jumna in a small boat, looking at the multitude on the banks of the rivers, thinking back over everything that had taken place in a few short weeks, I believe that I had some perception of the meaning of darshan. It is also my belief that I had experienced it, briefly but intensely, and had thereby acquired the most valid of reasons for pursuing the investigation wherever it might lead, since the darshan was that of Mahatma Gandhi.

For further discussion of Caste, Karma and Darshan, see page 259.

III

What Is the Battle?

Men of Athens, I honor and love you; but I shall obey
God rather than you, and while I have life and strength
I shall never cease from the practise and teaching of
philosophy.

The Apology of SOCRATES

What Is the Battle?

Mahatma Gandhi based his highest and clearest teaching, as well as the conduct of his entire life after the age of thirty-seven, upon the *Bhagavad Gita*. This great poem, the crown of classical Sanskrit literature, occupies a position in the Hindu scriptures rather like that of the New Testament in the Judæo-Christian Bible. It is later than the Upanishads, as the Upanishads are later than the Vedas; and in its advice to the despondent hero, the Aryan fighter, it sets forth a rule of life which has had the most immense influence upon Hindu development for about twenty-five hundred years. Until the Gita appeared and insinuated its divine harmonies into the consciousness of Hinduism, the ideas associated with specific incarnations of God, as well as of the salvation of mankind through divine grace, were unknown. It can be said with considerable assurance that although Hindu scriptures are many, and Hindu religious philosophy an immense realm, the Gita alone has meant more to Hinduism in the past thousand years, and means more today, than all the rest put together.

Gandhi declares in his autobiography that the *Bhagavad*

Gita is for him "the supreme book for the knowledge of truth." His reverence for it grew rather than lessened over the years, and for a long time before his death he had made the last nineteen verses of its second chapter a part of the normal procedure at his morning and evening prayer meetings. At other times the whole of the Gita was chanted by his followers, all of whom had familiarized themselves with the Sanskrit poem so that they could go through it with only an occasional glance at the book.

During the thirteen days which, according to Hindu ritual as prescribed for the Gandhi caste, elapsed between the cremation of the Mahatma and the immersion of his ashes in the sacred rivers, the Gita was chanted every morning beside the cremation platform on the banks of the Jumna near Delhi. One old member of the Congress Party told me that in the 1920's and 1930's a knowledge of the Gita and some ability to join in the chanting was almost a requisite for the greater number of Hindu nationalists—or at least that they felt it to be so; I am sure the Mahatma never really required it of anybody outside his own immediate circle. It is quite conceivable that the emphasis on the Gita was one of those things which Indian Muslims in general disliked in the nationalist movement—one of the things which "drove the Muslims out," as Mr. Jinnah used to say, along with other aspects of Gandhiji's profound Hinduism. This may be so, but if it is so, it is again a proof of Mr. Gandhi's supreme sincerity and the extent to which his behavior was governed by it. A more practical leader might have been less insistent upon the Gita at times when it was desired to keep the Muslims contented within the Congress. Mr. Gandhi could no more have suppressed the Gita to please the Muslims than he could have suppressed the Koran to please the Hindus. What he valued in the Koran, aside from its expressions of religious faith and devotion, was the absolute democracy it teaches and the universality of such texts as the great utterance, "All creatures are members of the one family of God." He found great and true statements of his own beliefs in the other canonical scriptures of the world, including the *Granth Saheb* of the Sikhs and the Buddhist books, which also contributed texts to his regular prayer meetings for many years. The influence of the idea of Jesus Christ, particularly as expressed in the Sermon on the Mount, is to be seen in an enormous part of his activity and teaching. But the Gita, which he must have known first in childhood without particularly understanding it, was the scripture which in his adult days came to mean most, so that it commanded his study and devotion more than any other. During his last term in jail he worked on it with his friend and secretary, the late Mahadev Desai, who had the Sanskrit scholarship Gandhiji lacked, and together they produced the volume (published in 1946) called *The Gospel of Selfless Action, or the Gita According to Gandhi,* in which his interpretation of the "song celestial" is interlarded with the Sanskrit text and its English translation. This English translation is itself a translation of his earlier translation from Sanskrit to his native Gujerati language, which he had sold at cost price so as to disseminate a knowledge of the divine poem among the people.

As I shall show later on, Mr. Gandhi appears in the very last period of his life to have gone still further back, to the Upanishads, for his quintessential truth. What he urged upon me was the *Isha Upanishad* and not the Gita, and he told me he had found its authority when he was looking for something to quote to Christians, on his visit to Travancore in 1946. It may be that something more fundamental, simpler than the Gita fitted the needs of his spirit in these months which accompanied and followed the liberation of India. However that may be, it is certainly true that through the larger part of his mission (from 1924 to 1946 or 1947) the Gita was for him the supreme scripture, and he never ceased to think of its lesson as the perfect expression (according to his interpretation) of *ahinsa* or non-violence as the final flower of truth. The Gandhi interpretation is open to much question, as we shall see, but just as there is little to be understood of modern India without some serious consideration of the *Bhagavad Gita,* so there is little to be understood of Gandhi's teaching unless his changing views upon the Gita and his ultimate conclusions upon its significance are taken into account.

It is, naturally, a prevalent and largely unconscious tendency on the part of all Christians, all of us who were born within and nurtured by the Christian world, to see in Gandhiji's life an immense Christian influence, and to interpret its essence as at least in part an example of the *imitatio Christi* (the "creative mimesis" of Professor Toynbee). This tendency is encouraged by the testimony he repeatedly gives to his love and reverence for the Sermon on the Mount, which became real to him in his early days in England. Once within two years he himself offered two varying bits of evidence on this point. In 1925, speaking to Christian missionaries in Calcutta, he said (as reported in *Young India* on August 6th of that year):

"I must tell you in all humility that Hinduism, as I know it, entirely satisfies my soul, fills my whole being, and I find a solace in the *Bhagavad Gita* and Upanishads that I miss even in the Sermon on the Mount. Not that I do not prize the ideal presented therein, not that some of the precious teachings in the Sermon on the Mount have not left a deep impression upon me, but I must confess to you that when doubts haunt me, when disappointments stare me in the face, and when I see not one ray of light on the horizon I turn to the *Bhagavad Gita* and find a verse to comfort me; and I immediately begin to smile in the midst of overwhelming sorrow. My life has been full of external tragedies and, if they have not left any visible and indelible effect on me, I owe it to the teaching of the *Bhagavad Gita*."

And yet two years later he wrote in *Young India* (Dec. 22, 1927):

"I have not been able to see any difference between the Sermon on the Mount and the *Bhagavad Gita*. What the Sermon describes in a graphic manner, the *Bhagavad Gita* reduces to a scientific formula. It may not be a scientific book in the accepted sense of the term, but it has argued out the law of love—the law of abandon as I would call it—in a scientific manner. The Sermon on the Mount gives the same law in a wonderful language. The New Testament gave me comfort and boundless joy, as it came after the repulsion that parts of the Old had given me. Today, supposing I was deprived of the Gita, and forgot all its contents but had a copy of the Sermon, I should derive the same joy from it as I do from the Gita."

Mr. Gandhi spoke and wrote constantly; the influence of the mood, of the occasion, and of the audience frequently determined variations in emphasis, and he did not always remember from one year to the next just what aspect of the truth he had chosen to emphasize on this or that occasion. Hence, although no true contradiction exists, it is always easy for the captious to dig out of his voluminous works some apparent fluctuation or deviation in views on any important subject. In the case of the Gita and the Sermon on the Mount we are compelled to see—as I shall hope to prove later—that they were intimately interwoven in his consciousness, so that he was probably never sure himself which would speak to him most imperatively in the difficult moments. No doubt there were times when the Sermon on the Mount "filled his whole being," and at other times it is extremely evident that the Gita had sovereign power for him. In the end, in the work which must be considered his final philosophical utterance, *The Gospel of Selfless Action*, he presents his matured view of the Gita in a form which shows the power of the great central document of Christianity. He said to me himself, three days before his death:

"I must warn you that my interpretation of the Gita has been criticized by orthodox scholars as being unduly influenced by the Sermon on the Mount."

My own view, for which I shall give evidence in the later chapter on his life, is that the Christian influence upon Mr. Gandhi—canalized chiefly through the Sermon on the Mount— came to him in 1888-1889 in England (when he was twenty) and was most powerful throughout his South African experience, but that the Gita, which was revealed to him at about the same period through the metrical English translation of Sir Edwin Arnold, never developed its full dominion over his mind and spirit until he came to know it in Sanskrit thirty-five years later. Thus the Sermon on the Mount illumined his spirit through many decisive years, youthful years at that, and naturally left its imprint upon his character and external action to the end of his days. But the revelation of the beauty of the Gita in Sanskrit, which came to him during the great fast of 1924 (the three weeks' fast undertaken for the sake of the Muslims), was a superimposed revelation which had even greater validity for one born from thousands of years of Hinduism; and as he thereafter grew ever more familiar with the sonorous Sanskrit, hearing it day in and day out at his prayer meetings, studying it and memorizing every vocable, he came in his old age to love the Gita beyond anything else known to him, transposing into it the gentle essence of the teaching of Jesus in a way all his own, so that the great Sanskrit poem, through which and by means of which he returned to his childhood and his ancestors, sang out with a new meaning. Whether this meaning is sustained by philologists and theologians or not makes no difference: it was Gandhi's truth. In the inconscient—which with him, as with all highly intuitive beings, was an enormous part of the consciousness—he must have felt a deep kinship to its view of action in the world, and even some obscure realization that his own life and work might be a tremendous expression of the very heart of the Gita. Mr. Gandhi was humble indeed, but his was far too great a mind to be modest; he knew quite well that lives like his do not often occur in history; and by dint of ceaseless effort he had come so close to the *karma-yoga* (the way to God through selfless action in the world) that he almost became a part of the Gita in the end.

We find him, in 1939, when he was seventy, writing in the *Harijan* as follows (August 24, 1939):

"Today the Gita is not only my Bible or my Koran, it is more than that—it is my mother. I lost my earthly mother who gave me birth long ago; but this eternal mother has completely filled her place by my side ever since. She has never changed, she has never failed me. When I am in difficulty or distress I seek refuge in her bosom."

2

The two ancient epics of India, *Mahabharata* and *Ramayana*, are often loosely compared to the *Iliad* and *Odyssey*, to which, indeed, they bear a certain vague generic resemblance. The *Mahabharata*, the older and more primitive of the two, "containing within itself productions of different dates and authorship . . . has become a miscellaneous encyclopædia of history and mythology, politics, law, theology and philosophy." [1] It describes the great war that took place at some time in prehistory between the branches of the royal house of the Bharatas: various scholars have thought that the historical war upon which the poetic legends are based took place during the fourteenth century B.C., while others date it a century or so later. The poem or poems

1 Radhakrishnan: *Indian Philosophy*, Vol. I, p. 481.

came into being through succeeding centuries, more or less at the same time as the Upanishads, and the later portions show a philo-sophical progression far beyond the simple Vedic gods and god-desses who abound in the earlier parts. No doubt ballads of the war grew up, were repeated and elaborated, and found their way eventually into a more or less connected narrative. The process must have been complete before the Age of Buddha (circa 500 B.C.), because Buddha is not mentioned in it.

The *Ramayana* in the form in which it has come down to us must be a little later in date, because Buddha is mentioned in it (as a "nastriya" or denying spirit).[2] It is much more correctly described as an epic, since it tells the exploits of the hero Rama, "the model of virtue, the pattern of perfection," who in later portions becomes an incarnation of Vishnu sent on earth to re-dress wrongs and teach virtue. In later centuries Rama, from the Ramayana, and Krishna from the *Mahabharata* were alike wor-shipped as incarnations of Vishnu, becoming the chief aspects of the divine for the Vaishnavite sect which includes such a huge proportion of the Hindu masses. The soteriology of modern Hin-duism is almost entirely concentrated upon these two figures from the epics, Rama and Krishna, whose beneficent and tender grace, humanizing the divine and reaching down to help men on their way, is far more sympathetic than the stern and sometimes ogre-like abstractions of the primitive Vedic nature-gods. Both the epics in consequence are sacred and have for millions of Hin-dus the canonical authority of revelation, like the Vedas them-selves or like the Homeric epics in the Age of Pericles. The *Ma-habharata*, in fact, was sometimes called, even in ancient time, "a fifth Veda," because it contained similar authority on conduct and society but, unlike the four original Vedas, was not re-stricted to the privileged—was open to all, including women and Shudras or working people, who were not permitted to know the Vedas for themselves.

In the midst of the vast and glittering agglomeration of the *Ma-habharata* some unknown genius inserted, at a time not definitely established, the single homogeneous poem called the *Bhagavad Gita*. Its eighteen songs or chants contain advice given to the despondent hero Arjuna by the Lord Shri Krishna just before the

[2] Radhakrishnan: *Indian Philosophy*, Vol. I, p. 483.

battle of Kurukshetra, and taken all together they constitute a
rule of life for the righteous and devoted warrior, a reconciliation of many variant philosophies, a goal for the Hindu spirit
and a Sanskrit poem of supernal beauty. Even though I myself
know no Sanskrit, I have followed the chanting of the Gita so
often with the English text in my hand that I have come to
recognize a great many of the Sanskrit words, can follow its development and have come to feel its astounding beauty as sheer
linguistic melody, pure sound, in a way which hitherto only
Dante and Shakespeare (and lesser poets in lesser measure) had
made possible. A gate opens with the chanting of the Gita unlike
any other gate in the mind's peregrination: Gandhi himself felt
it, although he had known the Gita for many years, when he first
heard its tremendous sonorities in the voice of the Pandit Madan
Mohan Malaviya in 1924. Even a stranger from across the seas
can feel it, although the circumstances of the chanting, beside the
cremation platform of the Mahatma, may have had some special
influence upon my own case.

3

The beauty of this poem as a centrally organized work by a
mature artist of genius made it stand out from the rest of the
Mahabharata at a very early period, and impressed something
quite new upon Vedic Hinduism. The idea of salvation through
faith, brought forward in the last two cantos, was indeed not to
be found in the Vedas themselves, although most of the other
ideas are scattered through the Upanishads. There was a period
when European scholars, scenting a debt to Christianity, tended
to date the Gita very late, somewhere perhaps in the second century A.D., thus allowing time for the concept to seep through
from the Mediterranean and be absorbed in India. Such notions
have been abandoned with increasing study of the ancient texts,
and it seems well agreed now among scholars that the whole of
the *Mahabharata* (including, of course, the Gita) was known
by about 500 B.C. and fully recognized by 300 B.C. as a canonical document.[3]

[3] Radhakrishnan: *Indian Philosophy*, Vol. I, p. 481, note.

For Gandhi, this commanding canonical position was not enough. He did not regard a love for the poem, a knowledge of it or any learned homage as being a spiritual achievement: "Learned men . . . may recite the Vedas from memory," he says, "yet they may be steeped in self-indulgence." [4] The claim he makes for himself with respect to the Gita is the claim of his life itself, its ethical basis and unceasing discipline in accordance with Krishna's words. "At the back of my reading," he says, "there is the claim of an endeavor to enforce the meaning in my own conduct for an unbroken period of forty years." These words, written in 1931 in introducing his Gujarati translation of the Gita, give the measure of his literal devotion. He took the Gita as his guide literally, simply, directly, as a "spiritual reference book," regarding it as practically a scientific system by which self-realization could eventually be attained. And with him, of course, self-realization was no mystical revelation or cataclysm of the consciousness, but a goal to be reached after a lifetime of steady, hard, unremitting effort. There was something toilsome and immense about his effort, like the struggle not of one man but of millions—for of course, as he freely discloses in many pages of his writing, the renunciation of the body and of all attachments, combined with the most rigorous control of his own thoughts, was in itself an unceasing battle. This is perhaps the simplest innermost reason why the battle of Kurukshetra came to mean, for him, the battle within the human heart, and why in the very end (in my conversation with him on January 27, 1948) he declared that even if the scholars could disprove this reading of the Gita he would still believe it.

We have to step with care as we approach the Gandhi-Gita. Too easy, indeed, is the external judgment in such a matter: on the face of it Gandhi was simply wrong. That is, if you read the text of the Gita and consider the plain meaning of the words as they are set in the frame of the great battle of Kurukshetra you will say that the non-violence Gandhi deduced from it is not there. Non-attachment, yes; renunciation of the fruits of action, yes; control of all the senses and passions, yes; but in sum, what is it that Krishna imposes upon the despondent hero Arjuna? It

[4] *Young India*, August 6, 1931.

is to arise and fight. Regardless of the consequences, considering neither pain nor pleasure, hoping as a sage to overcome all obstacles within his own body and nature so as to attain eventual union with Brahman, it is nevertheless Arjuna's duty—his selfless duty, his absolute duty—to fight. And the warfare in which he is to fight is the most terrible known to ancient India, so destructive that hardly any of the Pandavas or Kauravas survived it.

This is the letter of the poem, and can hardly be denied. Gandhi at various times did concede that physical battle was the framework of the Gita in the letter, but he always maintained that the spirit was profoundly non-violent. His reasoning as expressed on November 12, 1925, in *Young India*—prefaced by the remark that "ultimately one is guided not by the intellect but by the heart"—is briefly this: from the age of twenty he believed the last nineteen verses of the second chapter to contain the Gita's essential teaching, and if other verses seem to be in conflict they can be rejected; a humble student could reject nothing but simply say, "It is the limitation of my own intellect that I cannot resolve this inconsistency." Further, prayerful study and experience, plus spiritual discipline, are needed for the interpretation of scripture. Further, no interpretation can be true which conflicts with Truth, of which non-violence is the maturest fruit. Further, the way of self-realization as taught in the Gita rules out all those things such as anger and attachment which go with physical battle, and although killing and being killed in battle is better than cowardice (great admission for Gandhi!) the Gita shows how to rise above both.

Later (1931) he went further and declared that "warlike illustration" is taken in the Gita because in the time of its composition battle was not taboo and nobody had yet observed the contradiction between war and non-violence, and that for other times other and fuller meanings come to life in the great poem. At various periods Gandhi claimed that the very greatness of such a poem lies in the ceaseless revivifying reinterpretation to which it can be subjected in times of changed circumstance. Thus he was able to write as a note to the first *shloka* of the first canto of the Gita, in his Gujarati translation, these words:

"The human body is the battle-field where the eternal duel between Right and Wrong goes on. Therefore it is capable of being turned into the gateway to freedom. It is born in sin and becomes the seed-bed of sin. Hence it is also called the Field of Kuru (*Kurukshetra*). The Kauravas represent the forces of evil, the Pandavas the forces of good. Who is there that has not experienced the daily conflict within himself between the forces of evil and the forces of good?"

It is a bold beginning. Thus, at the very outset of his Gita, Mr. Gandhi transposed the physical carnage of the Kurufield, Kurukshetra, into the life of the individual human being. (In talking to me he called Kurukshetra "the heart of man": in the foregoing he calls it the "human body.") The whole of the Gita immediately becomes an allegory because the physical battle which is its setting is washed away: this is now "a heart-churning," as Gandhi said (a favorite phrase) and thereafter every turn of the discourse is subject to allegorical interpretation. And yet as we pursue our investigation of the Gandhi-Gita we see that in fact this is not so: he takes all of its great concepts and teachings quite literally, with the exception of the bloody framework in which they are set. And what is more, if we surrender to his view—which, in a creative interpretation as in an original creative work, seems almost necessary in order to understand it—then great stretches of the poem acquire an even higher beauty and truth than they might possess without his transposition. The reader is asked to postulate one thing: Kurukshetra is in my heart. Once he has done this, all the Gita remains as before, but enhanced and deepened and heightened as it could not have been if it referred merely to a prehistoric blood-bath in Northern India.

And yet, of course, the historic field called Kurukshetra has been at all ages a place of special sanctity to Indians; its situation and extent are well-defined; even in the *Mahabharata* it is described as a field dedicated for the performance of austerities (before 500 B.C., that is); at the present moment Kurukshetra, which is not far from Delhi, is the site of one of the largest concentration camps in the world, where Hindu refugees from Pakistan are housed. All through the centuries Kurukshetra has been perfectly well known to Indians as it is today. The historicity of the *Mahabharata* is not doubted by most Hindus.

How daring, then, of Gandhi, at one stroke and without further explanation, to transfer his Kurukshetra from epic prehistory into the life of man!

At this stage we cannot explore much further into the meaning of this immense creative transposition. We know that it took place and that from it Mr. Gandhi deduced non-violence as the highest truth and the rule of life. It will be necessary to know much more about his own life and thought, his iron discipline in obedience to the Gita, and the way in which he became himself an exponent and proof of the Gita before he died; at the end of such knowledge, if we can reach it, we shall at least understand that for him at the summit (esoterically, that is, if not exoterically) the battle was in the heart.

It was so, I believe, for him alone. Even his devoted Mahadev Desai does not go far in supporting the Gandhi view of Kurukshetra. And other scholars quite explicitly disown the allegory; they have done so through the centuries and still do so today, long after Gandhi's elevation of non-violence to supreme law had become universally known. The greatest of the moderns is no doubt Shri Aurobindo Ghose, in whose powerful *Essays on the Gita*, published from 1916 to 1918, we find a very different —and a more widely accepted—view. Aurobindo declares the battle of Kurukshetra to have been a plain, literal field of strife, of physical carnage, and holds that the entire Gita proceeds from a concept of nature in which such violent strife is seen to be necessary as an aspect of human activity in general.

We may take this to be the classical expression by a scholar, philosopher, saint and sage, of that view of Kurukshetra which Gandhi's non-violence compelled him to reject. It is abundantly justified in the text of the Gita itself and at the stage to which we have now arrived it may seem to be the only possible view. It may be said that Gandhi was by temperament, heredity, childhood training and lifelong effort so vowed to non-violence that this determined his view of the truth and hence of the Gita. It may also be said (although not by me) that his political genius recognized non-violence as the only possible means for the powerless Indian masses to achieve their freedom and that this influenced him to exalt it as the final fruit and flower of truth.

My own impression of his crystalline sincerity was absolute, and no such merely psychological treatment of his way to the truth would be adequate in my view. I hope to show that his was a *creative* truth—in other words, that it was the kind of truth which, by the miracle of genius, becomes true, is born of faith crossed with supreme intuitive power and in its becoming is enacted upon the stage of the world. To state it philosophically, Shri Aurobindo's Kurukshetra is a truth of being; Mahatma Gandhi's Kurukshetra is a truth of becoming. The liberation of India, if this is so, may be a prelude to the peace of the world.

For further discussion of the Gita, see The Gita and The Gandhi-Gita, page 279.

For an account of the forerunners of Gandhi, see page 299.

IV

The Way of Action

Lord, inspiration of sacrifice! May our ears hear the good. May our eyes see the good. May we serve Him with the whole strength of our body. May we, all our life, carry out His will. May peace and peace and peace be everywhere.

Mundaka Upanishad, I, *1*

The Way of Action

The instinct of mankind has always, I think correctly, held that a conjunction of circumstances was required for the formation and effective unfolding of historical greatness. In the most primitive times rites of magic were performed to influence these circumstances at the birth of a child; in mythologies of all nations, operating after greatness has declared itself, signs and portents, often in meteorology and almost always in visions, are assigned to the origin of any life which changes the course of whole peoples; and in astrology, which wore the cap and gown of science for many centuries in our own culture as it still does in many others, the stars themselves in their courses determined the fate of such a man from birth. Such expressions of the truth, although they may themselves be false and proceed upon a false concept of cause and effect, do give visible form to the deeply experienced reality of which all men and women are conscious, which is that every life is a nexus of circumstances, that much we do is done blindly, that our purest hopes and efforts often come to nothing and that the best, bravest and wisest of men cannot bring about a decisive change in the conditions of life unless time and space with their innumerable interweaving strands happen to be propitious in the hour of his struggle.

If the view taken in this book is correct, it can be seen that everything hitherto described—darshan, the Gita and its widespread modern influence, a Hindu revival and a political awakening, as well as a foreign rule which mitigated its severities by justice under law and bridled its exploitation by conscience—played a part in the historical situation which made the lifework of Mahatma Gandhi possible. Gandhi could not have done what he did if he had been born fifty years earlier; he could not have done it if the English had been Germans or Japanese; he could not have done it if his own people had not possessed their peculiar religious consciousness which made the "great soul" their leader, whatever their degree of political maturity or its opposite. The political part of his effort was, I believe, that which he valued least. It so appears in every expression of his views on all the main questions. What he hoped for was a spiritual awakening, union and peace in India, a "conversion" of the foreign rulers, and, in a word, the reign of God. The political revolution and the liberation of India were, so to speak, incidental results of the larger struggle to which he gave his life. If these results have for thirty years tended to obscure everything else in Gandhi's teaching, the reason is to be found in the minds of men, in the West and elsewhere, who value what can be seen and touched and measured, what has an effect on the stock market, what alters the prices of commodities and the rate of exchange at the bank. Gandhi, largely unconsciously, had a very decisive effect upon all such things for many years, and it is even said that some men made fortunes merely by watching his course and guessing what he was going to do next. But to all this he would have paid little attention even if he had been aware of it: he was concerned only with the truth in thought and action, regardless of consequences, and the rest—these incalculable results which even yet are difficult to measure—were the doing of history. Such an attitude is not only for him as an individual, in the strictest accordance with the teaching of the Gita, but also objectively speaking, conforms to what we know of the complication and interaction of economic, political, social and psychological forces as well as to the sense, deep in all of us, that one man can do little with these forces unless he stands at a crossroads of destiny, that is, in Einsteinian language, at an intersection of lines in the time-space continuum.

2

There were no signs or portents attending the birth of Mr. Gandhi, or if there were, he has since obliterated their traces. His autobiography, *My Experiments with Truth*—a singularly candid and pure narrative of the things he lived for and with up to the year 1921—shows the way in which reason can review a life of even the most religious motivation. There seems to have been a distaste for superstition in him from the beginning, and along with his profound religious feeling there went (even in his earliest days) a thoughtful concentration upon sane and healthy purposes, a refusal of excess, an almost Greek moderation of tone on all subjects.

His father was a prime minister in the Kathiawar states in Western India, north of Bombay—first in Porbandar and then in Rajkot. The Gandhi family belonged to the Bania, or tradesman caste, and Gandhi thought they were originally grocers, but for three generations they had been prime ministers for the Kathiawar princes. These little states—there is a patchwork of them, many of them tiny—are in a district where the Jain religion, that offshoot of Hinduism which refuses to take any life, even the most microscopic, is strong and exercises an influence over the orthodox Hindus of the neighborhood. The Gandhi family (orthodox Hindus) were all devout Vaishnavites to begin with, and growing up, as he did, in a Vaishnava family surrounded by Jain influences, Mr. Gandhi's devotion to non-violence, along with some of the other aspects of his religious personality (including the emphasis on fasting), dates from as early as he could remember.

He was born at Porbandar, October 2, 1869, and passed his childhood there. Kaba Gandhi, his father, was married four times and had six children (three daughters and three sons), of whom Mohandas Karamchand Gandhi was the youngest. Kaba

Gandhi was uneducated, according to his son's testimony, and could read the vernacular language (which, in that part of India, is Gujarati) up to the "fifth standard" (fifth grade). But if he was unlearned, he appears to have been competent and experienced to a high degree, capable of handling large numbers of men in public affairs and satisfying the requirements of the successive princes whom he served. It is obvious from Gandhi's autobiography that the youngest member of the family, at any rate, had a love and reverence for the father which survived in memory for many years. Gandhi says his father was "truthful, brave and generous, but short-tempered." Moreover: "To a certain extent he might have been even given to carnal pleasures, for he married for the fourth time when he was over forty." This fourth wife, Putlibai, was the Mahatma's mother and to her he attributed most of his early religious discipline as well as a good start in his assiduous practise of the virtues of restraint.

The mother was deeply religious in her way. Among the Vaishnavites fasting in various forms and degrees is a discipline greatly in favor, and Gandhi's mother practised them all. During the four months of the rainy season a sort of Lent is observed among the devout, with vows of fasting and semi-fasting. These Lenten practices are called the *Chaturmas*, and Gandhi could never remember his mother missing one. Another vow of fasting is called the *Chandrayana*, in which the quantity of food taken daily is increased or decreased according to the waxing or waning of the moon. During one *Chaturmas* the mother vowed not to eat unless she had seen the sun (which, in the rainy season, is not often): and one of the early memories of the boy who was to become Mahatma was of waiting outside, staring at the sky, so as to be able to announce the sun to his mother so that she could eat. These very early memories of disciplinary austerities (always in obedience to some vow) made the deepest impression on Gandhi's mind, and as we shall see, at the very end of his life they still played a part. He told me, in fact, that his bent toward what he called "disciplinary resolutions" was the result of his mother's saintliness and her influence upon his earliest awareness.

When the child was about seven the Gandhi family moved from Porbandar to Rajkot, where he went to primary school and high school (instruction being in English, of course). He was a shy boy, afraid of attention or companions, and used to run home as soon as school was over for fear that somebody might wish to talk to him. Some plays based on the Indian epics seem to have aroused his imagination more than anything else during those early years. One was the drama of *Harishchandra*, a story from the *Mahabharata* which he actually told me at some length two days before his death. He saw the dramatization once and thereafter acted it to himself time without number, saying: "Why should not all be truthful like Harishchandra?" The ordeals undergone by that king of old for his devotion to the truth made an impression which was never to be effaced, although in later years Gandhi came to see that the stories from the *Mahabharata* were not necessarily historic fact. In his childhood he believed every one of them literally, as do millions of other Hindus today.

The boy Gandhi was married at thirteen to a girl his own age, a stranger named Kasturbai who was totally illiterate. He is painfully candid on the subject and warns his readers: "I was married, not betrothed." The whole notion of child marriage was one which became very repugnant to him in after years, but in his autobiography he tells the story of what happened without concealment. In the Gandhi family there were three marriages to be made—Gandhi and one of his older brothers along with a cousin—and the elders decided to get all three done at once, thus producing a greater effect and combining the expenses. Hindu weddings, for which months of preparation sometimes scarcely suffice, are tremendous occasions on which many families spend the income of several years or—as Gandhi says—"bring themselves to ruin." The clothes, ornaments and food are all the product of immense effort, time and (relatively) money; there is incessant singing and banqueting and festivity. The boy Gandhi only came to know of his approaching marriage by these signs.

"I do not think it meant to me anything more than the prospect of good clothes to wear, drum beating, marriage processions, rich dinners and a strange girl to play with," he says. And, after describing the ceremonies, he goes on: "My brother's wife had thoroughly coached me about my behavior on the first night. I do not know who had coached my wife. I have never asked her about it, nor am I inclined to do so now. . . . How was I to talk to her, and what was I to say? The coaching could not carry me far. But no coaching is really necessary in such matters. The impressions of the former birth are potent enough to make all coaching superfluous."

The schoolboy husband had read some pamphlets on marriage and took them to heart. His own passion for truth was innate, and he had resolved to be faithful to Kasturbai for life; but he determined to exact the same fidelity from her, and became, apparently in no time at all, a jealous husband, watching over every excursion the girl made and quarreling for a trifle. Under the system of Hindu society at that time, the husband and wife met only at night, and for months at a time Kasturbai returned to her own parents to live. Gandhi found himself thinking of her at school and at all other times, longing for "nightfall and our subsequent meeting." Kasturbai's illiteracy disturbed him a little and he was "very anxious to teach her," but, as he says, "lustful love left me no time." Under the *purdah* system of that period, he could not visit her in the daytime at all. Kasturbai remained substantially illiterate to the end, although she later learned to make simple letters in Gujarati and read simple sentences.

The sins of Gandhi's youth involved eating meat and smoking. He acquired an elder friend, in the desire to reform him, and found himself corrupted instead: the friend had the habit of eating meat surreptitiously, and preached a "reform" of Hindu dietary habits. "We are a weak people because we do not eat meat," the friend said. "The English are able to rule over us because they are meat-eaters. You know how hardy I am, and how great a runner too. It is because I am a meat-eater."

Gandhi's elder brother had already succumbed to these arguments and supported the friend in his effort to get another convert. To their presentation of the case Gandhi added a reason of his own—that he was a coward. This was the last accusation anybody could have made against him in his later life, but he tells us that in childhood he was afraid of the dark and that he imagined ghosts coming from one side, thieves from another and serpents from a third. (He was even forced to sleep with a light in the room at this period.) Eating meat, he imagined—and his friend bore him out—would cure all fear. They had a piece of doggerel they used to quote, which goes as follows:

> "Behold the mighty Englishman
> He rules the Indian small,
> Because being a meat-eater
> He is five cubits tall."

Persuaded by all these false reasons, Gandhi yielded. With his friend he sought out a lonely spot by the river, where they ate some tough goat's meat and some baker's bread. Gandhi sickened in his attempt to eat the stuff and went home, where he had nightmares all night long, with a live goat bleating inside him. He was then forced to remind himself that meat-eating was a duty to India—a "reform"—and "so became more cheerful."

The disastrous first experience was repeated a number of times during the next year with better results. The insidious elder friend never again asked Gandhi to eat straight meat, but prepared the meat dishes with various other delicacies and savors, so that they were more appetizing. Since such dishes were expensive, the feasts were intermittent, and Gandhi believed there could have been only about six of them in the course of the year. He stopped eating meat because he found that it was leading him into telling lies to his parents, which he abhorred. He said to himself:

"Though it is essential to eat meat, and also essential to take up food 'reform' in the country, yet deceiving and lying to one's father and mother is worse than not eating meat. In their lifetime, therefore, meat-eating must be out of the question. When they are no more and I have found my freedom, I will eat meat openly, but until that moment arrives I will abstain from it."

Of course the "moment" never arrived, and Gandhi was a vegetarian ever afterward.

The same wicked friend, who seems to have been indefatigable in his efforts to corrupt the budding saint, once took Gandhi to a brothel. He had made all the arrangements and paid the bill in advance. The future Mahatma sat beside the prostitute on her bed, but was "almost struck blind and dumb in this den of vice." The woman eventually put him out "with insults and abuses." He gave thanks to God ever afterward for having saved him, although he points out that it was a moral lapse to have gone there anyhow, since "the carnal desire was there, and it was as good as the act."

At about the same period Gandhi fell into the habit of smoking cigarettes, and, what was worse, of pilfering stumps of his uncle's cigarettes and also the servants' coppers to pay for cigarettes. This in turn led him to a more serious theft: a bit of gold from the solid gold armlet of his meat-eating brother. He used this gold to pay his brother's debts, but the storm in his own conscience was great: he resolved to confess his sins in writing to his own father. In the confession he pledged himself never to repeat the offense, and trembled with emotion as he handed it to his father, who was then ill in bed. The elder Gandhi wept and said nothing, and young Gandhi was cured of these particular sins.

"A clean confession," says Gandhi, "combined with a promise never to commit the sin again, when offered before one who has the right to receive it, is the purest type of repentance."

It may be remarked that whether Mr. Gandhi knew it or not, this statement is almost precisely the doctrine of the Roman Catholic Church.

The last illness and death of the father Gandhi provided another instance of the youthful sins which so greatly exercised the Mahatma's conscience. The elder Gandhi was dying, and the boy gave him those services which are usual from son to father in India (or even from youth to elder). He massaged the father's legs every night until he fell asleep. The sin was that in the hour of his father's death he was in bed with his wife, indulging in "carnal desire," instead of being in attendance on the dying man. This was "a blot I have never been able to efface or forget," he says.

Religion played a great part in the life of the Gandhi household, as it does for most Hindus, but in the case of young Mohandas the influences brought to bear were of an exceptionally tolerant and unsectarian nature. The elder Gandhi, as a public official, had friends in all faiths, and all visited him from time to time. Young Gandhi was present (as nurse, during the last illness) in discussions with Jain monks, with Mohammedans, with Parsis and others. His own religious temperament was not fully awakened: he did not like temple worship, with its glitter and its hints of immorality, and his chief religious mentor appears to have been his old nurse Rambha, who used to give him advice. She told him to take refuge in *Ramanama* (repetitions of the name of the deity under the incarnation as Rama) from the fears that assailed him at night. He tried it, and finding it of no avail gave it up; but the mature Gandhi, and still more the Mahatma in his age, returned to that childhood lesson with gratitude. In some of his greatest agonies—as when he had fasted for many days or weeks and was suffering—he found repetitions of the name of the deity a source of strength. His last words, I am told, breathed on a sigh just after the assassin's bullets went home, but audible to those nearest him, were such a repetition: *"Hé, Ram! Hé, Ram!"* (Ah, God! Ah, God!—the word Rama standing for God in Ramanama.)

The exception to the Gandhi family tolerance was Christianity. In his childhood Christian missionaries used to preach in the streets, pouring out abuse on the Hindu religion and its gods. This was more than Gandhi could endure. He also found that Hindus converted to Christianity began at once to eat beef and drink alcohol, which gave him a poor opinion of the religion that brought about such changes.

He was, in fact, inclined toward atheism during these years (thirteen to seventeen, or so) and found little to answer his doubts in such Hindu scriptures as came his way. He found that Manu the Lawgiver approved of meat-eating, and at that time the young Gandhi considered that it was "quite moral to kill serpents, bugs and the like." Absolute non-violence was still far from his consciousness. What he had, even at that age, and retained in ever-increasing strength to the end of his days, was a regard for truth as the substance of all morality. "Truth became my sole objective," he says. "It began to grow in magnitude every day, and my definition of it also has been ever widening."

3

At eighteen Gandhi went to college in Ahmedabad but lasted out only a term. The teaching did not arouse his interest and he did not do well; but a revolutionary change was now in prospect. A Brahmin who was a friend of the family suggested that he go to college in England, become a barrister, and then return to Kathiawar fully prepared to take over the prime ministership of one of the princely states, thus succeeding his father and grandfather.

The suggestion was, in 1887, something to startle a devout Hindu family. In the first place those who crossed the sea were almost automatically expelled from their caste; in the second place a foreign country, with all its dangers to morals, was not thought fit for so young a man alone; and finally the expense of the undertaking was serious for the Gandhi family now that the father was dead.

Gandhi himself was on fire with the project, and it was clearly owing to his own insistence that the family councils finally decided to send him to London. If it was necessary to sell his wife's jewels, he was ready to do so, but his elder brother promised to find the money somehow. The devout mother only agreed to the idea when young Gandhi solemnly vowed that he would not touch wine, meat or women during his absence.

But there was one more hurdle before he could leave India. The Modh Bania caste, to which he belonged, had never yet had a member cross the seas. This was in itself regarded as against religion, but still worse was the constant exposure to Europeans, eating with them and drinking water with them. Young Gandhi in Bombay was summoned before a general meeting of the Modh Bania caste and was formally ordered not to proceed. Gandhi defied his caste in this matter and was therefore pronounced outcaste, which meant that no member of his own caste (or other caste Hindus) could help him or be friendly to him without also being expelled. He took this punishment without undue agitation and never afterward went through the formality of being restored to caste, so that—technically speaking—he was outcaste for a section of the Bania to the time of his death. (As a Mahatma, of course, he was apart from and above all caste anyhow.)

The only effect of this caste regulation on him was to hasten his departure from Bombay. His brother's contribution had not yet arrived, so he borrowed the necessary money and sailed at once—September 4, 1887.

At this time the young Gandhi, although educated in English, had very little practice in speaking the language and was seldom able to understand what his English fellow-passengers said to him. He records that even when he did understand he was unable to reply, not only because of his agonizing shyness, but also because he had to frame each English sentence precisely in his mind before he could begin to utter it. He heroically wore his black suit, European style, every day on shipboard, saving his white flannels for what he imagined to be the necessities of life in England. These clothes had been provided for him by his friends, and were uncomfortable; the short jacket seemed to him immodest; the necktie (which he confesses he afterward took pleasure in) was a form of torture. He stepped ashore at Southampton (in an English autumn) wearing white flannels, discovered too late that he was the only person so caparisoned, and had to travel thus to London because his luggage and keys had been delivered to the tourist agency.

In London he and the barrister who was his fellow-passenger went to the Victoria Hotel, where they stayed from Saturday to Monday, Gandhi in great shame over his white clothing and scarcely daring to eat anything for fear of breaking dietary rules. The bill at the hotel was three pounds, which gave the budding Mahatma his first shock in England. On Monday he and his fellow-passenger moved to rooms, the first of a series of such habitations rented from London landladies who could not understand his diet.

The diet became one of the dominant interests in life during the first weeks the young student spent in London. He was determined not to break his vegetarian vow. Other Indian students, including his roommates of the early days, broke all their dietary rules while they were in England and did their best to persuade Gandhi to do the same. Their arguments were based upon climate, custom and the ease of life, none of which made any difference to the obstinate young man who had taken the vow. With some of his companions he had painful disagreements just then, and he tells the story of one Indian friend who, having asked him to dine at the Holborn Restaurant, flew into a rage when he insisted on asking the waiter what was in the soup: young Gandhi went without dinner that night.

The misery of those early weeks is easy to discern through the

language of the Mahatma's autobiography. It was
ast, by a great discovery: by sheer accident he fell
tarian restaurant in Farrington Street. Up to then
eating in whatever cheap restaurant he could find,
ever could eat anything but bread. Now it was
reveal___ him that there were actually other people in England,
not Indians, who ate only vegetables, and did so on principles
which could be detailed and supported—moral, hygienic and
physical principles. In the first vegetarian restaurant he found
(the one in Farrington Street) where he had his "first hearty
meal in England," he also found a book for sale for one shilling:
Salt's *Plea for Vegetarianism*.

Up to the time of reading this book Gandhi had been a vegetarian out of regard for his mother, or in respect to his vow, but
had never been intellectually convinced of the value of such a
diet. He had thought, on the contrary, that Indians should become
meat-eaters to gain strength and win their freedom: he thought
so even when he was himself starving on bread and water in
London. But after Salt's book, which he read and re-read, he
was what he calls "a vegetarian by choice," and was henceforth
prepared to proselytize to win others to that belief. He went on
to a whole library of works on diet, hygiene and health, all
English, and all confirming, from the point of view of doctors of
science, what his ancestral religion had taught him. Dietary experiments became henceforth one of the main interests of Gandhi's personal life, at first for reasons of health and afterward as
an instrument of religion. There was never a time when he lost
interest in dietary theories or innovations, and only a few days
before his death he was on the track of some new vegetable-and-
fruit combination expounded in an American magazine. For the
greater part of his life he was himself engaged in trying out fixed
diets of one sort or another, sometimes all fruit, sometimes all
vegetables, sometimes combinations and variations. Once, for
instance, he tried giving up starchy foods, another time living
on bread and fruit alone, and still another time on cheese, milk
and eggs alone. This diet he abandoned in less than two weeks
because it became apparent to him that under his mother's definition (and it was his mother who had administered the vegetarian
vow) eggs were counted as meat.

He found three distinct varieties of vegetarianism among the English authors he consulted. In the first group only flesh-meat was rejected, and fish, eggs and milk were accepted. In the second group the flesh of all living creatures, including fish, was taboo, but eggs were allowed. In the third group—to which Gandhi soon belonged for life—even eggs were forbidden. (The milk problem was one he never really solved—owing, as he told me, to "the weakness of the body"—and we shall consider it in due course.) Once he had firmly made up his mind not to eat eggs, in view principally of his mother's definition of eggs as meat, his difficulties even in vegetarian restaurants were numerous, because many of the dishes even there contained eggs. He had to ask, for example, about the constitution of every pudding or cake that came his way, since many were made with the forbidden eggs.

The medical advice in the books he consulted—and most of his vegetarian authorities were doctors—was unanimous against spices and condiments. These are prominent in most Indian diets and govern the palate of the Hindu, no matter how severely he may restrict himself in the elements of food. Gandhi tried obeying the doctors' advice and found that in time his taste for condiments disappeared, and then, by compensation, the plain boiled vegetables which had seemed to him insipid on his first arrival in England acquired appetizing qualities. He concluded, thus early, that "the real seat of taste was not the tongue but the mind."

The motive for all this vegetarian enthusiasm was, he tells us, health and economy. He reached the point, a little later on, where he was able to live on one shilling and threepence a day, by making his own breakfast and dinner in a single room and lunching out in a cheap vegetarian restaurant. The religious motive, he says, did not play much part in his thinking on the subject at that time. This may be so, but even Gandhi was not wholly conscious of every element in his being, and we may quite easily see that his delight in the vegetarian discovery—in the revelation that there were scientific reasons for his religious diet—was essentially that of the devout believer who finds support from an unexpected direction.

He subscribed to a vegetarian magazine, joined the Vegetarian Society of England, and organized a vegetarian club in his own neighborhood, which at the time was Bayswater. (Sir Edwin

Arnold, the translator of the Gita, lived in the neighborhood and became vice-president of the club; Gandhi was secretary; Dr. Oldfield, President of the Vegetarian Society of England, was president.) It appears to have been vegetarianism which first conquered his appalling shyness and made him try to speak before strangers. In both the attempts he made, with his speech fully written out in advance, he failed utterly: when he rose, even to read his paper, no sound would come out of his throat and his speech had to be read by somebody else.

One of the parts of Gandhi's London experience which has caused much laughter among his friends is that which he calls "playing the English gentleman." He made up his mind that he had caused quite enough pain and embarrassment to his Indian friends through his obstinate vegetarianism, and he would make it up to them by cultivating some new airs and graces: he would become a "gentleman." He got rid of his Bombay clothes and bought some new ones at the Army and Navy Stores; he acquired a chimney-pot hat for the monstrous sum of nineteen shillings; he paid ten pounds for an evening suit made in Bond Street; he wrote to his brother in India and asked for a double watch-chain of gold. He learned how to tie a necktie (since it "was not correct to wear a ready-made tie") and wasted, as he mournfully records, ten whole minutes every day looking at himself in the mirror while he tied it and brushed his tough black hair into the correct style. He paid three pounds for a term at a dancing class, three pounds for a violin and some more for a violin teacher, and a guinea as down payment to an elocution teacher. All this extravagance lasted about three months. He discovered that no teaching could give him the faintest idea of how to dance or even to move rhythmically, and the elocution was, for his purposes, worse than useless. He abandoned the whole "gentleman" experiment and set to work in earnest on his studies. What remained of the episode was a photograph of Gandhiji at the age of eighteen which is unrecognizable and very funny—"aping the English gentleman" is the title he gives it in his autobiography—with slick hair, prim tie and the dark, thick-lipped, rather sullen face of an adolescent. The only element in this physiognomy that those who knew the Mahatma in his age would recognize is the ears, which, then as at all times, stuck out at right angles to his face.

Besides the examinations for the London matriculation, which he undertook and passed in his first months in England, Gandhi's studies for admission to the bar were in Roman Law and Common Law. Under the loose and antiquated system in use by the Inns of Court, the law students had to read certain textbooks and attend at least six out of the twenty-four dinners given during a term. The examinations (four times a year) were notoriously easy, and it would have been possible for Gandhi to become a barrister by skipping through a few books and going to the right number of dinners. His conscientiousness did not permit this, and he studied his way laboriously through all the books prescribed, reading Roman Law in Latin, for example (which was not necessary). He was afterwards grateful for this, since Justinian was the basis of the Roman-Dutch common law in South Africa. At the dinners he was always in demand, since he did not drink wine and two bottles were allowed to each group of four students; his share, especially on a "grand night" when champagne was added, was highly prized by the others.

In vegetarian restaurants and suchlike haunts the young Gandhi picked up quite a few acquaintances during his stay in London. One such acquisition, toward the end of his second year, was a pair of brothers who belonged to the Theosophical Society. They were then reading Sir Edwin Arnold's translation of the Gita, called *The Song Celestial*, and asked Gandhi to read the original with them. To his shame, Gandhi was obliged to confess that he had not read it either in Sanskrit or Gujarati, but offered his knowledge of Sanskrit (such as it was) for a reading along with the translation. This was his first acquaintance with the divine poem, and to the end of his days he regarded the Arnold translation as the best English version (probably because it was the medium through which he first knew the work). The theosophical brothers also took him to Madame Blavatsky's house, where he met Mrs. Besant; they likewise invited him to join the Theosophical Society, which he sagely refused to do.

He met a "good Christian" along about the same time, another chance acquaintance in a vegetarian boarding house, who opened up to him the other world which had hitherto been closed: that of the New Testament. The Christian was a vegetarian and did not drink alcohol, which in itself did something to dispel Gandhi's childhood notion that Christianity was a religion of meat-eating and drunkenness. On the advice of this man Gandhi bought and read the Bible, making no headway with the Old Testament, but stirred to excitement over the New Testament and above all by the Sermon on the Mount. Even then, when he was twenty, some fusion of that supreme Christian document with the Gita was established in his mind.

He came upon Carlyle's *Heroes and Hero-Worship* soon afterward and discovered Mohammed in the Hero as Prophet. He would have pursued his investigations of the great religious ideas, which obviously appealed to him beyond measure, but his efforts to learn something about the law precluded any great amount of reading on other subjects. He was thus—although no longer an atheist—still on the merest threshold of the subject which was afterward to engross his consciousness more than any other.

He passed his examinations at last, was called to the bar on June 10, 1891, enrolled in the High Court on June 11th, and sailed for India on June 12th.

4

His first shock on arriving in Bombay was to learn that his mother had died during his absence; the news had been concealed from him. The second—less concentrated—was the progressive discovery of his own unfitness for the practise of the law.

It was decided in the family that he should get his start in Bombay rather than in Rajkot, attending the High Court, studying Indian law and taking whatever briefs he could get. He tried this for six months with a lack of success which was practically absolute. The only case he got to try in court he was unable to handle: when he rose to cross-examine the plaintiff's witnesses his head reeled and he had the usual trouble of being unable to utter a sound. He gave up the case and told his client to engage Patel—Vallabhbhai Patel, later one of his stout adherents, then already a successful barrister. The only job of work he was able to perform during these six months was a written effort, a memorial for a poor Muslim whose land in Porbandar had been confiscated: this was good enough, apparently, but was done for no fee. The High Court put him to sleep, he was learning little of Indian law and there were no clients in prospect: therefore he gave up the struggle in Bombay and went home to Rajkot, where his brother and his brother's partner could throw a considerable amount of business his way.

The small Kathiawar states dwelt in an atmosphere of incessant intrigue which was repugnant to Gandhi. In addition, he ran afoul of an English officer whom he had known in England, whose manner (like that of others in the imperial days) was far different in India. The surroundings, the opportunities and the general tone of life were of a kind to depress the young man, even though he was earning enough money to pay his own expenses. At this juncture, when he was obviously pining for a break in the clouds, a Porbandar firm offered him a job in South Africa.

The firm was Dada Abdullah and Company, Muslim merchants with a big business in Natal and an outstanding claim for some 40,000 pounds sterling against another Muslim firm. It was suggested that Gandhi, as a barrister from London, could instruct the counsel (English or South African) for the Indian firm and could help the company in other ways as well, since much of its business was done in English. The terms were a first-class ticket to Durban and back, all expenses in Africa paid, and 105 pounds for a year's stay. Gandhi accepted at once, with apparently no remote notion of what conditions he would find in South Africa or what was about to befall him as a result.

He sailed from Bombay for Natal in April, 1893, and reached Durban toward the end of May.

5

Gandhi in his European dress and with his European manners—these were his "first-class days," as he says—was rather a shock to Abdullah Sheth, the old-fashioned Muslim merchant who was his new employer. He observed at the very outset that Indians were not treated with much respect in Durban. At the time the Indians there dressed in their own national style; Gandhi wore a frock coat and a Hindu turban, something like the Bengali *pugree.* That turban was soon to become famous in South Africa.

Abdullah Sheth tried to explain the case now pending—the great case for 40,000 pounds—and Gandhi perceived that with all his practical knowledge and experience, the Muslim merchant was in fact illiterate. He ran a big business, the biggest among Indians in the colony, but had never mastered English or book-keeping.

On the second or third day Abdullah Sheth took Gandhi to see the Durban court. Here began the struggle which was to engage all the rest of Gandhi's time in South Africa. The magistrate in the court, eyeing him, asked him to remove his turban. Gandhi refused to do so and left the court.

Under the schemes of differentiation and prejudice then in vogue, Muslims were permitted to wear turbans in court because it was their religious custom to do so, but Hindus, Parsis and other Indians were obliged to uncover their heads, like Europeans. South Africa was then, as now, a prey to racial prejudice of all sorts, attaining a complication of discriminating practices unknown elsewhere, and Gandhi had run into an example of its operation at the very outset of his experience there. The "turban incident" acquired immediate notoriety, was much discussed in the South African press, and induced Gandhi to write letters to the newspapers defending his course.

He discovered that the Indians in South Africa, surrounded by hostility and prejudice, fell into a number of groups, amongst whom the privileged made constant attempts to escape from their own nationality by calling themselves something else. The Muslim merchants, some of them very rich, called themselves "Arabs." The Parsi clerks called themselves "Persians" and the Hindu bank clerks and bookkeepers, unless they wished to call themselves "Arabs" too, were obliged to submit to the ordinary lot of the Indian immigrant to South Africa. This lot was not good. The bulk of the Indian immigrants consisted of South Indians (Tamil, Telugu) who had come over on contract to serve as common laborers for five years. There were North Indians and some free laborers among them, but all alike were known as "coolies," a term which was then extended to all Indians even of the more privileged classes. The Englishmen and South Africans also used the word "sami" as applied to all Indians, although the word actually is merely the Tamil version of the Sanskrit word *swami* (meaning "master") and was not at all what the white men had in mind in using it. Most probably those who addressed every Indian as *sami* thought they were using a collective nickname ("Sammy") and never realized that it was a term of respect in Tamil.

Gandhi was therefore a "coolie barrister," he says, and the Indian merchants were "coolie merchants." Muslims, by pretending to be Arabs, could sometimes escape from this nomenclature, but Hindus never.

A week after his arrival in Natal, Gandhi was sent off to Pretoria to represent his employer, Abdullah Sheth, in the great lawsuit. In the meantime he had familiarized himself with the case —undertaking a quick study of bookkeeping to clarify its details—and had formed the notion that a settlement out of court would be best for all concerned, especially since the defendant, Tyeb Sheth, was a close relative of Abdullah. He acquired a first-class ticket on the railway and set off for Pretoria.

From Durban to Maritzburg, the capital of Natal, all went well, but there, at about nine in the evening, a white passenger saw him in the first-class compartment, called a railway official and had him ordered out. "Coolies" were not allowed in the first class. Gandhi declared that he would have to be removed by force, as he had bought his ticket and was legally entitled to travel by it. A constable came and put him out of the train; he sat in the railway station all night, with his luggage (containing his overcoat) locked away by the inimical railway officials. It was bitter cold. He reviewed his situation and decided that he could not allow a superficial hardship to interfere with his performance of duty, and therefore made up his mind to take the train on to Pretoria the following night. During the day Indian merchants of Maritzburg called on him at the railway station and told him that his own mishap was a commonplace, that it nearly always happened thus, and that many worse things could befall an Indian in that country.

Gandhi went on as far as Charlestown the following night, but from there to Johannesburg it was necessary to take a stage-coach: here again no "coolies" were allowed, and Gandhi was obliged to ride on the driver's box with the coachman. The "leader" of the stagecoach, that is, the white man who was in charge of the trip, sat inside with the white passengers so that the "coolie" could have his seat. Later on the "leader" wanted to smoke, so he spread a piece of dirty sack-cloth on the footboard and said to Gandhi: "Here, *sami*, you sit on this, I want to sit beside the driver." Gandhi refused and was thereupon assaulted by the "leader," who boxed his ears brutally and began to beat him. Gandhi clung to the brass rails of the coachbox, refusing to move, although the man rained blows on him. The white passengers who were witnesses to the scene intervened; the "leader," breathless with curses and physical exertion, stopped beating Gandhi and moved to another seat vacated by the Hottentot servant of the coach.

At Standerton Gandhi made formal complaint to the coach company (as he had done to the railway company in Maritzburg) and was transferred to another coach the next day in which he traveled to Johannesburg with the other passengers. In the meantime, as at Maritzburg, the Indian colony had made him welcome, in response to a telegram from Abdullah Sheth, and regaled him with stories of their own misfortunes from race prejudice.

In Johannesburg he drove to the Grand National Hotel and was refused a room, which appears to have surprised him; he learned when he went on to Abdullah Sheth's local shop that "coolies" were not admitted to hotels either. He now faced the problem of the railway journey from Johannesburg to Pretoria, some thirty-seven miles, in a country (the Transvaal) which was even more bitter toward the Indian than was Natal. Against the advice of his friends, who had accepted the situation and never traveled except in third class, Gandhi wrote a letter to the station-master and declared his intention of coming to buy a first-class ticket. It was his calculation that if he gave the station-master time to reply in writing, the answer would be "no," but if he went in person in his best English clothes, it would be more difficult to refuse him. He also stated in the letter that he was a barrister and "always traveled first class."

The station-master was a Dutchman from Holland, somewhat freer from prejudice than the Transvaalers, and sold him the ticket. The train guard made an attempt to move him into a third-class carriage, but by luck there was an Englishman in the compartment who protested and declared that Gandhi should travel by the ticket he had paid for. "If you want to travel with a coolie," the guard said, "what do I care?" Thus Gandhi triumphantly entered Pretoria in a first-class compartment.

These episodes of his initiation into the life of the Indians in South Africa set the tone for much of Gandhi's earlier activity there. He was not personally either proud or pretentious, and of course the whole world knows that in after years he voluntarily adopted the standard of living of the poorest of poor Indians, including third-class travel at all times. But his national pride or patriotic feeling was another matter, and it was this that he felt to be insulted in all these discriminations. He was still so shy that any altercation gave him acute pain, and the thought that an inquiry might be answered by an insult kept him mute, tongue-tied. At Pretoria he was not met by Abdullah's representatives as he had expected, and he was afraid to ask anybody for the name of a hotel that might be willing to take him in. He waited until all the passengers had departed and then surrendered his ticket to the collector and asked for information. The expected insult did not come; instead, an American Negro who was providentially standing there in the station offered to take him to a small hotel kept by an American where he might be received. Gandhi went with him and found himself in Johnston's Family Hotel, the only "coolie" guest, but welcome so long as he would take his meals in his room. He consented to this gladly, but the American proprietor then took a sort of plebiscite of the other guests and, finding that they had no objections, permitted Gandhi to eat in the dining-room.

On the next day he made the acquaintance of Abdullah's lawyer, A. W. Baker, a devout Christian who was to play a considerable part in his life for years. Baker found him lodgings with a poor woman who understood his vegetarian tastes and took him as a boarder at thirty-five shillings a week. At their very first meeting Baker tried to find out Gandhi's religious views and invited him to a daily prayer-meeting at one o'clock. Gandhi's reply, as given in his autobiography, was this:

"I am a Hindu by birth. And yet I do not know much of Hinduism, and I know less of other religions. In fact I do not know where I am, and what is and what should be my belief. I intend to make a careful study of my own religion and, as far as I can, of other religions as well."

On that first night, before he went to sleep, Gandhi resolved to learn all he could about religions. Again, it appears to me, as in the case of the vegetarian discovery, he derived from experience —in this case the proselytizing zeal of Mr. Baker—merely a confirmation of what was already in his own nature: the desire for religious knowledge and harmony. He went to the prayer-meeting the next day and as often thereafter as he could, even though he was aware that one of the main purposes of the welcome given him was his conversion to Christianity. He began to keep a religious diary, met a variety of devout Christians, and acquired a friend (Mr. Coates) who was a Quaker. From this friend he received a stream of books on Christianity which he read and then discussed with others. The more he read, the more he separated the higher and permanent truths of religion (as a belief in God) from the exclusive claim of Christianity to be the only truth, and its doctrine of vicarious atonement for sin. His conversion was as far off after this course of instruction and discussion as it had been in the beginning, but he had initiated those studies of religious essence which were to become the dominating force of his life.

Meanwhile his sense of the injustice being done his fellow-Indians in Africa grew keener as he came to know the situation better. He found that in the Orange Free State Indians were in fact proscribed, except in menial employments, and in the Transvaal they were subjected to a number of discriminatory regulations under the special law governing Asiatics (1885, as amended in 1886). Indians had to pay a poll-tax of three pounds sterling on entering the Transvaal; they could not own land except in special locations (a sort of ghetto law); they were disenfranchised; they could not walk on public footpaths or sidewalks, but only in the street; they could not be out of doors after 9 P.M. without a special permit. (To the latter law the "Arabs," or Indians calling themselves that, were in practice exempt.)

Gandhi's public life may be said to have begun with a meeting he called of all the Indian colony in Pretoria. There he made his first public speech, telling his countrymen what their situation was and giving them some advice. He admonished them on their own conduct, saying that the obligation to truthfulness was greater upon them since all Indians would be judged by what they did; he called their attention to insanitary conditions amongst them; he asked them to forget the distinctions between Hindu, Muslim, Parsi and Christian, between Punjabi and Madrasi and the like, and to form an association of all Indians so as to present a united front to the authorities and obtain redress for some of the grievances of the Indian settlers. To this he offered his own services free. He also offered to teach English to anybody who was willing to study, and actually did obtain three pupils whom he instructed with assiduity in their own places of business for the next eight months. The success of this first meeting was such that it was repeated with regularity thereafter—once a week or once a month, with a growing attendance from the Indian colony. As a result Gandhi's acquaintance among the Indians of Pretoria became complete, and there was no member of the colony whose problems were not familiar to him before the year was out.

He also presented the Indian case to the railway authorities and received in reply a letter that first- and second-class tickets would be issued in future to Indians who were "properly dressed." This, of course, left it to the discretion of the station-master to decide who was and who was not properly dressed.

The curfew rule for Indians was personally awkward to Gandhi because he liked to walk in the evening with his Quaker friend, Mr. Coates. The difficulty was solved by a letter from the State Attorney, a Dr. Krause (a Boer) who had become a barrister at the same Inn as Gandhi. The rule about Indians walking in the street was not enforced in Gandhi's case, perhaps because of his English clothes, except on one occasion. He was walking out toward President Kruger's house when a policeman unknown to him kicked him into the street without a moment's warning. He did not take court action against the policeman (in spite of his friend Mr. Coates who had witnessed the incident from horseback) because he had now made up his mind not to go to court for any personal grievance.

His idea for solving the case that had brought him to Africa grew upon him the more he saw how the lawyers, like locusts, were eating away at the lawsuit. If the case came to trial it might last for a long time and ruin both plaintiff and defendant. He therefore bent every energy toward bringing the parties together, and finally, after prolonged effort, obtained a settlement in which Tyeb Sheth would pay Abdullah Sheth some 37,000 pounds in instalments over a period of years. This great success—his first in the law—gave him a fixed principle for all such activities, and in his twenty years as a barrister he never deviated from it: that was, to bring the opposing parties together whenever and however it might be possible. Thus his system became a peculiar one for any barrister, but the only correct one for his own personality, and he settled a great many cases—most of those that came to him—by the method of mediation and compromise.

During this year in Pretoria the earnest little dark-skinned man in the English frock-coat and Hindu turban must have become a personage of considerable interest to all who knew him. His interest in religion grew apace, and his Christian friends—particularly Baker—lavished upon him every persuasion in their power. His Muslim friends also saw in him a possible convert and under their influence he read the Koran for the first time, as well as numerous other Islamic works and works on Islam. He was only twenty-four and had by now passed well beyond the atheistic phase, but nothing his friends could produce for him shook his feeling that his own religion, when he came to know it better, would suit him best. He was reinforced in this by a letter from his friend Raychandbhai in Bombay—that businessman, jeweler and poet whom he thought the most wonderful character he had ever met, a spiritual guide whom he would have "enthroned in his heart as *guru*" if he had been capable of doing so—who said:

"On a dispassionate view of the question I am convinced that no other religion has the subtle and profound thought of Hinduism, its vision of the soul, or its charity."

The year for which he had contracted came to an end, the case was over, and he was ready to go back to India, even though the plight of his fellow-countrymen in Africa was heavy on his mind. His sense of responsibility toward them is not hard to understand: most of them were illiterate, few had an adequate knowledge of English, and he was the only Indian barrister in the country. They had come to rely upon him more than he yet

realized—old men, some of them, and rich, but dependent upon
the deep honesty and unselfish talent of the twenty-four-year-old
boy. Abdullah Sheth gave a farewell dinner for him at Durban,
to which a considerable number of the Indian merchants came.
In the course of talk Gandhi saw some newspapers and noticed
that the "Indian Franchise Bill" was before the Natal legislature.
This was a bill to deprive all Indians of the right to vote. He exclaimed at his discovery and asked Abdullah what he and his
friends intended to do. One thing led to another in the general
conversation, until one of the merchants said there was but one
thing to do: induce Gandhi to stay over another month and organize a movement to defend the franchise for his fellow-Indians.
After some discussion he agreed to do this, provided there was no
question of paying him for his services and that money for the
necessary expenses (printing, telegrams, etc.) would be found.

Thus he began what was to be a career of twenty years' hard
work for the Indians of South Africa.

He had to call for volunteers to get out the necessary petitions
and other papers in a hurry; the farewell dinner then and there
turned into a working committee, and the volunteers stayed up
all night to get the copies out and obtain the signatures. (The
Indian vote was about to be lost by default, Gandhi seems to have
thought; a point had been made in the press that the Indians did
not value their vote or use it.)

The Indian Franchise Bill passed, just the same, but the petition
to the legislature had a salutary effect and was widely printed.
Most of all, an example had been given of how Indians of all religions and races could work together for a cause common to all
of them. Gandhi had made a particular effort to reach the young
colonial-born Indians, most of whom had been educated in South
Africa, had become Christians and Europeanized, and were substantially lost to the rest of the Indian community. He had an
unprecedented success in enlisting their support, and they became
among the most enthusiastic of his volunteers in the following
period. Once the Indians had lost their vote, the next step was to
organize a propaganda campaign to regain it. Gandhi composed
a petition to the Secretary of State for the Colonies (then Lord
Ripon) and obtained ten thousand signatures to it in Natal in
the space of two weeks, using his young volunteers to scour the

countryside. Newspapers in India and in England took up the case, supported the claims of the Indians, and set going a worldwide interest in the matter which, with intervals of relative calm, has never since altogether died down.

It was now impossible for Gandhi to leave Natal. Too much depended upon him: he was too thoroughly the center of the new-born community sense which united all the breeds and sects of his people. His Indian friends wanted him to remain as a paid public worker, but he declared then (as he always did afterward) that he could not accept fees for work of that kind. To pay for it, he felt, was to devalue it, to rob it of its merit as service given. He calculated that to live in Natal in the style which—for patriotic reasons—he wished to maintain, that is, a style roughly equivalent to that of an English barrister, would cost him, even with his extremely simple tastes, three hundred pounds a year. He therefore agreed to stay if this sum could be guaranteed as barrister's fees from private practice—retainers from the merchants who dominated the Indian colony. His scruples were not fully understood but the arrangement was made as he desired.

He now had to get himself admitted as an advocate of the Supreme Court of Natal, the first Indian, in fact, the first "man of color," to be so admitted. He held a certificate of admission from the Bombay High Court, which had kept his English certificate on file with his application. He therefore submitted his Bombay certificate plus two affidavits of good character from European merchants, but ran into unexpected difficulties. At first he was told to get Indian character witnesses instead of European—"if I had had Indians they would have asked for Europeans," he reflected wryly—but he swallowed his resentment and complied. Then he discovered that the Law Society of Natal would oppose his application anyhow, on the ground that no colored man should practise at the bar. The Chief Justice, after hearing the Law Society's argument—which by this time was pure, naked Jim Crowism—dismissed it without even calling upon Gandhi's counter-argument. He swore Gandhi in as an advocate then and there, declaring that the law recognized no distinction between white and colored men, but after the oath had been administered he added:

"Now you must take off your turban, Mr. Gandhi. You must submit to the rules of the Court with regard to the dress to be worn by practising barristers."

The famous turban, which had seemed worth a struggle the year before, no longer seemed so important, and Gandhi's sense of justice recognized that if he was to be an officer of the Court he must obey its customs. He took off the turban and never wore it again.

His next step after this signal triumph was to establish the permanent organization of the Indian community. To continue the struggle for the franchise and against the poll-tax it was desirable to have a regular body which could speak for the community and work for it, contributing what funds might become necessary. The word "Congress" had come to be synonymous with nationalism in India by that time, and no other word carried quite the same connotations. Gandhi therefore recommended that the permanent organization bear that name: the Natal Indian Congress then came into existence on May 22, 1894.

It was at the outset (like the Indian National Congress) a body of middle-class people with wealthy contributors. The indentured laborers—five-year-contract men—who formed the mass of Indians in the colony, a peonage not far from slavery, were illiterate and desperately poor: the Congress could work for them but could not depend upon them for public effort or financial support at that stage. At an enthusiastic opening meeting the merchants and other prosperous Indians adopted a simple constitution and pledged generous subscriptions. It was decided to make each member pay five shillings a month, and the wealthier members were expected to give more. Abdullah Sheth pledged two pounds a month and was followed by others. Gandhi himself pledged a pound a month, which he could ill afford. He became the secretary (and to all practical intents the general director) of the Congress; it was his duty to see that these subscriptions were paid, and before long he discovered that his clerk was kept busy all day long attempting to make collections. He then decided to make the subscription annual instead of monthly, and thus simplified his financial task.

Gandhi had always been as careful as he was frugal; when he was a student in London he entered in a little book every expenditure he made, however tiny, and this remained his rule for many years. He insisted on the most cautious and detailed accounting for every penny received or paid, ruled that there must be receipts in all cases, and made it a point of pride to keep the books as clean as possible. "I learned at the outset not to carry on public work with borrowed money," he says. The funds had to be in hand before any expenditure was made, and the Natal Indian Congress—the only organization of the kind he ever ran—was never in debt.

"Without properly kept accounts," the Mahatma wrote long afterwards, "it is impossible to maintain truth in its pristine purity."

The Colonial-born Indian Education Association was one of the first children of the Congress: it arose from Gandhi's desire to enlist the interest and service of the second-generation Indians (mostly Christian) who had drifted away from the community. It became a sort of debating society with a library and social center, and in the result many of the educated youths were reintegrated into the community of their own people and did it great service in the years to come.

In propaganda, for which Gandhi had a natural bent, he was eminently successful from the beginning. He wrote two pamphlets, one called *An Appeal to Every Briton in South Africa*, and the other called *The Indian Franchise—An Appeal*. These were printed and widely circulated in South Africa, as well as going to a choice list in India and England.

The Natal Indian Congress, like the National Congress at home whose name it bore, was a middle-class organization. The mass of the Indian immigrants were indentured laborers and could not afford to belong to the agitating body. Gandhi had borne in mind all along that sooner or later the mass of peons had to be served by the Congress, but he was thrust into their consciousness a little earlier than he had planned when a Tamil worker, in tattered clothes and with a bleeding mouth, came into his office one day, weeping. The man's name was Balasundaram; he had been beaten by his white master, and Gandhi took him at once to a doctor from whom he obtained an affidavit of the injuries. The magistrate to whom he submitted this affidavit instantly issued a summons for the offending master, but Gandhi explained that he did not want anybody punished; he merely wanted the laborer released from his peonage to one European and transferred to another. This could be done by consent of the old and new masters, which Gandhi set about obtaining. It was not too difficult, but the result of the case was that Gandhi himself became famous among the indentured Indians as their friend, as the only Indian barrister in the country and their only defender: his office was the scene of a steady progression of these poor men for months to come, streaming through to see their friend and tell him their troubles. The Balasundaram case became celebrated for a time and was reported in India, where—particularly in Madras, the capital of South India—it aroused great interest. Gandhi was to hear of it a good deal thereafter, although, as he says, the case was in itself not remarkable.

The interest he was now acquiring in the difficulties of the very poor was enhanced when in that same year (1894) the Natal Government tried to impose a poll-tax of twenty-five pounds sterling on every indentured Indian. This astonishing sum was to be exacted from men whose average yearly income was thirteen pounds and four shillings. The Natal Indian Congress began a thorough campaign against such an iniquitous tax, sent leaflets and cries of alarm in all directions, and perhaps was thus instrumental in reducing the tax from twenty-five pounds per person per year to three pounds. Lord Elgin, Viceroy of India at the time—that same Viceroy who used to ask for instructions from London twice daily—agreed to Natal's proposal of a three-pound tax, although he disapproved of the twenty-five-pound figure. For a poor Indian there was not much difference, since he could not pay either one. (A man paid three pounds for himself and three for his wife, three for each male child over sixteen and each female child over thirteen, which for a family of four would come to twelve pounds a year, almost his total annual income.)

The Congress, with Gandhi as its indefatigable animator, waged war on this tax in season and out. It took twenty years to get it repealed, twenty years of "unflinching faith, great patience and incessant effort," Gandhi says. When justice was finally done, it was as a result of the struggle of all the Indians

of all South Africa, not of Natal alone. Many times during these
years, impulse or interest dictated a surrender on the part of
the Indians—a yielding to the inevitable—but Gandhi never gave
up; and we may be sure it was owing in large part, perhaps
entirely, to his own gentle but quite immovable obstinacy that
the struggle was carried on to the end.

During this period, while he lived in the "style" he thought
necessary for a barrister, Gandhi never stopped his readings in
various religions. His friend Raychandbhai in Bombay kept on
sending him books about Hinduism and long letters full of
advice: in Durban he met a Christian missionary, Spencer Wal-
ton, the head of the South Africa General Mission, who became
a real friend and welcomed Gandhi into his family as, practically speaking, a member of it; he made the acquaintance of one
of Professor Max Muller's books and continued to read about
Mohammed. Possibly the most decisive influence amongst those
presented to him at this period was Tolstoy.

He had read *The Kingdom of God Is Within You* during his
first year in Africa, while he lived at Pretoria. Its effect upon
him was profound and remained present in his consciousness to
the end. The preachment of that book—that the Sermon on the
Mount was a sufficient guide to life individually or in society—
along with its bitter sorrow over war, conscription, injustice and
oppression, was as if created for Gandhi. Here, as in the other
cases we have seen before or shall see afterwards, he *found*
what he needed—it was an expression he used himself—and what
he could not, in fact, do without. It was another case of authority, in this case the authority of the greatest writer then
living, for something which he already felt to be true, knew to
be true, and longed to see stated as powerfully as possible.

Now, in Durban, he went on to some other late works of
Tolstoy. *The Gospels in Brief* and *What to Do?* made a deep
impression on him; he wrote to their author. Tolstoy, far off
at Yasnaya Polyana, receiving a letter from an unknown young
man in South Africa, felt the presence of something sharply
individual in his immense correspondence, and eventually (as
was his custom) he reached that letter in its turn and answered
it. He answered all his letters, and by hand, too, although he

was sometimes weeks or months behind with the task. Gandhi answered again: there ensued a correspondence (although here I am a little ahead of my tale) in which genuine communication took place over intervening immensities of space, rank, nationality and education, and Tolstoy felt—and was perhaps the first to do so—the existence of a rare new spirit, an element of the most undeniable greatness, in the obscure young Hindu lawyer in Natal.

In 1896 Gandhi asked for a leave of absence for six months to return to India and settle his family affairs; he would now bring Kasturbai and their two children out to Natal and settle there indefinitely. He had been in South Africa for three years.

6

Gandhi's time in India was by no means consumed with family matters. He had brought into existence the question of the treatment of Indians in South Africa, and although interest in it was slight, it had been non-existent before: it was therefore his duty to stimulate that interest by any means in his power and enlist for those who had emigrated the support of their fellow-countrymen at home. In this design he wrote a pamphlet on the question, which, since it had a green cover, came to be known as the Green Pamphlet, in which he described the plight of the Indians in Africa as moderately and quietly as he could. He got ten thousand copies of this paper struck off and sent to all the newspapers of India and the leaders of all parties. A summary was cabled to London by Reuter's and from London to Natal (in still more summary form) at once. In Bombay, Poona, Madras and Calcutta Gandhi did what he could in the way of propaganda, spoke at a public meeting—or rather had his speech read for him—and met some of the national leaders of India at that time, including Sir Ferozeshah Mehta and the Lokamanya Tilak. Everywhere (especially in Bombay and Madras) he found great interest in the question, of which little was known except through his own pamphlet, and the groundwork was laid for a healthy support in India for the men who had gone overseas. He would have gone further in his initial effort if he had not received a cablegram from Durban asking him to return soon, as the Natal parliament was to meet in January.

He went back to Natal with his wife and two children on a boat belonging to the Dada Abdullah Company. He had decided that their own native dress would not do for Natal, where considerations of prestige—not personal, but national—dictated Gandhi's arrangements. European dress was too uncomfortable and difficult for them, so he compromised on Parsi clothing as being the nearest thing to it. He also insisted on shoes and stockings for the whole family, which, as none of them had ever worn such things, caused great pain and discomfort for a while. The docile Hindu wife, whose religious duty is to obey her husband without question at all times, can never have had a more perfect exemplar than Kasturbai: she made no complaint. It was more difficult for them to get used to a knife and fork, which Gandhi also imposed upon them—just as he later imposed upon them a return to their own native style of eating and dressing. He was at the same time beginning to teach—or try to teach—poor Kasturbai, who had remained illiterate during his forays in England and Africa. His own narrative of these things is touched with a gentle, tender regret, not so much for his own imperiousness in such matters (if he had not been imperious, his wife and family would have been disappointed) but because the institution of child-marriage had, in his own as in so many cases, combined a literate husband and an illiterate wife in union thus made unnecessarily difficult.

After a stormy passage the steamer reached Durban on December 18, 1896, and was put into five days' quarantine because there had been plague in Bombay when it sailed. It became clear almost immediately that health played little part in this quarantine, and that the real question was whether Gandhi and his hundreds of Indian fellow-passengers would be allowed to land. The white residents of Natal were in ferment; they had read the newspaper accounts of his activities in India and were determined that he should not return; they believed, quite baselessly, that he had brought hundreds of Indians with him to force them on the colony, and that his presence in Natal would disturb the white man's power. Gandhi refused to return to India, although his life was explicitly threatened, and he felt

deeply responsible for the danger to which he was now sub-
jecting his wife and children. At last, when nothing could be
done to make him or the other Indians return to India, the ships
(there were two belonging to Abdullah, both crowded with
passengers) were allowed to come into harbor and unload.

The angry whites had had five days to grow calmer, and
Abdullah's solicitor, who came aboard to see Gandhi, thought
there was no need to land surreptitiously or at night. On his
advice, Mrs. Gandhi and the two children landed by themselves
and drove to the house of an Indian Congress friend, quite un-
molested. Gandhi then landed with the English lawyer of Abdullah's firm, Mr. Laughton, who thought he could give sufficient protection.

Some boys around the dock recognized Gandhi and set up a
shout, "Gandhi, Gandhi!" which soon brought a crowd. Mr.
Laughton called a rickshaw in the hope of escaping quickly,
but the crowd grew rapidly, frightened the rickshaw boy away
and separated Gandhi from his protector. (Gandhi had never
used a rickshaw, of which he disapproved, and was grateful to
God for saving him from the necessity this time.) As soon as
Laughton was safely walled off by the mob, the attack on
Gandhi began. They threw stones, brickbats and rotten eggs,
tore off his turban and began to beat and kick him. He fainted
and, upon recovering consciousness, clung to the railings of a
house in front of him, trying to get his breath. The assault was
continuing when Mrs. Alexander, the English wife of the Police Superintendent, made her way through the crowd to
Gandhi and opened her parasol (although the day was sunless)
and stood in front of him. They could not continue the assault
without injuring the lady, and a pause ensued, during which the
police arrived. Under their escort Gandhi arrived at his friend
Rustomji's house without further mishap.

But here, as night was falling, the mob gathered again. The
police superintendent held them in check—mainly by joking
speeches—for a while, but their mood grew more threatening.
It was their wish to lynch Gandhi, and they might have done
so if Mr. Alexander had not handled the situation with considerable tact and skill. He hastily sent a message to Gandhi,
saying that Rustomji's property and the lives of all the others

might be destroyed if he did not leave at once, and gave directions for what was to be done. He stayed outside the house, holding the mob in control, while Gandhi inside the house was swiftly dressed as an Indian constable by two detectives who disguised themselves as Indians. They then made their escape through a neighboring shop and a by-lane to a carriage some distance away, which took them to the police station.

As soon as he knew Gandhi was safe, the police superintendent informed the crowd. They did not believe him but insisted on searching the house, and he agreed to permit a few representatives to do so. They found only the women and children, and the mob broke up.

Gandhi stayed at the police station for a few days and the popular excitement among the whites died down. In the meantime accounts of the riot had appeared in India and in England. Joseph Chamberlain was then Secretary for the Colonies and cabled an order to Natal to prosecute all those responsible for the attempted lynching. When the government's representative came to Gandhi to receive his complaint he declared that he would not prosecute anybody. In his view, the white people of Durban were simply misguided and misinformed, and had been told plain lies about his activity in India. He was asked to put this decision in writing so that it could be cabled to Joseph Chamberlain, and did so. It was a characteristic decision: it already foreshadowed the later Gandhi, as did the sermon on non-violence which he delivered on shipboard before landing to face the mob.

Gandhi made his position clear to the local press: he had said nothing in India that he had not said in Natal before leaving (except that in India he deliberately modified his language), he had copies of every speech he had made (or caused to be read) in India, and he had had nothing to do with the coming of the other passengers who arrived with him. This interview was printed in full, and, coupled with the news that he had refused to prosecute his assailants, worked in his favor. He was himself convinced that the lynching incident, by showing the white men how wrong they had been, definitely increased the prestige of the Indian community and made his own work henceforth less difficult.

Bills to penalize the Indian merchant and limit immigration were pending before the Natal parliament, and Gandhi was immediately absorbed in work to combat them. By this time there had been a decision that no laws could be passed against Indians as such—that is, that distinctions of race or color could not be enshrined in legislation—and this theoretical victory was, Gandhi thinks, due to the preceding agitation on the franchise. At the same time, by crafty phrasing, it was possible to make laws which seemed to be of general application and yet applied, or could be made to apply, only to Indians. This was the line taken by race prejudice in South Africa thereafter.

At this period Gandhi believed in "permanent funds" (i.e., some species of endowment or property yielding income) for public institutions, and set about collecting money so that the Congress could own property and subsist on income. His views in that matter soon changed, although at this period (1896) he successfully carried through his plan and saw the routine expenses of the Congress provided by rent. Later he was a firm believer in public subscriptions as the only right way of supporting public work. If public work has not public support it "forfeits its right to exist," in his belief. "I have no doubt that the ideal is for public institutions to live, like nature, from day to day." The knowledge later acquired of religious foundations which kept no accounts, were responsible to nobody and spent their income as they pleased, along with some regrettable litigations even in the Natal Congress on the disposal of funds, had something to do with Gandhi's view. His campaigns were, in any case, of a nature which aroused popular enthusiasm and the method of living from day to day provided all that was needed.

He now had a household consisting of his wife and two sons (nine and five years old) and his sister's son, who was ten. The problem of finding a school for them was one of his first. By special exception they could have gone to the schools for European white children, but he was unwilling to accept such favor. Christian missionary schools were open to Indian children, but this was also unsatisfactory: besides the proselytizing, the instruction itself was not good and had nothing Indian in it. His solution was to teach the boys himself in Gujarati, and at the same time to engage an English governess to give them lessons in English. The devices found were not adequate or satisfactory, and Gandhi often thought he had failed to give his sons a good enough education, but he was convinced—even then—that they should grow up at home, and the possible alternative of schools away from home, somewhere in India or South Africa, did not attract him.

His desire to be of service to his fellow-men was growing so much at this time that mere "public" work (i.e., agitation in behalf of the Indians) no longer satisfied him. From his busy day he succeeded in squeezing out two hours which he could give to a charitable hospital founded on money he had no doubt begged himself ("Rustomji's charity," he calls it). He acted as compounder in the dispensary attached to the hospital. Most of the patients were very poor Tamils, Telugus or North Indians, indentured laborers, speaking no English and afraid of the doctor. Gandhi had to hear their woes, explain them to the doctor and then fill the prescriptions and dispense them. He trained himself to take the place of almost any nurse on occasion, read books on nursing, midwifery and the care of children, and cared for his own two younger sons who were born in South Africa. His fourth and last son was, in fact, delivered by himself, since the labor came on suddenly and neither doctor nor midwife could be found in time.

It was in this period that Gandhi's mind began to turn to *brahmacharya*, the absolute chastity of body and mind to which Hindu students, philosophers and saints are sooner or later all vowed. He had already dedicated his life to *satya* (truth) and *ahinsa* (non-violence). An effort toward the third objective of his life, absolute self-control, began in the 1890's in Natal. At first the effort alone was not enough; repeatedly he failed; it was not until some ten years later, in 1906, that he perceived he would have to take a solemn vow. By that time the practice of taking vows, as what he called "disciplinary resolutions," had grown on him (all his first fasts and many of his dietary experiments were bound by vows); he was thirty-seven years old in 1906. At the period of his settling down in Durban with his family, ten years earlier, he was already beginning that self-control which was afterward to become a central part of his religion.

He also began to limit his physical needs and expenditure at the same time. Since his washerman was expensive and unpunctual, he bought some washing apparatus and a book on washing, "studied the art," as he says, and thereafter washed his own clothing. He also taught the art to his wife so that she could wash her own. He became so proficient that he could starch and iron a stiff white collar as well as any laundry in the town, or perhaps better. In the same way he made a study of hair-cutting and learned to cut his own hair with comparatively good results. In all this there were foreshadowings of the Mahatma that was to come, who believed in self-help, mutual help and the simple life as few on earth have ever believed in it or practised it.

When the Boer War broke out, Gandhi's conscience subjected him to a gruelling test. His sympathies were all with the Boers, but he did not believe he had a right to allow individual sympathies or even convictions to dominate action in a society. He came to the conclusion that since he was a barrister, engaged in season and out in demanding the rights of a British subject, not only for himself but for others, it was his duty to accept the decision of the British Government in such a matter and support it loyally. (This dilemma of conscience is exhaustively treated in his *Satyagraha in South Africa*.) He therefore organized an ambulance corps from Indian volunteers, trained it with his friend Dr. Booth, obtained medical certificates of fitness for service for all the men, and offered the body to the government. It was refused.

This was to be expected, from the attitude most South Africans had toward Indians, but Gandhi persevered. The Bishop of Natal took up his cause—since there were many Indian Christians in the Gandhi corps—and as the war continued to go badly for the British, Gandhi had his chance to serve.

He had 1100 men and 40 leaders under his command. The original orders called upon this body to work behind the lines, but in a critical moment the commanding general sent word that he would be grateful if the Indians would go into the line to rescue the wounded. Thus the Gandhi corps was engaged during the battle around Spion Kop and carried wounded men from twenty to twenty-five miles a day. After six weeks' service the corps was disbanded because a new strategic concept had

come into play: the British were no longer attempting to fight
the Boers, but merely to hold their lines and await reinforce-
ments. The experiment did, however, do the Indian community
good in many ways: it caused the white South Africans to think
and speak better of them, it caused them to be mentioned in
dispatches and awarded medals, and best of all, from Gandhi's
point of view, was that Indians of all the different breeds and
creeds had served together as brothers and borne danger well.

Another of his enterprises which helped to lift the status of
the Indian community was his voluntary campaign for sanitation. He found that this was not always easy. "I saw that I
could not so easily count on the help of the community in
getting it to do its own duty as I could in claiming for it rights,"
he says. He had had some experience in house-to-house inspec-
tion in Bombay during the plague there, on his last visit home;
he now proposed to put this to work in Durban when the plague
threatened. The principal requisite, he found, in an effort to
make poor people keep their houses clean when there is no
money and no equipment, is patience—endless, infinite patience.

In 1901, when the war was over, Gandhi wanted to return
to India but had the greatest difficulty persuading his friends in
Natal that he should do so. He thought his work in South Africa
was done; he felt that he could be of more service in India; he
was afraid that the rewards of his profession as a barrister in
Africa might turn him into a "money-maker," which he did not
want to happen. He succeeded in obtaining his release only on
condition that if he were needed within the year he would
pledge to return. This he did, against his own will; and his
farewell this time was an occasion in which the entire Indian
colony of Natal wished to participate. To his horror, Gandhi
received many presents, some of them of considerable value, and
there were jeweled ornaments for his wife besides. What was
the use, he asked himself, of doing public work as a service to
humanity if he was to be so rewarded for it? He decided to put
all these presents in the bank under trusteeship for the benefit
of the Indian community, but his wife, Kasturbai, took no such
view of the matter. She felt that he had no right to deprive her
and their children of valuables which might be of use later (for
her "daughters-in-law," she said, although their sons were still

children). Gandhi has faithfully recorded the family row on this subject, in which the children took his side of the argument. The jewels and valuables were put in trust.

In India his first purpose was to obtain passage by the Indian National Congress of a resolution of support to the Indians of South Africa. With this aim he attended the Congress of 1901 (a three-day meeting) in Calcutta, and had the highly qualified joy of seeing his resolution passed by acclamation, without a dissenting voice, but in such a perfunctory way that he doubted if anybody in the Congress had read it.

That was the way the Congress operated in those days. It was a middle-class organization which had originally started with British help and approval; it had no revolutionary or even pronouncedly nationalist tendency, and its annual meeting was as much a social occasion as anything else. Gandhi was deeply disturbed over the unsanitary conditions prevailing in the crowded camp of delegates, and when he saw the filth of the latrine he was supposed to use he cleaned it out himself. (Such work was done only by untouchables, and still is.) He had no luck in persuading others to do as he did, and it was his opinion that if the meeting had been prolonged there would be a good chance of an epidemic.

He also deplored the heavy reliance upon English as the language of the session (although fewer Indians spoke English then than today); he disliked the separate dining of certain castes and wondered at the plenitude of orotund speeches. He did, however, see Gokhale again, and it was owing to Gokhale's approval of his resolution that it passed through the Congress without debate.

Gokhale then asked him to come and stay in his house. Gandhi was too shy to accept at once. The celebrated nationalist leader went to the India Club, where Gandhi was staying, and fetched him.

Gopal Krishna Gokhale, a Chitpavan Brahmin, was one of the national leaders of India at the turn of the century. Gandhi afterward referred to him often as "my political *guru*," and the basis of the relationship thus indicated was built during the month he spent at Gokhale's house. He declares that he felt at home in Gokhale's house from the very first day—which, for a young man as shy, conscience-ridden and tongue-tied as

Gandhi, was altogether exceptional. Here for the first time he heard political discussion and the language of public service between men who were intellectually equal and ready to talk. Some of the discussion was a shock to Gandhi because from it he discovered that public figures whom he had reverenced were in fact less than heroes. But as he watched Gokhale work he was awed by the intensity, regularity and constancy of the man's devotion to public duty. The only qualifying element in his admiration was the feeling that any man should find time for some exercise, even if only a little walking, and he perceived that Gokhale had no time at all for it and was burning his health away.

Bengal was strange to Gandhi, and he took what opportunities he could to familiarize himself with it. He wanted to visit the Kali temple, for example, but was horrified when he got there to find that a lot of sheep were about to be sacrificed to the goddess on that day. He held, even then, the view he expressed so often afterward: "the life of a lamb is no less precious than that of a human being." He made some attempt to argue with the worshippers that day but saw that it was quite beyond his capacity to influence them, and went away sick with the smell of blood. Even twenty years later he could smell it when he wrote:

"It is my constant prayer that there may be born on earth some great spirit, man or woman, fired with divine pity, who will deliver us from this heinous sin, save the lives of the innocent creatures and purify the temple. How is it that Bengal with all its knowledge, intelligence, sacrifice and emotion tolerates this slaughter?"

On this visit Gandhi tried to interest some of the Indian Christians in South Africa, but found them more concerned with converting him; he tried to see old Tagore (that is, the Maharshi, Debendranath) but could not; he went out to the Belur monastery to see Swami Vivekananda but the Swami was lying ill in a house in Calcutta. He did succeed in meeting some members of the Brahmo Samaj and in forming an idea of the nature of their thinking. Wherever he went, whatever he did, it was his constant effort to awaken Indian and Bengali leaders to the plight of their fellow-countrymen in South Africa, and to a considerable extent—thanks to Gokhale's support in part, and thanks also to the sympathy of Mr. Saunders, the editor of *The Englishman*—he made some headway.

On leaving Gokhale and Bengal, Gandhi proposed to make a tour of India in third-class. The densely crowded third-class carriages were seldom, if ever, used by any but the poor, the very poor who are the immense majority of Indians, but Gandhi evidently felt that his knowledge of his own country would be deficient if he did not share that experience with them. He wanted to go first to Benares, where Mrs. Besant was at that time, ill; he would be a pilgrim to Benares for the first time, and then go on to Agra, Jaipur and Palanpur, sightseeing on his way home to Rajkot.

"The indifference of the railway authorities to the comforts of the third-class passengers, combined with the dirty and inconsiderate habits of the passengers themselves, makes third-class traveling a trial for a passenger of cleanly ways," says the gentle Gandhi. (Anybody who has ever seen an Indian third-class carriage will agree that this is a most moderate way of stating it!) "These unpleasant habits commonly include throwing of rubbish on the floor of the compartment, smoking at all hours and in all places, betel and tobacco chewing, converting of the whole carriage into a spittoon, shouting and yelling and using foul language, regardless of the convenience or comfort of fellow passengers. I have noticed little difference between my experience of the third-class travelling in 1902 and that of my unbroken third-class tours from 1915 to 1919.

"I can think of only one remedy for this awful state of things —that educated men should make a point of travelling third class and reforming the habits of the people, as also of never letting the railway authorities rest in peace, sending in complaints wherever necessary, never resorting to bribes or any unlawful means for obtaining their own comforts, and never putting up with infringements of rules on the part of anyone concerned. That, I am sure, would bring about considerable improvement."

It may be gathered from these comments that Gandhi's third-class travels in those days constituted a sort of mission in themselves.

His visit to the Kashi Vishvanath Temple (the Temple of the Master of the World) was a shock and a disappointment to him. The dirt, the stones, slippery with Ganges water, the shopkeepers and the tip-conscious priests, the masses of stale flowers stinking—all this revolted him. "I searched here for God but failed to find Him," he says bluntly. Twice in later years, when he had been "already afflicted with the title of Mahatma," he visited the great temple, but the experience he had as an unknown pilgrim was then denied him: the crowds seeking his own darshan would not permit him to have the darshan of the temple.

"The woes of Mahatmas are known to Mahatmas alone," he comments wryly. "Otherwise the dirt and the noise were the same."

He paid his visit to Mrs. Besant—the briefest possible—and went on home to Rajkot.

It had been Gokhale's idea that Gandhi should "settle down" as a barrister in Bombay to prepare himself for public life. Public life meant work in the Indian National Congress, the body of middle-class intellectuals—not yet a mass organization—which conducted what nationalist movement existed. Gandhi fell in with the ideas of his "political *guru*," as Gokhale henceforth was in his eyes, and tried to work at the bar, first in Rajkot and afterward in Bombay itself. He was not wholly without success this time, as he had spent much time in study of the Indian laws of evidence; his shyness was apparently being conquered at last. But he was not destined to be left long in that endeavor. His pledge to the Indian community of Natal still stood: if they needed him he would return. He received a cablegram saying that Joseph Chamberlain was expected for a tour of South Africa: the community needed him at once. He left as soon as he could make his arrangements, leaving his family again in India for what he thought might be a year's separation.

This second visit to South Africa, which extended over eleven years, created the "Mahatma." (It seems impossible to fix an exact date for the first use of this appellation, but it was undoubtedly given by the Indians in India on account of Gandhi's work in South Africa.) At first there was little success to be marked. Chamberlain, for instance, to whom Gandhi presented a memorial he had drawn up immediately on arrival, was not easily moved. He had come to South Africa to obtain a gift of thirty-five million pounds sterling and was consequently in no mood to alienate the South African Europeans' sentiment by espousing the cause of the Indians. He told Gandhi so with considerable frankness. The community then sent Gandhi to the Transvaal to prepare and repeat the petition in that country, which had suffered greatly from the war and was anxious to keep Indian immigration out, at least for the present.

Gandhi obtained a permit to go to the Transvaal from his old friend, the Police Superintendent in Durban, but on his arrival at Pretoria this time he found conditions much changed—from the Indian point of view, for the worse. A number of English officers from India ("the autocrats," he calls them) had come to South Africa during the Boer War and a good many of them had remained to set up what was called the "Asiatic department," to deal with the interests, or, at any rate, with the control, of the Indians. It was no part of their plan to allow an energetic young barrister from India to come in and organize the community or give it political advice. They therefore tried to exclude Gandhi, and, failing that, refused to permit him to present the Transvaal Indians' petition to Chamberlain. He was by this time accustomed to insult and it did not upset him as much as it had done some years before, but he perceived through this and other episodes that the new "Asiatic department" would be an oppressive influence upon the Indians of the Transvaal and that his immediate task must be here. Without some help, the Indians would be thoroughly robbed and eventually driven out. Already a corrupt traffic in permits for Indians to enter the Transvaal had been developed and accepted both by the Indians themselves and by the authorities. Gandhi therefore decided to stay and fight it out: he would open a law office in Johannesburg and get himself enrolled in the Transvaal Supreme Court.

Thus opened the decisive period of his life, upon which his subsequent struggle in India was based. He was approaching the formulation of his most original idea in human action, the translation of conflict into terms of non-violence, but he was still unaware of it. At the time when he began work in Johannesburg he was thirty-four, and although his inclinations toward religious thought, dietary reforms and sacrifice for others were all clearly marked—were there by nature and temperament— they had not matured into a system, and he had as yet no idea how to apply them in practical life. He was brought to it by a series of intellectual and spiritual discoveries, disciplines and ex- periences which in five years (1903-1908) formed the distinct nature and power of his genius as it was to be expressed upon the scene of history.

7

The earlier influences to which he had been exposed in Africa had been Christian; now he began to know and associate with some theosophists, and although he never became a member of their society, the extent to which they depended upon Hindu ideas turned him back again to his own scriptures. Above all the Gita now began to assume that place in his consciousness which grew in consequence to the very end of his life. He started memorizing it in Sanskrit, and since his day was rigidly worked out to schedule, the time he found best adapted to this was the thirty-five minutes allotted to his morning ablutions. He spent fifteen minutes brushing his teeth (a lavish allowance!) and discovered that he could memorize a verse or two of the Gita every morning while he was doing it. He stuck slips of paper all over the bathroom wall with lines from the Gita written on them, and before the great Transvaal struggle began he had thus committed to memory thirteen chapters of the poem.

This now began to be the rule of his life. Non-possession, non-attachment, the cardinal rule of the Gita, could not be merely a beautiful idea sonorously recited in ancient poetry. It had to be true. He therefore gave up his life insurance, which was his only property or guarantee for the future, and explained his course to his long-suffering brother in India. The life insur- ance was reprehensible to Gandhi because he thought it showed a lack of trust in God. His brother, unable to appreciate this, ceased writing to him and there ensued an estrangement for years. Gandhi now decided that everything that came into his hands—everything he earned, everything the community wished

him to have and everything that belonged to his wife or children—was his on trust alone, not as a possession, and that everything he might thus hold would in future be used for the good
of the community.

This, of course, involved still further economies and simplici-
ties in his personal existence, although at the time he was still
anxious, for the sake of the other Indians, to keep up appearances so far as his office and his European clothes were concerned. ("A barrister" had to live thus-and-so.) He was bent
upon doing every sort of work necessary in his own household,
including, for example, the emptying of chamber-pots, which
is a duty assigned in India to untouchables. He did this for all
who lived in the house—the clerks in his office and other helpers
—including one who had himself been born untouchable. This
was a little too much for Kasturbai and produced one of their
not infrequent quarrels: she did not understand, and it took her
years to accept without understanding the extremities of his
self-sacrifice.

A good deal of the money he was able to save by these austerities went into the publication of a weekly paper called *Indian
Opinion*, in which for the first time the point of view of the
Indian community was expressed in print in South Africa.
Gandhi not only helped to pay for the paper but wrote a great
part of it, and, in the years just ahead, it was the mirror of his
great campaign for his people. Without some such publication
he could not have developed and made clear, both to Indians
and to Europeans, the distinct and original nature of non-violent
struggle.

Nursing, work in hygiene and sanitation, experiments in
household remedies such as earth-and-water plasters—all this
continued concurrently with Gandhi's law work, his religious
development and his political organization. The Black Plague
broke out in Johannesburg: Gandhi at once set to work as a
nurse and organized a hospital. It was a time of terror and many
Indians died; their "location" (a sort of ghetto in which they
were permitted to live) had to be evacuated and burned to the
ground; Gandhi was with the Indians throughout, exposing himself without fear, and was apparently exempt from the terrible
contagion. One result of this episode was that the very poorest

of the Indians came to look upon him as a creature apart, and no doubt (although he does not say so), as God's messenger to them. He was at this time known as "Bhai," or Brother, to the whole Indian community, and in their distresses they entrusted to him the guardianship of everything they owned, so that sometimes very large sums, in the aggregate, were in his hands.

On one of his journeys to Durban a theosophical friend gave him a book to read on the train. Gandhi never was a great reader. (He told me I would be surprised if I knew how few books he had read in his life; it reminded me of Savonarola's remark: "My things have been few but great.") In South Africa he had consumed a few works on diet, hygiene and kindred subjects, and he spent years memorizing the Gita, but, aside from Tolstoy, no European writer had yet impressed his mind.

The book he read on the train to Durban was Ruskin's *Unto This Last*. He sat up all night reading it. It affected his life in its external aspect more immediately than any other. Then and there he decided that he could not carry out his work unless he led a life of labor, co-operative and communal upon a basis of absolute equality.

Now, of course, as we have observed repeatedly during this consideration of his life, Gandhi's great discoveries were always of things which already existed within him. Thus it was with the Sermon on the Mount, with vegetarianism, with Tolstoy, with the Gita: so it was now with Ruskin. But since he was a natural born *karma-yogin*, and for him action was the way, he could never accept a truth without putting it into practice immediately. He therefore wasted no time, but proposed at once to all his collaborators on *Indian Opinion* that they get a farm and live there co-operatively. Within two days the agreement was made and the ten co-workers, Indian and European, were pledged to an enterprise of which Ruskin himself would never have been capable. They advertised for a piece of land not too far from Durban, acquired twenty acres with a spring and some trees, and founded the Phoenix Settlement.

The Ruskinian notions as Gandhi interpreted them consisted of ideas which could have been found in Hinduism anyhow, and which aroused great echoes in his soul. His formulation of them is as follows:

"1. That the good of the individual is contained in the good of all.

"2. That a lawyer's work has the same value as the barber's, inasmuch as all have the same right of earning their livelihood from their work.

"3. That a life of labor, i.e., the life of the tiller of the soil and the handicraftsman, is the life worth living."

The job of moving the printing-press to the farm and getting out the first issue of *Indian Opinion* there was a high moment for Gandhi, because the little oil engine they had bought for the press failed at the critical moment and they were all forced to use the hand-wheel which Gandhi had favored from the first. They worked all night long and even got some of the sleeping carpenters who had been working on the building to get up and help. West, one of Gandhi's English collaborators, sang Christian hymns as they worked. In the morning, after the paper had at last been printed and folded, the engine which had refused to work the night before operated, as is often the way with engines, like a dream. Gandhi regarded this as a test of the courage and determination of his little band, and later on, when they were more numerous, he reverted to the hand-press entirely for the publication of his paper.

The Phoenix Settlement flourished for years on the principles of its foundation, but Gandhi could not live there himself for long at a time: his work in Johannesburg was now approaching a climax and was about to demand his fullest attention. But before this could come about the final step of his self-purification, as he saw it, had to take place. He took the vow of chastity for life in 1906, when he was thirty-seven years old.

He had been approaching this supremely difficult renunciation for about ten years. He had, in fact, made efforts at self-control which lasted for long periods at a time, and his rigid fidelity to his wife, combined with his long absences from her, had forced chastity upon him even against his will. He was now, however, to view it as a religious duty and impose it on himself by a solemn vow. Once the vow was taken he could never break it; there is no instance in which he ever broke a vow, although in the case of goat's milk, as we shall see in due course, he allowed a vow to be interpreted for him.

The origins of the Hindu belief in *brahmacharya* (God's teaching, control of body and thought) may be sought in innumerable ancient scriptures, but undoubtedly the idea itself antedates all records. We find it enjoined upon especially devoted or consecrated classes (monks, nuns, hermits, priests) in all societies and in all religions. St. Paul and the Lord Buddha do not greatly differ upon this point. Christian mysticism, of course, is full of it, including some very extreme cases, like those of St. Louis Gonzaga and others that come to mind. In Hinduism, the concept of chastity as necessary for all seekers after truth was modified, socially speaking, into the law of the "four ages of man" (the Four Ashrams), in which, at both extremes of life, his student period and his retirement from the world, a man was supposed to be bound to sexual abstinence in thought and deed. In countries like Burma, where practically every man passes through a stage as a monk, this is still the rule: it seems to have survived in Buddhism when it had become hardly more than a historical reference in Hindu society.

For the life Gandhi was destined to lead there was no possible evasion of this necessity. He must have known—however unconsciously or half-consciously—that his was a religious genius. He must also have known, although again we can only guess at how explicit it became in his own mind, that only a religious genius could arouse and unite the Indian masses and set them on a new road. Now, however it may be in other countries, the fact is that poverty, chastity and humility are inseparable from the religious genius in India, and the Indian masses could never accept a religious leader, reformer or saint who was not vowed to these renunciations. Thus Gandhi's own nature, which had brought him to this step, was never more powerfully Hindu than in the moment when he took it. Without it he could not have performed his historic task, objectively regarded; and without it he would not have become what he unquestionably was long before his death, a saint with tranquil mind and an absolute assurance of God.

Mrs. Gandhi does not appear to have objected to this: it may even be that it was to her a relief. Gandhi freely confessed to have imposed his lust upon her many times in his youth, and in later years he had familiarized her with the idea of a time when he would have to take the vow. By now she knew that her husband was very far from being an ordinary man, and although in earlier years she may have regretted it, by now she was ready to go with him in whatever way his conscience led. As a result she became—after the vow, not before—the most devoted and courageous of his fellow-workers, ready to brave anything and do anything in the epic drama which was now to begin. There is no evidence that she ever had a regret or a difficulty with sexual renunciation. (Gandhi himself had to struggle, mainly by prayer, for long years to come, not against any deed, against which his vow protected him, but against thoughts or dreams.)

To support *brahmacharya* Gandhi had been engaged in dietary experiments and variations—all fruit for a time, all vegetables for a time, nuts and fruits combined at another time —which he sometimes also regulated by vows. It was later on, while he was still troubled, that he discovered some other dietary aids to self-control: some of them he learned in jail. The absence of salt, tea and coffee, the rule that the evening meal should be eaten before sunset, and various other privations which aroused protest among the prisoners he found to be beneficial to him. And at the same period (1906-1908, roughly) he returned to the earliest memories of his life and began the occasional, but quite systematic and regular, practice of fasting. All of these restrictions had an underlying religious import, but on various other levels of the consciousness they performed other functions: thus he found that after a long abstinence from fruit he would relish it more when he returned to it, and with all his severity, it would appear from his own account that he took great pleasure in his meager food.

Kasturbai, loyal in all things, participated even in these dietary experiments and restrictions, although he was scrupulous not to force any of them upon her. During a certain illness he was even willing to give her beef tea when the doctor ordered it, but she protested that she would rather die in his arms as a true vegetarian than live by a product of another life. In this instance—as in others with himself and his sons—Gandhi's luck or, as he preferred to think of it, God's grace and his home nursing and household remedies, proved the doctors wrong.

All through these years of preparation for his mission Gandhi had been developing his great central idea of the possibility of struggle without violence. He had now reached the point at which the main lines were fairly clear in his own mind, but he still lacked a word for it. He was well aware that the introduction of a concept so novel—not to say revolutionary—demanded some precise term: otherwise the task of making people understand and inducing them to adopt such a sacrificial method of attaining ends would be doubly or trebly difficult. He thought of many terms and discarded them all; he offered a small prize in his paper, *Indian Opinion*, for a word and had many answers. One of his own cousins, Maganlal Gandhi, produced a word which seemed to him almost right. It was *sadagraha*, from *satya* (truth) and *agraha* (firmness, a kind of force). To make the meaning perfectly clear, Gandhi changed this to *satyagraha*, which, in a large group of related Indian languages, plainly says truth-force, the power of truth. (In after years it was often translated into English as soul-force.)

Up to this time Gandhi's ideas of the only kind of struggle permissible to the Indians, under the concept of *ahinsa* or non-violence, had been rather lamely expressed in the phrase "civil disobedience," borrowed from Henry Thoreau. Even in the Indian languages this phrase had been used, but it did not really describe what Gandhi had in mind. It was negative, to begin with, and did not contain the notion of voluntary sacrifice. And another objection to it in Gandhi's eyes was that "passive resistance" could so easily lead into violence or be the cause of violence. It was therefore his determination to find or create an Indian word which conveyed the full meaning of his great idea. *Satyagraha* was that word, and those who offered *satyagraha* became known as *satyagrahis*. If I may paraphrase the idea a little more boldly than Mr. Gandhi himself ever did, it is simply this: that in essence what a man can do is declare his truth and die for it. This any man can do; and there is no power on earth that can prevent it. (I often thought so long before I was familiar with Gandhi's teaching; so have innumerable others for centuries; it was Gandhi alone who knew the power latent in that simple truth.)

The great occasions for *satyagraha* now began. The Union of South Africa, formed after the Boer War out of five provinces, did not attempt to mitigate the racial laws of Natal and the Transvaal. Gokhale, then the acknowledged leader of the Indian National Congress, visited South Africa and departed with a pledge—or what he thought was a pledge—from General Smuts that the worst immediate abuse, the three-pound poll-tax, would be abolished. But Smuts told the legislative assembly that since the Europeans of Natal wanted to keep the tax, he could not interfere. Thus this iniquitous impost, designed to keep the Indians in slavery or peonage, was perpetuated. Any Indian who worked his way out of contract labor—the indentures—was immediately liable to a three-pound tax unless he indentured himself again.

Smuts' broken pledge coincided with another iniquity of a more intimately insulting nature to every Indian. A court judgment declared that no marriage could be legal unless it had been performed according to Christian rites and registered in South Africa. This made most Indian children illegitimate and reduced their mothers from wives to concubines. It seemed to Gandhi that the Indian women—whom he had hitherto held out of public life, although many had come to him and accepted his teachings—could now quite properly take their part in the movement, since they were so directly attacked.

He had founded another settlement, the Tolstoy Farm, some twenty miles from Johannesburg, a few years before, and in the period of his mounting concentration on *satyagraha* his time was divided between the two. There were eleven "sisters," as he called them, on Tolstoy Farm, who had been anxious for a long time to offer themselves in the kind of sacrifice called *satyagraha*. Gandhi had never wanted them to go to jail or suffer any other indignity, but now he felt that he could no longer refuse.

He had at the Phoenix Settlement his own closest and oldest collaborators, upon whose constancy he could always count. They were ready and willing to go to jail. When Gokhale wrote from India to ask how many persons Gandhi could count on to offer the sacrifice, Gandhi said sixteen as a minimum and sixty-five as a maximum. The treatment of the Indians in South Africa had become, by 1912 and 1913, a national grievance in India, and Gandhi's struggle in their behalf had already made him a hero among his people, although he was not to know it until his return home. In six years he had made his ideas of satyagraha and his appeal to all the religions, his use of all prayers, hymns and feasts or fasts, familiar to an immense public. The fact that Hindus, Parsis, Christians and Mohammedans all lived together in harmony at both Tolstoy Farm and the Phoenix Settlement, to a considerable extent sharing even their religious observances, was well known by now and Gandhi's course was watched with steadily increasing interest. He was resolved, however, not to ask for any help from India, but to carry through the war of non-violence on his own resources.

He followed his usual custom of writing first to the government to inquire if it would recognize the validity of Indian marriages. His request was declined.

It was forbidden for Indians to enter the Transvaal without a permit, as it was also for them to enter Natal from the Transvaal. The first satyagraha offered in the great campaign was by eleven women from the Tolstoy Farm, all but one Tamils from South India, who crossed the border without permits. The police ignored them. They then went to Newcastle, the mining center —all this in accordance with Gandhi's carefully prepared plan —and asked the Indian workers there to go on strike.

Gandhi's plan also involved his own family and fellow-workers at Phoenix, except children under sixteen. He did not intend to ask his wife to sacrifice herself but she overheard the talk and protested. She asked him what defect in her made her unfit for going to jail. The sixteen crossed the border into the Transvaal, were arrested and sentenced to three months' imprisonment at hard labor. The jailing of Indian women—one of them Mrs. Gandhi—startled and angered the whole of India, convinced many doubters that Gandhi's view of the grievances in South Africa was correct, and acquainted a large part of the world for the first time with the existence of a new form of struggle.

Meanwhile the "eleven sisters" from the Tolstoy Farm had had complete success with the mine workers at Newcastle: they had all gone out on strike. The government could no longer ignore them, and they, too, were put in prison for three months at hard labor.

Gandhi's plan had worked like clockwork so far. He now

realized that his place was at Newcastle and he went there to work for the strikers. The imprisonment of the women had greatly increased the strike movement and the mine-owners were fighting back with the methods of the time and place. Aside from cases of flogging and other violence administered to the strikers—which, under Gandhi's orders, they took without retaliating—the owners were cutting off the water supply and lights from the company houses in which the workers lived. Gandhi now found himself with a small-sized but constantly growing army on his hands—four to five thousand men—but fortunately the excitement among Indians of all classes had now risen to the point where many men and women came to him as volunteers to aid the workers.

In his predicament—having no money to feed all these people and no way of housing them—Gandhi decided to march them all to the Transvaal border, cross it and thus confront the authorities with about five thousand prisoners at once. He told the men what he had in mind and all were ready to go.

The march from Newcastle to Charlestown, the last town on the Natal side of the border, took two days and was accomplished in good order and discipline. Gandhi had, of course, as always in his life, a passion for cleanliness, and the unsanitary habits of these very poor laborers from South India were as serious in his eyes as they were in the eyes of any European doctor. He therefore used his own indefatigable energy and the lesser energies of his educated volunteers in an attempt to keep his army clean. He made one last attempt to convince the mine-owners that the poll-tax was wrong (they were its chief proponents and beneficiaries, since by forcing the Indians into slavery they obtained very cheap labor) but they were in no mood to discuss. When he went back to Newcastle from this trip to Durban there was nothing left to do but march and court imprisonment.

The march took place on October 28, 1913. By this time there were about six thousand men in the army. Gandhi made the rules to be obeyed by all: they were to take as little clothing as possible and accept an iron ration of a pound and half of bread a day; they were not to touch anybody's property on the way; they were to endure patiently any insult to which they might be subjected by Europeans; they were to endure flogging if it came; they were to submit to arrest. Then, as afterward became his custom in India too, Gandhi read them the list of those who should take his place, in consecutive order, if the authorities should arrest him too. (Then, as later, the authorities made every effort to avoid arresting Gandhi himself.)

When the army reached Charlestown, Gandhi formed a camp on the most sanitary basis he could, and there, as so often before and afterward, he set the example by himself doing the work of the untouchables—cleaning, sweeping, scavenging and the like. His volunteers, including some Europeans, were equally willing to set to work, and as always the example was far more effective than any rules or teaching could have been. The Indian miners had never in their lives learned the rules of sewage disposal or the relation between dirt and disease: they did now.

Gandhi again wrote to the government, which was now facing a predicament quite new to its experience. He told them that the indentured laborers' strikes—which were now spreading everywhere—would be called off if the poll-tax were repealed, and that the march of his "army of peace" into the Transvaal was only a protest against General Smuts' broken pledge. If the government wished to do so, it could arrest the army of peace right away in Charlestown, without waiting for it to march into the Transvaal.

The action taken was to arrest Gandhi himself, but on this occasion no case was ready to present against him and he was released on bail. He therefore returned to his "pilgrims," as he called them, and implacably began to march into the Transvaal. The government tried to ignore the situation for a few days but it became impossible: arrests began on November 8th, when Gandhi and some of his fellow-workers were arrested at Standerton. They were separated and sent to different jails, Gandhi to Bloemfontein.

But meanwhile there was no stopping the *satyagraha* movement. Indian men, women and children of all classes offered themselves for jail in large numbers. The South African Government's way of dealing with the miners was to drive them back to the mines, surround their miserable quarters with barbed wire and proclaim these compounds to be "out-stations of the Newcastle and Dundee jails." The European staff of the mines were appointed as warders. *Satyagraha* was now understood, however, even by the miners: they simply refused to go into the mines, and endured patiently all the floggings and other abuses to which they were subjected.

It must, of course, be clear to any who have read so far in this book that *satyagraha*, or a number of ideas closely approximating to it, had an overwhelming appeal to the Indian consciousness. All of Hindu religion and philosophy made it a natural growth: Gandhi invented the method of struggle and the precise way of using sacrifice, but the power of the invention arose from its ideal associations in the Indian mind. *Satyagraha* now began to run like a flame all over South Africa. Strikes and voluntary submission to arrest became everyday occurrences, and there was a danger that the entire Indian laboring population, some sixty thousand, would go on strike, which Gandhi had never desired.

Meanwhile in India and throughout the world there was a storm of criticism of the South African Government. The Viceroy of India, Lord Hardinge, made a public speech at Madras defending Gandhi's course, attacking the barbarism with which the Indians were treated in South Africa, and approving of civil disobedience as a defense against unjust legislation. Gokhale had, of course, seen to it that the press and public of India was fully informed on the whole movement, and the South African struggle became a unifying and enspiriting element in the national movement at home.

All this storm had been aroused by the little dark man who now sat in Bloemfontein jail, eating his "fruitarian" diet, studying a few books, and discussing hygiene with the jail doctor. The line and character of Gandhi's power in the life of his people were now becoming apparent to all. "Blood and iron" were tried on the Indian workers; there was a good deal of shooting and numbers of lives lost; but it made no difference to their determination. In the end General Smuts did what every government that ever opposed Gandhi had to do—he yielded.

His way of doing so was to appoint a Commission of three members to study the Indian grievances with special reference to the poll-tax. It was a foregone conclusion that the tax would be abolished, but the Commission served in part to save Smuts' face. The Indians would have nothing to do with this Commission until Gandhi and his fellow-workers were released from jail, and unless an Indian member were appointed to it.

Gandhi, who had been sent to jail for a year, was unconditionally released after six weeks. He was not pleased, for all of his Indian fellow-workers had been kept in prison—only he and three of his European friends were let out. He addressed a letter to General Smuts on December 21, 1913, demanding that the other *satyagrahis* be released from prison and that the Commission of inquiry should be enlarged. He was now prepared to make another march across a forbidden border and go to jail again.

But now arose an unexpected difficulty. Gokhale cabled him from India that he should not go to jail again, as this would place him and the Viceroy—who had been collaborating in support for Gandhi—in an awkward position. It was Gokhale's, and apparently therefore the Indian National Congress', hope that Gandhi would testify before the Commission.

This Gandhi could not do. He had taken a pledge to boycott the Commission, and he of all people could not break a pledge—it would have shipwrecked the whole movement, which was in essence based upon pledges, vows and moral concepts. He cabled Gokhale his reluctant refusal and asked that Lord Hardinge be shown the cablegram—for the Viceroy, too, had been an invaluable support for the campaign. Gokhale's health suffered a setback but he did not give up his support for Gandhi, and, as it appeared, Lord Hardinge also stood by his previous position.

Gandhi's principles came into play at this juncture in a way which caused a good many of the English in South Africa—and Smuts as well—to express appreciation of them. If he had started his march at this precise moment he could have landed the government in a very difficult position, because it so happened that the European railway workers of the whole Union of South Africa went on strike just then. They would have liked Gandhi's march to coincide with their own struggle, which must have meant easy victory for both and would have put a whole group of white workmen at least temporarily on the side of the Indians. Gandhi, however, refused. He thought the struggle of the Indians was a quite different matter and he was not attempting to harass the government unnecessarily. Here, as in a number of other instances during the same and later periods, he followed the *satyagraha* principle that the opponent must be considered and no unfair advantage taken. He went to Pretoria at Smuts' request and talked to the General, who was, he saw, now ready for a settlement. (Martial law had been proclaimed throughout South Africa and the railway workers were now increasing their demands.)

Gandhi's willingness to trust Smuts aroused criticism among the Indians, who could not forget that the General had made pledges in 1908 and broken them. But Gandhi's principle was always the same:

"No matter how often a *satyagrahi* is betrayed," he said, "he will repose his trust in the adversary so long as there are not cogent reasons for distrust."

Gandhi trusted Smuts and called off the whole *satyagraha* movement. In the resounding victory which followed during the spring of 1914, the main grievances which had called forth the movement, the poll-tax and the outlawing of Indian marriages, were set right. In the first historic test of the Gandhian principle on a big scale, it had won, and although it was not yet widely understood, by any means, it was clear that something new had appeared amongst the historic forces.

8

Gokhale summoned Gandhi to meet him in England after the triumph of *satyagraha* in South Africa. It was July, 1914, when Gandhi and his wife, with Walter Kallenbach, the German-South African friend who had worked with him throughout the struggle, sailed for Southampton. They reached it two days after England's declaration of war against Germany.

Gokhale was stranded in Paris by the declaration of war and Gandhi now had an indefinite period of waiting ahead of him. He did not wish to return to India without seeing the "political *guru*," the great leader. And his old sense of loyalty to the British Government, which had caused him to organize ambulance services during the Boer War and the Zulu rebellion, governed his action again. He proposed that the Indians living in the British Isles should volunteer their services to the government.

His course was opposed by many, and, indeed, under his own principles. *Ahinsa* made participation in a war impossible. And were the Indians not slaves to the English? Why should they rush to the aid of their masters? These arguments Gandhi opposed with his usual gentle insistence, and at that time put forward the view that British rule was "faulty but not intolerable." Then, as earlier, he blamed individual officials but not the system itself for whatever had been done wrong. His views prevailed; many Indians of all the provinces, races and religions came to him as volunteers; and he was soon at work again. An attack of pleurisy put all this to an end; he was ordered to return to India; in December, 1914, he sailed from England for home.

Gandhi was already Mahatma at this time. He had no doubt heard that immense numbers of people had begun to use that title in referring to him, but it seems probable that he had no real notion of what an impression his campaign in South Africa had made, or to what extent it had elevated him into a heroic or symbolic position in the eyes of the Indian masses. Certainly he did not like the title Mahatma and it took him years to get used to it, or to the extravagant reverence which it induced people to show toward him. He liked being called "Brother" (*Bhai*), as he had been in South Africa, and in later years he was reconciled to the title of "Father" (*Bapu*); Mahatma by then had become almost a part of Gandhi's name. At the end of his life I think the most affectionate and significant title given Gandhi by the whole Indian people, his closest followers as well as the millions who had never seen him except from afar, was "Father."

Now, however, in 1914, he was Mahatma for the first time for a whole people. How different this homecoming was from any previous one may be imagined. To Gandhi's astonishment there was a multitude on hand in the harbor and streets of Bombay to great the new Mahatma, whose struggle based on non-violence, love and truth had aroused historic memories unstirred for two thousand years among the people. There must have been a sign for many, English as well as Indians, in the scenes which took place during that second week of January, 1915, when Gandhi came home. It was clear that this mass demonstration was fundamentally of a religious nature, and yet it had so much political potentiality in it that no shrewd observer could remain unawares. Lord Willingdon, then Governor of Bombay, asked through Gokhale that Gandhi call upon him. When the fragile little man—still far from well—made his first visit to a British ruler in India, Willingdon asked him to promise one thing: to "come and see me" whenever he contemplated steps which concerned the government.

For Gandhi this was, indeed, easy. It had always been his principle to consider the opponent, to consult him, and never to undertake anything without letting the opponent know in advance. He was thus free to assure the courteous Willingdon that this would be his course in the future as well. In that interview both showed their mettle and perhaps—if there had been perceptive natures in Whitehall to consider the episode—the course of the coming epic might have been traced out substantially in advance.

Gokhale was living in Poona, the headquarters of the Servants of India, a society with principles in many respects quite different from Gandhi's, although their immediate objectives were much the same. It was Gokhale's wish that in spite of these differences the new Mahatma should join the Society. He did not do so—thus obviating a painful debate—and the Society was, in fact, grateful: for the establishment of his first Ashram they provided the funds and kept him—who was, as always, penniless —from an embarrassing search for money.

Gokhale by this time had a very adequate idea of the possibilities latent in this strange new genius. Gandhi was forty-six, and in spite of repeated illnesses he had always won out over the doctors. One of the most recent battles had been in London, with Gokhale on the side of the doctors. At that time the struggle was over milk, which Gandhi had given up in 1912. When he was finally convinced that Gandhi would rather die than drink milk, Gokhale gave in, but with disapproval. He now saw that in India a power of extraordinary quality had at last been added to the national treasure; he probably realized, from the time of the Bombay homecoming, that it would lie within Gandhi's capacity to convert the national movement from an affair of middle-class intellectuals, lawyers and the like, into something which would reach far out and down into the masses. But he wanted the new instrument of destiny to be fully matured before it came into use, and perhaps, also, he felt that Gandhi's long absence from India had made him unfamiliar with India's life. For whatever reason, he exacted a promise from the Mahatma not to speak on public questions or take any part in public life—not to join any political party either, which Gandhi was incapable of doing in any case—for a whole year. This was a sort of period of probation which Gokhale may have felt necessary, but which in any case Gandhi's own character would have imposed. Gandhi, in fact, felt that it might be five years before any occasion for bringing *satyagraha* to India would arise.

He left Gokhale at Poona and went on to his own family and friends at Rajkot and Porbandar—traveling third class, as had become his fixed custom since *satyagraha* began. As soon as he could do so he went on from there to Shantiniketan, the school and settlement (Ashram is the ordinary word for these colonies and will be used hereafter) of the poet Rabindranath Tagore. Here Tagore had been glad to welcome Gandhi's rather heterogeneous collection of followers from the Phoenix Settlement and the Tolstoy Farm, who belonged to more or less all religions and races. Among them were his faithful English friends, Pearson, and Andrews, who, with Maganlal Gandhi, had led the followers over from South Africa when the Mahatma had gone to London. Gandhi now had his reunion with that faithful band which had done so much for all his work of the past six or eight years.

It does not seem, however, that any great bond united him and Tagore at the time. The eloquent and beautiful Tagore came of a different strain; the Tagore family had always been rich and privileged, and even amidst the poetry of the Shantiniketan retreat there were things Gandhi did not particularly like. He thought, for example, that it would be better for the boys to do all their own work, as was the custom in his own settlements. They would learn self-help, save money and be much surer of seeing the work well done. There were a hundred and twenty-five boys in Tagore's school, all of whom welcomed the experiment with enthusiasm, but the teachers were at first a little reluctant. The Poet himself—referred to by Gandhi, as by all other

Indians during this period, simply thus: the Poet—had no objections, but it is easy to see that such ideas were not natural to him. He did say to his boys afterward: "This experiment contains the key to self-government." After Gandhi's departure the enthusiasm for cooking, washing and the like (not to mention scavenging) died down, and Shantiniketan returned to the older system of hired servants.

His own visit to Tagore's retreat was short, although he was obliged to leave his own "family" (that is, his relatives and followers) there for about three months more until he had found a place of his own for them. He was recalled to the other side of India by an event he had no doubt foreseen clearly during these last months, but which came as a shock of grief: the death of Gokhale. This left Gandhi without that "sure guide," the political *guru*, which at this stage of his life he felt he needed, but it also left him in a position of extraordinary historic insecurity—that is, he was already so far out in front as a leader that his course inevitably affected those of millions of others, but he did not see clearly what that course was to be. His pledge of a year's silence in public matters was thus a shield and a strength to him: he could found his own settlement, for his family, friends and followers, could conduct his school and continue his system of work, prayer and periodical fasting, without going forth upon the public stage or speaking his mind too soon.

The Satyagraha Ashram, as it was called, was founded on May 25, 1915, at Ahmedabad. Gandhi chose Ahmedabad because it was the capital of his native Gujarat and he believed that through his own region and people he could best serve India. He also hoped that funds for the support of the Ashram in the future might be forthcoming from the rich Gujaratis who were his fellow-countrymen. And, finally, since Ahmedabad had an ancient tradition as a center of handloom weaving, he hoped that it might be a favorable spot for his great project, the revival of hand-spinning.

The Ashram contained about twenty-five men and women in the beginning, all bound to the same vows of chastity, poverty and service. Their food was prepared in the same kitchen and all the work was shared in common, including, of course, that ordinarily done by untouchables.

Indeed, from the outset Gandhi had been determined to admit untouchables to his Ashram on a basis of complete equality as soon as any fitted for the service should present themselves. Untouchability had for years seemed to him the worst abuse in Hinduism, and he had taken every opportunity himself and through his followers to perform untouchables' work. At the great Kumbh Mela Fair, held that same spring shortly before the opening of the Ashram, Gandhi and his followers had volunteered to do the scavenging to the extent of their ability and had actually done so for one part of the vast encampment that gathers every twelve years by the sacred rivers.

Gandhi himself was in a curious intermediate stage of his mission. He was already Mahatma and was so addressed by everybody, including Tagore. The whole of India was aware of him and watched his course with close attention. At the same time he was still able to get into a crowded third-class compartment on a railway train and travel in that box of sardines, exposed to the same discomfort and indignity as every other passenger. It was a difficult period of adjustment for him, for he seems to have believed that it would actually be possible for him to dig latrines and bury excrement when he went to the great religious fair of the Kumbh Mela. Of course it was not: he had to sit in his tent hour after hour while the devout filed before him to obtain his darshan, and the throngs in their reverence even prevented him from moving to the sacred river to bathe. He was not alone even at his meals. The scavenging therefore had to be done by his friends and followers, which was not at all what he had had in mind. The woes of Mahatmas, as he said, are known to Mahatmas alone: he never revisited the religious fair of Kumbh Mela until his ashes were scattered at the confluence of the rivers in 1948.

Now, after that disillusioning experience at the fair, where he had seen enough superstition, dirt and hypocrisy to last him a lifetime, he was about to have his principles tested in a vital spot. A devout family of untouchables, father, mother and small daughter, applied for entrance to his Ashram.

After consultation with his followers, Gandhi accepted them. He could not have done otherwise. India was not yet used to him, however, and a storm arose. There were the usual troubles about water (the well used by an untouchable being "polluted"), and a sort of feud with the neighborhood, which Gandhi's firmness finally overcame. But, more serious than these, the Ashram was threatened with complete social boycott as being a settlement of untouchables, which meant that food, drink and all the usual services of the community would be denied it.

Then, finally, the rich of Ahmedabad, who had been finding the funds for the Ashram, decided to pay no more.

At this point one of Gandhi's typical experiences took place. He accepted his fate quite calmly and decided that he and his friends could move to the untouchables' quarter and earn their living as manual laborers, becoming themselves untouchables. While the plans were being drawn up for this move, one of the children of the colony came and told the Mahatma that a Sheth (that is, a Mohammedan of the middle class) was outside and wanted to speak to him. Gandhi went out and the Muslim asked him if he would accept help for the Ashram. The Mahatma said he certainly would. The Muslim made an appointment for the next day at the same hour, returned at the time appointed, placed thirteen thousand rupees in Gandhi's hand, and drove away again without another word. It was enough money to keep Gandhi's frugal establishment, large though it was, for a whole year.

"On all such occasions God has sent help at the last moment," is Gandhi's only comment on this remarkable episode.

The admission of the untouchable family, consisting of Dudabhai, an ex-teacher from Bombay, his wife Danibehn and their baby daughter Lakshmi (whom Gandhi adopted later), was an event of capital importance at the outset of his career in India. It served notice on the whole country that he would have nothing to do with the complicated and cruel system of bans upon untouchables. All Indian reformers before him had said the same things—Ramakrishna as well—but none had gone the length of taking an untouchable family into the house, living with them, dining with them and sharing the same water with them. From then on anybody who gave money for the support of Gandhi's Ashram had to do so with the knowledge that these practices, abhorrent to the orthodox, went on there. And yet more and more, as the years passed, the money for the support of his Ashram came from the orthodox. He took this to be an indication that the conscience of Hinduism had been moved and that the institution of untouchability was shaken to its depths. He lost no opportunity thereafter to shake it still further when the occasion arose.

The Mahatma left his retreat and his year of silence on February 4, 1916, for his first public address on public matters in India. He had been asked by Pandit Malaviya, the founder and first president of the Hindu University of Benares, to attend the opening of that institution, which was being set up with government help after public subscriptions throughout India to which maharajahs and others had contributed heavily.

By this time Gandhi had become himself. That is, he knew his course, he had worked and prayed, he had returned to native clothing of homespun cloth, he realized to some extent the power that was vested in him so long as he used it only for others. The experiment of hand-spinning, of which we shall hear more, was now well developed so far as his own Ashram was concerned, and he felt sure of what he could do with it. India had waited to hear what he would say when at last he was ready to speak. He accepted Pandit Malaviya's invitation and went to Benares.

The Hindu University is today a great institution with modern buildings covering a wide area: it was then small and experimental, but much money had been given and promised and a future of unlimited usefulness seemed to open before it. The opening ceremony was what is called an "all-India" occasion: the Viceroy (Lord Hardinge) had lent it his presence and there were representatives of every branch of Indian life in the crowd. The ceremony was, of course, in English, and English was the language of instruction for the new university (as it still is until 1952), as for all other institutions of higher learning in India. Gandhi, too, was obliged to speak in English—of which he had a perfect command by now—but he chose to begin by remarking upon that fact.

"It is a matter of deep humiliation and shame for me that I am compelled this evening," he said, "under the shadow of this great college, in this sacred city, to address my countrymen in a language that is foreign to me."

The bewilderment of his audience was at first extreme, but

he proceeded unfalteringly to make his points, one after the other.

"The charge against us is that we have no initiative. How can we have any if we devote precious years of our life to the mastery of a foreign tongue? We fail in this attempt also."

He then proceeded, in that resplendent gathering, to attack the splendor which had accompanied the opening ceremony. He was himself barefoot and dressed in the homespun garments of the very poor, which made his remarks about the jeweled show of the day before all the more pointed. The Indian princes who sat on the dais heard these remarks with discomfort, particularly as on the outskirts of the crowd there were murmurs of amusement at their predicament. (Actually Baroda and others had given most of the money for the university, and had dragged out the most gorgeous of their jewels for this show.) Gandhi went on to say that the maharajahs should clean their own streets, that the priests ought to clean the temples of the holy city of Benares, and that the high-caste Hindus should not ill-treat the low-castes on railway trains and elsewhere. "No amount of speeches will ever make us fit for self-government," he said. "It is only our conduct that will fit us for it."

However, and in the war year 1916 it was no light thing to say, the Mahatma declared: "If I found it necessary for the salvation of India that the English should retire, that they should be driven out, I would not hesitate to declare that they would have to go, and I hope I would be prepared to die in defense of that belief."

The first campaign of Gandhi in India, which followed soon after his startling speech before the notables at Benares, came, in his mind, under the head of "unfinished business." That is, the three-pound poll-tax on indentured Indians in South Africa had been abolished by the Smuts-Gandhi agreement of 1914 and was never again revived, but the abuse of the indentures themselves—that is, emigration from India under labor-contracts for a term of years—was still in existence. It was clearly a form of peonage, and Gandhi could not proceed to other questions until he had disposed of this one. He tried talking to some Indian leaders and wrote a few letters and articles in the press, and the response convinced him that India at large would support a campaign to abolish indentured emigration. As it was his way, at least for many years, to concentrate on one such question at a time, he spent a good part of the next year on the problem of how to get indentures abolished.

At first the friendly Viceroy, Lord Hardinge, had no objection: he accepted a motion made by Malaviya in the legislative council and promised abolition "in due course." This was much too vague to satisfy Gandhi. He made it obvious during his talks and press writings of the next few months that if the abolition did not come soon he would consider ways and means of bringing into play his terrifying weapon, *satyagraha*, which had never yet been used in India.

While he was coming near this decisive step he attended the meeting of the Indian National Congress at Christmas, 1916, at Lucknow, but took little part in its work and made no deep impression on the middle-class intellectuals who composed it. At this meeting he met a young man, Pandit Jawaharlal Nehru, a formidable collaborator in later days, but they do not seem to have had much to say to each other. Pandit Nehru, in his autobiography, records that he found Gandhi "very distant and different and unpolitical"—which, indeed, must have been the case and to some extent remained the case to the end.

In February, 1917, Pandit Malaviya tried to introduce a bill (in the legislative council) for the immediate abolition of the indenture system. Lord Chelmsford, the new Viceroy, refused permission. Gandhi then decided to start upon his first campaign throughout India.

Before he did so he asked to be received by the Viceroy, to whom he explained the plan with his usual gentle courtesy. Lord Chelmsford was by no means inimical; he promised to help if he could. Gandhi then started his tour, with Bombay as the point of departure, asking the Indian people to demand the abolition of indentures by May 31st of the same year. He chose a definite date because he had always found that such words as "in due course" or even "immediate" were subject to wide latitude of interpretation, and he felt that if the step were not taken by May 31st then it would be time to bring into play some form of outright *satyagraha*.

The tour aroused high excitement throughout India and the

government abolished indentured emigration before May 31st—thus ending a struggle Gandhi had first undertaken in 1894, twenty-three years before, as a completely unknown young barrister.

The hardships of the tour were not concerned with either the government or the people, but with the third-class system on the Indian railways. The Mahatma was then not recognizable to everybody, and as he would not give his name until he was asked, he often found himself cramped, shoved and stepped upon in the dense mass of humanity which overruns the third-class accommodation in India. In those days he traveled alone, except for the detectives of the Criminal Investigation Department who never left him. He treated these detectives with courtesy at all times, recognizing that it was their job to observe him, and even when they were unnecessarily intrusive (as when they kept on examining his railway ticket time after time) he made no objection. Later on, men in this general profession, that is, detectives, jailers, and persons employed in or about a jail, became as reverent and attentive to him as his own immediate followers.

The abolition of indentured emigration was Gandhi's first successful reform in India. It was in itself important, but more important as an indication of what was to follow. Viceroy and government were aware by now that the course of history depended most of all upon what he would do next.

9

He was at this period almost apolitical, or at least almost without ideas on political subjects, so far as one can tell from his own writing and other evidence. He wanted to reform abuses and help his people, but it does not seem that the central problem of colonial imperialism took up much of his mind. For example, he always considered himself—up to this period and for some time yet—to be a loyal subject of the British Crown and tried to behave as such, even when he was in opposition to a governmental body, as in South Africa. In the Boer War and the Zulu rebellion he had not agreed at all with government policy but he had formed his ambulance units just the same and worked for the wounded. In 1914 in London he considered that as he was living under the protection of the British fleet he had a duty in return, and for the third time organized an ambulance unit of Indians. Now, at home in India, he was gradually beginning to realize that many people, many millions, in fact, depended upon him for guidance, but the guidance he was as yet ready to give had little to do with the problems of government. It was only slowly, as he began to see how government concerned every one of these other problems—poverty, injustice, economic oppression and the general condition of the people—that he came to the inevitable steps toward "political" action.

His next campaign in 1917—running partly alongside the one for abolition of indentures—was in protection of the share-croppers of the Champaran district in the upper part of Bihar province. He knew nothing about the cultivation of indigo, but had been beset by a very insistent man from Champaran who wanted him to sponsor a resolution of sympathy at the Indian National Congress for the indigo workers (sharecroppers) of Champaran. Gandhi would do no such thing; somebody else had to present and sponsor the resolution; but he promised to go and look at the situation and see what he could do.

Gandhi found when he got to Bihar that innumerable cases had been brought to court. As usual in India, the lawyers were active in the matter but for considerable fees. It was then that he used a phrase afterwards to be used with immense effect by President Roosevelt: "to be free from fear," he said, was what the sharecroppers needed. This they could not be by going to law courts.

Under the system of land tenure obtaining in Champaran, each tenant farmer had to plant three parts out of twenty in the land he held for the benefit of his landlord. These three parts—called *tinkathia*—were to be cultivated in indigo.

The Mahatma now asked all the anxious lawyers, Congress members and others with whom he talked in Patna, to undertake the campaign for nothing, for love and service, and to be prepared to go to prison, if necessary. These were novel ideas and it took some time to get them accepted. At last he got the necessary pledges—full time from some, part time from others, prison, if necessary, for all. He could then go to work.

In accordance with his fixed principles, he called first upon the
Secretary of the Indigo Planters' Association and the (government) Commissioner of the Division to let them know that he
proposed to investigate the grievances of the tenant farmers. He
got a sharp reception from both and realized that he might soon
go to jail, but proceeded with the investigation.

Such a thing had never happened before and the abysmally
poor tenant-farmers flocked to Gandhi to tell him their stories.
He went on the first day to Bettiah, one of the poorest districts,
where the peasants were worst treated, and throngs of them surrounded him and filed before him to tell him. It required all of
his volunteers (the Biharis from Patna) to keep the crowds in
order and take the necessary notes. None of this was done because
he was Gandhi: nobody in that part of India knew who Gandhi
was or had any clear idea of the National Congress either. They
assembled merely because they realized that a friend had come
at last. It seemed to Gandhi that they had suddenly lost all their
fear of punishment, and, since there were so many of them, the
usual floggings would have been impossible.

On the first day he received a notice from the Police Superintendent that he must leave Champaran; he sent word that he
would not comply with it; he then received a summons to stand
trial for refusing to obey an order. He sat up all night giving
instructions, putting his notes in order, giving instructions for
the rest of the investigation and hearing stories. What he was
doing was done merely privately, not in the name of the Indian
National Congress, and he was careful not to involve the Congress
in any of it. Beyond any doubt he was not deeply in sympathy
with the Congress of those days, so lawyer-like and paper-ridden,
and it was a relief to him to be able to do something useful by
himself.

When he appeared in court the next day to stand trial he read
a brief statement explaining why he could not obey the order to
leave Champaran until he had investigated the grievances of the
peasants. He asked that the trial not be postponed, but judgment
given at once, as he pleaded guilty to refusal to obey the order.

The embarrassed magistrate postponed judgment just the same,
and in the meanwhile the government ordered the case with-

drawn. (Gandhi had informed the Viceroy of the situation, which may have had something to do with this.)

This was the first occurrence of civil disobedience in its form as *satyagraha*, voluntary and non-violent, in the history of India. It was discussed all over India, where the principles of the new form of struggle were still very imperfectly understood. Gandhi had taken each step with such care—with such friendly respect toward all the government officials involved, such deference toward the Viceroy and all who might be concerned—that the essentially new character of *satyagraha*, its character of love for both sides in a dispute, began to dawn upon innumerable surprised observers. To keep this situation going, to teach *satyagraha* step by step, required even more delicate attention then than at later periods, particularly since (as Gandhi knew well) the planters of Champaran were now furious at the government for permitting him to go on with his investigation.

He therefore wrote to the Indian press and urged them not to send reporters to the scene, as the appearance of excited articles might make matters worse; he promised to send them information himself from time to time.

In this first experiment with his own methods he could not really rely upon anybody but himself. The methods were too new; at every turn they ran the danger of being misunderstood or misinterpreted; it took him hours every day to explain to his own fellow-workers why they must do this or that in that or this way. He patiently insisted day after day that only the most rigid truth must be spoken, that anything else would weaken the strength of *satyagraha;* every day he insisted upon non-violence under all conditions, even under violence. Thus the investigation proceeded, although with constant efforts on Gandhi's part to mold his new fellow-workers (Biharis all) to his way of living and working.

Thus the Patna lawyers each had a servant and a cook and had meals at all hours; it took some time for Gandhi to persuade them that it was simpler for one kitchen to be run for all of them, and that, a vegetarian kitchen. Then, too, they thought he should take money from the peasants to run the operation—a thing he was resolved never to do: he got the necessary funds, instead, from a few wealthy Patna residents and a friend in Rangoon. In the style in which he lived no great sums were ever necessary, but whatever was necessary must not, he was determined, come from such poor people as the *ryots* or landless peasants of the district.

Again, as always, he was not content with merely taking the depositions of the thousands who came to him. This work went on all day every day. It required from five to seven volunteers on fairly constant duty taking down the notes. Much of it was unnecessary, since there was so much repetition of misery and injustice, but the Mahatma had seen from the outset that these people were finding a friend for the first time in their lives, and he therefore permitted them all to tell their stories, whether necessary or not. A detective from the Criminal Investigation Department stood alongside and listened, but the peasants had now overcome their fear and poured it all out anyhow.

Yet Gandhi saw that their condition required more than a reforming action on the part of the indigo planters. They needed village schools of some kind, for their children were either put to work too soon or allowed to roam about like animals. They needed, above all, some kind of notion of sanitation, for their lives were passed in terrible filth. He therefore sent to other parts of India for volunteers, obtained them, and set to work on six village schools and the usual scavenging, cleaning and sweeping operations to go with them. He hoped that the example, even of only a few months, would last among the indigo slaves; he was afterward of the opinion that it had lasted in part.

His presence in the indigo country was an embarrassment to the government and eventually they wrote to ask when he would leave. He said he would leave only when the government recognized that the grievances of these unhappy people were real and set about redressing them. The government then set up a committee of inquiry (of which Gandhi was a member), which made a report in favor of the tenant-farmers; the system of three-twentieths sharecropping was abolished by law; it was another triumph for *satyagraha*, although the *satyagraha* was not yet fully formed and was mainly Gandhi's alone.

Upon the accomplishment of the work for Champaran, Gandhi returned home to his Ashram, which by now had grown to some forty men, women and children. Its original situation was no

longer healthy because of a plague outbreak, and at this juncture
the Mahatma found a new piece of ground at Sabarmati, not far
away. (It remained there for years.) The new ground was full of
snakes and had to be cleared, but he stuck to his principle—which
he had already put into effect at Phoenix Settlement and Tolstoy
Farm in Africa—that no reptile was to be killed. In spite of this
rule there never was a loss of life caused by snakebite. The
Mahatma attributed this to the mercy of God. (One is reminded
of the Lord Buddha, who said, when one of his disciples was
killed by a snake: "It was because his mind was unfriendly toward
the snake.")

While he was making the move and resettling his "family"
in the new Ashram, the Mahatma was called upon to help the
mill-hands in the textile industry of Ahmedabad, who had grievances which the mill-owners were unwilling to redress. After
talking to the mill-owners, the Mahatma advised the workers to
go on strike, providing they were willing to take a pledge of
non-violence. They were not to molest strikebreakers and not
to accept alms, but to earn their daily bread by some other form
of labor so long as the strike lasted. The pledge was freely taken
by the leaders of the strike and accepted by the whole mass of
workers, who thereafter, for about two weeks, paraded the streets
declaring their adherence to the pledge. Every day the mill-
hands, or delegations from them, went to the Mahatma and
repeated their vow. Although his relations with the mill-owners
were cordial—some had been benefactors of the Ashram, and he
never lost his feeling of friendliness toward them—he regarded
himself as responsible for the mill-hands and their strike because
of this vow.

Then the strikers' zeal began to flag, there were signs of
declining enthusiasm for the vow, and the Mahatma began to be
afraid of violence to strikebreakers. He therefore told the workers
that until they rallied to their vow and continued the strike until
a settlement was reached, he would touch no food.

He had a considerable struggle with his own conscience over
this fast, because he did not then (or at any other time) want a
fast to become a form of coercion. He felt himself to be responsible for the behavior of the workers and therefore could find

no means in his own mind of atoning for their lapses except by fasting; at the same time he was reluctant to have even the appearance of forcing his friends, the mill-owners, into a settlement.

Under these circumstances the fast began. At first others (in the Ashram and amongst the laborers) wished to fast with him, and many did so on the first day, but as usual he dissuaded them. Vallabhbhai Patel had by now joined him—not as a member of the Ashram; he was a successful Ahmedabad lawyer even then— but as a devoted visitor and follower. Patel and others organized a means of labor for the strikers which would give them employment and help the Ashram: they carried sand from the river for the new weaving school which was to be built.

The Mahatma fasted for three days ("Only three days," as he says). Then the mill-owners and mill-workers had a meeting, agreed on an arbitration, and settled the strike in no time at all, amid general rejoicing.

He began almost at once upon a campaign of *satyagraha* for the starving peasants of Kheda District, in his own Gujarati country, who were on the brink of famine but were still being held responsible for their annual tax assessment. The law declared that a peasant did not have to pay his assessment if his crop was worth four annas (perhaps ten cents at the time) or less. The peasants of Kheda, who had been hit by very adverse weather and crop failure, declared that their crop was under four annas (per unit) and the government insisted that it was over that value. There was no disposition on the part of the government to argue the question or accept arbitration. Gandhi therefore advised the peasants of Kheda to declare *satyagraha,* and he went to the district to explain it and help them.

The pledge taken on this occasion was by all the peasants, well-to-do or very poor, that they would withhold tax payments until the remaining three assessments for the year were remitted from the very poor. Once the government had remitted for the helpless, those able to pay promised to pay in full. (The reason for this was that the poorest might, in fear and confusion, sell everything they possessed in an effort to pay, leaving themselves without a pot or a pan, and thus depress still further the level of ordinary life.) Those who signed the pledge had to be willing to suffer any punishment the government might offer, including (of course) jail and, more serious to them, the forfeiting of their land.

Gandhi and his fellow-workers had to explain to these peasants all the principles of *satyagraha*, not only its non-violence and its perfect friendliness toward the adversary, but the nature of voluntary sacrifice. As in Champaran at the other end of India, it was a startling novelty, but the difference was that in Kheda, so near to Bombay with its many big newspapers, every move in the campaign was chronicled fully in the press.

At one point—the high point in this campaign—while the government was seizing cattle and movables, attaching crops and going through other forms of coercion upon the people, Gandhi advised that a certain onion crop, which in his opinion had been wrongly attached by the government, should be removed. Eight or nine volunteers removed the crop, were promptly arrested, and their trial and imprisonment aroused the people to great demonstrations of enthusiasm. The campaign came to an end soon afterward when the government issued an order suspending the tax assessment for the poor peasants, providing the wealthier ones paid.

Gandhi was not satisfied with the ending of the Kheda *satyagraha;* it failed to meet most of his requirements, the chief of which was that the end of a non-violent campaign should leave the participants "stronger and more spirited" than they were in the beginning. It certainly had not the dramatic coherence, rising action and climax which characterized so many of his great campaigns, but the circumstances did not conspire in his favor as they so often did afterward. In any case, he introduced the idea to the Gujarat country and it was never forgotten, although neither had it fully penetrated all minds, as was to be seen later. The Kheda campaign did receive full attention throughout India, and even though it was not a perfect example of the Mahatma's principles in action, it was worth doing, above all, because it brought the middle-class intellectuals for the first time into a direct connection with the peasantry and allied them in a common cause. A number of things about it displeased the Mahatma (too much money was spent, for example, by the rich Bombay sympathizers, and there was actually some money left over after the goal was won). These errors and defects arose from a lack of comprehension of the principles, and he was to spend much of his energy for years in an attempt to get them understood so that a *satyagraha* campaign might at last be pure.

Champaran and Kheda were in the nature of a prelude to what was to follow. They were a prelude of such consequence, however, that it was no longer possible for anything of an All-India nature, involving the whole sub-continent, to be undertaken again without some consultation of Gandhi's views. He had already become so central in the consciousness of the people, Hindu as well as Muslim, that nobody could afford to ignore him. Therefore when the Viceroy, Lord Chelmsford, wished to undertake a recruiting campaign in India (1917), it was necessary to call upon Gandhi to support it.

The request tested his principles and the relations between them. Under *ahinsa* he could not support a war, and yet he felt himself to be a loyal subject of the British Empire, enjoying its protection and concerned in its fate. He had supported the Boer War to the extent of creating an Indian ambulance unit; he had done the same in the Zulu rebellion and in 1914 in England; he was now called upon to follow out the logical consequences of these previous acts. And yet he felt strongly that the Indian Muslims, who were deeply disturbed over the collapse of the Ottoman Empire and the breakdown of Islam's temporal power, should be placated. He had been convinced in South Africa, he says, that "It would be on the question of Hindu-Muslim unity that my *ahinsa* would be put to its severest test, and that the question presented the widest field for my experiments in *ahinsa*." Truer words were never written.

He therefore linked the questions of the Muslim Khilafat, home rule for India, and the recruiting campaign, all together in his mind, and made of the whole a kind of summary statement of the Indian case, which he intended to present together to the Viceroy. When he got to Delhi he discovered another moral obstacle: there were undenied reports in the press that England had made some secret treaties with Italy and others. How could he support a war of which even the objectives were thrown into doubt by secret treaties?

Lord Chelmsford persuaded him by saying that he knew no more of the matter than Mr. Gandhi, and that such moral questions should be brought up after the war, not in the crisis. He put it on a broader and simpler basis: if Mr. Gandhi felt that the British Empire had been, on the whole, a power for good, and if India had benefited by the British connection, then India should help the Empire.

On this basis Mr. Gandhi agreed to enter the War Conference and support the resolution for the recruiting of Indians. He spoke in Hindustani, for the first time in a viceregal meeting, and said but one sentence: "With a full sense of my responsibility I beg to support the resolution."

That he had spoken in Hindustani rather than in English was made a matter of congratulation to Gandhi, which, he says, hurt his national pride. He had apparently not realized that the language of these exalted levels in the government of India was exclusively English. And not only the language, but the sense of that one sentence gave him much trouble. Certain Indian national leaders who were thought "extreme" had been excluded from the conference; the Muslim demands had not been heard; there was no clear pledge of home rule. The Mahatma, therefore, wrote a letter to Lord Chelmsford on all these points and made it public throughout India. He was, at this stage of his life, going much further in friendship toward the British than most Indian national leaders would have wished, but he did so in the clearest expectation that advantage to India would result.

"Ours is a peculiar position," he told the Viceroy in that famous war letter. "We are today outside the partnership. Ours is a consecration based on the hope of a better future. I should be untrue to you and to my country if I did not clearly and unequivocally tell you what that hope is. I do not bargain for its fulfilment, but you should know that disappointment of hope means disillusion."

This warning of the results if India's desire for home rule should be frustrated was followed by a passage in which Gandhi stated his inability to "sink domestic differences," as the Viceroy had asked, if this should mean acquiescence in tyranny. "Ask me to suspend my activities in that direction," he said, "and you ask me to suspend my life. If I could popularize the use of soul-force, which is but another name for love-force, in place of brute force,

I know that I could present you with an India that could defy the whole world to do its worst. In season and out of season, therefore, I shall discipline myself to express in my life this eternal law of suffering, and present it for acceptance to those who care, and if I take part in any other activity, the motive is to show the matchless superiority of that law."

The letter concluded by requesting the Viceroy to ask the London government to give definite assurances on the postwar status of the Moslem countries, the question which most powerfully interested the Indian Mohammedans at the moment.

Gandhi now had, in pursuance of his usual logic, to suit the action to the words, and embark on the incongruous enterprise of recruiting soldiers for the Indian Army. He did so in his usual way, walking from village to village and talking to the people in his own Gujarat country, until his health collapsed and he fell into his first long illness. He was still very weak and in great pain when the news of Germany's surrender arrived, along with a governmental message to tell him that recruiting for the army was no longer necessary—"a great relief." He lingered on in that illness for months, trying remedies of one sort or another and, for some weeks, fully expecting death. Most of his time was spent in listening to the Gita chanted by members of his Ashram, familiarizing himself still further with the language of the poem in the original. He was so extremely weakened by prolonged dysentery that the doctors told him he could not recover at all without some radical innovation in diet. Since he refused eggs or any other animal food, the remedy proposed was milk. Against this recourse he had a simple answer: he had vowed in 1912 not to drink milk and the vow was unbreakable.

(The milk vow was an important matter in Gandhi's mind to the very end, and he spoke to me at some length about it two days before his death.)

Kasturbai, his devoted wife, was standing by the bed during his talk with the doctor. She interposed her suggestion: his vow had been only against cow's milk and buffalo's milk. There was therefore no reason, she said, why he should not drink goat's milk.

Her pleading and Gandhi's own desire to live prevailed. He accepted goat's milk and drank it ever afterward—"because of the body's weakness," he said to me—although he actually felt that his vow against buffalo and cow milk should, in nature, have included all other kinds of milk as well.

As he was regaining strength that first winter after the war, Gandhi in his retreat picked up a newspaper which contained the report of the Rowlatt Committee. This was a committee of inquiry, under an English jurist, to study sedition in India and means to deal with it. Its recommendations were of an oppressive character with respect to the liberties of speech, press and assembly, which had in any case been restricted throughout the war, and it looked to Gandhi like an ominous breach of faith: if the liberties of the people were to be curtailed even after the war, what became of the chance of home rule?

This was the decisive phase, it appears to me, in the relationship of Gandhi to Indian politics and to the British government of India. Up to now he had been a loyal subject even when he opposed specific officials or specific acts. It was the Rowlatt Committee's report and the legislation which followed (the Rowlatt Bill—January, 1919) that forced the Mahatma into political action and before long made him into a rebel against the British Raj—an entirely new kind of rebel, it is true, filled with love and devoted to non-violence, always faithfully warning his opponents of what he was going to do before he did it, but a rebel just the same. The process took some three years and transformed the nature of the Indian situation: when it ended with Gandhi's trial and imprisonment for a six years' term (March, 1922), the lines were drawn and the general character of the Gandhian movement had been proved in action before the whole world.

This period of Gandhi's life (1919-1922) gave it a color which could never again be altered, whatever he did. His life from then on was a form of political action and his slightest word or deed had political significance in the immense revolutionary development which was at hand. That this should be so did, at times, obscure the wider significance of his search for truth and his struggle to deal directly with the terrible poverty and suffering of India. He was known to many in England and the whole West (particularly to politicians) as "a politician," and although I cannot see that this was ever correct as a description of his activity, it prevailed for a long time in the popular mind outside of India.

He was himself unchanged; there never was a moment when the spinning-wheel, cottage industries, the emancipation of women, the spread of knowledge on sanitation, hygiene and diet, the improvement of agriculture, and innumerable other practical forms of service, did not occupy his mind—not to speak of his daily and unceasing effort to reach God through prayer and meditation—but in spite of all this, or perhaps even partly because of it, his activity could never again be separated from the political struggle of India. Even his silence became a form of speech and his occasional retirements, illnesses or withdrawals themselves a form of action. When he wished to abstain from any participation in politics (as he often did), the abstention itself was taken by the masses to indicate an attitude. He thus became, and remained for almost thirty years, a living proof of the intimate union of religion, politics and society in the Indian consciousness, and the most powerful single influence upon the development of that consciousness in its epic phase.

Gandhi himself must often have regretted the demands politics made upon his time. We know, indeed, that this was so, and that the inhabitants of his Ashram—students, followers, "patients"—took up an equal share of his attention with matters of national and international importance. Nothing was ever permitted to interfere with his morning and evening prayer meetings, the chanting of hymns, the meditation and the sermon. At any moment he was ready to interrupt a political conference to devote himself to some follower who was ill or troubled, to put his household remedies (mud-packs and the like) to work, or even to give an enema. His very simple, homely advice to the Indian people on health, sanitation and hygiene—much of it contained in the book called *Guide to Health*, but also frequently renewed in newspapers or sermons—was at least as consequential in his eyes as any of the complicated political difficulties which were brought to him for consideration. And most of all the spinning-wheel, with all that it represented for the poorest of the poor peasants, came to represent to him the most useful of his services, a solution for the pauperization of the Indian masses. With all this we may say that if Gandhiji was in fact a politician, he was the only one of his particular kind that ever lived; and we need not be surprised to find that he did not think of himself in that way at all. He thought of life as a whole, and regarded it as impossible to separate the elements of religion, politics and society ("politics without religion is dead," he said) but if there must be three categories, and these are the three, then clearly politics came off a poor third in his eyes.

From the point of view deliberately taken at the beginning of this book, Gandhi's political activity, although historically great, was only one aspect of his life, and although it changed the world and brought him to martyrdom, I still do not consider that it was the principal element of his significance. I shall therefore make no attempt to treat the thirty years which led to the liberation of India in any detail. There are political histories both existent and in the making which take good care of that subject. I shall recall only the main steps in the development, and even these rather summarily, in order to get the external events in their correct order as a basis for some consideration of what does seem to me vital: the creative ideas of the Mahatma.

10

Shocked as he was by the Rowlatt Bill, Gandhi could not at first see what there was to be done about it. He could only offer civil disobedience if the government gave him some opportunity to do so. In his dilemma, although he was still very weak, he undertook a journey to Madras, where he had always had a multitude of devoted followers since his South African days. There he stayed with Rajagopalachari—whom he was to value later as one of the finest of his fellow-workers—and discussed the situation. He reached his first idea of tentative *satyagraha* (an inspired one, as it turned out) one night after one of these discussions; in the twilight region between sleep and consciousness, he says, the idea came to him. He would ask all India to observe a day of national mourning, fasting and prayer, as self-purification in preparation for the struggle which was now inevitable.

His appeal to the people was brief and he gave them very little time. At first he fixed the day of mourning—*hartal*, it is called in India—for March 30th, but then, deciding that this gave too little time for preparation, changed it to April 6th. He did not expect more than a few provinces (Bombay, Madras, Bihar and Sind) to respond fully, but he thought that if these few did, the meaning of the demonstration would be clear.

As a matter of fact, all India observed the *hartal* with an astonishing completeness, Muslims as well as Hindus, towns as well as villages. All work ceased and all places of business were closed. In Delhi the change of date became known too late, and the *hartal* was observed on March 30th with some disorder when the police fired on a procession. There were casualties, and incidents of a similar character occurred also in Lahore and Amritsar. Gandhi himself was at Bombay for the *hartal* of April 6th, which was an immense demonstration of national unity. Never before had Hindus and Muslim acted together so successfully. Gandhi and Mrs. Naidu, who was with him, delivered speeches in a mosque and sold forbidden books in the public streets. The books chosen were two by himself, one, his *Hind Swaraj*, and the other his Gujarati translation of Ruskin's *Unto This Last*, both of which had been proscribed by the government. An army of volunteers helped to sell the books, and it was thought that this form of civil disobedience might bring punishment. The government, however, decided that the books being sold were mere reprints, and not to be considered the same as the books which had been proscribed, so no arrests took place.

Gandhi, however, was now in demand both in the Punjab and in Delhi. The dimensions of the movement he had set off with the *hartal* surprised everybody, including himself. He started the next day on his journey to Delhi and Amritsar, but when the train got to Palwal station he was served with a written order forbidding him to cross the borders of the Punjab province on the ground that his presence there would disturb the peace. He refused to obey the order, was taken off the train, put under arrest and returned to Bombay.

The news of this arrest spread like wildfire; immense crowds gathered in Bombay and other cities; Gandhi himself went to the center of the city to try to quiet the mob and was there when the mounted police charged, causing a good many casualties. In the meantime there were disorders in a number of other cities, including his own Ahmedabad, where the mill-hands whom he felt to be his particular charge had gone mad with anger and killed a police officer. Gandhi addressed a mass meeting on the beach at Bombay—although he was still not strong and could not speak standing up—asking them to keep peace and explaining again the principles of *satyagraha*. He then left for Ahmedabad, saw what had happened there, and immediately declared that *satyagraha* must now be abandoned because the people had not sufficiently understood its meaning and its essential character as non-violence. He also undertook a three-day fast in penitence for the violence committed by his people.

Now the whole of India was in turmoil. The government was engaged in repressive activity on a big scale, some of it savage in severity; the nationalists who had swarmed into the streets on April 6th were now (April 13th-14th) suddenly told that they must abandon the movement because there had been violence; Gandhi's own position, in the midst of his prayer and fasting, was unclear to millions of people who did not understand what it was he wanted them to do. As soon as he could do so, he made another speech (at Nadiad) on the subject of violence and non-violence, using for the first time a phrase which became famous in India and was to be heard from his lips more than once—"a Himalayan miscalculation." He said he had made a "Himalayan miscalculation" by asking the people to offer non-violent civil disobedience, or *satyagraha*, before they were ready for it and before they truly understood it. The phrase exposed him to a good deal of ridicule, because at that time it was quite true that his ideas had not really penetrated enough to be quite clear and to many of the young hotheads it seemed that he was abandoning them without sufficient reason.

On April 13, 1919, the very day when Gandhi was giving up *satyagraha* and declaring his fast, the British General Dyer at Amritsar fired upon a meeting of some 20,000 Indians at the Jallianwala Bagh in that city. The Jallianwala Bagh is a garden with only one exit; Dyer and his fifty soldiers stood in the exit and fired over 1600 rounds of ammunition in ten minutes into the death-trap. The figures of the massacre have always been disputed; there were 1200 dead and 3600 wounded, according to the report later made by the non-official (Gandhi's) committee of inquiry. The official committee (governmental) reported about 400 killed and between 1000 and 2000 wounded.

The Amritsar massacre made a tremendous stir both in India and in the world outside, but what was in some respects even worse was the savage repression and humiliation to which the living were subjected afterward. No Indian could pass a certain street except by crawling on his belly; there was martial law; there were special tribunals, wholesale arrests, floggings and heavy prison sentences. Gandhi wanted to go to the Punjab at once but could not obtain permission to do so. As he received the news from Amritsar and Lahore and tried to keep calm he had two organs of opinion put at his service—*Young India*, a weekly in English, and *Navajivan*, a monthly in Gujarati. Since he felt in this situation how greatly the public needed education in the principles of non-violence, and since he wanted some opportunity to comment regularly on the state of the nation, these periodicals were what he needed. He published them from the same press in Ahmedabad, and their owners were ready and willing, for patriotic reasons, to do without advertisements and give the Mahatma a free hand. Both jumped to big circulation at once, and enabled Gandhi to make his views and advice heard at a time when his own freedom of movement was limited and the whole Indian sub-continent was going through a time of trouble.

The Mahatma was not permitted to go to the Punjab until October of that momentous year. He had repeatedly asked the Viceroy for permission and had been repeatedly asked by other Indian leaders to go. He was, actually, held responsible for all the disasters by some British officials (particularly Sir Michael O'Dwyer, the Governor of the Punjab) and by a good many of the young Indian nationalists as well: O'Dwyer because Gandhi had ordered the movement for civil disobedience, the young nationalists because he had called it off. But whatever these scattered elements of opinion might be, Gandhi's hold upon the masses of the people was now secure, and on his arrival at Lahore, the Punjab capital, the entire population turned out to greet him. He had never been in the Punjab before and had even said to a police official during his brief Bombay arrest, "Nobody knows me there." He was now to see how wrong that statement was. Thousands of Punjabis filed before him during the next three months to tell their stories; innumerable women came to give him yarn for his spinning; his committee of inquiry (non-official) became far more important than the government's own and amassed far more evidence. It was undoubtedly a source of great embarrassment to the government of India that Gandhi should be conducting an inquiry at all, but the state of public feeling at the time was such that no serious interference with him could be contemplated. He was, it seems, an austere judge of evidence, and rejected everything that seemed to him exaggerated or unproved, so that the final report of his committee stood, he believed, as a sober and exact account of the atrocities. Since he and all the other Indian leaders had boycotted the government's inquiry, and since most of the Punjabi leaders were in jail, his own report was bound to stand as a more likely document than the official version prepared upon much slimmer evidence.

And this, too, served still further to entangle Gandhi in the web of politics. He had never really taken part in meetings of the Indian National Congress before: he had attended them more or less as a matter of showing his allegiance, but was, as they all thought, "remote and unpolitical." He had annually made a speech, but chiefly so that he could use a national language in that body which, for all its nationalism, conducted its meetings in English.

Now he could not refuse to take part: he had had too much to do with the Punjab investigation. Moreover, the Montagu-Chelmsford Reform, which promised a constitution to India along certain well-defined lines, which meant (in Gandhi's eyes) definite progress, had just been announced, and the Mahatma thought it should be accepted. Many or perhaps most Indian national leaders did not agree with him. However, the time had now come when it was hardly possible to disagree with Gandhi on any matter of primary importance: his sway over the masses was too great. After some maneuvers and a compromise amendment, his resolution accepting the constitutional reform was passed. He had not wished to impose his views, and suggested instead that he might absent himself from the Congress as soon as his report on the Punjab had been disposed of; but such an absence would have looked like disapproval and the leaders implored him to stay. Once he did stay it was inevitable that he should be consulted on every question, and he acquired for the first time some practical knowledge of how the Congress worked and what its divisions of opinion were.

The political power of the Mahatma over the Congress became still more apparent in the special session at Calcutta (1920) and the ordinary annual session at Nagpur soon afterward, when he presented for the first time a resolution in favor of non-violent non-co-operation with the British government and succeeded in getting it passed. Considerable disagreement existed upon the question: a good many seasoned leaders thought the Indian people could not be trained in such a novel form of struggle in time to obtain results. Gandhi himself had wanted to limit the struggle to two objectives, redress of the wrongs done in the Punjab and a settlement of the Islamic caliphate in a way acceptable to Indian Muslims. (In those days some of his strongest support in the Congress came from Muslims, and specifically from Mr. Jinnah.) He yielded to other opinions and included self-government (Swaraj) as an objective, although he had originally intended to postpone it. By his gentle patience and willingness to discuss any opposing views, he thus committed the Congress, by 1921, to support his own program, including the abolition of untouchability, the introduction of homespun cloth (khadi) as a substitute for foreign cloth, and the unity of Hindus and Muslims. Upon all of this there were misgivings, but the hour of Gandhi's irresistibility in these matters had arrived and it was not possible to disregard his advice. The whole Congress went into homespun from then on, and it became possible to tell a Congressman by his clothing or his cap (the "Gandhi cap," it was called, although the Mahatma did not wear head-coverings).

The campaign then began. Gandhi wrote to the Viceroy, resigning the various honors and decorations he had received from the government; he asked all Indians to do likewise. He poured out a stream of speeches, articles in the press, interviews and other communications designed to educate the people in the principles of *satyagraha*, under which there must be no disorder or violence and the opponent is to be treated with respect. In the first stage of the movement Indians were to remain away from government positions, schools or law courts, and very generally did so. There were four stages, the fourth of which was refusal to pay taxes, but again the movement was stopped by Gandhi himself before it had gone so far. His reason was the same as in 1919: his own people committed violence.

The outbreak this time was at Chauri Chaura, where a crowd grew wild with excitement and murdered several police officers. Gandhi at once undertook a fast for five days in atonement for the crime committed by others, and refused to continue the civil disobedience into its further stages. The British government, which had hesitated for months what to do about him, now decided to put him on trial for "exciting disaffection toward His Majesty's Government as established by law in India."

Amidst tremendous excitement throughout the sub-continent, this extraordinary trial took place at Ahmedabad in a circuit court before District and Sessions Judge C. N. Broomsfield on Saturday, March 18, 1922. Mr. Gandhi, courteous and respectful in his homespun cloth, pleaded guilty and refused to be defended, but the English Advocate-General arraigned him at great length as a lifelong rebel and agitator. When he rose to answer, Gandhi refused to defend himself but he did enunciate, in his weak, thoughtful voice, a few principles which were new in their expression before a court.

"If one has no affection for a person or a system," he said, "one should be free to give the fullest expression to his disaffection so long as he does not contemplate, promote or incite to violence."

"I wanted to avoid violence," he said again. "But I had to make my choice. I had either to submit to a system which I considered had done an irreparable harm to my country or incur the risk of the mad fury of my people bursting forth when they understood the truth from my lips. I know that my people have sometimes gone mad. I am deeply sorry for it, and

I am, therefore, here to submit not to a light penalty but to the highest penalty. I do not ask for mercy or plead any extenuating act. I am here, therefore, to invite and cheerfully submit to the highest penalty that can be inflicted upon me for what in law is a deliberate crime, and what appears to me the highest duty of a citizen."

He reviewed his thirty years of loyalty to England and his transformation from "a staunch loyalist and co-operator" into "an uncompromising disaffectionist and non-co-operator."

"I have no personal ill-will," he said, "against any single administrator, much less can I have any disaffection toward the King's person. But I hold it a virtue to be disaffected toward a government which in its totality has done more harm to India than any previous system. India is less manly under British rule than ever before. Holding such a belief, I consider it a sin to have affection for the system. And it has been a precious privilege to me to be able to write what I have written in the various articles tendered in evidence against me."

As he finished his short speech, he said to the Judge:

"The only course open to you, the Judge, is either to resign your post and thus dissociate yourself from evil, if you feel that the law you are called upon to administer is an evil and that in reality I am innocent; or to inflict on me the severest penalty if you believe that the system and the law you are assisting to administer are good for the people of this country, and that my activity is, therefore, injurious to the public weal."

The Judge, conscious of his own unenviable position, used language not often heard in a criminal court.

"It will be impossible to ignore the fact that you are in a different category from any person I have ever tried or am likely to have to try," he said. And at a later stage of his talk: "There are probably few people in India who do not sincerely regret that you should have made it impossible for any government to leave you at liberty. But it is so." And, after sentencing the Mahatma to six years' "simple imprisonment," he ended: "If the course of events in India should make it possible for the government to reduce the period and release you, no one will be better pleased than I."

11

In Yervada jail, Gandhi, in solitary confinement but treated with great courtesy by the British, spent his day in prayer, study and spinning. It took some persuasion to get permission for the spinning-wheel, but Gandhi was bound by a vow to spin every day, and the director of the jail yielded. He rose at four and slept at eight, dividing his time between the Gita, certain Christian books, the spinning-wheel and carding, which he had just learned. In a letter from Yervada he speaks with eloquence of what the spinning-wheel (the *charkha*) had come to mean to him:

"Spinning becomes more and more an inner need with me. Every day I come nearer to the poorest of the poor, and in them to God. The four hours I devote to this work are more important to me than all the others. The fruits of my labor lie before my eyes. Not one impure thought haunts me in these four hours. While I read the Gita, the Koran or the Ramayana, my thoughts fly far away. But when I turn to the spinning-wheel or work at the hackle my attention is directed on a single point. The spinning-wheel, I know, cannot mean so much to everyone. But to me the spinning-wheel and the economic salvation of impoverished India are so much one that spinning has for me a charm all its own. My heart is drawn backwards and forwards between the spinning-wheel and books. And it is not impossible that in my next letter I will have to tell you that I am spending even more time on spinning and carding."

The whole of India watched over Gandhi in prison, but he was himself "happy as a bird," as he said in his letters: solitude agreed with him and he had practically never been alone for years. He refused to be assigned to a special section in May, 1923, because he wanted no privileges not shared by others, and on November 12, 1923, he wrote to the governor of the prison that he could not have dietary privileges if his fellow-prisoners did not. This letter is signed, "M. K. Gandhi, No. 827."

When he fell ill and the prison authorities decided he must undergo an operation, he was transferred to a hospital at Poona, from which he was later released amidst national rejoicing. But during his enforced withdrawal from public life other counsels had prevailed both among the populace and among the leaders of India: his cherished Hindu-Muslim unity had fallen to bits, there were communal disorders, and in addition the National Congress, under the leadership of C. R. Das, had decided not to carry out the boycott of governmental legislative councils as Gandhi had wished.

It was at this time (1924) that Gandhi undertook his mammoth fast of twenty-one days, in Delhi, to atone for the sins of his people against the Muslims. Long before it was ended, even the bitterest of the opponents had regretted their violence, and the pledges of amity poured in upon the Mahatma. He then tended for a while to concentrate more and more upon the spinning-wheel and the spread of his *swadeshi* doctrine, leaving practical politics to others—at least so far as he was able to do so. It was impossible for him to avoid influencing the course of events, but his main desire at the time was to see Indian people in their masses abandoning the foreign cloth which, he was convinced, had been the principal agent of their pauperization. He founded the All-India Spinners' Association in 1925 and it remained until his death one of the most cherished (perhaps the most) of what he called his "constructive institutions." After we have traced out the principal phases of his strictly political activity—or those activities which had defined political results—we shall return to the spinning-wheel, for amongst his innumerable inventions, revivals and originations this was probably the most characteristic on a strictly practical plane.

An opposition had developed in the Indian National Congress between those who, like Gandhi and the elder Nehru (then President of the Congress), wished to attain self-government within the British Empire if possible, and the younger men who wanted a declaration of independence at once. Gandhi had consistently used the phrase "Swaraj within the Empire if possible and outside it if necessary." He now saw that a wave of more impetuous opinion was swelling up and could not be resisted: Jawaharlal Nehru, whom he had chosen as secretary-general of the Congress and who was always his favorite son in politics, led this rising of the young against both his fathers, Motilal Nehru and Gandhi. Gandhi accepted the will of the majority: if dominion status were not granted by the end of 1929 it would be moved that the Congress advocated independence as India's goal. At the stroke of midnight on December 31, 1929, Gandhi moved the resolution and retired to his Ashram to draw up the pledge. The American Declaration of Independence and a passage in Abraham Lincoln's second inaugural address both echo in this document, which declared inalienable rights for the people and among them the right to abolish a government which denies them. This was the pledge of *"Purna Swaraj,"* complete independence, taken by millions throughout India on the following January 26, 1930, which has ever since been celebrated as Indian Independence Day.

It now became necessary, the Mahatma saw, to release the forces he had been preparing for so many years: civil disobedience, *satyagraha*, peaceful *swadeshi* (as distinct from a vengeful boycott) and the non-violent revolution. He was not quite sure, could never be quite sure, that his people fully understood non-violence at all times and places, and this was, as he told the Viceroy, "the risk I have dreaded to take all these years." He wrote to Lord Irwin—afterward Lord Halifax—to warn him of his intention, and received the Viceroy's polite regrets "to hear that Mr. Gandhi intended to contravene the law."

The Salt March—Gandhi's March to the Sea—began on the morning of March 12, 1930, and ended at Port Dandi, two hundred miles away, on April 6th. During those three weeks of his pilgrimage the whole world watched him while India was in turmoil. Immense mass meetings took place in the cities; arrests took place on a scale never seen before; *satyagrahis* offered themselves for punishment everywhere. Meanwhile the little great man went steadily on walking to the sea, followed at times by immense multitudes, but in good order and without violence. The crowds that followed him changed from village to village in a sort of relay race, but he pursued his way as usual, trying to ignore the adoration that now surrounded him. At the sea he made a handful of salt out of sea-water—a symbol instantly understood in all languages: the foreign government claimed a monopoly of salt, which was God's gift to everybody, and Gandhi had therefore broken the law of the foreigner but obeyed the law of God. When he was arrested Mrs. Naidu and a succession of others took his place and did likewise.

The campaign continued until more than one hundred thousand people were imprisoned. There had been disorders in most parts of India, but the fault this time lay chiefly with the police. There was a general paralysis of the British administration in India and every indication that it would continue indefinitely.

On January 25, 1931, Lord Irwin released the Indian leaders and opened negotiations with Gandhi. These conversations would seem to have ended in an atmosphere of great friendliness between Mr. Gandhi and Lord Halifax. (Lord Halifax is himself deeply religious and cannot have failed to be impressed with the purity of Gandhi's intentions.) Gandhi agreed to call off the movement of civil disobedience; the Viceroy agreed to abolish the salt monopoly, declare a general amnesty, withdraw the emergency ordinances, and ask the Congress to send representatives to a Round-Table Conference in London for the drafting of a new constitution for India.

Among the colloquies of our time, these nine or ten conversations between the tall Englishman and the little Indian, who were so oddly alike in their extreme courtesy and gentleness, would have been, I think, among the most suggestive: no historical imagination could fail to hear in them the rhythm of destiny. And it was, in fact, from this time onward that the independence of India became primarily a constitutional and tactical question, a question of how and when, although its echoes of a revolutionary past were long in dying down and still reverberate in many minds.

Gandhi went to London. His visit to the Round-Table Conference will not soon be forgotten. For one thing, he traveled third class on the boat from Bombay, accompanied by his goat: this had long been his custom, but now that he had set out to negotiate with a mighty empire the world apparently expected something else. When he got to London he went straight to Kingsley Hall, a settlement house in the East End run by a friend of his, Muriel Lester, pacifist and social worker. He remained there during his stay, traveling when necessary to Buckingham Palace or St. James's, and the settlement house in the

East End was visited by a stream of the great, the devout and the curious, in about equal proportions.

The Round-Table Conference was itself a failure, in that it did not produce a constitution for India, but it marked the transition to the constitutional phase so unmistakably in the eyes of the whole world that it was never again possible to revert to the old state of things. After much trial and error concerning the voting system ("separate electorates" for Muslims and Hindus, even for untouchables, provided the subjects of argument) and the separation of powers, the rights of the Indian princes and those of the Crown, a constitution for India was finally adopted, went into effect in 1935, and resulted in Indian National Congress governments in eight out of eleven provinces. The Congress had decided to participate in government even though the constitution was not acceptable and independence still remained their goal. Gandhi, in accordance with his principles, had nothing to do with these operations, but nothing could prevent the constant pilgrimage of national leaders to his retreat to ask his advice on every step of their way.

During this period he was able to withdraw from day-to-day politics altogether so as to devote himself to his Ashram, which was now at Wardha in the Central Provinces. From there he could direct his "constructive institutions," the work for the villagers and women, and, above all, the All-India Spinners' Association, which since 1925 had made immense progress. (It now produces more textiles from hand-spinning and weaving than are produced in the mills of India.)

The Second World War forced him back into the arena again: he had supported wars in the days of his loyalty to the British Empire but he refused to support this one. The Indian National Congress was anti-Fascist by doctrine, but the long delays in fulfillment of British promises, the retention of many aspects of viceregal dictatorship, the headlong commitment of India to war in 1939 with no consultation of Indian opinion, all this made Gandhi unwilling to compromise again. He had seen too much of the process; he was too wise. The Congress leaders were more willing than he to support the war, and would have done so gladly, as they proclaimed often, if they could do it as equal partners. The culmination of these currents of thought and feeling came on August 8, 1942, when the Mahatma, speaking to the All-India Congress Committee meeting at Bombay, declared at last that the British must "Quit India." He was ready to start a new campaign of civil disobedience to obtain satisfaction of this demand, but said that it would take some weeks to prepare. He wished first to give full warning to the heads of the allied nations, and sat up all night writing letters to the Viceroy, President Roosevelt, Chiang Kai-shek and to Ivan Maisky, Soviet Ambassador to London. In the early morning he was arrested again.

With him, this time, all the leaders of the Indian National Congress were also nipped off at one time, so that the national movement was without direction or guidance. Gandhi had intended a movement of civil disobedience: what ensued after his arrest was a chaotic outburst of popular rage and a great deal of violence. The government's repressive measures were savage in nature and on a great scale: the clock seemed to have been turned back eighty years. For the first time since Gandhi had been drawn into the movement, Indian nationalism lost a good deal of its broad sympathy and support in Western countries: the war situation of 1942 made victory over Germany and Japan seem more important and much less certain than the ultimate independence of India. From the sequence of events, however, it is easy to see now that Gandhi's arrest precipitated the disorder which he could have prevented if he had been at liberty, and his final appeals before the projected civil disobedience might have produced a settlement.

In any case he had parted company with the Congress Working Committee on the war question, and it seems likely to me that he hoped to devote himself to his "constructive work" after the eventual settlement. It had taken more and more of his time and attention, and in the routine of his indefatigable days politics played no great part except on special occasions. Now, confined to the Aga Khan palace in Bombay, he devoted himself again to the Gita and looked over the English text prepared from his Gujarati by Mahadev Desai. There in prison, on February 22, 1944, Kasturbai Gandhi died. Faithful and devoted from beginning to end, traversing her astonishing destiny with no thought except for his good, Mrs. Gandhi was perhaps the only being whose death could have shaken the Mahatma out of that "non-attachment," that Gita-born serenity, for which he had striven for fifty years. It is recorded that when Kasturbai was cremated in the prison compound the Mahatma wept.

Gandhi was released on May 6, 1944, "solely on medical grounds," as the Government put it. His immediate effort, as soon as he could arrange it, was to come to terms with the Muslim League, which had grown into a separatist institution in the last seven years under the leadership of Mr. Mohammed Ali Jinnah. In this effort Gandhi failed altogether after long, patient and humble trials. Jinnah stuck to his demand for a separate Muslim country called Pakistan, to be carved out of India, and in the end even Gandhi had to accept it.

He did so on June 4, 1947, at his evening prayer meeting in Delhi. It seems probable that this finally broke his heart, politically speaking, and that his struggle to the end for peace and amity was weighed down by the oppressive consciousness of having failed to preserve the unity of India. "You can cut me in two," he said to Jinnah, "but don't cut India in two." Jinnah, whose historical existence may be said to be a negative function of Gandhi's, was deaf to the appeal.

On the day when India became independent, and the British powers were transferred to the new countries of Pakistan and India (August 15, 1947), to stay in the British association or go out of it as they wished, Gandhi took no part in the celebrations which went on throughout the sub-continent. He spent the day in fasting, prayer, silence and spinning. I believe he knew then that his end would not long be delayed.

12

In the main aspects of Gandhi's thinking the most practical advice he had to give India is that which has been most misunderstood in the West. His economic scheme of thought was not intended to be of universal application. He had universals: non-violence was one. But the whole cycle of the ideas which revolve about the spinning-wheel—those ideas which are collectively called "the economics of the *charkha*"—depended upon

Indian conditions and arose principally from his aching sense
of the poverty, disease and suffering of his people. India's population is 83 percent agricultural and the average annual income
is estimated at about $26 a year. This average is struck between
immense extremes, for some of the richest men in the world live
in India, as well as millions of the poorest. The landless peasant,
the untouchable, the half-starved villager—these are the dominant types in Indian society, if it is considered from the point
of view of number: these are the people for whom Gandhi
gave his whole life. He cared next to nothing for intellectuals,
unless they in some way served the people; he disregarded the
princes and potentates unless they came forward (as some did)
to serve; he was not much interested in artists or in form; philosophy itself engaged him only in so far as he felt it could lead
him to God, and even in this primary purpose he always believed that service to humanity was more important. In the end
the extremes met: that is, Hindu philosophy with its final emphasis on self-realization and union with God appeared to him
to be precisely the same thing as the dissolution of the personality (his own) in service to humanity. It was his ambition,
as he said more than once (particularly in the last passage of his
autobiography) to reach zero as a personality and merge himself into the life of all others, making their miseries his and
devotedly lightening their sorrow in any way open to him. This
is, in fact, the same thing as the self-realization of the Vedanta
philosophy in the end, although reached by a means externally
quite different from that of the purely meditative and withdrawn sages who have abounded in the world. Selfless action
as defined in the Gita, action for others, for the truth and for
God, without regard for its fruits, was the sovereign aim of his
life. It resulted—when seen from an alien point of view—in a
sort of *Drang nach Unten*, an attempt to drive down deep into
the mass, living in every tangible respect like the poorest of the
poor, walking like a beggar from village to village, staff in hand,
like the Lord Buddha or St. Francis of Assisi, and serving them
in any way his mind, talents, experience or belief could suggest. In this the end determined the means: he would make mud-
packs for a beggar's stomach with the same humble and devoted
sincerity he gave to the problems of the nations. A leper lived

in his Ashram in the hut next to Mahatmaji's and was attended
by Mahatmaji as his own son. For the accursed he had special
care, and insane or partially crazed people were never turned
from his door. For the prostitutes of the great cities, who adored
him, he did everything he could do for many long years, or-
ganizing work for them so as to help them escape their lot,
inveighing in speeches and print against the men who brought
about their degradation, and effectively bringing about a great
change in that particular social dilemma within two decades.
For the lower order of creation—which as a good Hindu he
took to be particularly symbolized in the cow, foster-mother
of the human race—he made patient and undiscourageable efforts, even though he realized that complete *ahinsa* was, under
the conditions of life, unattainable. Mr. Gandhi was in fact well
aware of how difficult nature itself made some if not all of his
ideals: he would not, like the Lord Buddha, sit immured throughout the rainy season for fear of stepping on some small beast
if he ventured out. No doubt in the course of his existence he
killed as many of the smaller forms of life as most of us do, but
the point is that he did it inadvertently, and held as his inflexible
rule (for himself alone) an absolute non-violence toward all
forms of life. This non-violence was transformed by his own
temperament and discipline into a positive element, precisely, I
think, that to which St. Paul referred in the thirteenth chapter
of Corinthians by the word variously translated as charity or
love.

Therefore, when he saw the chief worldly suffering of India
to be the problem of poverty, of poverty abysmal and grinding,
worse than any other in the world, he set himself to find solutions as definite and as practical as he could attain. His reading,
observation and experience led him in the early part of this
century to the conclusion that some, at least, of the poverty of
India was due to the disappearance of diversified work among
the peasantry. As long ago as 1908 he suggested, in his book
called *Hind Swaraj*, that a revival of the home spinning and
weaving that had once flourished in India might help his country to rise again. The trouble was at that time that he knew no
spinners or weavers and had never seen an Indian spinning-
wheel; moreover, he was so immured in his South African strug-

gle that he had no time to undertake the search. But the idea never left him; in fact, it haunted him for years until he could get at it and turn it into a practical demonstration upon the most literal stage of human experience, that of economics.

It should always be remembered that the notion of "boycott" was alien to Gandhi's thinking in this respect and originally did not even appear. As it turned out in practical action, the revival of home spinning and weaving did develop into a boycott of foreign cloth and well-nigh ruined the Midlands of England, or at least turned them into "depressed areas": yet when Gandhi went to Manchester in 1931, at the time of the Round-Table Conference, he was cheered by a vast crowd of the very workers whose unemployment was in part his doing. It is a tribute both to those workers and to him that they understood each other.

In fact the idea that colonial imperialism (not individual Englishman and not really England itself, but the system which developed in the nineteenth century) had organized the pauperization of India by taking its cotton, milling it abroad and sending it back to India to sell for several times its natural price, so far as I can make out, developed in Gandhi very late. He was more than fifty years old before he reached that conclusion. In earlier years his slowly evolving "economics of the *charkha*" had to do with the direct good of the Indian villager: that this villager, condemned by the climate of India to idleness half the year and hard agricultural labor the other half, should eke out his pitiful resources by finding the means to clothe himself. Ruskin's *Unto This Last*—which seems indeed a feckless and dilettante bit of paper compared to what Gandhi made it into— contributed an animating element to Gandhi's ideas, but we may be sure that they were dormant in any case in that universal compassion he embodied.

Even in 1915, when he returned from South Africa, Gandhi had not yet seen a spinning-wheel. But, as we have noted before, one reason why he chose the neighborhood of the city of Ahmedabad for his first Ashram was that a hand-loom industry used to exist there and he hoped the citizens might help him find his way back to it. He was able to install a few hand-looms in the Ashram, but there ensued a search for a weaver who could tell the "family" how to use them. Maganlal Gandhi, the factotum of the Ashram, learned quickest and was able to teach others, just as he was later to become such an expert at the wheel and the loom that he could design improvements.

From the very outset Gandhi was bent upon wearing only hand-woven cloth made from Indian cotton. The effort brought him into close contact with the spinning and weaving industry of the Indian mills, and he saw that the objective of the mill-owners was as far as possible to weave the yarn they spun—in other words, to have as little as possible to do with hand-weavers. The Gandhi weavers could get only poor yarn and were unable to clothe themselves, and it proved difficult indeed to induce hand-weavers outside to produce cloth for them. Gandhi grew more and more impatient to find a spinning-wheel and learn to spin, but the art of spinning had been, as he says, "all but exterminated." When it flourished in India it had been practically confined to women, and it therefore seemed to him that what he needed was some woman who would undertake the search for him.

He found the woman. It was Gangabehn Majmundar, a Gujarati widow who had freed herself of the ordinary prejudices about untouchability and caste, had undertaken a great deal of social work and was ready to make Gandhi's search for him. She eventually discovered a considerable number of spinning-wheels in the homes of people living in the state of Baroda, although nobody used them any more. A number of people were willing to get them out of the lofts and begin to spin yarn for Gandhi (whose name was already magic then), if he would send them "slivers" of cotton regularly and buy the yarn when it was spun.

Gandhi, in his usual accidental way, got the "slivers" from a mill-owner—Umar Sobani, the generous capitalist who put up half of the money for *Young India*. But this—although it worked beautifully, providing a plentiful supply of yarn for the Ashram —did not seem quite right to the Mahatma. He did not like taking slivers from a mill: if he took the slivers he might as well take the yarn and the woven cloth as well, according to his relentless logic. Therefore he had to find a way to get his own slivers. He asked Gandabehn if she could find him a cotton-carder, and one was found. The carder carded the cotton and some of the young people of the Ashram were trained to make slivers out of it. The cotton itself the Mahatma obtained by begging in Bombay, he says. The slivers then went to Baroda state (to Vijapur) where they were spun into yarn and thereafter hand-woven into *khadi*—that is, the completely home-produced cloth which will always be associated with Gandhi.

All of this was too complicated and diffuse for the Mahatma. He wanted to do it all in his own Ashram and still did not know how to spin. After considerable search he found two spinners who would teach some of his followers how to spin. He was then too ill to begin learning himself, but as soon as he was able to do so he began to try. The idea of *khadi* as a solution for India's poverty by now obsessed him to such a degree that he thought his recovery from illness was in part caused by the cheerful hum of the spinning in his room, although he was prepared to admit that this effect was "more psychological than physical." (Wise is the doctor who can distinguish!)

The search for the various elements of an abandoned industry and their assembly into a workable whole took a good deal of money, and Mr. Gandhi found out later that the prices asked in almost every case were much too high, but patriotic friends were producing the money and he considered the cause worth any expense. In due course he had made enough headway to achieve one ambition, which was to clothe himself entirely in home-produced cloth which was at no point indebted to the foreigner. This formidable example was presented to the Indian sub-continent from 1919 onwards.

The next step was to extend as widely as possible the practices of spinning and weaving and to familiarize the whole of India with the idea that Indian cotton could become cloth without ever going abroad in the process. Originally there was one specific objective: to give work and clothing to the half-starved women of India. To this was related, from the beginning, the larger objective of *khadi*—the cloth itself—as a means of economic self-sufficiency (*swadeshi*), which in turn must inevitably produce self-government (*swaraj*). This progression, *khadi-swadeshi-swaraj*, was Gandhi's incessant preachment for the rest of his life, and for long periods at a time—as for example during the last four years of the 1920's—it appeared to be the chief practical object of his whole activity.

It had momentous effects upon the scene of history. During the 1920's the movement for *khadi* swept India, was adopted as an integral part of the national movement by the Congress, and produced, under Gandhi's anxious care, hundreds of thousands of persons newly trained to the various processes of home-textiles, particularly spinning. Spinning-wheels, once absolete and forgotten, were produced in ever larger numbers. From the time of the foundation of the All-India Spinners' Association (1925) there was a nation-wide organization to foster the development of the movement and make it relatively easy for those who wished to join it to take part.

So, in 1930, when the "Gandhian war" began, the time was ripe for a further step: the renunciation of foreign cloth. Great fires burned for days in the cities and towns, destroying materials of English or Japanese manufacture which their owners now wished to give up for the motherland. This was, from the point of view of the British Government, perhaps a "boycott," but Gandhi did not so regard it. He regarded it as a sacrifice for India, and since most of those who burned their fine garments were the rich, he did not consider that any real wealth had gone. The "boycott" notion was repellent to him because it contained vengeful notions, concepts of hatred and violence, whereas for him *khadi* was a symbol of national rebirth and self-reliance, with malice toward none and with charity for all.

Objectively considered, the results were much the same as those of a boycott, and England's textile industry suffered greatly indeed. But Gandhi's notion of *khadi* had by now gone far beyond any such immediate and incidental results. For one thing, he had himself become an expert spinner, and although the spinning-wheel was still chiefly reserved for women and the hand-loom for men, he, who had learned both, had taken a vow to spin for at least half an hour every day. This became four hours a day when he was in jail, as we have seen, and at times of fasting or on days of silence it could become any number of hours. The Mahatma understood very well that he could not preach any such revolutionary doctrine unless he practised it himself, and he would have considered it untruthful to try. He did not, perhaps, follow out this process of example to its end—he would have considered it vain to permit himself such thoughts—but in effect what it came to was this: if the greatest and best of India's sons is willing, in the midst of his innumerable preoccupations, to devote regular hours to spinning, what woman in India, high or low, can refuse to do the same? And this is how *khadi* became *swadeshi* and *swadeshi* became *swaraj*, although at each step in the process perfection (the ideal completeness) was never attained.

Over the years the power wielded by *khadi-swadeshi-swaraj* naturally produced a great deal of speculation, argument and theoretical extensions of the principle. Volumes have been written about the "economics of the *charkha*," and in those volumes one can find a good deal of extravagation, although not from Gandhi. His genius had found a tremendous symbol which was at the same time a practical weapon of the first importance for the liberation of India, but he never at any time generalized it into a rule of economics for the whole world. Some of his followers may have done so: some, I know, carried their enthusiasm so far as to believe that industrialism was doomed or would bring the West to destruction, and to believe further that a retreat from industrialism was possible in other countries as in India. These extremists opposed industrialism in any form even in India.

Gandhi did not. He hoped that India's industrialization, or such industrialization as might become socially and economically necessary, could take place under safeguards which would protect the helpless masses from exploitation and misery worse than those they already had to bear. He thought, for example, that the necessary industry might be decentralized so as to avoid the packing of the poor into blighted slums. But even this he hoped to delay or possibly avoid, in important respects, for India. He thought that necessary heavy industry should be owned and controlled, with fullest consideration for the workers, by the state, and he hoped by the development of cottage and village industry to get India past the dangers which beset Western Europe with the industrial revolution. The machine in general was "satanic" and had produced the enslavement of the masses: this was an idea which was not Gandhi's alone, but has recurred all over the world in many places since the industrial revolution. Something very like it is to be found in Karl Marx, although what he wished to do about it was very different.

Gandhi was at pains to make his opposition to the machine practical and limited, without the sweeping applications of "principle" which had been read into it. To a disciple of Tagore's who asked him if he opposed all machinery on principle, he replied:

"How could that be possible? I know that my own body is nothing but an extraordinarily delicately constructed machine. The spinning-wheel is also a machine, and so is every toothpick even. I am not fighting machinery as such, but the madness of thinking that machinery saves labor. Men 'save labor' until thousands of them are without work and die of hunger on the streets. I want to secure employment and livelihood not only to part of the human race, but for all. I will not have the enrichment of a few at the expense of the community. At present the machine is helping a small minority to live on the exploitation of the masses. The motive force of this minority is not humanity and love of their kind, but greed and avarice. This state of things I am attacking with all my might."

To this must be added another element which I find clearly displayed in much of what Gandhi said about the spinning-wheel—an element which in one respect can be called mystical. That is, the more he got into the movement for homespun cloth the more it obsessed him. The symbol he had found, the wheel itself, assumed enormous importance with the passage of time: it related itself to the whole of life, to God, to the pilgrimage of the spirit. The actual spinning itself fascinated him beyond measure, and he found a kind of solace in it unobtainable elsewhere. All his symbols had universal aspects: salt, the spinning-wheel, the voluntary sacrifice of *satyagraha*. It was the distinguishing character of his genius that he found each one of them for practical reasons and only afterward discovered how wide and deep was their meaning. But in the case of the spinning-wheel something else was added, something beyond economics, sociology or politics, a kind of mystical concentration upon service as a form (and to him the pervading form) of religion.

When Adam delved and Eve span
Who was then the gentleman?

13

The life of Mahatma Gandhi was, he told a colleague of mine shortly before his death, a "failure." He had set India free but had to accept partition; there had been great violence; the lesson he had tried to teach all through his long, tireless life was apparently not understood even in his own country. And yet this "failure" had had great results. If I am not mistaken, its chain of consequences still goes on and will go on for a long time to come. His spirit, humble, pure and exalted, was vowed to martyrdom and achieved it in the end with a logic as inexorable as that displayed in all the rest of his life. In its mountainous but selfless activity his was surely the life of the *karmayogin*, that one who makes his way to God through action.

V

Upanishad, 1948

If you could only persuade everybody, Socrates, as you
do me, of the truth of your words, there would be more
peace and fewer evils among men.

PLATO: *Theætetus*

There are connections. Quite apart from and beyond the observed phenomena of natural science, and in a realm which has as yet been scarcely explored by even the most intrepid psychologists, the affairs of mankind are connected. It is quite impossible for a phenomenon like Gandhi to occur without producing innumerable effects of which he himself never dreamed —effects far and wide, altering the composition and direction of lives unknown to him, touching the very soul of the world.

Thus it is not remarkable that my own consciousness of him and of his work was aroused early. I am by profession concerned with such matters. I know that I had some awareness of him long ago, and that this was brought into focus by René Fulop-Miller's book called *Lenin and Gandhi*, published in the United States in 1927. (I reviewed that book for the *New Republic* and probably caused to be printed some rare nonsense on the subject.) At that time I took the rather jocular view of him which was prevalent in the West—the view summarized by Winston Churchill when he called Gandhi a "naked fakir." It was all too strange and new; moreover, in the 1920's material-

ism was in its heyday, producing nightmarish excesses in the
United States. I was young and unready.

The first serious shock administered to my own consciousness
by the Gandhi phenomenon was the Salt March (1930). I was
then in New York and remember well how tenaciously the
thing clung to my mind. I bought newspapers chiefly to find
out what happened next in that extraordinary drama. And of
course it is also true that the imagination of the entire world
was seized and almost obsessed for a time by the Salt March.
I doubt very much if Gandhi himself had any idea, when he
originated the notion, of what it would mean—of how the
echoes would roll, and of how the languages would be transcended, the values transvaluated. There is no Hottentot or
Eskimo who could not understand the Salt March. I go to the
ocean of God, he said, and I make salt with my hands, and the
foreign government will arrest me and put me in prison for it,
but this is my truth and I will die for it.

We all understood. Last year in Delhi I met a man, an agricultural laborer from that province, who had marched to the
sea with Gandhi. This was on the great plain beside the river
Jumna, where the Mahatma's body had been cremated, and the
salt marcher and I were among the people who gathered there
every morning beside the cremation platform to listen to the
chanting of the Gita. (The Salt March had taken place seventeen years before.) When I was introduced to this man by Brij
Krishna, one of Gandhi's most devoted followers, and was told
that he had been on the Salt March, I know that my immediate
response produced a communication between us—no more than
a smile and a shake of the hand, but a genuine communication
quite independent of language. He knew that the Salt March
had also meant something to me.

Again, some time later at Almora in the Himalayas, I met a
man who had been on the Salt March. He was a prisoner in
the jail there, which I had wished to visit because it was Mr.
Nehru's last prison before the liberation of India. The man
stood behind bars and talked to me eagerly, smiling with tears
in his eyes. He also knew that I understood about the Salt
March. (He was in prison through some mistake, he said, and

was soon afterward released; the jail warden told me that this poor man had chanted the Gita when Gandhi died.)

My own self-indulgent and frivolous life did not allow for any concentration on Gandhi's ideas for many years. They were still too remote. The Salt March clung to my mind, as it still does and always will, but I did not generalize or apply its meanings.

Then, in 1944, when I was an officer in the Air Forces, I was sent to India on the project which had been approved at the Cairo Conference, under which we undertook to bomb Japan from China if Chiang Kai-shek could give us the airfields and the British would accommodate us in India. Chiang fulfilled his part of the bargain with unbelievable rapidity; we had fields in the province of Szechuan and used to fly the gasoline and bombs over the Himalaya to these distant outposts. There was little I could see or know of India then, even though I was living in Bengal except for the monthly mission to Szechuan; but it was impossible even to be in that country without feeling in some respects the quality of its consciousness, its view of life, however imperfectly understood. I knew then that I should be obliged to come back, although I was obscurely afraid and hoped to postpone that return as long as possible.

In the spring and summer of 1947 events moved in India with a rapidity which astonished me and no doubt millions of other people throughout the world. Lord Mountbatten's task in the spring was to bring about a transfer of power to Indian hands, and after laborious negotiation and effort it became clear that nothing would be accepted by the Muslim League which did not provide for partition of the sub-continent and creation of the new country to be called Pakistan. On the fourth of June, at his prayer meeting in Delhi, where he was then living in the untouchables' quarter, Gandhi accepted the partition of India after reading from the Koran. This was the last thing he had ever expected to do, the last we in general, the people of the world, had ever expected of him. He saw that the time had come when he could do nothing else.

There followed the swift preparations for the partition and independence of India, the delineation of new frontiers, the setting up of projects for the division of properties, assets and

liabilities. An immense undertaking was put through in a bare
two months, and on August 15th the power was ceremoniously
transferred from British to Indian hands, with Lord Mountbatten—rare in the experience of viceroys—wildly cheered by
vast Indian crowds in the streets of Delhi.

All this was accompanied by considerable violence between
Muslims and Hindus. There is not much use tracing back the
origins of the 1947 rioting. If one date is taken, the Hindus
were at fault; if you go further back the Muslims were at fault;
if you go further back still, the Hindus are again responsible.
Thus it goes. The only thing that can be said with certainty is
that there were outbreaks here, there and the next place in the
sub-continent from 1946 onward, mounting to a climax when
the two new countries came into being. All this Mahatma
Gandhi struggled against as well as he could, by precept and
example, tirelessly urging his people to remember their pledges,
and no doubt himself never forgetting what he had written long
before—that the conflict between Muslim and Hindu would be
the final test of his non-violence.

On August 15th, when India and Pakistan became self-gov-
erning nations with the right to leave the British Empire or stay
in it as they pleased, with full control over all their own affairs,
domestic or foreign, it might have seemed to most men that the
principal aim of Gandhi's long life had been achieved. To him,
however, partition robbed independence of its savor, and the
future, in view of disturbances between the communities, looked
less than rosy. He spent the day in silence, praying and spinning,
and the tremendous outburst of rejoicing throughout India was
without his participation.

To a good many sympathetic observers his anxiety seemed
well-founded and his conduct on August 15th was understood.
I myself, so ignorant then (or even now) of Indian things,
could not escape anxiety even at a great distance. I was in a
Vermont farmhouse when the India League of America—in
late July—asked me to come to New York and speak at its meeting on August 15th which would mark the independence of
India. I could not go, but I wrote a brief message which—even
though it did not contain the note of celebration which was
expected—was read to the meeting and printed afterward in a

pamphlet of such messages. I quote it now only to show that my
sense of approaching trouble in India was strong even before
August 15th:

"India has given the world first of all its religions: those oldest
forms which substantially remained Indian under various guises,
and those later forms which in passing to West and East be‚
came modified and sometimes transformed by local conditions.
In all of these forms there subsists the concept of prayer, which,
to anybody who has even set foot in India for five minutes,
must seem to express a potent reality of co-consciousness amongst
a people welded together by thousands of years of suffering. If
this should be so, then, at this moment when the power in India
passes from Western into Indian hands, all the religions of India
should together pray as never before—pray for India or for whatever idea India represents to them. In their brief passage across
India the British did some good and left some traces, but their
hour, compared to the whole history of India, was too short to
count. India now returns to the forces that arose in the dark forest
many thousands of years ago, and to them the religions, separately and together, should pray, for the dangers ahead are
many."

The premonitions indicated in this message were not long in
being verified. Soon after August 15th the violent antagonism of
Muslim and Hindu broke into the open and there were disorders
in Bengal, leading in September to the terrible carnage of the
Punjab and (a little later) to wholesale murders in the streets of
Delhi itself. Millions of Hindus fled from Pakistan and millions
of Muslims from India. I was not only aghast at the extent of the
disaster—greater by far than I had thought it would be—but was,
for some reason or for some unreason, perturbed and anxious
about Gandhi. It may seem absurd that this should be so. I was
at a great and safe distance; a farmhouse in Vermont has little
to do with India; yet for weeks I read everything I could in the
newspapers, clinging also to the radio at the hours when the
B.B.C. was relayed from London by way of Toronto, following,
as best I could, Gandhi's course. His attempts to stop the carnage
were partly and locally successful. In Calcutta in September he
moved his Ashram into the devastated quarter of the Muslims,
called on Hindus and Muslims to make peace, and said he would

not move from there until peace had come. I was afraid for him, and it was then, in September, that the conviction came upon me that he would certainly be martyred by his own people.

On one occasion the house he occupied was stoned by Hindus, although he was not in it then; and on another occasion a crowd of young men came to see him and told him he must leave the Muslim quarter. The Mahatma said then: "If you want to take me out of here you must take me as a corpse." They went away, ashamed, and the Calcutta miracle occurred: the disorders ceased, Hindus and Muslims paraded the streets under banners calling for peace, and Gandhi had won again.

It was only a partial victory, although it was real so far as Calcutta was concerned. In the rest of the country, particularly in the Punjab, the lesson had not been learned. Whatever the word used—"genocide" came into favor later at the United Nations—there can be nothing but horror for the mass murders and migrations which then took place. The Mahatma started out for the Punjab, but was obliged to stop at Delhi. In October, while the situation between the communities was still as bad as possible, the Maharajah of Kashmir acceded to the Indian Union and asked for help against Muslim raiders from Pakistan; Indian troops occupied Kashmir and engaged in a battle for its defense; and now it seemed that not only communal slaughter and internal cruelty, but actual war between the two new countries, might be the results of freedom.

My own interest was centered about Gandhi, because by this time I was well aware of his great spirit and what it had done in the world. I had intended for years past to get to him sometime, somehow, and although the war and other preoccupations intervened, the intention never faded. Now my anxiety had grown so that I felt (at times during that September) that I was too late: that I could never ask him any questions at all, that martyrdom was upon him. I was so convinced of his martyrdom that I actually discussed it in considerable detail with New York editors before I set forth for India. It seemed to me implicit in the whole logic of his life and in the objective conditions which now surrounded him. America's interest in India has never been keen, but I found one editor, Mr. Ted Patrick of *Holiday* magazine, who believed my account of the importance of these events and was willing to give me a contract which would pay my expenses for the winter.

I left New York on November 13th for London, Paris, Prague, Vienna, Rome, Cairo and Karachi, stopping for a few days or weeks in each of those cities. By this crablike progression even the airplane can be made into a slow means of transport, so that I actually reached Karachi only on the evening of December 26th, Mohammed Ali Jinnah's birthday. The city had been celebrating the birthday of Pakistan's founder and first ruler without a thought, I suppose, that it would be his last.

Pakistan and its problems interested me, and I began to see, from conversations with ministers and others, that the case for India was perhaps not as overwhelming as it had seemed in preceding years—that there had, in fact, been injustices. Not to speak of the communal disorders, which involved the gravest faults on both sides, the Pakistan ministers spoke of a good many ways in which India had displayed hostile intentions—"strangling Pakistan at birth," was the phrase used. In my surprise at these revelations I decided to stay longer in Karachi than I had originally intended, and even to visit the rest of Western Pakistan up to the Northwest Frontier, before going on to Delhi. An outburst of communal disorder in Karachi itself put the whole city under martial law for some days and effectively arrested all my movements.

During this time I was reading every morning what Gandhi (in Delhi) had said the night before at his prayer-meetings. Aside from steadily deploring the disorders, asking for help for refugees, and commenting on a variety of specific subjects connected with these, he did not attack the central problems of the day. His speeches (or sermons) at the end of his prayer-meetings were rambling dissertations, often consisting simply of replies to individual correspondents. He received a mountain of letters every day, and if a point of general interest arose among these he was accustomed to answering it after his prayer-meeting. When I first started to read these accounts in the English-language newspapers in Karachi, I did not understand Gandhi's way, his technique (so to speak) or his tremendous simplicity, and the daily sermon seemed to lack organization and point. It was never a "speech": it was a sequence of remarks, of divagations. In the atmosphere of Karachi it was not possible to understand.

Then, on January 13th, the Mahatma began to fast "for Hindu-Muslim unity." This was his last fast, and from all the context of his utterances it could be seen to be a form of penance or atonement, although what was its precise purpose, or what might be done to induce him to stop it, the newspapers did not say. (At that time I really did not understand the Mahatma's fasting: I thought some of it had been a simple method of bringing pressure on others, or obtaining a desirable social result. I did not know then what I know now, that in his own mind it was always a form of prayer to God and not a form of coercion, even though often great actions were taken to persuade him to desist.)

At once all my interest in Pakistan evaporated. I had, after all, come to India primarily to see Gandhi and ask him some questions of a fundamental nature. Nothing else could be of any importance compared to this. I went on the morning of January 13th to the Pakistan Foreign Office and asked for a government priority on the first airplane to Delhi. The official to whom I talked thought me foolish: a bright young westernized Muslim, he did not share my agitation and thought Gandhi's life was in no danger whatever. Even so, he gave me the Foreign Office order without demur, and as it was now too late for that day's aircraft I booked myself for the next day, January 14th, arriving in Delhi in the evening, the second day of Gandhi's fast.

Delhi was crowded; there was no room in any hotel. I took refuge in the American Embassy's compound opposite the Imperial Hotel, intending to go to the military attaché and ask for a bed. My feet took me to the naval attaché's apartment (or bungalow) instead, and there Captain Atkins, U.N. (known, of course, as "Tommy Atkins") took me in. Here I stayed during the next few days, in as odd a frame of mind as I can remember, tense but not nervous, waiting for something but uncertain of what it was, and abusing myself bitterly for all my delays in getting here. I should have been in Delhi by early December; why had I dawdled until mid-January? I wrote to Mr. Nehru, took the letter to his house, went home and waited.

2

Gandhi's fast was shaking all India. The Stock Exchanges in Bombay and Calcutta closed on the day the fast began; the government of India—which had been withholding almost $200,000,000 of the gold reserve allotted to Pakistan on the ground that this would be used to support the campaign in Kashmir—now presented Pakistan with this huge sum of money, hoping to ease Mr. Gandhi's mind thereby. Gestures of repentance, of peaceful intention, of desire to return to non-violence, were made throughout the country. There were parades in the streets with great frequency, calling on the people to "save our Bapu" by making peace. Various persons (both Indian and foreign) in Delhi told me that talk of war with Pakistan had been quite common only a few days before; it now vanished utterly. On January 15th, the third day of the fast, the Prime Minister, Mr. Nehru, made a great peace speech in which he announced that India was turning over to Pakistan the famous "55 crores" (the sum of gold reserve mentioned before); the fifth day of the fast (Saturday, January 17th) was a day of prayer throughout India—prayer for Hindu-Muslim peace and for the ending of the Mahatma's fast.

During this extraordinary week I lived at "the Taj," as it was called, the compound in which a good many members of the American Embassy staff had their quarters. I saw press colleagues—Bob Neville of *Time;* Edgar Snow of *The Saturday Evening Post*, and others—along with some few Indians, but my chief anxiety was when, or if, I might see Gandhi. I was in fact very much afraid that I never could, and this fast, at the age of seventy-eight, had such aspects of finality that I was afraid and depressed. It did not seem to me that there was anybody else in the world who could tell me just the things I most needed to hear. I kept a journal during those days, as I have done off and on for years. It makes curious reading now—a mixture of things read (*Coriolanus*, the Theban Plays of Sophocles, a little book on ancient Mexican religion) and incessant references to Gandhi and his fast. This is a sample:

"Here in the Taj this afternoon I sat in the latticed veranda off my room and read *Œdipus the King* and while I was doing so—curiously appropriate accompaniment—the cries, shouts and prayers of a crowd kept swelling up over the lines of Sophocles. It was one of the peace processions, I assume—must have been; they go about the city proclaiming their wish for peace between Muslim and Hindu and calling upon the Mahatma to cease his fast."

There are lines of *Coriolanus* thrust into this day's entry, merely, I suppose, because they struck my eye. (I was certainly not thinking of Gandhi, in any case.) One is from Act III, Scene 2:

> *You might have been enough the man you are,*
> *With striving less to be so.*

Another occurs in Act V, Scene 4, in prose:

> *He wants nothing of a god but eternity and a*
> *heaven to throne in.*

During my absence that evening Mr. Nehru's secretaries telephoned me no less than seven times. I received the message at ten o'clock at night and went out to York Road where the Prime Minister lived. At that time—it was soon to be different —there were no guards visible and one rang the doorbell as in any other house. I found Mr. Nehru with the celebrated American photographer, Miss Margaret Bourke-White, who was asking him questions and taking notes. I waited until she had finished and gone before I tried to talk to him. It was a rather desultory conversation with a good many intervals of silence; I felt that Mr. Nehru was tired and I did not want to weary him further. I did convey, I think, my extreme anxiety over the Mahatma's fast, and at one point, as if to reassure me, Mr. Nehru said with a sudden gleaming smile that illumined his tired face: "I cannot believe that his work is done yet." He quite understood my desire to ask Gandhiji many questions; I think he knew that it was a kind of quest, brought on by the failure of every human institution to supply hope for the future, and that in a sense I had nowhere else to go. In any case, although these foregoing things were not made explicit, what was clear was

Mr. Nehru's idea—coinciding exactly with my own—that the best thing I could do would be to go with Gandhi wherever he went and ask him my questions (obtain my lessons, in fact) as best I could. It seemed clear that Gandhi would, in fact, go somewhere, after he had recovered from his present fast, although not to Wardha. (To go to his Ashram at Wardha had been my highest hope.)

A delegation representing all the main bodies in orthodox Hinduism had waited upon the Mahatma that very evening and had told him they were ready to pledge anything for peace if he would resume eating. Mr. Gandhi had listed for them seven main points, all looking toward the peace, protection and well-being of the Muslims in Delhi, their freedom of worship and the restoration of their mosques. These were not conditions, but they were his idea of what the suppliants could do to restore peace. He did not say he would stop fasting even if these seven points were all pledged.

However, from what Nehru said I received some hope that the fast would soon end. Nehru, after so long a knowledge of Gandhi, realized that the Mahatma would not prolong a fast after its purpose was attained, above all since to do so might mean suicide. (I did not realize until afterward that he, like the Christians, regarded suicide as a great sin.)

That evening when I drove home through the cool night of New Delhi I felt for the first time that my journey to India was not going to be quite useless. Above all I felt some assurance that the Mahatma would live and would answer my questions.

On the following day the heads of the Hindu organizations all took the peace pledge, following the seven conditions laid down by the Mahatma. At 12:30 on that day—Sunday, January 18th—he broke his fast, accepting a glass of lime juice from the great Muslim divine, the Maulana Sahib, his friend of many years. The breaking of the fast, like its initiation, was accompanied by hymns and prayers, in which "Lead Kindly Light" figured as always.

During this week I had not wished to see Gandhi suffering and I remained away from Birla House, although as a matter of fact that house and garden were never closed and the press

representatives went there often. I had some inexplicable un-
willingness to do so. I had not as yet understood very much, but
I knew that this was a great and suffering spirit. It was my hope
to go into his presence at a time when he was well and alert to
answer the questions I had come across half the world to ask
him. So I remained away, and listened to the accounts given by
others of how they filed past the glass doors and looked in at his
poor body.

On the day when the fast was broken I went to lunch with
Edgar Snow at the Imperial Hotel before an afternoon of sightseeing in Old Delhi—the Jumna Masjid (the Great Mosque) and
the Old Fort. It was there, at lunch, that we learned of the ending of the fast. We learned it in the language of our colleagues,
deliberately irreverent, but, I think, meaning no harm. The press
correspondents all seemed to think it strange that Gandhi had
ended the fast at this particular moment: they regarded the seven-
point pledge as being meaningless (which it was not), and were
inclined to see something a little calculated or calculating in the
whole business.

As I sat there listening to them, and feeling helpless to counter-
act what seemed to me great incomprehension, I felt suddenly
that I knew why the fast had ended. I turned to Ed Snow and
told him under my breath, and after lunch I was able to explain
it to him more fully.

In my opinion Gandhi ended his last fast because the sun did
not shine that day. This is much too simple a reason for most
people and would have been (probably) too simple even for his
own conscious mind, although it arose from the bottomless well
of his own simplicity. The fact of the matter is, as we have seen
—as is shown in his autobiography—some of his earliest memories
were connected with his mother's fasts and the sun. He used to
watch for the sun to come out so that his mother could eat, during the Hindu Lent. (She fasted when the sun did *not* shine.)
Now, it so happens that during this last fast, January 13-18, the
sun shone every day in Delhi until the late morning of the 18th.
It was the Mahatma's practice to spend most of the day lying
out in the sun on a cot, in the garden of Birla House. The absence of the sun on that day—which is in any case unusual in
Delhi—must have stricken deep into his unconscious mind, which

had all the more power in that his whole organism was weakened by the long fast. I think it powerfully supported the pledge of the Hindu organizations to keep the peace. In fact I think the darkness of the morning, the pledge to peace and the memory of his mother all combined together to make up the utterance which he called "the inner voice," that which guided him through all the last thirty or forty years of his life, and said imperiously: "Fast no more."

This explanation I would never have dared to give to Gandhi, but, as will be seen later, he somehow knew (perhaps by telepathy) that this was my idea: otherwise I cannot explain the long dissertation he gave me on the uselessness of precise astronomical knowledge about the sun. Still later, after his death, I spoke to Mrs. Naidu about it; she said that she did not believe the absence of the sun would have been decisive without the pledge to peace, but that combined with that pledge it may have called forth the "inner voice."

Furthermore—another point my American press colleagues did not at all consider—throughout his long life the Mahatma always believed in trusting the pledges of others. He did it repeatedly, on the theory that a man who betrays you must be trusted again and again until he becomes worthy of your trust.

In any case this is my unsupported belief. I think the meteorological phenomena play a great part in the religious consciousness, as they do in all religious poetry and literature. Every sacred scripture abounds in examples. Since Mahatma Gandhi's was primarily a religious consciousness, the absence of the sun on January 18th, played a part, subliminally or otherwise, in his decision to cease fasting.

3

India rejoiced. All talk of war had ceased, not only in Delhi but everywhere. The Deputy Prime Minister, Mr. Patel, was in Bombay, making a speech a day, but the belligerent tone he had used ten days before was completely gone. The Mahatma was, according to the newspapers, regaining strength.

On Tuesday evening, January 20th, he was carried to the

prayer-ground in a wooden chair to take part in the evening prayer-meeting, although he could not yet walk. I did not go to this prayer-meeting because I was unaware that he would be there; I did actually think of going anyhow, as a preparation for later on when he would return, but it was too late when the thought crossed my mind. That evening some poor wretch threw a bomb which exploded harmlessly somewhere in the neighborhood but did not even engage Gandhi's attention. (They told him about it afterward.) As I was soon to see, motor backfires and airplane noises were quite common in the neighborhood of Birla House; the Mahatma was extremely weak, ill and old; no doubt he took the noise to be an ordinary one, if he heard it at all. He proceeded that evening to make his usual remarks after the service, but his voice (the papers said) was so weak that they had to be repeated after him by one of "the girls," his granddaughters. In my diary for the 21st I find:

"He will only go to Pakistan if the government there welcomes him as a friend of the Muslims, he says. (I don't believe Jinnah could keep him out if he tried.)"

The next paragraph of this entry in my diary is as follows:

"This episode confirms me in the opinion that it would be rash to stray very far from Gandhi at this time. Some great climax in the sacred drama which he is (partly consciously, partly unconsciously) enacting, and which has been lifted to the tragic height of a last act since August, is surely approaching. The fact that he is so uncannily able, by the instinct of genius, to assist the operation of fate, merely makes this climax inevitable. I have believed since last summer that if he is to be killed it must be (for India's sake) by a Hindu and not by a Muslim. This is in the logic of every sacred drama in the entire history of religion, and I believe it will take place."

At about this time I wrote to Mr. Patrick, the editor of *Holiday* magazine, in much the same vein, saying that the tragedy was at hand: this letter arrived in New York the day before it happened.

It will be observed that in the language of my diary (and I believe still more in the letter to Mr. Patrick) I preserved a sort of externality, as if I were not myself concerned very deeply in the matter except as a spectator. I must for the sake of a perfectly explicit record explain that this externality was more apparent than real. My vision of Gandhi's martyrdom was usually accompanied by an idea that I might be able to do something to prevent it. In recurrent dreams I saw myself interposing between him and an assassin. I have no record of dreams, of course, and cannot tell now how many times this happened, but I know it had occurred even before I left the United States. Since dreams are a useful key to the consciousness, I believe that I was myself far more deeply concerned and engaged, far more aware of the meaning of the drama, than I was willing to express in language. And in another sense—or on another plane—there was also fear: the fear that this inevitable tragedy would take place before I could obtain from him some clue to the meaning of our struggle. A good deal of this I could not possibly have told anybody a year ago. Now it does not matter.

In the afternoon of that day, January 21st (Wednesday) I went to Birla House for the first time to stand at the back of the crowd at the Mahatma's evening prayers.

Birla House was the residence in Delhi of Mr. G. D. Birla, a very rich man who had been for a long time, although rather uncomprehendingly, a follower of Gandhi's. It was a large establishment and Gandhi had used it often before on his visits to Delhi. The house stood inside sandstone walls with a long garden stretching behind it to a raised terrace which was well-suited to the purpose of Gandhi's evening prayer-meeting. At this time of the year a long arbor stretched from the house itself to the prayer ground at the end of the garden, and alongside the arbor there were thick beds of petunias. At one end of the house, directly at the end of the arbor, there was a rose garden, and just inside the rose garden Mr. Gandhi had his room.

On the other side of the house from the rose garden there was a driveway which led to the prayer-ground. The public came in that way, and of course there were policemen to see that there was no disorder, although in deference to Gandhi's ideas they were made as unobtrusive as possible. (He wanted nobody barred from wherever he was staying.)

The character of Birla House—its chateau architecture, its carefully tended lawns and gardens, its general air of wealth and pleasaunce—was inappropriate to the Mahatma, but it is doubt-

ful if he ever noticed. He was unaware of his surroundings to a
remarkable degree. Every room he stayed in was the same—the
bare, clean room and the pallet in a corner—and it did not matter
where he found it; on his previous visit to Delhi he had been in
the untouchables' quarter. Whoever offered him hospitality had
to be prepared to transform his house (as Gandhi said) "into a
caravanserai," and Mr. Birla seemed willing to do this. (No doubt
there were advantages also to him in so offering.)

On my first day at the prayer meeting I was with Mrs. Neville,
the wife of a colleague, and we stood at the back of the crowd.
We were a little late, which discomfited me greatly until I saw
that people came and went quite freely all through the service.
I quote my diary:

"The prayer-meeting takes place in the garden of Birla House
in a sort of summer-house built of red sandstone against the sandstone wall.

"Gandhi was seated in a very light-looking wooden chair,
portable, in the middle of the summer-house. In front of him on
the steps were the women who sing the hymns, the women of his
entourage. They sing sometimes one by one, sometimes in chorus.
In front of them other women sit on the ground, facing the
Mahatma. Men are farther back and then there is a fairly thick
circle of men (chiefly men, that is) who stand around all this
and enclose it. The faces, some rapt, some indifferent and some
merely curious, are fascinating. There were half a dozen Europeans, no Muslims that I saw, many Sikhs among the Hindus.

"Gandhi was thickly wrapped in white homespun, muffling
him up to the mouth. He looked very small and frail and, until
the very end of the hymn-singing, seemed to be deep in meditation or abstraction with his head sunk. With the last hymn he
began to move his hands rhythmically under his wrappings. One
or two of 'the girls' facing the audience did so too—it was a
sort of rhythmical handclapping without any noise. At the end
of this last hymn the microphones were brought up to the old
man's lips and he began to speak in a husky voice, not weak exactly, but certainly not strong. His face was obscured by the
microphone, which had an advertisement on either side of it.

"The incongruous word 'Chicago' was all that could be seen
while the Mahatma was talking. It is the name of a radio company

in Delhi which sells instruments. These prayer-meetings are all broadcast and have an immense unseen audience.

"What he said I have no idea, but the words Hindu and Sikh and Mussulman kept recurring, so one could guess. There was a slight disturbance (very slight) and a man was arrested. According to Sharma, Bob's chauffeur, this man was a member of the Hindu Mahasabha.

"When he had finished speaking Gandhi was carried back to Birla House in this improvised *sedia gestatoria* of his. He seemed to be sunk again in meditation, with his chin in the folds of the white homespun. It was strangely moving, just as a spectacle, to see him pass through the arbored walk up to the house. He looks so small, fragile and abstracted, half in heaven, I suppose, as the Bard says. There is a great sadness in this somewhere."

There follows an episode which requires a little explaining. Sharma was Bob Neville's chauffeur; he had been in the Indian Army and was a prisoner of war in Germany for some years. Consequently his language to me was a weird mixture of German and English. He asked me: "Wass denken Sie von Mahatma Gandhi und die atomic bomb?" The entry in my diary continues:

"He was laughing: I think it seems to him—as to many young Indians—that Gandhi has little or nothing to do with the contemporary world. I told him I thought Gandhi would win over the atomic bomb. However, I am not really so sure. I have spent the whole day, or most of it, reading Griswold's two books, *The Religion of the Rig Veda* and *Insights into Modern Hinduism*, and certainly it seems to me that the religious heritage is terrific and Gandhi the best of the lot (the moderns), but none of the others could convince the world, why should he?"

On Thursday, January 22:

"To animadvert: Gandhi's left hand emerged from his *khadi* wrappings and emphasized what he had to say with a curious vehemence, like that of a teacher before recalcitrant little boys. It was as if he knew that what he had to say was not being accepted, or was being accepted only for the sake of form or *à contre-coeur*. This morning I have read what it was. He expressed pity for the 'misguided youth' who threw the bomb on Tuesday and said that those who formed his mind should be won over from error. He spoke indeed of Hindu, Sikh and Mussulman, saying that it did not matter which the young man was."

Friday, January 23:

"Another thing Gandhi said the other night about the young man who threw the bomb was, 'He must learn that those who disagree with him are not necessarily evil.'"

I went to Agra that week-end with the Nevilles to see the Taj Mahal and the Old Fort with its palaces (it was the night of the full moon). On my return on Monday afternoon I found a note from one of Mr. Nehru's secretaries summoning me for seven o'clock that evening. I just had time for a bath and a change from the dust of the road before going out to his house, where there had been a reception for the anniversary of India's Declaration of Independence. Mr. Nehru had retained Jai Prakash Narain, the general secretary of the Indian Socialist Party, for a few moments, and it was thus that I first made his acquaintance. We were to meet fairly often thereafter, at least for a while, as he was staying across the street from me in the house of Shri Krishna, the Indian journalist. (I had moved to Parliament Street by now, to Wenger's Flats.)

In brief, Mr. Nehru was angry. He had seen the text of the article I had written from Karachi on January 7th (printed in New York on January 16th) and it infuriated him. He contested it point by point. I could hardly dispute his facts; all I could say was that this was the Pakistan case as given me in Karachi. I was particularly startled to find that a piece of information I had passed on about the Sheikh Abdullah—head of the Kashmir government supported by India—was made of the whole cloth, without a word of truth in it.

The discussion was long and, to say the least, animated. I can hardly doubt that Mr. Nehru was in a full flood of indignation and anger—many things about the Kashmir dispute had the power to arouse these feelings in him—and yet the surprising outcome of all this was as follows: he had spoken to Gandhiji about me and Gandhiji was ready to talk to me now if I would telephone for an appointment.

I did so on the following morning and Mr. Pyarelal, the secretary, told me to come to Birla House after the evening prayers.

4

On Tuesday, January 27th, I was accompanied to the prayer ground at Birla House by Rangaswami, a Madrassi Brahmin who was then acting as secretary to *Time* and *Life*. He stood beside me and translated in an undertone, so that I obtained a much clearer notion of the proceedings than before. The first prayer or chant was from Buddhist scripture, the second was Vedanta (I learned much later that it was the first *shloka* of the *Isha Upanishad*); the third was Parsi; the fourth was from the Koran. This was followed by the chanting of verses 54 to 72 of the second chapter of the Gita. There was some hymn or devotional song between these which Rangaswami did not recognize, but he thought it was Islamic. The *Ramadunh* (devotional singing with rhythmical hand-clapping) ended the choral part of the prayer-meeting. Mr. Gandhi then spoke in his gentle, husky voice with a pleading note in it, asking those present to bring their Muslim friends when they came to the evening prayer. He had asked this before, and tonight when he began to speak he inquired how many Muslims there were present. No hands went up; nobody made a sign; but somebody called out from the crowd that there was a Muslim present. The Mahatma shook his head sadly and I can well remember his disappointed voice as he repeated: *"Ek? Ek?"* (One? One?) And added, as translated: "That is not enough."

When the Mahatma ceased speaking he walked from the prayer-ground, leaning lightly on two of "the girls." He no longer needed the portable chair, and seemed, in fact, to be in as good health as ever—the familiar figure, the familiar face, which it seemed to me I had known for thirty years or more and could hardly believe now that it was before me. He made his way back to the house by the arbor-walk; Rangaswami and I took the driveway on the other side, rounded the house and came out in the rose garden not long after the Mahatma had gone inside. We were accompanied now by the French photographer, Henri Cartier-Bresson and his wife, who is Javanese; they had also been at the prayers. I was grateful for the helpful presence of these three young people from the corners of the earth, both before and after the conversation, for I have never been so nervous in my life. In spite of long experience, heady and dangerous some of it, of this one above all I could say with perfect truth that I was afraid.

Rangaswami spoke to Mr. Pyarelal and introduced me; after a few moments, as we stood on the steps, Mr. Pyarelal came back to the glass doors and signaled to me. "You must take off your shoes," said Rangaswami. "I know there will be a hole in my sock," I said in terror to Madame Cartier-Bresson, and removed my shoes, and there was the hole. I went into the room.

It was a small rectangular room with glass doors or French windows on one side, where the steps were, and long windows on the other two. The fourth wall was the wall of Birla House, against which this room was as a sort of annex, but an almost transparent annex: curious persons were peering through the windows or doors at all times and the Mahatma, through long training, did not even notice.

As I came in he was walking up and down on a rectangular blue carpet which covered less than half the floor. This, and his white pallet in the corner, made the only furniture of the room. In the corner at the right were three or four of "the girls": granddaughters, grandnieces, seated on the floor and talking in whispers.

I began by saying that I wanted to make a rather extensive study of his system of thought and action. (I think I actually said "Good evening, sir," at the outset.) He said: "Yes, Pandit Nehru told me." He paused and looked up at me with a curious birdlike motion (I was much taller). "Pandit Nehru did not tell me," he said, "whether you wished to see me *absolutely* alone." The delicate emphasis on *absolutely* was full of meaning; I knew quite well that Mr. Gandhi never saw anybody "absolutely" alone.

"No, sir," I said. "I make no conditions."

"Very well," he said. "Would you like to walk or to sit?"

"Whatever you wish," I said. "Perhaps you are tired after the meeting . . . ?"

"On the contrary," he said with a sort of gentle decision (oddly, I can still hear this phrase when some more important ones are preserved only by written notes). "At this hour I prefer to walk a little."

We walked up and down the blue carpet. I was absurdly conscious of the hole in my sock, which I hardly suppose Gandhi saw. I was also aware that his swift steps up and down the carpet were much more numerous than mine. For me walking up and down that carpet was hardly walking at all; in three steps I had reached the end of it and turned back with him.

"Then you would not object," he went on, "if some notes were taken . . . ?" He motioned with his hand toward Mr. Pyarelal, who was keeping pace with him on the other side.

"No, sir," I said. "On the contrary . . ."

"They might even be useful?" He finished the sentence for me on a rising note, with a curious half-smile.

"I have been reading your edition of the Gita," I said, "and my questions are based on that."

He smiled and exclaimed something ("*Acha, Acha!*" I believe, conveying assent). I went on:

"I propose to begin with action and the fruits of action."

He stopped still in his walk and looked up at me with his head slightly on one side. This is the characteristic motion I have called birdlike. He then straightened his head and pointed a long finger at the carpet.

"Let me get one thing clear," he said. "I have typhoid fever. Doctors are sent for and by means of injections of sulpha drugs or something of the kind they save my life. This, however, proves nothing. It might be that it would be more valuable to humanity for me to die."

He stopped again for a few seconds; we were both standing still now. The moment was of tremendous importance.

"Is that quite clear?" he asked, looking at me with his head up. "If it is not, I will repeat it."

This was the nearest thing to asperity—a very gentle kind of asperity—in the whole conversation.

"No, sir," I said. "I think I understand it."

We resumed the walk.

"What I wish to ask is this: how can a righteous battle produce a catastrophic result?" I said. "The battle is righteous in the terms of the Gita. The result is a disaster. How can this be?"

"Because of the means used," he said. "Means are not to be distinguished from ends. If violent means are used there will be a bad result."

"Is this true at all times and places?" I asked.

"*I* say so," he said with his curious lisp, and rather shyly, too, as if he had never gone quite so far before (as indeed he had not). Then he produced a statement which was much bolder.

"As I read the Gita, even the first chapter, the battlefield of Kurukshetra is in the heart of man. I must tell you that orthodox scholars have criticized my interpretation of the Gita as being unduly influenced by the Sermon on the Mount."

He took a few more steps and then made a really defiant profession of faith.

"There is one learned book in existence," he said, "which supports my interpretation of the Gita. But even if there were no such book, and even if it could be *proved* that my interpretation was wrong, I would still believe it."

I was so taken aback by this certainty that I could not get out another question for the moment. Gandhi smiled and said: "Now I think we might sit down. Shall we?"

He made his way over to the pallet in the corner and sat near the end of it, leaning against the wall. I sat cross-legged on the floor beside him, with Mr. Pyarelal in front of him. I was now quite close to him and saw that his face had assumed an expression of concern, almost of anxiety.

"You should not be sitting there," he said. "You should have a chair."

"No, sir, please," I said.

"There are chairs in the house," he said, inclining his body forward a little, as if to emphasize the offer. "We can send for a chair."

"No, sir, I'm comfortable, thanks," I said.

The question of the chair came up twice more, I think, as he imagined me to be uncomfortable on the floor. As a matter of fact, I did begin to get a bit cramped before the end, but I could never have admitted it. The idea of sitting on a chair with Mr. Gandhi on the floor at my feet was something impossible for me to conceive. I was finally obliged to tell him that I did not want a chair; and after that he abandoned the notion.

"Are the means and the ends not to be distinguished?" I asked. "If the end is good . . ."

"The terms are convertible," he said. "No good act can produce an evil result. Evil means, even for a good end, produce evil results."

He spoke further on the harmony or even identity of means and ends, but this part of the talk does not appear in the written notes (various and incomplete as they are) at my disposal, and I shall not attempt to reproduce exactly what he said. At this time he did not even distinguish means from ends in a temporal sense, although he did so the next day.

I put before him the case of a good action: that is, in the sense of the Gita, an action undertaken selflessly and without desire for the fruits of action. How can such an action produce a disastrous or catastrophic result? He said that if a good action involved the use of violence to achieve its purpose then it could not be a good action. At one point in this part of the talk he leaned over and looked at me very close, through his glasses, and then took them off and wiped them and said: "Mind you, ordinary governments cannot do without force."

Another interjection along in this part of the hour came when he said: "Renunciation of the fruits of action does not mean that there can be no fruits. Fruits are not forbidden. But no action must be undertaken for the sake of its fruits. That is what the Gita means."

After a considerable amplification of these ideas of means and ends, action and the fruits of action, I came to the specific case I had in mind all the time, which was our war against Hitlerism. The instance was my own—he may have had some other instance in mind—but I had avoided mentioning it before because I wanted to get the principles straight to begin with.

I told him that I was thinking of our war, which, in my view, had been a righteous battle.

"I knew some of the leaders on our side," I told him. He nodded his head slowly, accepting by that nod both Roosevelt and Churchill as being righteous in intention. (I did not mention their names; he knew.)

"How can such a truly righteous battle as our fight against the evil of Fascism produce the result which now faces us?"

That was my question as my diary records it on the following day. (Even this may not be quite accurate; the memory even from one day to the next can hardly be literal.)

With great sadness, leaning toward me and speaking almost in a whisper (so gentle was his voice) he said that our ends may have been good but our means were bad, and that this was not the way of truth. Then he made a few direct remarks which I remember verbatim (I can hear them now).

"You cannot destroy a great nation like Germany," he said.

"I know it, sir," I replied. "It is madness to try."

"You cannot destroy the spirit of Japan."

"I know it, sir."

"You are heading straight into a third world war."

It was just here, I think, that I returned to my main subject. (The possibility of a third world war was not included.)

"Those who govern us are obviously concerned with the fruits of action rather than with the truth of action," I said. "How, then, are we to be well governed?"

"You must give up the worship of Mammon," he said.

(Here, I believe, he was speaking of America, whereas by "we" I had meant all the people everywhere.)

He proceeded to outline a theory of representative democracy in characteristic terms, using the first person generically.

"I am ten million people," he said. "I send into government certain men to represent me. They may be corrupted. If they are corrupted I will recall them. I cannot recall myself."

He paused and leaned forward in a way which I could only regard as a little mysterious. (These movements forward and back, with the putting on and taking off of his spectacles, are beyond description: they indicate in retrospect that he was almost as tense by this time in his contemplation of the questions as I was.)

"Have nothing to do with power," he said, again as a sort of aside from the main discussion.

"Do you mean that power corrupts?" I asked him. (I was quoting Lord Acton, I suppose, but did not think it necessary to say so.)

He leaned back on the cushion with a sigh and said: "Yes, I

am afraid I do mean that power corrupts." Then he sat up again
and resumed his discourse:

"I have five constructive institutions. In all of these five constructive institutions I have constantly told the workers to have
nothing to do with power. I do not send them to Parliament.
They are to educate and guide those who vote, so that they may
do so well."

(The five constructive institutions to which he referred were
undoubtedly the organizations he had founded for village
women, cottage industries, the All-India Spinners' Association,
and the like.)

At this point Mr. Gandhi went into a long discourse about
the uselessness of scientific measurements and lifelong devotion
to research into facts, as compared with the true business of man,
which I took to be his relation to the truth and hence, to God.
The specific example he used at some length was the sun, its distance from the earth, place and function in the system, and other
facts which, the Mahatma said, might be true as facts but not as
truth. (This reference to astronomical precision made me think,
rightly or wrongly, that he understood me to understand him as
having ceased his fast because the sun did not shine.) I then
asked:

"Your own disciplinary resolutions are originally due to family, are they not?"

He understood me to say "memory," not family, and answered:

"No, not to memory. I owe them first of all to my saintly
mother and to my good nurse. These were noble women. They
taught me to tell the truth and not to fear."

I then asked him, on impulse, how he could explain how quite
different persons, such as Bernard Shaw, for example, could get
at the same disciplinary resolutions without religion. The sentence was so phrased that "disciplinary resolutions" came at the
end of it, and before I had pronounced the words Mahatmaji
caught me up with his sudden smile and the substitute word
"conclusions." I let that pass, although I had meant chiefly vegetarianism, abstinence from stimulants, self-control in general, and
not anything quite so large as "conclusions." I then added: "Unless you say that Mr. Shaw is himself religious."

The Mahatma, still smiling almost playfully at the thought, said with his slow, careful enunciation:

"I was just about to say that it would be difficult for anybody to say that Bernard Shaw had no religion. In everything of his that I have read there has been a religious center."

I think it was at this point that he said to me: "You would be astonished if you knew how few books I have read." This was a sort of aside, almost in an undertone, and I answered in the same way: "I don't see what difference the number makes if they were good ones."

Then we began upon the nature of reality. I wanted to know which of the two classical schools of Vedanta philosophy most engaged Gandhi's thought, that of Shankara or that of Ramanuja. I mentioned Shankara and asked if the world—"all this," I said, touching with my finger the pallet on which he was sitting—was illusion.

"If you are using the word illusion as a translation of Maya," he said, "it is wrong. There is no correct English translation for the word Maya."

"Could we use some other word? Form or forms? Differentiated forms? Appearances?"

He accepted the word "appearances" but then said—most earnestly, coming close to me and speaking in a whisper at the end:

"God is in everything. Even in the stone. Even in the stone."

(This is one of the phrases I can still hear in my own head—"even in the stone.")

"Well, then," said I, more or less in these words, "I gather that the disappearance of the appearances . . ."

He interrupted to say: "The dissolution of matter?"

I nodded and went on: ". . . may occur, owing to the atomic energy which has been or may be released, or owing to some other cause? May I take it that atomic energy itself does not surprise you?"

Never could I forget the tranquillity with which he answered the question.

"On the contrary," he said, "I consider that the dissolution of matter is absolutely certain at some point. If there were any survivors of such a thing—if you can imagine survivors—they would undoubtedly say, 'What a wondrous spectacle!'"

There was a little more about the "disappearance of the appearances," but either in Hindu philosophy or in modern science
there was obviously nothing that Gandhi did not accept without
a tremor. We returned, then, to the problem of non-violence and
he confirmed again the absolute nature of its necessity for a good
result. Hearing himself assert this so clearly he was assailed by
some thought of India (of the campaign in Kashmir, no doubt),
and leaned back upon the cushions to say in an undertone, and
almost, I thought, in an accent of despair: "Look at what India
is doing now. And with my tacit consent. I cannot deny that it
is with my tacit consent." This was the only time the word India
was pronounced in this conversation.

He himself spoke of the failure of the United Nations—which
was one of the reasons that had brought me to him—and I said:
"I have hoped in the past year that perhaps you could be persuaded to come to Lake Success and talk to the United Nations.
Then they would be forced to listen."

He laughed; the idea seemed to him funny for a moment. He
then said, more seriously: "Perhaps, if I were spared for more
years of service . . ." It sounded as if he did not regard this as
probable, and we dropped the subject.

I then asked him why he was certain when the "inner voice"
spoke to him. Others have inner voices and are not sure.

He answered in terms of the formless God: God is the spirit
within, both law and law-giver.

"At Lausanne in Switzerland," he said (I suppose this was in
1931 when he visited Romain Rolland on his way home from
the Round-Table Conference), "I said that I had hitherto
thought God was Truth, whereas now I was inclined to say that
Truth was God."

He proceeded to affirm again that non-violence was the "final
flower of Truth," and that as Truth was within and above (i.e.,
immanent and transcendent) so by non-violence could the soul
perceive its law. Taking as an example his last fast, he told me
that every reason was against it, but the law which was above all
reason (which spoke to him in the "inner voice") commanded
it against reason. When this happened, he obeyed, for, against
that living law within, nothing could stand.

I then asked precisely this (I remember it well): "Does the

certainty precede the renunciation?" And he replied precisely this: "No, the renunciation precedes the certainty." The words were said with vivacity, as if I had misunderstood something vital—as indeed I apparently had, for he immediately began to talk to me about renunciation.

"Renunciation is itself the law of life," he said. "When we speak of action undertaken without regard for the fruits of action we *mean* renunciation. That is renunciation of fruits. I eat to live, to serve, and also, if it so happens, to enjoy, but I do not eat for the sake of enjoyment."

There was a phrase here which I distinctly remember but cannot find in any of the assorted sets of notes which were taken. He was speaking of his last fast and of its certainty both in beginning and end: he used the phrase—glancing at me through his spectacles with a look of the most earnest wisdom—"without committing suicide." In his slow, half-whispered utterance the accent of abhorrence which he gave to the idea of suicide was deep and great.

"I find the sum of wisdom on this subject in the *Isha Upanishad*," he said. "Do you know it?"

"No, sir," I said, "but I will get an English translation tomorrow."

"Where will you find it?"

"I shall look through all the bookshops in New Delhi. I have found other books there."

"If you cannot find it let me know," he said, "and I shall find it for you. When I went to Travancore I spoke to Christians, large numbers of Christians. I looked for authority with which to convince them, and what I found was the *Isha Upanishad*. It is, you know, the shortest of the Upanishads. Is there a copy of the *Isha* . . . ?"

He looked into the room and somebody did something. While he continued to talk about renunciation a small book in Sanskrit was thrust into his hands. He swooped upon it with a curiously agile movement and held it up before his spectacled eyes with an appearance of both gratitude and reverence which cannot be conveyed in words.

"It is not in English," he said, "so it will not do. But I shall tell you what the first *shloka* says. It says: The whole world is the garment of the Lord. Renounce it, then, and receive it back as the gift of God."

He paused and seemed to consider.

"There is another line which may puzzle you. It says that thereafter you are not to covet. You may inquire how you could covet, having renounced and received back again as God's gift. This is added because even those who have renounced sometimes covet. I find in this *shloka* the greatest truth of renunciation. There is no other way. Since I found it in Travancore I have been using it regularly at my evening prayer-meeting, as regularly as the Gita."

At about this point we all looked at our watches—that is, Mr. Gandhi, Mr. Pyarelal and I. Almost a full hour had passed, and I realized that there must be many people waiting for appointments. I said: "I'm afraid . . ."

Gandhi, looking at that enormous and very cheap watch he wore in his shawl—the kind that was called a "turnip" in America when I was young—said: "Well, this is more than I had bargained for. Do you want to come back again tomorrow?"

"Whenever I can, whenever you have time for me," I said, rising from the floor. He looked up at me and smiled.

"You can come every day," he said. "You can move into the house if you like. I will find the time somehow. But in a few days I hope to go to Wardha, and perhaps it is better if you come to Wardha."

"At what hour shall I come tomorrow?" I asked.

"At this hour," he said, "after the prayer-meeting."

"I'll come to the prayer-meeting," I said.

This made him laugh.

"Come to the prayer-meeting!" he said, with an almost disembodied gayety. "And consider that a standing invitation!"

As I said: "Thank you, sir," he added very gently, in a voice that would have melted the heart of an enemy (and I was no enemy): "If there is no time, will you understand?"

I stumbled out. The door was beside me. On the stone steps outside the glass door it was very dark. I could hardly get into my shoes. My friends, the Madrassi Brahmin, the Frenchman and his Javanese wife, had waited for me. Without their help I do not think I could have got out of the dark garden.

5

So bald and clumsy a paraphrase can give little of the true meaning of this interview. I have not Gandhi's precise words, except
in those small phrases which I can still hear many months later;
I have certainly not my own precise words except where I have
indicated. I have my diary, not nearly detailed enough, some very
telescoped and partial notes which were salvaged and transcribed
by Mr. Pyarelal many weeks later, and a newspaper version
written under great emotional strain four days later while the
Mahatma was being cremated. None is quite right; only a dicta-
phone would have given the exact words.

But even the exact words would not mean the same in cold
print. The fact is that Gandhi had some extraordinary faculty
of speaking from the depths to the depths, with no intervening
irrelevancy, so that every word, every turn of phrase, had suggestions and reverberations in the consciousness. For example,
when he told me that, "Renunciation is the only way," it is my
impression now that he said: "Believe me, renunciation is the
only way." But the phenomenal expressive quality of his tired,
husky voice was such that the "believe me" may only have been
implied by his tone, not physically pronounced on the corporeal
air. It had, in any case, the cadence of an entreaty to be believed,
whether the words fell in that form or not.

It is the same with the passages about illusion, appearance, form
and reality. In this whole part of the conversation Mahatmaji was
earnestly entreating me not to consider the world as an illusion,
but to give the appearances (or forms) what reality they possess.
It was obvious that he considered this to be only relative and
transitory, and that the essence, which he called God, might be
called atomic energy or some other term in other systems, but
that in any case I should not lose grasp of the forms. All of this
was conveyed more by the anxious and pitying and earnest manner (voice, gesture, look) than by the actual words. He *wanted*
me to understand; he knew, somehow or other, how deep was my
trouble, and he cared about it. The startling thing was that we
communicated. On these subjects—so beset by the jargon of the
professional philosopher that they are almost forbidden to ordi-

nary inhabitants of the earth, although they concern us most
—it is well-nigh impossible to communicate with anybody.
Gandhiji knew my trouble (supposedly) because he had been
through it all long before, or perhaps by his unrivaled intuition;
but whatever it was he understood and *he wanted to help me*.
That is the point: that was what shattered my self-control for
the time that it took for me to find my way out of the garden
and back (aided by my friends) in a bus to the center of New
Delhi. No matter what I had expected—and I had expected greatness of some incomparable kind—this was more. He knew that I
had come across half the world in a state approaching despair to
ask him to tell me the truth—this much he knew within a few
minutes, by intuition—and he set out to do so without regard for
the consequences. What I had encountered, quite beyond expectation or probability, was a manifestation of divine pity.

There were many small asides, sometimes only of a word or
two, which I have not put into the foregoing account of the conversation because I do not know quite where they came and
because they somewhat interrupted the continuity. I shall mention them now because they are examples of the kind of communication to which I have referred, a very special kind indeed.
He had made some mention of the lower creation, which, as I
knew, he took to be chiefly symbolized in the cow. He leaned
over and looked at me very straight through his glasses.

"You know," he said, "that I am a cow-lover?"

"Yes, sir," I said.

Now, by his question, so tentative and yet so piercing, he was
actually inquiring whether I had the usual Western attitude of
derision toward the Hindu cult of the cow. By my reply, which
was entirely submissive, he perceived that I had no disposition
to doubt the truth or *ahinsa* of this conception (even though
much might have been said of it at a later stage). The cow was
not mentioned again.

In the part of the talk concerning Maya, the world as illusion,
he puckered his brow at me and said: "Things are not what they
seem. That's all it means. There's a line of poetry, I remember—
'Things are not what they seem.' It's your own poetry. Is it
Whittier?"

The line is actually from Longfellow's "Psalm of Life," which

schoolboys in America used to learn by heart, but I was much
too concentrated on Gandhi to remember it then. (I found it out
days later too.)

There were many small words of this kind scattered through
the whole hour. When he said that I could move into the house
(Birla House) he added the word "but" and left the sentence
hanging. I knew what he meant, just as he knew what I meant
when I said, "Yes, sir," to the cow.

In another moment broken off from the main current of the
talk he leaned toward me to explain his dietary system.

"I eat only innocent food," he said gently. And then, looking
straight into my face, very close, he added in the merest thread
of voice, a sort of whisper not to be forgotten: "That is, if one
may impute innocence."

And once when he was talking of the self, wishing to differen-
tiate it from the body, he said: "Not the body, of course—the
body is a prison. Only a prison."

Much more decisive is the question he posed to me at the very
outset of the interview: that is the question of value. The saving
of a life by drugs or medical intervention is one thing, but it does
not settle the question of value: "perhaps it is more valuable for
humanity that I should die." I understood this, I think, perfectly,
and he knew that I did. A kind of integument of comprehension
was established between us after the first two or three minutes
which made any elaboration of either my questions or his answers
wholly unnecessary: the bare bones were enough. Perhaps after
a time—if there had been time—we might have achieved an ever
barer structure of verbalization, in which a look, a tone or a sign
would have taken the place of whole paragraphs. How this could
be—how it was, in fact—passes my comprehension, because nothing in my experience of life had really prepared me for Mahatma
Gandhi. No amount of reading could have done it. There was
something else: at a later stage I may be able to formulate a concept of what it was.

What overwhelmed me most, of course, was the perfectly
clear intimation that he, as *guru*, had accepted me as *chela*—not
completely and permanently in the Hindu sense, by which the
guru makes a sort of life compact with the student, but in so far
as the immense distances between us would permit. My sense of

astonished gratitude must have escaped me at some point or other, because I remember vividly how he leaned toward me and gave a serious warning. "You must not consider me to be perfect," he said in a worried voice. "I have not achieved perfection."

"Yes, sir, but your struggle has been in that direction," I said.

There was a light, faint sigh and he said: "Yes, that has been my struggle."

Hardest of all for me to believe was that so great a saint could take so great a sinner for his *chela*.

6

On that very day I had been given an opportunity to test what I had begun to learn in India. The Criminal Investigation Department summoned me to the police station in Old Delhi for not having registered with the police during my first twenty-four hours in the city (a regulation of which I had been unaware). To the accompaniment of a good deal of insolence and a number of bad jokes, I was informed that I was liable to arrest. The whole business took about an hour and a half, most of it waiting while a police clerk smoked my cigarettes and made sharp comments about American policy in the United Nations. I was resolved not to get impatient or angry whatever happened. Even when I was made to fill out the papers for the clerk—papers clearly marked "to be filled out by the officer in charge"—I did so without complaint. Considering how many centuries these people had been patient, I thought I could devote an hour and a half to the same discipline. There was nobody else in the police station except those on duty. When they perceived—rather to their surprise, I think—that I was not to be goaded, they signed my papers and let me go. If the same thing had happened in Europe I should have been telephoning all sorts of august protectors to intervene for me. It was the first time I had really learned a Gandhian lesson, and on my way back to New Delhi I felt inordinately proud of it. The details went into my journal the next day with the comment:

"All this I record at such length because the principal event of

the day—or of many days or perhaps of all my days—is so difficult
to write down at all. This was my first meeting with Gandhi.
Perhaps I shall have more time and energy later, or tomorrow, to
describe it."

That afternoon I went to the prayer-meeting at Birla House,
again with Rangaswami to translate the proceedings for me.
What I wrote about that in the journal later the same day
(Wednesday, January 28th) follows:

"I have had my second conversation with Gandhi today and
have just come from it. It was in a much more familiar and ordinary vein. The terrific tension and extreme altitude of yesterday's talk couldn't be kept up for long, and as we are to talk a
little every day, it was necessary to bring it down to earth.
Gandhiji felt this instinctively, I am sure, and achieved it by
assuming a quite different tone and telling a few—two, actually—
stories, one from the *Mahabharata* about a king who gave up
everything and went into the lowest slavery for the truth, and
the other (in detail, apropos of a question of mine) about the
drinking of goat's milk, which, he says, honors the letter of his
old South African vow against drinking cow's or buffalo's milk
but kills its spirit."

The fact was that I had found—or thought I had found—in
the milk vow the one example of a conflict between truth and
ahinsa in Gandhi's life and thought. To eat animal food was, he
explicitly decided long ago, *hinsa* or volence, although it was
not until 1912 that he made the vow which extended such *hinsa*
to the drinking of milk. (The drinking of milk is permitted even
to the most rigid vegetarians in India.) How could the drinking
of goat's milk be reconciled, in truth, with his other concepts of
hinsa and *ahinsa* as applied to food?

I put it to him as an example of conflict, but he would not
allow the word.

"Conflict is too strong," he said. "It isn't conflict."

"It worries you."

"Yes, it worries me. I have never been reconciled to it. But
it is because of the vow rather than because of *ahinsa*."

Then he told me the story of the vow, describing the very
scene in all its details. He and his friend Kallenbach, the South
African German, were eating rice from the same bowl and

drinking milk with it. They had often discussed the question before: Kallenbach had followed Gandhi in all his dietary experiments and theories, and perhaps even outdone his master at times. On this day in 1912 Kallenbach, after taking a drink of milk, said to Gandhi: "If you will give it up I will do so too." Gandhi was moved by one of those inner necessities which governed his whole life to take the vow then and there. The vow was not to drink the milk of the cow or the buffalo again.

It was kept. But during his first great illness, already described, his wife found the loophole: goat's milk was not forbidden by the vow. Gandhi did not want to drink even goat's milk, but she stood at the foot of the bed and looked at him pleadingly.

"I see her before me now," he said, with his hand outstretched in the air as if he really did see her. "She for whom I did it is gone, while I . . ."

He was in a subdued and reminiscent mood, perhaps a little tired and perhaps a little melancholy. He talked a good deal about his wife, and although I have forgotten the transition, it was undoubtedly the shade of Kasturbai that turned his mind on to the story of Harishchandra from the *Mahabharata*. This he told me at considerable length—the king who gave up everything for the truth, became the lowest of slaves, in that out-caste which burns the corpses, and was restored to life through spiritual reunion with his wife.

The incidental remarks during this conversation were, as on the day before, as illuminating as his main discourse. At one moment, distinguishing the self from the body, he said to me in an admonitory way: "Not the body, you understand. The body is only a prison."

At another moment, when he was declaring that for him nothing could conflict with or interfere with the truth, he remembered an episode of some years before, when a Frenchman had come to stay at his Ashram.

"What was the name of the Frenchman?" he asked.

Somebody among those seated on the floor around us (more numerous today) pronounced the name of Sartre—which, of course, to me meant Jean-Paul Sartre. It was apparently another Sartre.

"You've never heard of him?" Gandhi asked. "Well, of course

not. But he was very celebrated out here. He ran a magazine; he was a friend of Asia. We afterward heard that his life was not at all straight. . . ."

Here the Mahatma's face contracted in a grimace of what I can only describe as woe: it gave him suffering to contemplate the kind of error to which he was now so delicately referring.

". . . we learned that he had divorced his wife. His life was not at all straight."

He recovered himself and went on: "However, he was a friend of Asia, so we took him to the Ashram and he spent a couple of weeks with us. When he went away he wrote some articles in which he quoted me as having said that I would sacrifice even my country to the truth. I did indeed say so, but he omitted to add that I also said that the contingency could not arise."

Of all the *obiter dicta*, the meaningful odds and ends which were sprinkled along the main road of his discourse, this was probably the one I expanded most fully in my own reflections during the months that followed. He meant, of course, that any man's truth is very largely created by his own country and indissoluble from it: that to speak of sacrificing one's country to the truth is to speak of an impossibility. The ideas put in being by that one remark could fill pages.

On this second day Mr. Gandhi began, before I could ask a question, by setting me straight on one point.

"When I said yesterday that means and ends were convertible and indistinguishable," he said, "of course I did not mean temporally. Naturally the means precede the ends in the sense of time. They are otherwise of the same nature."

There were more people in the room today and more of them took notes. (I learned afterward that the Minister of Health, Rajkumari Amrit Kaur, was one of those who took notes.) I was aware that there were people, but did not distinguish between them; I was concentrated upon Gandhi as I have never been concentrated in my life. On this second day I do not even remember if there were people looking in through the windows. (There had been on the first day, and one of "the girls" had drawn the curtains when she saw that this distracted me.)

At the very end of this conversation I wanted to return to the milk vow for one more question, but the Mahatma said—very gently, but looking at his watch just the same—"Now, that'll do for tomorrow, won't it?"

"I can't come tomorrow, sir," I said, getting up. "I am going to Amritsar with Mr. Nehru. I'll come the next day."

He looked up at me from his pallet with a sudden glowing smile as if this was wonderful news. Perhaps my questions tired him; perhaps a reprieve of one day was welcome; but I think it was mostly because I was going with Mr. Nehru to Amritsar. He raised both his hands in the air with the palms toward me in an unmistakable attitude of blessing.

"Go! Go!" he said.

Those were the last words I heard him say.

During these two meetings I had addressed him as "sir" and had given, I suppose, every outward sign of the respect I so deeply felt. But I did not kneel or bow or touch his feet, and unless a sign of this sort was given, Mr. Gandhi was not in the habit of giving blessings. He was obliged to do so innumerable times over the years—"The woes of Mahatmas are known to Mahatmas alone," he says—but only because he knew the people wanted it and felt comforted by it. Why he gave me his blessing when I was going to Amritsar I do not really know, but I suppose it must have been chiefly for Mr. Nehru.

At any rate we went to Amritsar. Mr. Nehru took me in his airplane the next morning and there followed such a day of reviews, inspections, parades and public ceremonies as I have seldom seen. How the Prime Minister got through it without fatigue I do not know, but in the evening, after dinner with officers of the Indian Army, he made a long improvised speech which was up to the best of his public efforts for skill, sincerity and force, although all delivered in a conversational tone. The Amritsar mass meeting, two hundred thousand strong, was a small thing as Indian crowds go, but I had never seen anything like it. Since Amritsar is the holy city of the Sikhs and was the scene of some of the most dreadful mass killings during the communal uprisings only a few months before—and since it was full of disgruntled Hindu and Sikh refugees from Pakistan who thought not enough was being done for them and were full of a desire for revenge, meaning war on Pakistan—it was half-expected that there would be trouble. In spite of this atmosphere Pandit Nehru in his speech there attacked the proto-Fascist organizations of the Hindus with considerable force; it was the first time he or any other high dignitary of the Indian Government had done so. The strength of these organizations—who were to take the life of the Mahatma within twenty-four hours—came from white-collar workers and befuddled young men, precisely the classes from which European Fascism had been recruited fifteen or twenty years before. The two in question were the R.S.S.S. (Rashtriya Swayam Sewak Sangh—National Self-Servant Association) and the Hindu Mahasabha (Great Society of Hindus). The R.S.S.S. was political and para-military, with indeed a bloody history in recent months; but it was the Hindu Mahasabha, with a respectable past as an organ of the revival of Hindu culture, which was now become more rabid than any other in its desire for Hindu empire over the whole sub-continent. These organizations had publicly trampled on the flag of India only three days before during the independence day celebrations at Amritsar. Their strength in the country was said to be great, and they were known to believe that the Mahatma—aided by Nehru, of course—was responsible for keeping the peace which they longed to see broken.

Mr. Nehru attacked them both boldly, by name. One of the young Indian journalists told me it was a brave speech, but impolitic, since these organizations were so strong. Within another week they had been suppressed throughout India, and their future is now all in the past. Amongst the innumerable results of the Mahatma's martyrdom the dissolution of the Hindu Fascist movement must be counted as one.

We slept the night at Amritsar and flew back to Delhi the next morning. It was well after one o'clock when we landed; one of the generals drove me in to New Delhi in his car. I then had a cold bath, shave, and sat down to consider what I should ask the Mahatma this evening.

I had intended on this day (Friday, January 30th) to continue with the questioning on the possibility of conflict between truth and *ahinsa*. But the more I thought of it the more it seemed to me that this line of questioning was painful to Mr. Gandhi. He did not like to consider even the possibility of such a conflict. As for the milk vow (which I had taken as the only example I could find) it was decidedly an ache in his tender conscience. He had said to me the other day: "I drink goat's milk even now. They say I cannot live without it. It is the weakness of the body."

I determined, therefore, to drop the subject and go on to the next, which—as I had already told him—was *The Kingdom of God Is Within You*. I had also told my friend Edgar Snow that this subject was coming next, and asked him if he wanted to come and listen. (Since there were so many people in the room already I was sure the Mahatma would not mind.) Owing to his interest in Tolstoy, I thought this would appeal to Ed, and it did. However, it was now Friday and there was no chance of getting Snow in time. (He was inaccessible by telephone.) The following subject, which I had intended for Sunday, would now come on Saturday. It was Jesus of Nazareth as a creative artist. To this I had thought of asking Margaret Parton of the *Herald Tribune*, who had great reverence for Gandhi.

Since these subjects were never to be reached, I may note here what the inquiry would have been, although I cannot even guess at Gandhiji's possible answers. The Tolstoy book, which influenced him deeply in his South African days and contributed a good deal to his distinctive invention of *satyagraha*, I had read only the year before. It is that late work in which Tolstoy condemns all the institutions of the state, including police and courts and law (besides, of course, conscription), on the confident assertion that the Sermon on the Mount contains all the rule that is necessary for man in society. When I read it I was taken aback by what I thought was naked anarchism, and neither then nor now could I see how this might be true in any society known to us. However, I knew that Gandhi had felt the weight of the book very much in his youth, and I wanted to know what he thought of it today.

The next subject—Jesus of Nazareth as an artist—was drawn from remarks Gandhi had made years before, published in *Young India* on November 13, 1924. These were:

"Jesus was, to my mind, a supreme artist, because he saw and expressed Truth; and so was Mohammed, the Koran being the most perfect composition in all Arabic literature—at any rate that is what scholars say. It is because both of them strove first for Truth that the grace of expression naturally came in; and yet neither Jesus nor Mohammed wrote on art. That is the Truth and Beauty I crave for, live for and would die for."

On the Wednesday he had said to me of the *Mahabharata* and the *Ramayana:* "I regard the stories in these epics as fictions, significant fictions, but not historical. Millions of Hindus regard them as strictly historical. I do not."

It was my intention to discover his opinion of the historicity of the Gospel narrative in the New Testament and then to find out what he meant by Jesus as supreme artist. I had an idea that it might be something akin to my own about him—that is, that he collaborated with destiny, helped fate to shape its course and his own, by some penetration of the truth of things.

I had no copy of *The Kingdom of God Is Within You,* but Tolstoy's argumentation was fairly fresh in my mind. I got a taxi and went out to Birla House in time for the prayer-meeting. This time I was alone. I stationed my taxi under a tree opposite the gate of Birla House and walked down the drive to the prayer-ground. It was not yet five o'clock and people were still streaming in on foot, in cars and with tongas. As I came on to the prayer-ground at the end of the garden I ran into Bob Stimson, the Delhi correspondent of the B.B.C. We fell into talk and I told him about the journey to Amritsar and what had taken place there. It was unusual to see any representatives of the press at the prayer-meeting; Bob explained that he had submitted some questions to the Mahatma for the B.B.C. and thought he might as well stay for the prayers since he was on the premises. He looked at his watch and said: "Well, this is strange. Gandhi's late. He's practically never late."

We both looked at our watches again. It was 5:12 by my watch when Bob said: "There he is." We stood near the corner of the wall, on the side of the garden where he was coming, and watched the evening light fall on his shining dark-brown head. He did not walk under the arbor this evening but across the grass, in the open lawn on the other side of the flower-beds. (There was the arbored walk, and a strip of lawn, and a long strip of flower-bed, and then the open lawn.) It was one of those shining Delhi evenings, not at all warm but alight with the promise of spring. I felt well and happy and grateful to be here. Bob and I stood idly talking, I do not remember about what, and watching the

Mahatma advance toward us over the grass, leaning lightly on
two of "the girls," with two or three other members of his
"family" (family or followers) behind them. I read afterward
that he had sandals on his feet but I did not see them. To me it
looked as if he walked barefoot on the grass. It was not a warm
evening and he was wrapped in homespun shawls. He passed by
us on the other side and turned to ascend the four or five brick
steps which led to the terrace or prayer-ground.

Here, as usual, there was a clump of people, some of whom
were standing and some of whom had gone on their knees or
bent low before him. Bob and I turned to watch—we were
perhaps ten feet away from the steps—but the clump of people
cut off our view of the Mahatma now; he was so small. Then I
heard four small, dull, dark explosions. "What's that?" I said to
Bob in sudden horror. "I don't know," he said. I remember that
he grew pale in an instant. "Not the Mahatma!" I said, and then
I knew.

What followed must be told just as it happened (*to me—me*)
or there is no truth in it.

Inside my own head there occurred a wavelike disturbance
which I can only compare to a storm at sea—wind and wave
surging tremendously back and forth. I remember all this distinctly; I do not believe that I lost consciousness even for a
moment, although there may have been an instant or two of
half-consciousness. I recoiled upon the brick wall and leaned
against it, bent almost in two. I felt the consciousness of the
Mahatma leave me then—I know of no other way of expressing
this: he left me. The storm inside my head continued for some
little time—minutes, perhaps; I have no way of reckoning. Then
I was aware of two things at once, a burning and stinging in the
fingers of my right hand and a similar burning and stinging in
my eyes. In the eyes it was tears, although of some more acid
mixture than I had known, and on my fingers I did not know
for a while what it was, because I put them in my mouth (like
a child) to ease the burning. In the wildness and confusion of
that moment a young Indian—unknown to me—came to where I
was doubled up against the wall and said: "Is he dead? Is he
dead?" The young Indian had staring eyes and was as filled with
horror as I was, I suppose, although I do not know why he asked

me such a question. "I don't know," I said, taking my fingers out of my mouth to do so.

Then I looked at my fingers. On the third and fourth fingers of my right hand blisters had appeared. They were facing each other, on the sides of those fingers which touch. The blister on the third finger was rather large and was already filled with water. The blister on the fourth or little finger was smaller. They had not been there before I heard the shots.

The storm returned inside my head, but briefly, very briefly. I sat on the edge of the wall and looked at my fingers and then put them back into my mouth: they burned far worse than is usual with blisters. What was this?

Then flooding into my memory came the visions in Vermont the summer before, the dreams since, the many, many dreams in which I had endeavored to interpose myself, my arm, my leg or my body between the inevitable murderer and Mahatma Gandhi. How could such things be? That was the question that streamed through my head incessantly. *How can such things be?* was the exact form in which it appeared, and came back again and again through the next hour and a half (or indeed at decreasing intervals for two or three days).

Now, of course, I know that the blisters were a psychosomatic phenomenon which, although curious and interesting, present no great element of novelty to science. For me, however, at that moment, they were an overwhelming evidence of connection with this dreadful deed—of my failure, at least, to die for the Mahatma, the last best hope of earth. An unspeakable misery consumed me.

It was during this time, apparently, that many things happened: a whole external series of events took place in my immediate neighborhood—a few yards away—and I was unaware of them. A doctor was found; the police took charge; the body of the Mahatma was carried away; the crowd melted, perhaps urged to do so by the police. I saw none of this. The last I saw of the Mahatma he was advancing over the grass in the evening light, approaching the steps. When I finally took my fingers out of my mouth and stood up, dry-eyed, there were police and soldiers and not many people, and there was Bob Stimson. He was rather breathless; he had gone somewhere to telephone to the B.B.C.

He came with me down the steps to the lawn, where we walked up and down beside the flower-bed for a while. The room with the glass doors and windows, by the rose garden at the end of the arbor, had a crowd of people around it. Many were weeping. The police were endeavoring to make them leave. Bob could not tell me anything except that the Mahatma had been taken inside that room. (On the following day he told me that he had seen him carried away, and that the *khadi* which he wore was heavily stained with blood.)

Presently Bob had to go and I was left alone in the garden. Almost everybody else vanished too; I think the police cleared the place several times. Why they did not put me out I do not know. (Since then I have thought that perhaps Mr. Nehru, who must have been there by then, told them to ignore me—it would consort with his great and subtle kindness.) I walked up and down beside the flower-bed, which I now observed to be filled with petunias of the same kind and colors as those which I had lately seen stretching beside the fountains and streams in front of the Taj Mahal. At this point I was numb with horror and went through these motions meaninglessly, only the surface of mind and body engaged. Underneath there was a deadness, a kind of suspended animation.

A young American came there and spoke to me. I took him to be a representative of the United Press. He said that he was not; that he was from the American Embassy and had never been to the prayer-meeting before; he had just arrived in India from China. He went away, and after a while he came back again. This time I thought he was from the Associated Press (confusing him, each time, with young Americans whom I actually had met). He told me again that he was from the embassy. I took in nothing that he said to me, but later on I learned that it was this young man who, at the moment of the assassination, actually captured the assassin and held him for the Indian police, and after turning the assassin over, searched the crowd for a doctor. When I knew this in the following week it gave me a sort of tribal pride to think that although I had been paralyzed and helpless, there was one of my breed who had been useful.

The garden now was almost empty and the sun was going

down behind the prayer-ground. There were two more people who came and spoke to me. One was a young Indian—perhaps the same one who had spoken to me on the prayer-ground—who was weeping bitterly. He said: "He will recover, won't he? He will recover?" I said these words exactly: "If he still has consciousness he may recover. He has great resources. But if he has lost consciousness he cannot recover. There is nothing the consciousness can do against a bullet." (I believed that his consciousness had gone because it had left me, but I did not want to say so to the woe-stricken young man.) Another Indian, much older, but also weeping bitterly, said: "This means some great disaster for the world, does it not?" I said: "I am afraid that you may be right."

Then they, too, went, as did the police, and the garden was absolutely empty except for me. This was the state of things for about an hour. Why I remained (and why I was allowed to remain) I do not know. I had some vague idea that perhaps Mr. Nehru would pass by and I could ask him if it was true or not. But this could not have been the real reason; it was what is called unconscious behavior. (Actually Nehru was on the other side of the house some of the time, speaking to the vast crowd that had assembled outside the walls; and part of the time he was in the room with the glass doors and windows, where the Mahatma lay, a few feet away from me.) I wandered between the rose garden and the petunia beds. With one part of my mind I was noticing these flowers and the neat little wooden labels that Mr. Birla's gardeners had stuck into the ground beside the roses. One yellowish rose was called "Lord Lonsdale," I remember, and even then (so peculiar is the human brain) I wondered why.

But most of the time I was prey to an unexampled misery. At times it submerged me so utterly that I lost all but the faintest surface consciousness of my surroundings. There was a small summer-house or perhaps family temple beyond the rose garden, a few feet beyond the glass room where the Mahatma lay. When I could no longer stand up or walk I had recourse to the steps of this small, closed house, leaning or sitting on the edge of them, more often than not bent in two. Words went through my head in two ways—two forms of what the behaviorists so naïvely call "talking with concealed musculature." One was the ordinary way of words pronounced, words sounding in the inner air. The other was precisely like ticker tape—words visible in the mind but unheard. Most of them were from Shakespeare or the Bible, and were undoubtedly thrown up by the unconscious memory, but with an agonizing suddenness and an effect of unbearable truth each time. One was quite incongruous, from Macbeth: *She should have died hereafter; there would have been a time for such a word.* (Incongruous, that is, for the pronoun *she*, but otherwise quite applicable.) Another was: *I cried to him from the depths and he answered me.* Another was: *Father, why hast thou forsaken me?* These last two appeared both verbally and visually in my mind many times, shaking my whole being each time.

I was helped out of this traumatic condition by the appearance of Bob Neville's wife and sister on the other side of the garden wall. His sister called: "Jimmy! Jimmy!" and I looked for the source of the sound. The wall of the garden was in baroque style with decorative circles. Through one of these I saw Bob's sister and wife, neither of whom spoke further; by their mere presence and their look I knew that they had felt something about my unfathomable unhappiness and wanted to help me. I therefore tried, with some success, the operation we call "pulling ourselves together"—I stood straight, breathed deep, dried my eyes and tried walking up and down beside the house, that is, on the side between the house and the garden wall. Here, in due course, Edgar Snow appeared. He was as shaken, I suppose, as everybody else in Delhi must have been on that day. I said to him: "I've lost my only *guru*. I'll never learn anything now." [1] He told me about Nehru's speech to the great crowd outside the walls.

We walked around the garden once, and even up to the prayer-ground, where Ed showed me the place where the Mahatma fell. The prayer-ground was empty, except for a soldier standing guard over that spot and the cartridge-shells which lay there at his feet.

Swirling and dense and immeasurable, like all Indian crowds, the great mass of people surrounded the house outside the garden

[1] Edgar Snow, in an article printed in *The Saturday Evening Post*, quoted me as saying: "The Western world has lost its only *guru*." I am sorry to say his memory is at fault: I neither said nor thought nor felt anything about the Western world on that day, but only inside myself. In that state I was incapable of generalization.

walls. It was very difficult to get through and out, but when we succeeded in doing so we found my taxi where I had left it two hours before, under the tree. I had, of course, forgotten it. It took us back to the city.

7

The Mahatma was cremated on the following day (Saturday, January 31, 1948) on the immense plain beside the river Jumna outside of Delhi in the presence of a vast multitude. There followed the thirteen days of mourning prescribed for orthodox Hindus of his particular caste. On the thirteenth day, which was February 12, 1948, his ashes were distributed to the seven sacred rivers of India.

VI

The River Flows to the Sea

Such was the end, Echecrates, of our friend: concerning
whom I may truly say, that of all men of his time whom
I have known, he was the wisest and justest and best.

PLATO: *Phaedo*

The River Flows to the Sea

*A*cross the street from where I lived in New Delhi was the house of the Krishna family—Shri Krishna, a leading economic and financial journalist, who (perhaps in self-defense against the aura of his own name) was an advanced free-thinker or professed to be such; his brother, Brij Krishna, a devout follower of Gandhi and a member of the Ashram for twenty-five years; Shri Krishna's wife and children and certain guests. Among these guests were Jai Prakash Narain, the leader of the Indian Socialist Party, and his silent, grief-stricken wife, who had been devoted to the Mahatma and spent a good deal of her day spinning. Jai Prakash had been educated in America. He became a Communist at one university (I think the University of Wisconsin) and later on a Socialist at another (I believe the University of Ohio). He was a quiet, thoughtful man, perhaps a year younger than myself (although he looked ten years younger), concerned not only with the Socialist and trade-union movement in India but with the general affairs of the world. I had met him first in Nehru's house and had two or three talks with him about his own subjects before the Mahatma's death. Jai Prakash wore homespun and

was, of course, a member of the Indian National Congress—it was
not until some months later that the Socialists left the Congress
for good—with a record of loyalty to the Congress in national
matters. There was something about him which vaguely reminded
me both of Gandhi and of Nehru, so that I had a tendency to
go to him in difficulty.

Thus it was now. From the time of Gandhi's death until the
following Wednesday—some four or five days—I was undoubtedly suffering from some kind of shock which disturbed
every part of my being. For two of these days I could not leave
my room, and when I did go out there seemed an unearthly
quality to every sight and sound, as if I had ceased to be there.
Once or twice I emerged to a fair degree of normality, as on the
evening four days after Gandhi's death when I dined with friends
in Old Delhi and to my astonishment faced an enormous beef-
steak. I had and have no prejudice against eating meat, naturally,
but I was amazed that the slaughter of cows and the sale of their
flesh was going on in the midst of this unparalleled national
mourning. (As a matter of fact it stopped the next day.) Another
time I went around Connaught Circle in the shops and saw
distinct signs of terror on the part of two or three Hindus who
worked in them. I realize now that this must have been because
of my appearance; I no doubt had a wild look in my eye. At the
time I took it to be a fear of the evil eye, or something of that
sort, since neither then nor afterward did I meet anybody in
India who had not somehow heard that I was at the prayer-
ground on that terrible evening.

These were fancies. But they were accompanied by some inner
experiences, during the many hours I spent alone, which can
hardly be described for a Western reader at all. During that
week I was very seldom out of my room, and except when Edgar
Snow came to tell me what was going on I had no idea of the
succession of events. On the day after the assassination (January
31) I had, at the request of the *Herald Tribune* correspondent,
Miss Margaret Parton, written some kind of account of what
my testimony in the matter might be, but although it took about
ten hours to write and seemed (in that condition) to be a form
of auto-vivisection, I kept no copy and have never read it since.

After some days of this chaos and misery, alternating, it is true, with hours of unprecedented clarity in which I understood more than I had ever understood in my life, I knew what I had to do: adopt some modified version of Gandhi's rules and join his followers for whatever the devotional aspects of their mourning might be until the immersion of his ashes in the river. It was then that I went across the street to see Jai Prakash.

He was sitting on the floor by a long open glass door through which the sun, warm that day, was flooding in. I sat on the sill and talked to him.

"I have rejected historic materialism once and for all," I said. "I believe in God."

This was, of course, the tremendous realization to which I had come in those sleepless nights.

What I expected of Jai Prakash after such an announcement I do not know, but what he actually said surprised me and sticks in my memory with all its surrounding circumstances. Shri Krishna's garden was full of flowers; it lay directly outside the door in which we sat; the sun was warm and bright. Jai Prakash looked out into the garden and said calmly: "Well, I believe in God too."

He surveyed the garden impassively for a moment or two, as if to indicate the kind of God he meant, and then turned his face back to me and smiled.

"What can I do for you?" he asked.

On that day I lunched with Shri Krishna and Jai Prakash and Brij Krishna and the rest. The food in time of mourning was "bland"—that is, it did not have all the peppers and spices which ordinarily appeal to Indian taste. (It was Gita food, in fact.) It was also vegetarian, and I liked it very much. Brij Krishna then explained to me the whole of the mourning customs—simplified a great deal, I believe, from more orthodox Hindu customs, but in any case beautiful and in the pure spirit of Gandhi. It consisted of morning and evening prayers and chants around the cremation platform beside the Jumna River.

From then on I went to the river every day from the Krishna house. There were always Brij Krishna, Mrs. Jai Prakash Narain and Ramdas or Devadas Gandhi, sons of the Mahatma. There were sometimes others. I do not know where the car came from;

it seemed to be different every day. We left at half-past eight in the morning and the service was at nine.

The great plain beside the Jumna was empty and arid except in the place where the Mahatma had been cremated four days earlier. There a rectangle of barbed wire had been built around the cremation platform and soldiers stood on guard. The plain stretched with an air of limitless space under the winter morning sun; you could not have guessed that a great city was near. The Jumna was barely visible from the place of cremation (the Rajghat). It was more inferred from the iron arch of its railway bridge in the distance than actually seen. The Gandhi family and followers sat on a mat or grass carpet which was spread in front of the cremation platform. The platform itself was buried under marigolds, and everybody who came there brought more. There were marigolds sold in the plain outside this enclosure. When I first entered the enclosure Krishna put some marigolds in my hand and told me to strew them on the platform. I did so; there was no other rite or ceremony that I was ever asked to perform during this time.

I brought with me Purohit Swami's English translation of the Gita, which, although I knew it to be rather distant from the original, was the one best known to me and most flowingly written. And it was for me, even the first time, a strange and penetrating pleasure to hear the Sanskrit sounds as I read the English. My ear is fairly just and has been much accustomed to music over the years, so that it was not long before I could fit the ancient chant to the English words with considerable precision. I grew to recognize a good many Sanskrit words by their sound—not only the names in the epic, of course, which are unmistakable, but the important words themselves—and derived an extraordinary peace and solace from their beauty. The chanting of the Gita was the main part of the morning service. The Gandhi girls knew it well, and one of them—one of the granddaughters or possibly Dr. Sushila Nayar—knew it exceptionally well and chanted in a pure, unfaltering voice from beginning to end, seldom looking at the book. Krishna, to whom I adhered like a leech, was the best of all: he held a book in his hands but I doubt if he ever even glanced at it. He sat in the true Gita position with a perfectly straight spine and never looked to right or left until the poem was finished.

After this there was a devotional hymn to Rama, in which the mourners encircled the cremation platform several times, clapping their hands rhythmically without sound, throwing marigolds upon it occasionally, or sometimes touching or re-arranging the marigolds already there. I did not take part in this on any occasion because I did not understand it, and, quite aside from my general insensitiveness to the devotional aspects of religion, I could not take part in a ceremony of which the sense was unknown to me. I therefore slipped out to the barbed-wire gate, put on my shoes and walked over by the river. On some of the other days I merely retired from the enclosure and stood there, watching the slow, graceful and calm progress of the procession around the platform. It was not sad, although its very calmness had a certain touch of melancholy; and at no time did I see evidence of emotion among these people—Gandhi's family and friends—for whom the light and warmth of their lives had gone. It would have been unworthy of their beliefs and his to show such emotion. And yet it was there—then and later at the Ganges I knew it was there.

My own thoughts kept me company on those mornings when the Gita was not wholly filling my mind. Words of Gandhi's as spoken to me kept coming back into my head, sometimes in his own imagined voice, sometimes as soundless words. Of these, by far the most common was: "Kurukshetra is in the heart of man." (Or, sometimes, "The battle of Kurukshetra.") To this my own consciousness set up a kind of response, as in a litany: "And there let it remain." This occurred a very large number of times during the days of mourning and afterward; I am still not exempt from such repetitions and probably never shall be. On one morning in particular there seemed to be some unusual aviation activity going on in the neighborhood of Delhi and planes flew over our heads repeatedly as we sat by the cremation platform. The closer the aircraft came the more insistently did this litany repeat itself in my mind:

"The battle of Kurukshetra is in the heart of man."
"And there let it remain."

The sacred books of the Muslims and Sikhs were read on some of these days in the afternoons, alternating with a chapter of the Bhagavad Purana (the eleventh) and parts of the Ramayana. I believe there were readings from the Koran on two days and from the Granth Saheb (the Sikh scripture) on two days. On one day (the Friday following Mahatmaji's death) the Gita was chanted through twice over.

On that Friday I fasted—as, indeed, I had fasted on the Friday preceding his death—not through any belief in the moral efficacy of fasting, but because it seemed to me an aid to understanding the point of view of those who had followed Gandhi for so long, and in whom, quite without speech, I was beginning to recognize friends. It is very curious that during this whole period I hardly spoke once to any of the people with whom I was so constantly in company. I knew all of their faces and should know them twenty years from now, but there did not seem to be any need for speaking. They included the entire Gandhi family, of course, and at various times coming and going to the Rajghat I did speak briefly with two of the Mahatma's sons, but in general I relied upon Krishna for my communication and such explanation as was necessary.

On the very first day he asked me if I had yet found the *Isha Upanishad*. I then learned that he, too, had been sitting on the floor and listening to my conversations with the Mahatma. (I shall never know exactly who was in that room: I was really conscious of nobody but Gandhi.) I told him that I had not found it, although I had searched every bookshop in New Delhi and had finally cabled to London for it. He took me to an establishment—not a bookshop at all; in fact it sold herbal concoctions and sanitary appliances—where the works of Aurobindo Ghose were for sale at a stall; there I obtained Aurobindo's edition of the *Isha*, which I hope I shall never lose.

Most of my time during these days I spent reading. At night, when I occasionally dined with European or American friends, it was like going into a different house, a different world. I suppose what I should have done was, in logic and common sense, to cease for a time from my ordinary frequentations, since they were so alien to what chiefly interested me (not to say obsessed). But I could not do that—I have never yet been able to do that.

The conversation of my Western friends on this precise subject seemed to me extraordinary. They were all very much interested in the assassin, for example. I had never had the slightest interest in the assassin from the moment I heard the shots. I knew it could only be some poor misguided ultra-nationalist (Hindu) youth, of the sort who commit such crimes all over the world, forever killing their truest friends for the sake of some hideous tribal misconception. It could not possibly have been anybody else, as I knew long before it happened (as I knew in Vermont before I went to India). When Edgar Snow came to my room on the second or third day after the martyrdom to tell me who the individual instrument was I received that information as something I had always known. In comparison with the tremendous objective and subjective earthquake of Gandhi's disappearance, what conceivable difference did it make about the assassin? I never heard any Hindu mention that young man then or afterwards, which was perhaps another thing that made the Hindu point of view in such matters so sympathetic to mine.

One day at the cremation platform I saw, to my surprise, Jai Prakash Narain. He came with the secretary-general of the Socialist Party of Bihar, who was also in Krishna's house and used to go out with us frequently. I do not know why I did not expect Jai Prakash to come to this place; he had loved Gandhi too, as did all Indians (including, probably, the youth who killed him). But my mind connected the notion of doctrinaire socialism with at least an anti-traditional, if not anti-religious intellectual position, and was surprised. (Some time earlier, before the assassination, I asked Jai Prakash if Gandhiji had ever read Karl Marx: he said that the Mahatma had read the first volume of *Das Kapital* during his last imprisonment—1942—and had not "liked" it.) The Socialist leader came into the enclosure like all the others, threw marigolds and went through the entire ceremony, including the Rama-chanting, with the impassive dignity which seems to be part of him.

On the night of February 10th, I was all packed for departure and went to bed early. The "bearer" who took care of me in that establishment—a Rajput from up in the hillls—and the Babu who managed the office were by this time my friends, privy to all my doings, and I told them both I had to be up at two in the morning to go to Birla House. They promised to get me out in time and to provide a taxi. Even yet I had not quite realized the uncompromising devotion of Indians to the things which touch their consciousness. They did it for the Mahatma, not for me, but at any rate they neither one went home that night and must have had very little sleep in their chairs in the entrance hall. At two o'clock they were both in my room, and—a thing unheard of at that hour in Delhi—Devi Singh, the bearer, brought hot water.

2

The streets were dark, empty, silent. At Birla House there were soldiers on guard but they did not stop us. The Babu and the bearer both had come with me. With my Western sense of how things are done I was uncertain about this, but after they had waited all night I could not refuse. In the dark garden we passed along between the wall and the house and reached the well-remembered rose garden. The glass doors of the Mahatma's room were open. Inside there was a little light. I took off my shoes and slipped in. There were perhaps eight or ten people in the room, chanting the Gita. I had not my English book with me, and there was not enough light to read it by even if I had had it; but by this time I had learned to recognize by the sound what part of the Gita was being chanted. There were the same faces—"the girls"; Mrs. Narain; Brij Krishna; a few others—and the same beautiful language with the accent of eternity in it.

The urn containing the Mahatma's ashes was in front of me. There were a few marigolds and other objects on the floor around it. There was nothing else in the room; the pallet was gone.

When I opened my eyes a moment or two later, after listening for the meaning of the Gita as well as for its sound, I saw that the Babu and the bearer had both crept into the room after me and were now sitting on the floor. I looked at the family in some alarm. I was afraid that this intrusion of total strangers was too much. And yet I need not have worried; they did not even notice. In retrospect I find it odd that at no time was I ever asked a question, except once at Rasulabad by an Indian journalist, during the period between the Mahatma's death and the immersion of his ashes, although the presence of so vast and red a foreigner (with such big feet, too) was obviously not ordinary.

The Gita proceeded to its sonorous end. I sat looking at the brass urn before me, remembering the gentle body that had been in that space so short a time (or was it long?) before. The battlefield of Kurukshetra is in the heart of man: *and there let it remain*.

After the Gita I asked Krishna if it would not be better for me to go to the station at once to avoid the crowd. He told me to go. The Babu and the bearer went with me. I thought as I left it that there was no place on earth I knew better than this garden.

The special train which was to carry the Mahatma's ashes to the confluence of the rivers was made up of third-class carriages, all swept and garnished but otherwise no different from the ordinary carriages used by the Indian poor. The difference was that on this train each place was reserved, with tickets which had been given out by Ramdas Gandhi the evening before, and the unimaginable overcrowding which is the chief characteristic of Indian third-class carriages was avoided. In the center of the train one carriage had been arranged as a sort of catafalque, with a platform or table covered with marigolds in the middle, on which the urn with Gandhiji's ashes would rest. This carriage containing the ashes was brightly lighted throughout the journey, so that any who beheld it, even by chance, could receive the darshan of that mighty spirit.

As a matter of fact it was to darshan—the darshan I had myself received from Gandhi—that I owed my presence on this train at all. The tickets were greatly in demand. The cabinet ministers, press correspondents and other busy people were going to fly to Allahabad on February 12th for the ceremony itself, and the train with the ashes was, in fact, for the family and immediate followers of Gandhi; but it was quite fabulous how many immediate followers there seemed to be when it came time to distribute tickets. Krishna had put me on the list but I never really felt sure of my place until I had occupied it.

In my compartment there were five Indian gentlemen, none of whom I knew; one of them, Roop Narain, a merchant in Old Delhi, was a devout Gandhian dressed completely in *khadi*

(without even a mill-made vest or jacket). He took my education in hand and we had some hours of discussion about the
"economics of the *charkha*," upon which he had strong opinions.
I had my Gita and some other books, with a few nuts, Baghdad
dates and tangerines to eat. There was a rule that no smoking or
chewing of betel-leaf should take place, which was quite easy
for me, as I had stopped smoking anyhow for this period. There
would be food at the end of the first day—*puris* and vegetables—
and some tea the following morning at Rasulabad. Otherwise the
Mahatma's own austerity would prevail.

Even at that early hour a crowd had begun to assemble and
await the darshan of the Mahatma's ashes. As I wandered along
the platform I saw some members of government circles as well
as Jai Prakash Narain. There were the daughters of Mrs. Pandit,
the Prime Minister's sister; there were some cabinet ministers
and the Gandhi family. There was also the very distinctive
apparition of Mrs. Asaf Ali, wife of the Indian Ambassador to
Washington at the time. (She had received a cablegram from
Gandhi saying: "Your place is in India." She had gone to the
New York airport to take a plane and heard the news of his
assassination on the radio there as she waited for it.) For the
most part, however, those who occupied the train with the ashes
(the "Asthi Special" it was called) were the immediate followers
of Gandhi, many or indeed most of them persons without political interest or activity.

The long journey of the train across the central plain of India
was an evidence—if any were needed—of how every inhabitant,
whatever his condition, felt this loss. I quote from my diary as
written in Benares on Friday, the 13th:

"Wherever the train stopped, and in a great many places where
it did not stop, crowds of people had assembled for darshan. In
many towns the behavior was impressively solemn. In empty
fields, at small villages and at crossroads it was even more impressive to see the peasants standing with their hands joined in
the attitude of prayer (this has become also an attitude of ordinary salutation) as the train passed. The terrific demonstration
was at Cawnpore, which we reached at about five o'clock on
Wednesday evening. An immense multitude, said to have been
at least half a million, had gathered there, in and around the rail-

road station and along the tracks into and out of the town. We stayed in Cawnpore Station two hours for the darshan and then had to leave before more than a proportion of the people had obtained it. As we pulled out, the excitement of the people could no longer be contained and their instinct moved them to cries of *"Mahatma Gandhi ki-jai!"* (Victory, or Triumph, to Mahatma Gandhi!) which was what they used to cry out to him in life. I thought this very thrilling, especially as it rose to a great height as we slowly pulled out of the city. Essentially the instinct of the people was right, although Jai Prakash told me he would have preferred silent reverence. . . .

"Bonfires and torches burned along our way during the night until we reached Rasulabad (how Muslim all these names are!) where we stopped for the night. In the morning at seven we resumed the journey and reached Allahabad at 9 A.M. (Thursday). Nehru, Mrs. Naidu, Pandit Pant, Patel and other dignitaries were there on the platform to receive the ashes. We then started the long march to the Sangam, the confluence of the rivers. I don't know how many miles it was but I felt exhausted at the end. (We had eaten only some fruit at noon the day before, vegetables at night, and nothing at all on Thursday, which may have had something to do with it.) By the Christian cathedral a choir sang 'Lead, Kindly Light.' Our procession was completely enclosed by lines of infantry soldiers, but children and other determined persons succeeded in infiltrating and joining the march."

That march was a long, dusty and (in the end) sweltering pilgrimage. An assemblage of people which may indeed have formed the greatest single crowd ever known had converged upon Allahabad. Hundreds of thousands had already been there for the religious fair (the "miniature" or at least minor replica of the great twelve-year fair called the Kumbh Mela which the Mahatma had so disliked in 1915). They had remained for the immersion of their Father's ashes, and millions had joined them. The whole crowd, from Allahabad station to the confluence of the sacred rivers, about seven miles away (as I later learned), was said to have numbered four million, the greater part of which had assembled in a dense mass on the great plain at the Prayag. (The word Prayag in Sanskrit usually means a coming-together of rivers, a confluence, but it can also mean pre-creation, and also a place of rites; as a place-name it is common in India and usually signifies confluence of rivers.)

It was a very long trudge, and I was grateful for the sturdy presence of Ganga Sharan, the Socialist Secretary-General for Bihar, who was my point of reference in the rather fluid mob which the procession became. Jai Prakash marched too, but I lost him before we had gone far. At the cathedral (Anglican, I suppose) where the choir of young Indian girls and boys sang "Lead, Kindly Light," the march was joined by what might be called a grimly Christian figure. This was an English gentleman in black-and-white striped trousers and a morning coat, with a solar topee on his head. He had a prognathous jaw and an air of defiance, as if to ward off all criticism. Besides myself, he was the only other foreigner marching in that procession so far as I know, but, unlike myself, he was obviously self-conscious at doing so. I thought he could only possibly be a clergyman from that cathedral, or rector of the church, if it was a church. A more inspissatedly English figure I have never seen.

The procession was preceded by the great white catafalque, covered with flowers, in the center of which Gandhiji's ashes had been placed. Accompanying the ashes on this vehicle were Mr. Nehru, Mr. Patel and other high officers of the government. The diary continues:

"As we came over a ridge and saw the Ganges and Jumna flowing together (having passed through a long stretch of tents and bazaars of the Kumbh Mela) the sight was indescribable: all that space was filled with people, the greatest concourse of people I have ever seen. . . . I saw the urn transferred from the flower-covered catafalque to an American amphibious truck which had been painted white. By now I was too tired to push forward and argue my way on to one of the boats. I sat on a convenient wooden platform and watched the duck go into the river and head upstream to the Jumna looking for deep water to come down in. Then I thought I could bear no more: I had seen Gandhiji to the river. I tried to get out to get back to Allahabad, but the enclosure had by now been sealed by ranks of soldiers with barbed wire beyond them and millions of people beyond that. I was disconsolately standing there wondering what

to do, by the gate, when two Americans with the same idea came
up and talked to one of the soldiers. I thought they were American photographers (one had a camera) and believed they would
get out if anybody could, so I joined forces with them. They
turned out to be two teachers from the Ewing Christian College
on the Jumna, a short distance away—one named James Alter
and the other John Bathgate. (Alter and Bathgate, of all things!)
After various combined efforts had failed they said the only way
would be by boat around the masses of people. By this time
thousands had gone into the river to bathe during the time of the
immersion of the ashes. James Alter, who speaks excellent Hindustani (he was born in India), haggled for a boat and we got it.
The sight from the river was extraordinary—a sort of religious
regatta, a combination of sorrow, joy, self-offering or dedica-
tion, and sheer pantheism in visible form."

This bald diary-language gives no hint of the scene's wonder
and beauty. It would at any time be strange to see two great
rivers, one bright yellow and one bright blue, coming together in
a sort of combative but ultimately harmonious union and thus
pursuing as one their way to the sea. But to see it on that day,
when so far as vision could reach on the Prayag side there was
an unexampled crush and density of human life, with thousands
of men, women and children advancing from it into the river,
was an experience of almost dreamlike singularity, unlike any
other. One had to think, too, that for all of these people there
was also a third river, the Sarasvati, coming in somehow or somewhere underground, filling with its mystic powers the already
sacred waters of the Jumna and Ganges, so that the "Triveni"—
the place of meeting of the three—was by all odds the most
powerful of such bathing-places in its power of suggestion to the
popular imagination. The Sarasvati was a real river in ancient
times, although I am not sure that it converged with the others
just here. It was obviously part of the Ganges system, although
I do not believe the scholars can agree on its course; but it has
long since vanished. That makes no difference. Its name is also
the name of the goddess of learning in the popular pantheon.
What these wholly mythical entities add to the physical water
of the Jumna and Ganges in the consciousness of those who bathe
there I do not know, but the mystic three was all-important in

everything written about it in India, and the word "Triveni" has survived the riparian trinity to which it refers. The sun was very bright; it was by now late afternoon; the boatmen who rowed Alter and Bathgate and me up the blue Jumna obviously took a purely professional view of the occasion, which had enabled them to charge a price which my Christian friends regarded as extortionate.

We introduced ourselves actually after we got into the boat; I still thought my new friends were photographers until then. Alter picked up my Gita and saw my name in it, which he knew because of another book, and new avenues of conversation opened. Among other things, these missionary teachers told me that "Lead, Kindly Light" and "When I Survey the Wondrous Cross," the two Christian hymns Gandhi loved above all others, were constantly sung in their college whenever Gandhi was uppermost in the mind of India, which was extremely often. During the past month, they said, these hymns had been sung at every chapel service. The association of these hymns with Gandhi was, and for many years had been, implicit to all Indian Christians and other Christians living in India—no explanations were ever required.

We came at last to the Christian College, which had great sweetness and calm after the mass-passion we had just traversed. It was, of course, empty, since students and faculty alike had gone to the Triveni. Mr. and Mrs. Alter gave me some food, the first I had had that day, and although neither one of them smoked, their household servant—a Hindu untouchable—gave me two cigarettes. Afterward Alter succeeded in finding an *ekka*, an astonishing little platform drawn by a horse, on which the passenger perches most insecurely; on this I was conveyed into Allahabad through the teeming mob, with Alter valiantly escorting me on his bicycle.

The station at Allahabad was pandemonium. All trains were late, very late, and crowded to suffocation with people. It was quite impossible even to get near a ticket window. I could not find my own carriage in the special train from Delhi for a long time; information was unobtainable; even to walk along a platform was well-nigh impossible because of the throngs that had settled there in little whirlpools of movement and rest, some

patiently seated on their belongings and others aimlessly agitated
and shouting. In this predicament Jai Prakash—it was getting to
be a habit—came to my rescue. When I saw him in the station
dining-room I told him my troubles: I wanted to go to Benares.
He said he had a compartment to Mogul Serai, the junction for
Benares (he was going on home to Patna), and could give me a
bunk in it if I would be at the station at eleven that night. Jai
Prakash, calm and unruffled, looked as if he had not, like the
rest of us, been through a harrowing day.

I went back to dinner with my Christian friends and returned
to the station at the appointed hour. I found Jai Prakash's compartment filled to overflowing with visiting Socialists from Allahabad. I did not know until later that night that among other
things Mr. Narain was also head of the Indian railway workers'
union, which explained his ability to work miracles in this tu-
multuous hour. The train finally departed and we all went to
sleep on our bunks (Mrs. Jai Prakash had been asleep all along,
the sleep of exhaustion). Before he turned in, Jai Prakash wrote
a letter of introduction for me to Bhagavan Das, the author of
The Essential Unity of All Religions, at Benares.

Then at Mogul Serai he had to turn out again because I had
no ticket (this was at three in the morning). He worked his
usual magic with the station-master and I was allowed to buy my
ticket there. I did not see him again in India that year.

The train from Mogul Serai reached Benares in the fresh,
bright morning hours, seven o'clock perhaps, and I had my first
impression of the holy city in the correct light. It was much later
when I went out on the Ganges in a boat, with a guide, and saw
for the first time that famous row of hostels and temples, burning ghats and bathing places, which edge the sacred shore. During
my days there I did a fairly assiduous amount of sightseeing, including a visit to the Temple of the Master of the World and
actually a glimpse of the worship of the Shiva-linga through a
hole in the wall. The phallic symbol (if it be called phallic—a
great block of stone) was worshipped with flowers and Ganges
water: there was nothing in it to shock the most captious, so far
as I could see. I did not even sympathize much with the criticisms
that had been made by the Mahatma himself. The temple did not
seem to me particularly dirty, and as for the flower-vendors,

souvenir hawkers and priests, they were much less troublesome
than their breed often are in the West (not to speak of the Church
of the Holy Sepulchre in Jerusalem). It is also true that my own
imagination was more stirred by the ruins at Sarnath, where the
Lord Buddha preached his first sermon, than at the great temple
in Benares; a ruin has always an advantage in this respect over
the continuing and living thing, ever at the mercy of temporary
failures in taste.

From Benares I went on by plane to Lucknow, where I stopped
a few hours to see Mrs. Naidu. She had been ill ever since the
immersion of the Mahatma's ashes; but she received me at once,
sitting up in bed and displaying no sign of debility. The charm
and wit of her commerce have been celebrated in India for many
years, and I understood why. She it was who succeeded Mahatma
Gandhi in the Salt March, made salt after him and went to jail
for it. She told me now that at the time she had not really understood the full power of the symbol—she had done it because it
was what he wanted done, but without the comprehension that
came later. She also told me how she had first met him—in London
in 1914, when he was staying in some boarding house in Blooms-
bury of which she could remember even the stair carpet. She went
to see him—she, rich and fashionable and already celebrated as a
poet—because Gokhale had told her about him. She found him
seated on the floor on what she described as a worn-out black
blanket, with various small dishes and pots around him. He was
eating his midday meal. He looked up at her (quite an apparition,
she must have been: I see her in a gorgeous brocaded sari, with
jewels) and said: "Well, you must be Mrs. Naidu. Will you
share my meal?" She looked down at the assorted experimentation which surrounded him and replied: "Certainly not." Thus
began an association of the deepest affection and esteem on both
sides. Mrs. Naidu told me a number of wonderful things about
the Mahatma—including a story or two which managed to touch
and amuse at the same time, in the peculiar way Gandhi had—
and of these there is one remark I am not likely to forget so long
as I can remember anything. "He taught us to be just," she said,
"when it is so much easier to be generous."

From Lucknow I proceeded on the night train to Kathgodam,

at the end of the railway, and thence by bus up through the mountains to Almora. Here, in the house of Boshi Sen and his wife (Gertrude Emerson), I had a week of unexampled tranquillity. They had asked me to come there at a time when I did not know in the very least where Almora was; I had some vague notion (because it was in the United Provinces) that it was down in the plain; although I had known Gertrude for many years, since she had been an editor of *Asia* magazine, I had only met her husband once in New York and had no idea of what his work was. He was and is, of course (as many know), a plant physiologist of international reputation, whose laboratory work at present is partly supported by the Government of India. He had been a student of J. C. Bose and worked with him on the experiments which proved the "irritability" (as scientists say—I should have preferred "sensitivity") of plants. But he was also, as I now discovered, a *chela* of the Swami Sadananda, the first disciple of Vivekananda, and felt not the slightest contradiction between his philosophical idealism or monism and scientific work. The universalist aspect of the Ramakrishna-Vivekananda movement was implicit in all that he said of it, and Gertrude—who had been married to him for twenty years—was as familiar with this all-embracing will to harmony as he himself. The house looked out across an intervening valley to the sweep of the Himalaya, crowned directly opposite by the shining whiteness of Shiva's Trident. The Trident was not always visible, but when it was it asserted something which, by means of beauty but beyond beauty, compelled the imagination of man to consider the long road of his destiny. No wonder that the whole of the Hindu view of life comes at some point or other to the contemplation of the Himalaya. These towers of ice and snow, the abode of the gods in the primitive mind, cannot be compared to any other mountain range. There hangs about them the air of an origin and a terminus, the beginning and the end, confronting the bold manikin with an earth-spectacle no less intimidating than the parade of the stars in heaven, but more immediate to his perception, as beneath the unmelting snow of the ultimate barrier there lies also the dust that is akin to the dust of his feet.

3

In Almora it was necessary to think. It probably would have been necessary in any place where a breathing-spell was afforded; it was more necessary here. Indeed, the weight of evidence suggested that this discovery had been made before. Almost every Indian thinker or leader mentioned in these pages had been to Almora for a stage of its own peculiar repose. This was true of a number of those who brought about the Hindu revival, including Vivekananda but not Ramakrishna; it was certainly true of Gandhi; he had even once (in 1924) thought of retiring to the hills in this neighborhood to meditate and study for the rest of his life. According to a friend in the Ramakrishna Mission, Gandhi at this period had actually prayed for retirement; if his counsels had been rejected by the country (and chiefly by the Congress) he could have withdrawn with a clear conscience and devoted himself to the Himalayan preoccupation with God. Mr. Nehru, too—although involuntarily—had experienced Almora's encouragement of meditation: his last jail sentence before he became Prime Minister was served here, in the prison high on a hill at the other end of the town. We visited that prison partly because I was curious about one statement made in Nehru's last book (it was made either of this prison or of the one at Dehra Dun): that the clouds came into his cell. This may have been chilly to the body, but was in itself an idea of such curiously poetic suggestion that I wanted to see it for myself. The prison warder took us to see his cell, and—lo!—the clouds came in. They drifted along wispily, gently, and I do not suppose they ever amounted to a really full-bodied cloud, but there they were, just the same, striating the whole prison toward the end of the day.

In my room—where Tagore had stayed for some time, years before—there was a place for me to work. I wrote there the article about Gandhi which I was expected to do for *Holiday* magazine, and sent it all from the post-office in the town, by radio to America. Nothing of the kind had occurred in Almora before, but it was remarkable how impassively they all took it. The lengthy telegrams, one a day, were sent over a period of five or six days and must have clogged the wires to Bombay, but there was no protest. I have an idea that it was again the magic of Gandhi's name that subdued all difficulty. In any case this work obliged me, just as the surroundings obliged me, to consider what had been the meaning of the events I had just traversed.

In the first place it was clear that some kind of precognitive or premonitory pulsation of far more than ordinary power had been at work here. There are dozens of witnesses to the certainty with which I had foreseen Gandhi's martyrdom. (I must have told my theory of the "theophanic moment" to everybody I knew in Delhi—the theory will be explained in a moment.) Journalistic "prescience," as they call it, which is a sort of inference from known facts, could not account for these phenomena. I must therefore suppose some instinctive attachment of unusual strength to the idea of Gandhi not only as an embodiment but as a *persona*—that is, to the idea of Gandhi as distinguished from, or continuing out of, the physical life which had now come to an end. This idea must have wielded far more sovereign influence upon my inconscient (subconscious, unconscious, subliminal or transmarginal consciousness) than I had ever supposed: how else could the blisters on my fingers have happened? More than any other one thing in the whole nexus of experience, inner and outer, those blisters convinced me: they were a simple physical fact of (it is true) psychological origin, but at the same time a very ordinary fact, as plain as a broken leg even if less drastic.

I had to face two such facts of colossal importance to any human being in search of a clue to the meaning of life. One was concrete and irrefutable, small but with incalculable consequences in one's attempt to achieve coherence in a view of the world: the blisters. These flatly contradicted a whole array of supposed knowledge about the human body. If it was possible for those blisters to appear for no physical reason within a few minutes (very few) after the shots were fired at Gandhi, then what impossibility can one name with assurance in all the strange stories of the past? What of "faith healing" and what of Lourdes? And if you begged the question by introducing the word "psychosomatic" what had you done? Nothing at all: nobody really knows what psychosomatic phenomena are. It is a realm so shadowy that the best work on the subject fails to convince.

I, at any rate, had no choice in the matter: there were blisters. Therefore much is unknown.

The second fact I had to face was that the solitary or inner experience through which I had passed between February 1st and February 5th in my room in New Delhi—not continuously, of course, but at certain hours in the middle of some of those nights—had given me the absolute certainty of the existence of what is called, in general, God. By God I mean the transcendent and immanent spirit: a field of being above and beyond ours but accessible to it under given conditions. The experience is not at all rare; it was rare only to me, because I had never had it in forty-eight years. When I encountered it in books (in variant forms—I have never encountered in any book just what happened to me) I had always disbelieved it flatly or else "interpreted" it in accordance with the supposed laws of Freud, Jung, or some other system-builder.

I was now compelled to see that whatever these analyses might yield, they could never explain away a stubborn thing like a fact. A fact is a fact is a fact. I had two facts which nothing on earth could shake: blisters on my fingers and a realization of God.

Now, of course, when I pursue this further and make a more precise delimitation of what I mean by God, it becomes evident that my own experience was a poor thing. When I say God I am using the word which, in the considered opinion of mankind, most fundamentally applies to the field of being which has been recognized at all times and places, by the generality of men, as beyond physical nature. With me this did not mean a named deity or a personification of any sort: the experience was quite devoid of anthropomorphic aspects. It was a lifting of my own being into another field: no more. To devout members of exclusive religious organizations, each with a set of consecrated and revealed truths contradicting each other, this may not seem like a realization of God at all. And to the Hindu mystic, who goes at that goal as a lifework of passionate asceticism and aspiration, it would also seem that these few hours during a few nights could mean nothing. I can only repeat that for me they are a fact because they happened, and there is no part of my view of life that does not require rearrangement or at least adjustment as a result of them. I found myself, in Almora, awkward and astonished and novice-like at the job, actually talking to Boshi Sen about such things in a totally new vocabulary, as if I were learning a new language. There is a delight in speaking a new language, but much time must pass before it can come easily and naturally to the unaccustomed tongue.

However, even though my "spiritual" experience (if that is the correct name for it) was of the most rudimentary character —not to be compared to those tremendous revelations which are to be found in religious literature—it was nevertheless so real, so overwhelmingly real, that it compelled me to reject an entire set of pseudo-sciences and partial sciences as aids to the comprehension of life. I could no longer believe, for example, that the relations of the classes in society, the means of production or the economic system, governed the acts of men and therefore all human history. I had always had my doubts about dialectical materialism because it was too machine-like, too dogmatic; I now knew that it was simply wrong. It left out of human history the chief element: its humanity. Humanity by definition is that part of nature which is distinguished from the rest by an ability to think and feel. By thought and feeling it has very often reached perceptions of the kind I had in Delhi in February, 1948, but I had not hitherto been able to treat them with the seriousness they deserved. It was quite clear to me now that these communications between soul and oversoul, as Emerson would have said, really do take place and that in the case of gifted and powerful personalities such as that of Mr. Gandhi they play a tremendous part in the history of the world—a part which it is downright childish to explain away in terms either of Marx or of Freud. The third and most majestic analysis, that of Einstein, did not attempt to explain away any part of human life, but even at Almora I thought I was aware that its estimate of the universe was in perfect accord with that which might be reached by the ways of thinking which had now been opened to me.

Let me go back from Almora to the farmhouse in Vermont where all this started in the summer of 1947. At that time I was attempting to subject the purposive patterns (accidentally or delusionally purposive, I thought) of human destiny to the analyses of Marx, Freud and Einstein, whom I called—with that jocularity we often apply to our most serious preoccupations,

thinking to make them less portentous thereby—"my three Jew-
ish doctors." By much effort and, to be frank, very bitter suffering, I succeeded in getting all teleological notions out of my head,
thoroughly expelled any lingering or intrusive idea of God, and
finally arrived at a formula which, it seemed to me, deprived
destiny of its power over the mind. This formula was as follows:

"The concatenation of the circumstances sometimes, or even
quite often, becomes snarled in a way which produces indications
of pattern in the incidence of the occurrences."

This was the best I could do in the way of showing how, in
terms which had nothing contingent about them, one could explain away the unfolding of an almost *composed*—logically unfolding and therefore quite predictable—drama such as that of
Hitler. I was attempting to explain the appearance of destiny
without introducing ideas of God, fate or other extra-physical
forces. It was this formula which I had hoped sooner or later to
present to Gandhi, after much preliminary exploration, to see if
he could accept it as offering an alternative to the supernatural.

Well, as a matter of fact, I not only had been unable to present
my formula, but Gandhi himself, by his words, acts and death,
had conclusively disproved it. He had not only disproved it but
had set up such a tremendous earthquake in my own being that
I was compelled, from now on and henceforth, to accept his
central truth as being not only his view, but, by compelling evidence imposed upon me after his death, the simple truth as it is
and ever will be.

It was necessary to consider, therefore, what Gandhi had most
decisively communicated to me and whether his "theophanic
moment," as I called it, had taken place according to the logic of
the sacred drama as I had understood it.

The principal thing he communicated to me was the necessity
of the renunciation of the world. He was at great pains to show
that the fruits of action are not forbidden and that the world
could be enjoyed, providing it is first renounced. This means, of
course, that a man must at all times be ready to give his life for
his truth. It involves a great decision, which, once made, can
never be retracted. Gandhi had himself decided long ago and
since then had never been afraid. Centrally, over-riding every-

thing else, the truth was for him sovereign and identified with the idea of God. The fruits of action might be anything; the world received as a gift of God might be anything; but if the renunciation had first taken place, thoroughly, fully, in the heart, then the consequences, good or ill, could not affect the steadfastness of the soul. This was what aroused him to his most earnest effort with me; it was then that he sent for the *Isha Upanishad*.

Now, it is quite evident that upon this supreme principle he lived out his whole life in its last forty-five or fifty years, constantly purifying the concepts, it is true, and reaching an almost unearthly purity at the end. Was this his "theophanic moment"?

According to my understanding of certain rare spirits, they attain a moment in which their own communication with the higher field of being becomes so absorbing that it is evident even to others, at some point or other in their activity upon the stage of history. We may discern a series of "theophanic moments" in the life of St. Francis of Assisi, for example, beginning with his service to the lepers and going on through the sermon to the birds (even if it is only a legend) to the extraordinary episode in which the Saracen commander permitted him to pass from the Crusaders' lines through the army of Islam and in to Jerusalem. I think in another sphere, unrelated to ecclesiastical establishments and therefore of a plainer nature, Abraham Lincoln's "theophanic moment" occupied the last year and a half, roughly, of his life, producing state papers, public speeches and even private letters from which there exhales a species of prayer. I have had the idea that this took place—or rather came from the private realm of being into the external manifestation—because of the death of Lincoln's own son, which connected a personal grief with the grief of a whole nation over its sons, and, combining with all the circumstances of a fratricidal struggle and an unknown future, in the end lifted his genius to a generalization both deep and high, giving him the permanent quality (from the roots to the firmament) of man aspiring. Once he had taken on this dimension of larger-than-life and more-than-life, martyrdom was demanded by the inner logic of his drama, which was also, in its way, sacred.

This way of thinking was empirical in origin: it arose from my own observation of the tendency in certain kinds and configura-

tions of human affairs toward enactment, as in a drama written
by a playwright, of inexorable developments. It did not presup-
pose the drama, it merely observed it. The question then became
imperative: *how could such things be?* It was the question that
imposed itself over the hurricane of my mind after I had heard
the shots that ended Gandhi's life.

But I was quite clear in Almora—and clearer during the months
of reflection that followed—about one thing, which was that
Gandhi's great, personal and peculiar genius, so clear-eyed and
sane in its treatment of the phenomenal world, had understood
all this long ago and faced it in January, 1948, with an equanimity greater than courage. How tranquilly he walked to his
death! One of the secrets of his influence upon Christians was
that he was incessantly reminding them of Christ, whether he
wished to do so or not; and for all who were born into Christian‐
ity there must be a mighty substratum in the consciousness which
stirs to respond at such reminders. But what he had communicated to me—*renounce the world and receive it back again as the
gift of God*—was not Christian, but Hindu. It was the kind of
Hinduism Christians might be expected to understand, but it was
profoundly Hindu just the same. The whole of Hinduism since
remote antiquity had based its estimate of the validity of a search
for God upon renunciation of the world. ("No man could hope
to get a hearing in religious matters in India," says Sir Charles
Eliot, "unless he has first renounced the world.") And yet this
death of a Hindu saint and hero, accomplished in a manner recognizable to Christians as being a Christian manner, was, in fact, for
the sake of Islam. Gandhi died for all of us, but primarily for the
Muslims. Now, although it is quite true—as Gandhi tirelessly
pointed out—that the Prophet Mohammed never undertook a
jihad or holy war without fasting and prayer and prolonged consultation of the higher field of being to which he had access, and
although it is also true that he never undertook a war which was
not *jihad*, or holy war, under the will of God as he knew it, still,
by and large, the sacrifice of the one for the many is not an
Islamic idea. Outside of certain mystics (chiefly Persian or under
Persian influence), Islamic writers and leaders have not been
averse to violence; many have treated it as a high good in the

test of man's virtue, and the Gandhian view of life, which is intimately related both to the traditional Hindu view and the purer or earlier Christian view, does not harmonize well with the ruling ideas of Islam. And yet this sacrifice, offered for peace— peace everywhere, the peace of the world—was, in its most precise and limited immediate sense, poured out for Islam.

"Does the certainty precede the renunciation?" I had asked.

"*No, no. The renunciation precedes the certainty.*"

And of course at Almora even more than elsewhere, the litany of Gandhi's truth, as it had occurred to me innumerable times beside his cremation platform, came back with the force of prayer:

> "Kurukshetra is in the heart of man."
> *And there let it remain. And there let it remain.*

4

In the house of Gertrude and Boshi it was possible to bring the whole subject of Gandhi's life and death down to a humane comprehension which included many tender reminiscences. Both had known him and remembered episodes here and there over the past decades. (Neither was inclined to accept his interpretation of the Gita—indeed, I have found nobody yet who does.) At this time, extraordinary events were taking place all over India, testifying to the depth with which the departure of the country's father was felt. To most Indians, life without Gandhi was very nearly inconceivable. In the first onrush of grief, after the ashes had gone into the river, there were determined efforts on the part of many thousands of Hindus to get the gates of the temples opened to the untouchables. This had been one of Gandhi's projects, urged upon his compatriots in and out of season as a means of breaking down untouchability. In various parts of India Hindus of high caste joined with untouchables in attempts to penetrate the temples, and large numbers of them offered *satyagraha*—submitted to arrest and imprisonment—in this cause. In the result, laws were passed in several provinces opening the temple doors to the outcasts and another step was taken toward the abolition of Hinduism's most unlovely excrescence.

The Sens and I used to sit in the evening and listen to the radio telling of this and other manifestations of the nation's profound sorrow. Boshi talked to me a good deal about Tagore—the "Gurudev," or divine teacher—whom he had known well. He had a good many volumes of Tagore in his library, including one of fugitive poems collected and published posthumously by the Shantiniketan school. I tried to imagine, as Boshi talked, what Tagore and Gandhi must have been like together—Tagore, so beautiful, with magnificent hair and beard luxuriating around the countenance of a king, and Gandhi, the poor, the humble, the meek and merciful, with his ears at right angles and his beggar's garments. I think they did not understand each other very well for some years after Gandhi's return to India. But there came a time when the resplendent Tagore, a prince out of the *Mahabharata*, went to the courtyard of a jail and sang his songs for the meek little hero. That was at Yervada prison, in the 1930's, after Gandhi had fasted to prevent a separate electorate for untouchability (a perpetuation of the system he hoped to destroy). What songs Tagore sang I know now (I found it in a book: thanks to many books, I am not quite so ignorant as I was in Almora). But at Almora I did not know. I found a poem of Tagore's in that posthumously printed volume which seemed to me to fit the case. It was one of his Bengali patriotic songs, written for music and dated 1905. It sang out from the page at me— it seemed to me then precisely written for Gandhi, and not only for Gandhi but for the very Gandhi I had seen on the afternoon of Friday, January 30th, walking into the sunset. It was the Gandhi of India, without any of those innumerable other meanings (O world, O life, O time!) which beset the Western mind in contemplating him. I liked to think—even against the evidence —that one of the songs Tagore sang to Gandhi was this:

> *Blessed am I that I am born to this land*
> *and that I had the luck to love her.*
> *What care I if queenly treasure is not in her store?*
> *Precious enough is for me the living wealth of her love.*

The best gift of fragrance to my heart is from her own flowers
and I know not where else shines the moon
that can flood my being with such loveliness.
The first light revealed to my eyes
was from her own sky
and let the same light kiss them
before they are closed for ever.

VII

The Appeal to Spirit

I fear our mistakes far more than the strategy of our
enemies.

THUCYDIDES: *The Funeral Oration of Pericles*

O Will, remember, that which was done, remember!
O Will, remember, that which was done, remember!

Isha Upanishad, 17

The Appeal to Spirit

When we consider Gandhi's teaching as a whole we see plainly that it falls into two distinct categories, that which concerns all men and that which concerns the special condition of India in the twentieth century. For Indian conditions as he found them, his revival of the spinning-wheel was a leap of creative genius, serving a dozen or more ends at once, helping to clothe the nakedness of the poor—which was its original object—and at the same time serving mightily as an instrument in the struggle for freedom against a foreign government, inculcating self-reliance and taking the whole Indian national movement to the very root of the matter, the seven hundred thousand impoverished villages of India. In the same way the Salt March, a symbolization of imperishable power over the imaginations of all men, was primarily effective in the specific Indian condition of 1930 and is unlikely to have progeny in the Western world unless it is translated into other terms. In like manner we could go through a long list of ideas, organizations, activities and velleities in which Gandhi manifested his unceasing care for the half-starving millions of a country which received back from him what it had bestowed upon him, the gift of life.

But it has been our business to inquire, in this book, not only into those aspects of his teaching which aroused and effectively created the Indian nation, but also into the more general aspects of truth which profoundly concern the life and future of humanity. If we consult the literature of the subject, which is already very large, we shall find that estimates of the value of Gandhi's message in this respect vary widely between one extreme—ably expressed in Richard Gregg's book called *The Power of Non-Violence* (1934)—which would generalize to all the earth the exact techniques of mass non-violence as they were practised in India, and another extreme, expressed in a considerable number of books and in the lectures of Professor Toynbee, which regard Gandhi's teaching as unsuited to the world outside of India, impractical and impracticable, a mere saintly aspiration.

Any Western mind acquainted with the way of the world will concede at once that a good deal of Gandhi's ethical and moral teaching was much too ascetic for general acceptance, either in India or anywhere else. He always insisted that he was not a saint and that anybody could do what he did; he never made a rule for others that he did not obey himself, and it therefore seemed to him that the others could do likewise. He was wrong, just as Socrates, the Buddha and Jesus Christ were wrong: humanity may esteem all the virtues but it is incapable of attaining them except in individual examples. The very respect paid to saints in the West and in the East is a proof of their rarity. The three aims of Gandhi's endeavor—*satya, ahinsa, brahmacharya*—truth, non-violence (or love) and chastity—are alike in one thing, which is that the overwhelming majority of men cannot reach them in a pure form for long at a time. Moreover, "disciplinary resolutions" and the like are quite outside the chosen range of any ordinary life, which is, as a rule, much too taken up with the simple business of living to indulge in such interruptive (or disruptive) experiments. A learned monk of the Ramakrishna Order, writing to me recently about Gandhi, said that in his opinion the Mahatma had attempted to generalize, and to introduce into the ordinary life of the workaday world, a set of spiritual values which throughout Hinduism's long history has always been restricted to the monastic orders. This is certainly true from the standpoint of objective history: until Gandhi came along no great Hindu teacher ever tried to make ordinary men behave like monks. The Lord Buddha made a sharp distinction between those who followed his rule and those who lived in the ordinary world. Gandhi's effect as an ethical teacher and moralist was profound (as witness what he did to the institution of prostitution in the great cities, tremendously mitigating its conditions and limiting its extent); he shook every abuse and evil that had grown up around Hinduism; his influence upon millions of individual lives was great; but on the whole it can be said that he aimed too high, and that what he asked his people to do was beyond their capacity. In the celebrated argument between Gandhi and Margaret Sanger on birth control, for example—abstinence or self-restraint as against contraceptives—it is clear that Mrs. Sanger won. In India today, what birth control there is is accomplished by her methods, not his.

And, further, some of the other lessons he had to teach by precept and example were of so general a nature that the world was quite content to admire without emulating, as it had done many times before. Such virtues as poverty (and I agree with William James that poverty of the voluntary, the heroic kind, is indeed a virtue) are not envied in the West, and even in India the esteem given to the holy beggar is limited. Humility is difficult, so immensely difficult that when it occurs in a pure state, as it did in Gandhi all through the last part of his life, it arouses a form of affectionate reverence (not unmixed with amusement); but it is not a steady influence upon the consciousness of men. The same may be said of meekness, mercy, compassion, willingness to serve all human beings—all this has been seen repeatedly through the history of the human race and has produced little or no social effect. The most one can discern is, as in St. Francis, Ramakrishna and some others, the origination of a new stream of pity which takes the form of a new monastic order, a new body of men specifically vowed to perpetuate these qualities by an organized life of service. In the case of Gandhi not even that result will be seen, because he was at all times opposed to anything savoring of sect, faction, or indeed of any Gandhian religious particularity. It is easy to guess that he had a dread of being made into some sort of god after his death (the process had gone pretty far even during his lifetime); this is why his family, in obedience to what they knew to be his wishes, destroyed every relic and every part of his body, excepting only the blood-stained *khadi* that he wore on that Friday. Superstition will have no Gandhi relics to serve as pretext for the building of vast temples in a land of abject poverty: this was what he would most have disliked. If it be that the irresistible instinct of the people decides he was an incarnation of Vishnu or Krishna—as is more than likely—then there will be nothing the government of India or the Gandhi family or anybody else can do about it; but at least this development will not be encouraged. Although Gandhi, as he said, "did not disbelieve in idol worship," it is perfectly clear that the sense in which he believed in it (or tolerated it) was that of compassion for the illiterate mass of the very poor, dependent upon little figures of clay to represent the pantheistic presence which they all—under the incrustations of superstition—really worship.

What, then, remains? If the great virtues of Gandhi arouse no emulation—or at least no more than did the similar virtues of Buddha, Jesus Christ and a long line of Buddhist and Christian saints—and if his specifically Indian mission was accomplished at the time of his death (in so far as it ever will be); and if, moreover, the careful and elaborate techniques of non-violence as put into practise in political struggles during his lifetime cannot or do not apply to Western conditions, what is to be retained from his teaching for the benefit of all men? Is it merely another *imitatio Christi*, a beautiful and inspiring mystic poem, a vain oblation? Out of the indefatigable creative activity of so great a genius—so great a spirit, let us say boldly—is there no surviving principle to animate the struggle of men who come after him?

I think there is. I believe that Gandhi's supreme invention, discovery or creation was *satyagraha*. Whether we translate this word as soul-force or as truth-force, as "the firmness of truth" or "the resolution of the soul," we know now what it means. It consists of voluntary sacrifice for the truth. It is one of those ideas which appear on earth with the utmost rarity, and I am unable to discover any precedent or parallel to it in the whole of history. There are baffling cross-currents and vague resemblances, but nothing that approaches *satyagraha* in its completeness. The English expressions "civil disobedience" and "passive resistance" —although for lack of proper equivalents to *satyagraha* they have often been used, and even by Gandhi—give no true notion of what this concept is. Civil disobedience, as defined and first practised by Henry Thoreau in his opposition to American slavery and the war against Mexico, consisted chiefly in a refusal to pay taxes. (Thoreau fared well enough—he spent twenty-four hours in jail and then one of his neighbors, no doubt Emerson, went and paid his taxes for him.) "Passive resistance," as it has been practised in many places during even this century (as in the Ruhr and Rhineland during the allied occupation in 1923-1924), is only a form of strike undertaken for political or patriotic reasons. *Satyagraha* is something much more positive, involving a perfect or complete willingness to die for the truth.

Gandhi's method of employing this original means of struggle was, as we have seen, to explain it as carefully and fully as possible over a period of time and then to call upon the people to execute it. Except in South Africa in the first *satyagraha* struggle, it was never properly executed; there was always violence; and when there was violence, the Mahatma, in accordance with his principles, had to abandon the movement. (In 1930 the violence was all on the side of the police, or nearly all, but before that *satyagraha* had not been understood.) It was, nevertheless, an instrument of the most tremendous power, and amongst the forces which freed India it was certainly the greatest.

Now, in what respect can *satyagraha* be accepted or practised outside of India? Clearly the Western world is not by temperament, social and economic condition, philosophical adaptation or mass-consciousness in any way prepared for *satyagraha*. Richard Gregg's book on *The Power of Non-Violence*, even though it was written with the advantage of Gandhi's own advice and explanations, does not convince me that Western peoples can carry out such a program. Except in the single case of Peter the Hermit and the first crusade, I know of no time when sacrifice, as such, has widely appealed to Western populations. But the Western world is, above all things, the world of the individual, in which the ideal is for society to interfere as little as possible with individual development, and in which freedom for the single person, so long as he does no damage to others, is the explicit purpose of the social and political arrangements. In such a comity the power of the individual is great because he affects

other individuals in an endless chain; all the psychological forces
—let us say, with Professor Toynbee, "creative mimesis"—can
be brought to bear through a relatively small number of individuals if they engage the sympathy (even inactive) of others.

It is my belief that *satyagraha* can reach the Western world—
that is, the world of individual freedom—through individuals and
not masses. What the co-conscious Indian people, participating,
beneath their multifarious external differences, in a common
awareness of soul and over-soul, were able to do under the
magnetic influence of Gandhi, individual citizens of the democratic West may do by harkening to the word of Gandhi, by
relating it to other words spoken in ages past, by considering the
extremity of the world's peril and by obeying the dictates of the
individual conscience.

In what remains of this book I shall attempt to indicate what
seems to me the most significant fact, historically speaking, in
all the array of Gandhi's thought and action, deeds and results,
which is its incidence in time. Aside from *satyagraha*, the body
of the teaching is not new ("old as the hills," Gandhi once said).
The Gita, the Sermon on the Mount, the Buddha—all this has
been known for many centuries. But the reiteration of the
lesson in the form of a whole, long human life, enacted in the
plain view of the whole world under modern conditions of
limitless publicity, happens to come (happens?) at a time when
the alternatives to the lesson seem in any direction to lead to
disaster. We have arrived at a point where the famous "active
principles" of Isaac Newton—"the sun continues violently hot
and lucid," for example—are mathematically endangered. If we
do not learn to translate conflicts into non-violent terms there
may soon be no conflicts left because there will be no persons
left to engage in them. Supposing the universe to be a mere
happenstance, a meaningless army of atoms storming through
the void, it is at the very least worthy of remark that the most
literal and downright of all apostles of peace—the only one of his
line who made no exceptions and no qualifications—should have
taught his lesson in the exact time-area which also produced the
limitless destructive power of modern physical experiment.
Mahatma Gandhi, in other words, addresses one side of man's
nature at the moment when Professor Einstein addresses another,

and both say the same thing: make peace or perish. The spiritual exhortation is given greater power for the grossest minds by the fact that it falls in a day so dark: it may be, indeed, a final warning.

2

Among the formulae given by the general and special theories of relativity—confirmed so overwhelmingly in physical experiment —one in particular, which declares that energy equals mass multiplied by the square of the velocity of light, has received wide attention. It is, in fact, the general statement from which the specific phenomenon of an explosion of atomic energy is derived. But there are other mathematical expressions of no less startling a nature, including the one which figures inside the title page of this book. It is:

$$\frac{mc^2}{\sqrt{1 - \dfrac{v^2}{c^2}}}$$

What this means is that when or if a mass—however tiny— should equal the velocity of light, its magnitude must become infinite. Even an electron, so unimaginably minute, is a mass. The electron has, as all know, approached the velocity of light. It does so in each experiment of atomic explosion. Its capacity for destruction is, therefore, well on the way toward infinity.

The fact is quite simple, although it takes some time to get used to it. When we read or hear of nations "stock-piling" atomic bombs, that is to say, accumulating potential explosions of this incalculable kind, we know that few among the persons responsible have fully considered the possibilities. Scientists are able to predict, with fair accuracy, the results of one or two or three such explosions, but there is nobody living who could hazard a guess at what might result from fifty or sixty such explosions. So new and awe-inspiring a force is entrusted to military and political temperaments which have not yet fully realized the dangers of the war before the last, and whose attitude toward the unknown and unguessable has the cheerful simplicity of 1914.

Morally, intellectually and spiritually there is no difference between the national powers, since all who can do so are working on the techniques of these explosions and all would use them if the "necessity" (real or imagined) arose. The most that can be said is that some nations seem a little more fitted for responsibility —that is, a little less likely to destroy the world deliberately— than some others. It was for this precise reason, a belief that the dreadful power released by atomic fission was safer in American than in German hands, that so many great scientists of all nations gave their best efforts to the United States before 1945.

There is no agreement between scientists on what results may be expected from further explosions of atomic energy. The effects upon human morphology are as unknown as any others: all that seems sure is that there will be such effects. The behavior of the atomic cloud, the effects upon climate, the results for agriculture and conditions of human habitation, all are unknown. Yet into this realm of the unimaginable, of which all that can be said is that it contains great disasters, "planners" are ready to go, as go they must unless peace can be maintained.

This, then, is the situation into which Mahatma Gandhi's central idea of struggle conducted in non-violent terms has been thrust as a moral alternative to war. I should like to ask, briefly, whether there is anything inherent in either the system of modified capitalism in the West or modified Communism in the East (the two opposing materialisms) which demands violent struggle or rules out the possibility of non-violent struggle.

Under the Marxian analysis, capitalism periodically makes war and must make war either through competition for markets— as in the wars of rival empires—or through an effort to escape from internal economic crisis or by various combinations of these impelling motives. But the Marxian analysis has never been accepted in Western democratic societies (even the British Labor Party is not Marxist), and, in fact, some of its leading tenets have been conclusively disproved by the industrial society of the United States. What has become of surplus value, for instance? What of the idea that a worker must earn less and less, and what of the "subsistence level" to which capitalism is supposed to doom the proletariat? The industrial workers of the United States live far beyond any conceivable "subsistence level," and the Marxian description of the English factory system in the 1840's does not apply to them in any way. Why, therefore, should the Marxian notion of the inevitability of war be any more correct than other Marxian notions which have faded with the years?

In the modified capitalism of the West, there are, in fact, a great many forces which make for peace and not war. By and large, the Christian churches, although their influence upon practical life is not great, have worked for peace. The great capitalist interests have learned in two wars that whatever profits they make are too precarious to be worth the terrible dangers they incur for their own form of society. The mass of the people wields a mighty political power both in the United States and in England, and this general mass is more disillusioned with the results of war than ever before. All of these elements, in their simple human aspect, mourn and hope and despair alike, whatever their social and economic condition. As Croesus told Cyrus in the story related by Herodotus, all men prefer peace to war —war in which the fathers bury the sons instead of the sons the fathers.

I am unable to see any reason in the social and economic system of the West which makes war necessary or rules out a less destructive form of conflict. And when I read the literature of international Communism or of the Russian Revolution I can see no imperative reason why men formed by the other materialist society should want war either. Dialectical materialism is itself a process which continues in war or in peace: it interprets the whole history of mankind as being determined by the material conditions (the means of production and the class relations) in society, but it does not say that the necessary and inevitable oppositions which it incessantly produces have to be settled by war. There is opposition and clash between thesis and antithesis; from the struggle there results a synthesis which then becomes the new thesis and clashes with the new antithesis; but in all this apparatus there is no distinction between war and peace. Since there is no distinction, there can be no necessity for struggle to take the form of war—and above all in a period when the material relations themselves so vastly increase its dangers.

If the Russians, therefore, believed their own theories (which is another question altogether), they could struggle for them without war. Something very like dialectical materialism, with all its mechanical inevitability and predetermined cadence, has occurred throughout the story of thinking men, although usually in mystical forms. The fragments preserved of Heraclitus—roughly contemporary with Buddha—indicate a belief in "opposite tensions" of the same kind, producing a rhythm in events and an order in change. As Aurobindo Ghose paraphrases the system of Heraclitus, peace in any sense, except a balance of power between hostile forces, would be the end of the world. "A periodic end there may be," he says, "not by peace or reconciliation, but by conflagration, by an attack of Fire, a fiery judgment and conviction. Force created the world, Force is the world, Force by its violence maintains the world, Force shall end the world—and eternally recreate it." All the way from Heraclitus to Hegel this tension of opposites has been supposed by many philosophers to be the meaning and process of life: but even they (and most of them were mystics, not materialists) would hardly say that such tension should take the form of war in a moment when war means total destruction. Least of all should a materialist (i.e., a person who believes in matter alone and denies the existence of spirit) deliberately affront the material force of the physical universe.

There exists, to the best of my ascertainment, no theoretical validity to the argument that war between opposing materialist societies is inevitable. Individuals may think so, but there is no doctrinal command to that effect in either group of societies, nations or states. Lenin, above all, never ceased preaching that a changed situation demanded changes of approach; his *Collected Works* are full of speeches inculcating this necessity. Faced with the material impossibility of war-making in an era of ungovernable forces, he would be inculcating it again today if he were alive.

3

A knowledge of even the most rudimentary and general lines of relativity physics is still rare among us, so that these considerations will not—for a long time to come—carry their full weight with masses of men. They should weigh with individuals who think, who bear responsibility and who exert themselves to govern; but these, too, are often at the mercy of passion or prejudice. Politics in general, both of parties and of nations, would appear to be the human activity in which error is most common because reason is least esteemed. That is how leaders and masses are alike carried away by their own emotion: for impersonal emotion, the strongest to which numbers of men can be subjected, is lifted to a great height by the patriotic and national instincts. We find Hindus (many of them) on fire with the patriotic wish to "unite India" by conquering Pakistan, and Muslims who would give their lives to achieve the same end by conquering India: and this within a year of Gandhi's martyrdom for peace. When this is the case even in India, with all its past and present contradicted by such blind passions, what is to be expected elsewhere? The peace is kept only by luck in some places, by careful management in others, and by averting the attention from breaches in still others. It is insecure everywhere and there is hardly a man or woman to be found who does not feel this insecurity in the recesses of the consciousness.

Is there any use proposing specific schemes, "movements" or organizations, in a situation which has grown to be, if not universal, at least planetary? There are many such schemes in existence already and it would be difficult indeed to discern any results from them. They are like the churches: the more there are of them the less there is of religion. The spirit of the thing itself flees from the stones.

We should be well within the meaning of Gandhi's lifelong effort if we said that schemes and organizations are useful for specific purposes. He had "constructive organizations" of his own, of which the leading example is the All-India Spinners' Association. But peace in a world of nation-states does not fall into the category of such enterprises: it is saved or lost by the accidents of government, and in the really critical moments— the moments of decision—all government, even the most democratic, is and must be absolute. That is, a whole people can never decide the act which leads to war. That is always the work of an individual—some individual, somewhere.

This is another reason why I believe that the lesson of *satyagraha*, the greatest of Gandhi's lessons, can be learned only by the individual. Just as religion, or love, or mystical experience in general, has its deepest reality in a region of the individual consciousness to which nothing else can penetrate—and just as these experiences are in themselves incommunicable, or what is called "ineffable"—so the individual who has learned what *satyagraha* means will find his way toward an enactment of it when his time comes. Only a few such individual men could make a great difference in the world: Gandhi himself is the proof. Nine months after Gandhi's death another example of voluntary sacrifice, *satyagraha*, was offered in Jerusalem when Count Bernadotte was murdered. This was also a voluntary sacrifice for peace, made with open eyes and a steady heart. There have been one or two others in the single year since the Mahatma died (to avoid polemics I shall not name them, but they have occurred and many know it). It is my belief that Gandhi's teaching has been far more generally understood and accepted by perceptive individuals throughout the world than is yet supposed. So great an example could not pass unperceived even in the most materialist societies, and every one of us could name persons we know who are quite capable, singly, of *satyagraha*. Is there any doubt, therefore, that the individual effort has been made and will be made, whether it is called by Gandhi's Sanskrit word or not? And, furthermore, has any step forward in the life of thinking mankind been made in any other way than by individuals? I do not take to the idea of an élite in any society, above all, an élite which calls itself that and consciously endeavors to impose solutions; but there is the other kind of élite which H. G. Wells had in mind when he spoke of the "Open conspiracy of men of good will." This open conspiracy has existed for some time, and can only be quickened and strengthened by the influence exerted upon men's imaginations by the life and death of Gandhi.

For, essentially, what he led us back to was the concept of our own highest truth. This may differ widely: we should hardly expect the highest truth of a physicist, an astronomer or a biologist to be precisely the same as the highest truth of a Buddhist monk, an Italian priest or a Russian bureaucrat. Anthropology and climate have about as much to do with our concepts of the highest truths as do our educations, our social environment and external experience. It has sometimes occurred to me that St.

Paul's three Christian virtues, faith, hope and charity, might go by the name of dialectical materialism in a society which was founded upon that idea. But whatever it may be, a man's highest truth is most often forgotten or obscured in the heat of the day. What Gandhi did was to lead us all—that is, all who are accessible to his lesson—back to that central core of being in which we communicate with an idea higher and greater than ourselves. Thus, among his Islamic followers it can be said that they were better Muslims because of him, as his Christian friends were better Christians. He, the greatest of Hindus, expressed above all that all-embracing impersonal truth-absorbing catholicity of Hinduism, in which whatever garment the truth has worn makes no difference, and the worship itself (as the Gita says) is more important than the forms it takes. Thus a powerful impetus toward essential religion, as distinct from ecclesiastical orthodoxies, is one clear result of the Mahatma's life struggle.

By this I hope not to be understood as suggesting any Gandhian cult, creed or synthesis. Gandhi was himself always opposed to anything of the sort. He had nothing new to say—it was all ancient indeed; but he lived it and exemplified it. Those who believe in revelations are of course at liberty to see in him an element of proof for their particular creeds; many have already done so. But he did not himself desire to formulate, or to have formulated for him, any specific body of doctrine supplanting the great world religions for which he had such reverence. He was always content to let the believer return to his own forms with—he hoped—a new perception of their essential element. That is one reason why the prayers and hymns of all the great religions figured in his devotions for so many years: in all of them he saw aspects of the God which was, as he told me, "in everything—even in the stone."

It is easy to see that the orthodoxies of both science and religion must by nature reject most of Mr. Gandhi's ideas. What they cannot reject is his tremendous appeal to the imagination of mankind—the way in which he makes the Buddhist think of Gautama Buddha, the Christian think of Christ, the Catholic of St. Francis or the Hindu of Shri Krishna. This quality in him is, indeed, universal, and the most illiterate villager felt it during his lifetime as strongly as did the learned churchmen who visited him in London in 1931 to discuss questions of divinity. All the great symbols of the religious instinct for centuries seemed to be summed up in this one life. That is why it will not be possible for organizations, however great, to stifle the impulse he has released into the modern world. In a metaphor which ha. occurred to many of us, he was an "atomic man"—the chain reaction started by him, from individual to individual, has begun indeed, but nobody can say how far it will go or what will be its end. And if, in spite of everything, this too shall have been in vain, and men prove to be determined upon their own destruction, the spirit from which he came and to which he returned was, in his own belief, that which has exhaled worlds before this and will exhale others when this is gone. Such was his conviction.

4

Western scientific culture, now uneasily conscious that nineteenth-century materialism was much too positive even for science, has undergone many modifications in the past thirty or forty years. A considerable number of philosophical and scientific writers (Whitehead, Eddington, Jeans, Sullivan and others) have abandoned most of the precise claims made by their predecessors. It is fairly clear that science can describe processes and calculate relations but is now, more than ever, quite incapable of fundamental statements on the nature of reality. The present tendency is to avoid trying. Whitehead, as a matter of fact, seeking for a vivid illustration of what he means by the character of modern scientific thought, finds it in Greek tragedy.

"The pilgrim fathers of the scientific imagination as it exists today are the great tragedians of ancient Athens, Aeschylus, Sophocles, Euripides," he says.[1] "Their vision of fate, remorseless and indifferent, urging a tragic incident to its inevitable issue, is the vision possessed by science. Fate in Greek tragedy becomes the order of nature in modern thought. The absorbing interest in the particular heroic incidents, as an example and a verification of the workings of fate, reappears in our epoch as concentration of interest on the crucial experiments. It was my good fortune to

[1] *Science and the Modern World*, p. 15.

be present at the meeting of the Royal Society in London when the Astronomer Royal for England announced that the photographic plates of the famous eclipse, as measured by his colleagues in Greenwich Observatory, had verified the prediction of Einstein that rays of light are bent as they pass in the neighborhood of the sun. The whole atmosphere of tense interest was exactly that of the Greek drama: we were the chorus commenting on the decree of destiny as disclosed in the development of a supreme incident. There was dramatic quality in the very staging— the traditional ceremonial, and in the background the picture of Newton to remind us that the greatest of scientific generalizations was now, after more than two centuries, to receive its first modification. Nor was the personal interest wanting: a great adventure in thought had at length come safe to shore."

If we can find fate in relativity physics, and the logic of Greek tragedy in astronomical discovery, I think it is even easier to perceive them in the high incidents of the human drama as it unfolds before us. The oldest and simplest truths are sometimes re-enacted in a way which makes us feel that we have never seen or heard them before. One fragment of Heraclitus (it is the 121st) says: "Man's character is his fate." [2] If this is so, then there is nothing surprising in the fact that Gandhi's martyrdom was known to me in advance, or that he knew that I knew it, or that I knew that he knew that I knew it: it was contained within his character, and was there for all to read. In addition, I am persuaded that there are connections on the plane of human events which have not yet been studied by scientific methods and may never be so studied because their nature does not permit it. The unknown lies all around us, and beyond that, the unknowable. It is not the Gandhian way, therefore, to reject the hypotheses of any belief sincerely held by men, however alien they may be to us, and if the world we live in (the world of Einstein, Marx and Freud) is indeed a Greek tragedy, then we do well to remember that the old gods, too, those of Aeschylus no less than those of India, spoke for the truth, that to which man has forever aspired and to which he gives the name divine. For Gandhi and for Socrates, as for others of their band, I think

[2] Tr. by Burnet: *Early Greek Philosophy*, p. 217.

the third-century, neo-Platonist Maximus of Tyre spoke words that abide. The English translation is by Gilbert Murray.

"God Himself," says Maximus, "the Father and fashioner of all that is, older than the Sun or the Sky, greater than time and eternity and all the flow of being, is unnameable by any law-giver, unutterable by any voice, not to be seen by any eye. But we, being unable to apprehend His essence, use the help of sounds and names and pictures, of beaten gold and ivory and silver, of plants and rivers, mountain peaks and torrents, yearning for the knowledge of Him, and in our weakness naming all that is beautiful in this world after His nature—just as happens to earthly lovers. To them the most beautiful sight will be the actual lineaments of the beloved, but for remembrance's sake they will be happy in the sight of a lyre, a little spear, a chair, perhaps, or a running-ground, or anything in the world that wakens the memory of the beloved. Why should I further examine and pass judgment about Images? Let men know what is divine, let them know: that is all. If a Greek is stirred to the remembrance of God by the art of Pheidias, an Egyptian by paying worship to animals, another man by a river, another by fire—I have no anger for their divergences; only let them know, let them love, let them remember."

The End

Appendix

For those who wish to go a little farther

CASTE, KARMA AND DARSHAN

The activity of the Brahmins in the development of the caste system, and hence of Hinduism through the ages, was immense. The Brahmin went along with the warrior to perform rites and give counsel. It was no doubt the earliest Brahmins (rishis or seers) who composed the earliest Vedic hymns, those (over a thousand in number) which are called the *Rig Veda*. There are four Vedas or collections of these ancient hymns, and the language in which they were composed differs from the later classical Sanskrit, philologists tell us, "very much as Homeric differs from classical Greek or as the language of Chaucer differs from that of Milton." [1] The Brahmins not only composed these hymns but memorized them so that they could be preserved through centuries with a minimum of corruption. The prodigious verbal memory of the ancient Brahmin was trained by dozens of complicated techniques so that he could recite Vedic hymns backward or forward, with various skips or jumps and other standardized dislocations, in order never to lose the 1028 hymns, 10,402 verses, 153,826 words and 432,000 syllables [2] which it was his sacred duty to preserve.

[1] Griswold: *The Religion of the Rig Veda,* p. 65.
[2] Max Muller: *Physical Religion,* p. 66.

By this means, unique in all history, the four Vedas came down through the ages, perhaps from as long ago as 4,000 B.C., perhaps from as recently as 1,000 B.C., but in any case from long before there was any form of writing in India. There are, of course, almost as many opinions as there are scholars, and the argument will no doubt go on for ever unless some really scientific and comprehensive effort is made to get at the archaeological evidence which must lie buried in the Punjab. So far, Indian archaeology has scarcely existed, and until it does provide the evidence we cannot be sure even within a millennium of when the Vedic creative age was.

From its misty antiquity, however, the priestly Brahmin comes into history as the most powerful element in the social consciousness. Warriors and rulers listened to his counsel and depended upon his knowledge. Only the Brahmin knew the ceremonies in full, and above all only the Brahmin had in his treasured possession the full text of the sacred hymns. It is quite possible, as some scholars have suggested, that the Brahmin prolonged his exclusive possession of the Veda texts for centuries after the necessity to do so had vanished with the introduction of writing. The position of the Brahmin had economic as well as social advantages, all depending to a great extent upon his custody of the divine poetry. (Orthodox Hindus believed, and most of them still believe, that the four Vedas were revealed by the supreme spirit at the very beginning of the present world era.) When, sometime after about 600 B.C. the four Vedas were in fact collected in writing, there came into existence a sacred book (or books) which in theory anybody could read; but in fact it was already incomprehensibly archaic then and became more archaic with the passage of the centuries, so that the Brahmin still—in spite of the arts of reading and writing—retained his Vedic monopoly.

The four Vedas are not wholly separate: the primitive collection, the *Rig Veda*, is repeated to a large extent in two of the other three. And since the Vedic language was already antique by the time it was written down and the texts became settled, it is hardly surprising that by 500 B.C., when Yaska wrote the first Sanskrit etymology, a good deal of its vocabulary had already become impossible to understand. To this unintelligibility in the original sacred texts there was added the philosophical difficulty of the various expositions and interpretations which had already been added to them and which continued to be added through successive centuries up to the present. The Brahmanas, or earliest expositions and elaborations of the ritual elements in the Vedas, were amplified by the Upanishads (the Vedanta—end of the Vedas), which struck forth boldly into pure philosophy and constitute, taken together, the foundation of Indian thought. All of the ideas I have tried to outline as essential elements in the Hindu consciousness can be found in the Upanishads.

Now the Brahmin was not only custodian of all this, but he was its authorized interpreter. He spoke for a kind of learning so specialized that in effect he spoke for God. His prestige and power in prehistoric society must have been great, and, as the caste system developed, he hedged himself around with a large number of special rites, privileges, taboos and observances which set his group apart as innately superior to every other element in its environment. The economic consequences of such aggrandizement are obvious, and although Hinduism is not itself, philosophically speaking, conducive to materialist ways of thought, the accretion of wealth to some Brahmin families was inevitable. There thus grew up in remote centuries a high caste—the highest —of persons with no warlike duties, many social and economic privileges, and no particular social obligations except the principal one of keeping themselves "uncontaminated" by contact with the lesser breeds. The Brahmin caste, as it emerged from prehistory into history, at least had the aura of scholarship, but even this disappeared as the centuries rolled on, and by modern times all the practices designed to keep the Brahmins' purity and superiority survived, as it were, in a vacuum, without social, intellectual, religious or economic base. There are millions of Brahmins, all pure and superior in their own eyes, all occupying a special position in Hinduism considered as a social and religious complex, but no longer doing anything, or obliged to do anything, of special value to the society. Some are rich, some are poor, many are very poor, but all (except the relatively few who have become westernized) hang onto the marks, signs, rites and practices which encase and protect their Brahminism.

It is this circumstance which leads some Indians with an ill-digested reading in Western economics to say that India's history from the beginning to the present has been one long narrative of exploitation for the benefit of the Brahmins. The thesis will not withstand examination at the present day, since the possessing and exploiting classes in industry and agriculture show only a small Brahmin element. Indeed hardly any economic theory which leaves out the anthropological and religious base of the Indian consciousness can be applied, in any but the most superficial way, to the objective reality in India. Capitalism, socialism, communism are alike inappropriate because they are formed by the intellectual apparatus of the West and cannot even deal with the governing motives of the Indian mind. The social prestige of the Brahmin subsists today by religious association, and if a Brahmin should happen to be educated and capable he probably has a better chance in the struggle for existence than a member of a lower caste: no more can be said of his economic power than that. The Brahmins of Madras, for example, have been in modern times particularly apt at stenography, bookkeeping, and the like: they have supplied the best secretaries and clerks in the Indian Civil Service for quite a while, so much so that a quota system had to be introduced to keep them from dominating the government offices. And it is still true that among the scholars, philosophers, sages and saints who have at all periods flourished in India, and who flourish there today, a large number are Brahmins. Tradition is suggestive to young minds, and in Brahmin families, however poor, the scholar and saint are the traditional images presented to children. The holy and the learned, however, have seldom amassed wealth or exercised economic power even in Western countries; in India their asceticism usually leads them to the extremes of voluntary poverty.

Even so, the Brahmins had for thousands of years a vested interest, real though not simply economic, in the caste system. And since they were the source of its highest authority, it is only reasonable to expect what the evidence shows, that they have been at all periods an influence pressing for greater rather than for lesser rigidity and for the most unquestioning adherence to Hindu *dharma*. They succeeded long ago, for all the various reasons and motives which have been indicated, in making the caste system the very basis of Hindu *dharma*, which means that caste is as imperative as anything in life. As caste resulted from the concepts of karma and rebirth in the soul's pilgrimage toward union with God, the more it acquired irresistible force the more these causational concepts became necessary at both ends of the world-view, so as to explain the origins of life, to give it meaning and to illuminate it with an ultimate hope. Rebirth, karma and caste are philosophical concepts which arise when the universality and oneness of the soul have been profoundly felt to be true, and they refer to that oneness as the source and destination of their being. Socrates felt it himself and tried to prove it, but it is clear from his words (or from those with which Plato supplies him) that he had little hope of making even his friends and disciples understand his reasoning. In India there is no need of reasoning; all believe (or, they would say, *know*) because of the long historical development that has made religion, philosophy, society and even to a certain degree economics part of a single indivisible whole called Hindu *dharma*.

Such a close-knit web of being for individual and society makes it impossible to disturb any of the fundamental elements in the Hindu system without upsetting the rest. That is, perhaps, why so little evidence of dissent has appeared through the ages, and it is also why even the most oppressed classes make the best of their lot, in accordance with Hindu *dharma*, since these social rigors have been determined by past lives and will be mitigated in future ones. It is easy to see why the Brahmin labored through the centuries to make this so; and the Kshatriya, providing warriors and government to the polity, had no reason to question his lot. The Vaishya division and, above all, the Shudra, might have provided the elements of rebellion against Hinduism at some point, but nothing of the kind has occurred on any scale because the integration of the whole was too successful: a man or group of men might wish to revolt against some particular aspect of the caste system, or indeed against that system in its entirety, but it would be difficult for him to revolt against the general structure of Hinduism without being treated as insane: too much is involved.

I have tried to say why it seems to me that the basic belief in an immanent and transcendent spirit, universal and one under many forms, reaches throughout the Hindu mass. The second

question—has there never been any dissent?—is best answered by
a simple negative. There has been plenty of dissent from Brahmin
doctrines, from theologies and rituals and ethical systems as well,
and all such dissents are equably contained within the capacious
bosom of Hinduism. The range of possible belief is enormous;
the variety in all such respects seems almost limitless. Notions of
heresy and heretics do not obtain in the Hindu world. Both the
Lord Buddha and Mahatma Gandhi would have been, in any
other homogeneous world society, regarded as heretical. In Hinduism Buddha was first revered, then adored, then substantially
forgotten, but his name still appears in every list of the avatars
(or reincarnations) of God; and although Buddhism itself mi-
grated centuries ago from India to China, Japan and Southeast
Asia, educated Hindus regard Buddha today as one of the glories
of India. His refusal to answer final questions on the nature of
the absolute caused certain modern Western materialists to claim
him as an atheist, which, in view of the transcendentalism implicit in all his teaching, seems absurd; and yet, even if he had
been an atheist, Hinduism would not have rejected him. There
is room even for atheism in the Hindu system so long as the
immanent and transcendent spirit is admitted, assumed or acted
upon as if it were. (The necessity and utility of an atheistic doubt
to vanquish seems to be the theme of some of the stories in the
Ramayana.)

But if there has been no dissent to the "formulable essence"
of Hinduism, there has been plenty to everything else. There
have been disputes, wrangles and century-long antinomies about
doctrines in theology, epistemology and devotional ethics; the
Vedic exegesis is a worse battleground than are similar fields in
Christianity; every sort of variant belief is held and none is heretical. For example, it is possible to believe in the simple clay
images of the village potter and attribute to them divinity in
almost unrelieved idolatry, but it is also possible to contemplate
none but the unimaginable and formless One (which the mystics
call That) containing and contained in the present universe. Both
kinds of worship are Hindu. The phallus-worship which the
Rig Veda scornfully attributes to the inferior dark-skinned
Dasyu has long since made itself at home in the combined Aryan-
Dravidian race, and for thousands of years it has been the chief

form of the worship of Shiva in his temples, great or small. The phallus is, of course, a mere block of stone with no representational quality at all, and is worshipped by the pouring of water and the casting of flowers—as I saw at the Temple of the Master of the World—but it is still, in the eyes of Western scholars like Professor Toynbee, a "contradiction" to the lofty spirituality of Hindu philosophy. I see no such contradiction. The life-force can quite comprehensibly be worshipped by those who wish to do so, without detracting from the ultimate truths of which it is but one expression.

Disagreement among the sages has always been prevalent, and perhaps if Hinduism had ever acquired a "church" with the full apparatus of irresistible authority to enforce dogma, a great deal of this disagreement might have taken the form of dissent from it. But it is practically impossible to dissent from a world view which regards your very dissent as an element of its own being. Consequently the disagreements are between men, not between men and gods, men and institutions or men and divine revelation.

The luxuriant mass of these opinions does not concern us here, since it does not touch the fundament which produced modern darshan. One divergence of view only can be said to affect the matter. This is the great and philosophically permanent divergence between those who regard the world as pure illusion and those who take it to possess a reality of its own. The two views have their starting point in the Upanishads, which abound in contrasts between the formal extant universe and the formless eternal—between time-space and the timeless void—or between, as Kant said, phenomenon and noumenon. It was possible, therefore, for subsequent generations of Hindu thinkers to ride a philosophical high-horse straight into what looks to us like the solipsism of Bishop Berkeley, a world which is the figment of our own imagination. This purely logical view of physical existence is associated with the name of Shankara, one of the great teachers of Hinduism (deified of old), who lived and taught in the eighth century of our era. The inevitable revolt against a view so contradictory to experience came three centuries later under Ramanuja, a southern Brahmin whose influence upon the whole subsequent course of Hindu thought was immense. (Among other things, the prevalent cult of Vishnu and all his incarnations comes from that influence.) Ramanuja taught that the multiplicity of forms revealed by our senses had its own reality, and developed a kind of scale of mounting realities between the lowest, simplest awareness and the highest. Aurobindo Ghose, at the present time, in his "ascending terms of being," seems to start from the Ramanuja tradition and end with Shankara, although he enriches the whole by Western science.

Does this divergence affect the mass of the people enough to have any effect on their behavior? I am unable to prove it by evidence because of the language barrier, and yet I believe, from what I have observed and from what I have been told by friends, that the monistic view of Shankara is more popular among the masses—even though it contradicts every experience of daily life —than the reasonable system developed by Ramanuja.

Let me hasten to say that I do not suppose the generality of the people of India (who are 87% illiterate) to know anything about Shankara or Ramanuja. But I am convinced that they are broadly aware of monism, which is dramatized for them in ordinary existence by the "holy men" whose contempt for the world takes extreme forms and arouses their deep respect. I believe a phenomenon familiar in all countries has occurred in India, which is that the heart's belief and aspiring hope of the people has little to do with their daily lives. In every village there is somebody who holds forth on the world's illusion, on the only supreme reality: the great text, "One only without a second," [3] is familiar to millions. Such ideas appeal to Indians, perhaps because of the dreadful poverty and struggle of their existence, and they are never so poor that they cannot find something to give to the poor *sadhu* who lies in a trance sometimes for days on end in the village street. It is illogical but it seems to me very likely that most Indians—if they could deal with the philosophical disputation—would contend that Shankara was right, that the world is illusion, that this was what the Upanishads meant and that it will all be amply proved some day. Shankara consigned the phenomenal world to the realm of "lower knowledge," that is to say, to the knowledge we get by means of our senses, and admitted that many were enmeshed in that "lower knowledge" throughout life. It seems to me that the Indian peasant, if he

[3] *Chhandogya Upanishad, VI, 2, 1.*

could consider the dilemma and speak, would say very much the same thing: that he is enmeshed in the "lower knowledge," that this is a misfortune due to karma, but that he knows it is all illusion and he hopes to reach the realm of pure spirit after the requisite number of rebirths. ("We can't all be saints," is a familiar Western form of this pattern.) If a car is rushing at me at sixty miles an hour I will instinctively get out of its way if I can, but this does not deter me (if I am a follower of Shankara) from looking at the back of the disappearing car and telling it that it does not really exist.

The much more reasonable gradation of relative realities associated with the name of Ramanuja is too complicated for the popular mind. Among the educated it has tended to prevail in whole or in part, because nothing else will satisfy the common sense in ordinary existence. But Ramanuja, too, was a thorough-going transcendentalist who believed that God dwelt in everything, and his acceptance of the temporary reality of the physical universe in no way denied it. His innovation in Hindu theology was the concept of God as an infinite good—instead of containing all natures—and as bestowing grace upon men whether they merit it or not. The *bhakti* or whole-souled love and devotion which he introduced became a principal characteristic of certain aspects of Hinduism thereafter. In the great development of Vishnu-worship (which brings with it Krishna-worship and other forms of the same devotion to a benevolent deity who is the fountain of grace) Ramanuja probably did more for the ordinary Hindu than in his philosophical system itself. It is ironically true that his moderate and sensible view of the physical world, which would seem to be the only one that might reconcile transcendentalism and daily experience, is the view on which everybody acts; but the pure and uncompromising *Advaita* of Shankara, absolute oneness, is what most Hindus either believe, think they believe or would like to believe. There is no means of proving this: I depend upon my own impressions and information given me by friends, since a philosophical census of the population of India is not available. The educated, westernized Indian has a rather defensive dislike for the deep-rooted mysticism of his own country, shrinks at the words yoga and yogi, and would be the first to deny that the illiterate peasants and workers of the country had an instinctive and co-conscious sense of unity in one spirit: yet this is the probability according to any light I could get on the subject.

Shri Aurobindo Ghose, the sage and mystic of Pondichéry, seems [4] to belong to the tradition of Ramanuja, as I have said, and yet at the upper limit of his "ascending terms of being" he joins hands with Shankara. He has a sort of affectionate toleration for materialism, which in its scientific caution and painstaking method seems to him to have served knowledge most usefully; and in modern science he finds remarkable confirmations of the Vedanta. For example, one seed arranged by the universal energy in multitudinous forms [5] is only another way of stating the discoveries of twentieth-century physics, in which essential matter is no longer capable of being seized by the senses or even by the imagination; any worker in a laboratory of nuclear physics knows that this is the fact; matter has become what the ancient Sankhyas thought it was, a "conceptual form of substance." Shri Aurobindo pushes on beyond this "lower knowledge," however, from matter to life to mind to spirit, and sees in the science of the day a kind of ladder which leads to an ancient truth, "that which is immortal in mortals is a God and established inwardly as an energy working out in our divine powers." [6] As he goes on in his reconciliation of opposing views upon our present space-time and that which gave it birth and will survive it, we perceive that at its height his system is every bit as austere and uncompromising as the view of Shankara: he reaches what is called in Sanskrit *sanyag-darshana*, universal cognition, in which the soul (*Atman*) is identical with the supreme and unimaginable source of all being (Brahman), that which exhales and will absorb the successive illusory worlds. Shri Aurobindo thus manages to combine and harmonize the elements which have been at variance for seven centuries in Hindu philosophy, and in doing so demonstrates again how endlessly Hinduism can make dialectical progressions and still remain itself.

And it is with Shri Aurobindo that we reach a node or nexus of the phenomena we have been considering. These come from

[4] In *The Life Divine* (1914-1916: revised and enlarged edition, Calcutta, 1939).
[5] *Svetasvatara Upanishad VI, 12.*
[6] *Rig Veda IV, 2, 1.*

diverse realms: ancient religion and perennial philosophy, modern politics and the untaught observations of a stranger to India. It was with the last-named that we began: the great crowds assembled for the purpose of obtaining darshan.

If we have been together so far, we now know that darshan, which brings these unique mass assemblies together, arises from a general conviction among Hindus of the existence of one universal spirit to which they all belong, either absolutely (in the sense of Shankara), or in kindred and fellowship under a benign origin and destination (as Ramanuja would have it). To receive the darshan of the One, the many come together to behold or to be in the presence of an embodiment of their own spirit which they recognize to be noble, to which sometimes the masses spontaneously give the appellation Mahatma (*Maha*-great; *Atman*-soul), but which in other cases is recognized without any non-secular significance at all (as with Mr. Nehru). If I have made my reasoning clear, it will be seen that these vast assemblies, unique in the world, could take place just as well with an engineer, scientist or other beneficent embodiment, if the general spirit of the people perceived one amongst its millions of forms. It is therefore not "religious" in the Western sense, in the separate or classificatory sense, because everything in India is permeated by the religious consciousness and no such classifications are valid there. Darshan, as we have seen, sums up in a single act of the masses what their entire intellectual and spiritual life for thousands of years has proclaimed as its highest truth. Among the innumerable strands woven together in the contemporary phenomenon must be counted an element of that which, in the Christian world, is called the doctrine of salvation—"soteriology" in theological language—arising not from the particular source of darshan, but from the larger reality. That is, the glow of happiness I have described, which I have seen often at such close quarters that error in the observation was improbable, is essentially based upon hope: hope perhaps for a future life rather than for this one, but hope just the same. In the long round of rebirths (called *Sansara*, another word known to all Indians from the most withdrawn philosopher to the illiterate peasant) the great embodiment which can be seen and heard gives assurance that a time will come when this self, too, however earth-bound, will reach an advanced stage on the long way.

In the cases of Mahatma Gandhi and Mr. Nehru, the two I have given as specific examples, it may be said that too many other elements are present to make my analysis anything more than a plausible speculation. I should deny this on the basis of observation: that is, I should say that the great mass of the crowds assembled for both these great men came for darshan, and that the other motives or determinants influenced only a small number. Politics and nationalism, all-powerful motives, themselves derive their mass support in India from this darshan concept, and, without great embodiments to evoke it, the Indian national revolution, in a people so overwhelmingly unschooled, could not have occurred. The thing which underlies even the nationalism of the masses is an identification with Hindu *dharma*, and the distinctive or in fact unprecedented dynamic force of Mr. Gandhi's genius in action, as I shall hope to show later on, came precisely from the fact that he became some forty years ago (instinctively and not deliberately) *Maha-Atman*, a great soul, an embodiment of the spirit of the whole people, and thus a source of darshan. Through him, to put it in its plainest terms, the whole people became more aware of God, and from his darshan derived new hope.

The Western mind is obstinate and has thitherto encountered transcendentalism only in a few cranks like Emerson, Schopenhauer and the like; therefore it refuses (even in India) to admit the extent and complexity of this phenomenon. I have heard English and American residents of India speak of darshan crowds as if they were a riotous expression of superstitious ignorance. In such cases one's pity for the mind that can be so smug in its insularity is tempered by the reflection that most of us are the same. I am obliged to confess that until only last winter I regarded both Gandhi and Nehru as essentially political manifestations, and although I had for years followed their course with the deepest sympathy across the world, the nature of their power over the masses had completely escaped me. Perhaps it is impossible to be convinced of the reality of darshan as something much deeper than either politics or nationalism without actually having formed, at some time or other, part of a darshan crowd and attempted to perceive its meaning by such perceptions as are given us. I have reserved Shri Aurobindo as a proof of pure darshan, since in his case none of the other elements (nationalism, politics, worldly interest or curiosity) could possibly affect the matter. If this form of mass darshan is experienced with him, then there can be no doubt of its reality in the Hindu consciousness, however strange it may seem to us.

2

Shri Aurobindo Ghose retired from the world in 1910. He was then thirty-eight years old and had led an active life in the nationalist movement of his native Bengal. He was born in Calcutta (August 15, 1872), went to England at the age of seven and received there a completely occidental education. When he was twenty-one, he met the Maharajah Gaekwar of Baroda (the great Baroda) and returned to India in that prince's service, first in the secretariat and afterwards as Professor of English Literature in the Baroda College. During his thirteen years in Baroda he began and pursued his Indian studies, learning Sanskrit and a number of the modern Indian languages. (At King's College, Cambridge, he had been particularly good in Latin and Greek; French he knew from childhood; he taught himself German and Italian to read Goethe and Dante.) A good deal of his English poetry comes from his Baroda years, and some of his critical work, published much later, was also written then. From 1902 on, for a number of years, he was engaged in the underground preparation of the Bengali nationalist movement, and in 1906 he openly left Baroda for Calcutta to play his brief but spectacular part in Indian politics. He was one of the leaders of the Bengali nationalist extremists who called themselves the New Party and advocated direct action with the hope of accelerating the historic development. He was prosecuted for sedition in 1907 and acquitted; for about a year, 1908-1909, he was in jail awaiting trial on another charge of the same kind; and in 1910, when he had already left the world for good, a third prosecution was begun and eventually quashed by the High Court. It was the period of the "Bengali terrorists," and Aurobindo was one of their intellectual leaders if not himself a terrorist. The daily news-paper, *Bande Mataram*, named after the forbidden national song of the revolution, was edited by him during its short year of life. Aurobindo's political plan seems to have been to capture the Indian National Congress—then dominated by veteran "moder-ates" who contemplated a slow development over a century or two—and convert it into a revolutionary force arousing and directing a mass movement. (This was more or less what after-wards happened under Gandhi.) The spiritual crisis which brought all this to an end has not been described: in April, 1910, Aurobindo sailed for the French colony of Pondichéry, and there he has been ever since.

His retirement from the world was, under the circumstances, extraordinary. Aurobindo had possibilities of the rarest kind, and had already made such an impression upon Indian political thought that it never again returned to the relatively static con-dition in which he found it. He was only thirty-eight and had seemed to be engrossed in the most engrossing of pursuits, a patri-otic (and perhaps conspiratorial) struggle for freedom. But dur-ing this same period he had been increasingly taken up by the practices of yoga, which he began in 1905. By 1910 he had ap-parently come to the conclusion that one person could not live two such different lives at the same time; it was then that he went to Pondichéry.

There are four yogas or ways toward union with God recog-nized and systematically developed in Hinduism. (The word yoga literally means union but is used for any spiritual exercise showing a way toward union.) *Raja-yoga*, unfortunately the one best-known in the West, is a progressive series of exercises in control of the body, the breathing and the mind, leading toward concentration, stillness and finally realization. *Jnana-yoga*, the way of knowledge, is a directly intellectual approach through meditation: its word of command is "Know thyself," [7] precisely as was inscribed over the shrine of the oracle at Delphi. Then, since "The real self of man is verily the same as the Great One," [8] the realization of union takes place. *Bhakti-yoga*, the way of love, is a process of concentration through love and

7 *Mundaka Upanishad II, 2, 5.*
8 *Brihadaranyaka Upanishad II, 5, 19.*

devotion, by prayer, chanting, and all the forms of worship, including the study of the scriptures; it tends to concentrate on one of the personal forms or incarnations of God (Krishna and Rama are the favorites among the Vaishnavites, those chiefly given to *bhakti-yoga*); this path has strong similarities to the devotional practices of Christianity and Islam. *Karma-yoga*, the way of action or deeds, the fourth way toward union, demands the fulfillment of the duties of life in the world selflessly, without regard for rewards and in obedience to the will of God. The fourth or *karma-yoga* draws its scriptural inspiration from the *Bhagavad Gita*, that "song celestial," which, although it occurs in the Sanskrit epic *Mahabharata*, has in subsequent centuries been elevated to canonical status. The way of action in the world is, on the face of it, the most difficult yoga of all, and is regarded by Hindu teachers as being made easier by combination with one or more of the other yogas. The most conspicuous follower of the *karma-yoga* in modern times, perhaps in all times, was Mahatma Gandhi, who relied heavily upon the other systems—prayer, devotional exercises, love, meditation—to help him on his way. All four of the yogas, it should be made clear, must begin only after a moral and ethical preparation has taken place, involving truthfulness, non-violence, cleanliness, continence and various austerities. *Raja-yoga*, the system which includes elaborate disciplines for the control of the body, has attracted most attention in the West because some of its achievements look like a form of wizardry or physical impossibility. It is also the system which most lends itself to the deceptions (deliberate or unconscious) of charlatans, a breed for which the idle and prosperous elements of the Western bourgeoisie have always been easy prey. But even *Raja-yoga*, if pursued with caution and patience over a sufficient number of years, does result in the equanimity of spirit and subjugation of body in which the adept is said to find union with God.

What precise combination of these yogas was evolved by Shri Aurobindo as most suited to himself we do not know, but in all probability all played their part. For the first four years after he left the world he remained in silence and solitude. Then (1914) he began to publish some philosophical and critical work in a magazine called *Arya*, in Calcutta, and continued to do so for nearly seven years. This work, the fruit of his reflections in solitude, was collected into various books afterwards, the most comprehensive of which is *The Life Divine*. Gradually a number of disciples gathered around him, and from time to time he spoke to them; their number increased through the years until it became necessary to make a sort of colony of the students who came seeking clues to wisdom. His retreat thus acquired fame by word of mouth through all India, and after the passage of so much time (he had been withdrawn for thirty-seven years when I was in India last winter) it was probably better known than any other.

Through all this expanse of time, Shri Aurobindo always refused to "come out," as they say, although great inducements were offered. More than once he refused the presidency of the Indian National Congress. His hermitage is accessible only to those chosen by his immediate associates for conversation with the anchorite; others go to Pondichéry and remain for weeks or months without ever catching a glimpse of him. Most of them are content if they can receive instruction or suggestions from one of the half dozen persons closest to Aurobindo. At other periods—for months at a time, I have been told—Shri Aurobindo does not even see his closest associates, those who have been with him for a quarter-century or more. He communicates with them in writing, by small notes reduced to the barest necessities, and spends the whole of his time in communion with what we may suppose to be "knowledge absolute in existence absolute." [9] What distinguishes him from the hermits and "holy men" who have abounded in India at all times, as they do today, is that his meditations do eventuate in works of philosophical range, depth and validity, in which he returns to the world that which he has found in the upper reaches of the aspiring consciousness. In this way he is an almost perfect example of what Professor Toynbee, in *A Study of History*, has familiarized to a large public as "withdrawal-and-return."

Aurobindo's philosophical work is not easy to read. His English writing style borrows heavily from Sanskrit literature, so that when he says "the Ignorance" one is supposed to apprehend the concept *avidya*, and when he says "the Knowledge" we are supposed to understand the concept of *vidya*. (In Shan-

[9] Plato: *Phaedrus*.

kara all "lower knowledge," including personal gods, theology, the personal soul and its transmigration, etc., etc., belongs to and is created by *avidya;* the "higher knowledge," which is absorption into the formless, impersonal Brahman, is *vidya.*) Some acquaintance with Western science, philosophy and history would seem necessary for the most superficial understanding of what he writes, along with at least an awareness of the divergences and dichotomies in Hinduism. In this writing the atmosphere at times gets so rarefied that one wonders if any other person besides Aurobindo fully understands his precise meaning. In spite of the cloudy realms to which it rises, his work does make a sustained effort to link the two forms of knowledge and others which are not spiritual at all into a system of "ascending terms of being," in which we find, for the first time, a comprehensive account of the possibilities of matter, life, mind and spirit. The system of Aurobindo would accommodate such investigators and discoverers as Darwin, Marx and Freud in its lower areas without any trouble, as it would take Ramanuja also on its ascension to *sanyag-darshana,* the final cognition which is union with Brahman. One of the difficulties in obtaining a coherent view of Hinduism has always been that its multitude of forms and variety of concepts fall, roughly, into two great systems, one esoteric and one exoteric, one for the initiate and one for the vulgar. Under the latter form, almost any extreme of idolatry and, indeed, degraded practice, can be justified; under the former, ending in universal cognition, the soul itself is identical with Brahman and is indifferent to the life of this mundane era in all its forms. Aurobindo's thirty-eight years of retirement from the world have produced a statement of the consciousness which provides for the relative and conditional realities of both extremes and of all their intervening gradations. If Hinduism is "syncretistic" at all—which, in spite of Professor Toynbee and a number of other writers, I take leave to doubt—then this might be called a triumph of syncretism. However, that word, which means the deliberate adaptation of foreign gods into the system of one given religion (such as Christianity), is hardly applicable to the long and all-inclusive natural growth called Hinduism. Even Shri Aurobindo's inclusiveness, the most complete to be found in print so far as I know, is Hindu in every aspect and derives none of its essential character from that which he includes but rather from the very breadth of the inclusion.

Now, then, would you expect a hermit sage who was also a recondite metaphysician to be the object of wide popular interest on the part of a largely unschooled mass of people? I have said that Aurobindo's works are difficult to read: I will go further and say that they would be unintelligible to most readers without some preparation. And yet what we find is that three times a year immense multitudes gather at Pondichéry from all over India, as they have done for a good many years, to receive darshan from this anchorite. He comes out of his retirement (the Platonic "cave") on his own birthday—which happened to be the day chosen for the liberation of India in 1947—on his mother's birthday and on the anniversary of his "realization." (Realization is the universal cognition, *sanyag-darshana*, in which the soul is at one with God.) On each of these occasions people journey from all over India, some of them going a large part of the way on foot, to catch a remote glimpse of the sage. Nothing is expected of him except his visible presence. Three, four, five hundred thousand people make this pilgrimage for the concept they call darshan. It must, therefore, have a reality in the Hindu mind which has nothing to do with the ordinary motives of curiosity or collective excitement, little or nothing to do with the emotions of nationalism, patriotism and even religion as the West understands religion. It occurs because such proof of the existence of a great embodiment of the spirit is itself a source of happiness to those who deeply feel and intimately believe themselves to share in that spirit.

I must, of course, mention the legend which plays a part here. Aurobindo is widely supposed to possess mystic "powers," that is, the ability to contravene supposed physical laws by efforts of concentration and will. However this may be, it is certain that he never makes such claims publicly and if there should be some who expect strange occurrences (what the Christian world calls miracles) at Pondichéry, they are likely to be disappointed. I doubt if this legend plays much part in the case, although of course miracles may occur—they are not unusual in disturbances or exaltations of the mass consciousness—and be magnified by legend. On the whole I believe the Pondichéry phenomenon is a pure and simple case of Hindu multitudes seeking darshan. And, as it happens, since Shri Aurobindo spends so much of his time in the *sanyag-darshana*, the absolute cognition, we have here an example, I think the only contemporary example, which is subject to intellectual tests acceptable in the West, of a meeting of the two darshans, the cognition of God according to ancient philosophy, and the modern cognition by the multitude of one who has known God. This, then, is pure darshan, and since it occurs on such a scale, we can have no doubt that our interpretation of the sense and meaning of the vast crowds assembled around Gandhi and Nehru is correct on the same principle. "I do not believe in an exclusive political interest," said Tagore.[10] For India he was right: there may be many forms, but there is only one spirit.

3

Aurobindo Ghose was chosen to exemplify pure darshan because any Western mind, however unfamiliar with Indian conditions, can see that no other reason will explain the annual pilgrimages made to his retreat. And his case is subject to intellectual tests acceptable to this same Western skepticism because his work is written and published, his system of ideas can be explored, and some connection can be established between what he attempts to do and the response it evokes from the population.

In many other cases—where there is no published work, where the "holy man" is not a scholar or philosopher of quality, where the entire phenomenon is beclouded by myth—pilgrimages also occur or have occurred, and on the lower levels of this kind of experience gross deceptions are common. Thousands of ascetics and mystics in India impose upon the people by means of claims they make, or claims made for them, to *sanyag-darshana* (the cognition of Brahman), or—much more simply and commonly—to special perceptions and supraphysical powers. The credulity of the masses is great, and is in part a result of these very lofty philosophical ideas which tower over all Indian thought: by the time philosophy reaches the village it is often difficult to identify. And, moreover, the claims made for all these *yogin* and *sann-*

[10] *Nationalism*, p. 117.

yasin are by no means wholly unfounded. Prolonged asceticism combined with certain specified kinds of physical training does give an extraordinary control over the body, which the adept appears to be able to leave at will. Any traveler in India must have seen numerous examples of this. On my first visit there, when I was still in the army, the village nearest our airfield had a "holy man" who used to lie in an extremely uncomfortable position in the dust of the street through the hottest hours of the day, stark naked, in what presented every evidence of trance. He had "left his body," and anybody who doubted it was at liberty to duplicate the experience and see what happened. To an ordinary Indian even half an hour in such a place and position would have produced torture and illness. At Benares I saw such ascetics, smeared with mud from the Ganges, immobile day after day with lemons sewn to their naked skins, insensible, so far as one could see. Some kind of reverence, or at least of social consideration—not to speak of sustenance on the most limited scale—accrues to the poor wretches who engage in these enterprises. In the hills, where hermits and ascetics abound, mystical experience is thought to be more easily attained than elsewhere. In the south, a considerable amount of commercialized imposition on the people's credulity is said to exist in the neighborhood of the temples. In all these cases (there are scores of thousands) some low, crude form of darshan may be considered to take place between the "holy man" and the people. On ascending planes it takes place all through Indian life, reaching into fields quite unrelated to religion as we understand it; it is a powerful element in the influence of Ramakrishna's followers, has much to do with the prestige of all elderly scholars and philosophers, and blends quite naturally into the long Indian tradition of reverence for age. The Upanishads, after all, were always supposed to be mystic knowledge imparted by a master to a student living in the master's house (or by father to son), and the whole chain of Vedic thought has come from the darkness of prehistory by this means. Whether it is at the level of superstition and idolatry or the highest philosophical truth the essence of the darshan happiness is the same.

THE GITA AND THE GANDHI-GITA

THE *Mahabharata* contains over 100,000 *shlokas* (a certain kind of couplet), is equal to about eight times as much as the *Iliad* and *Odyssey* put together, and is by far the longest poem known to literary history.[1] It contains eighteen books with a nineteenth as supplement, and in this vast collection of material may be found everything from ballads and legends about gods, kings and heroes, to didactic discourses about many forms of thought and activity. There are manuscripts of the great work in Oxford, London, Paris and Berlin, and many others in India, but printed editions of the whole have appeared only in India; no translation of the entire work—and, in my view, no satisfactory translation even of its main parts—can be obtained in English. The exception is the *Bhagavad Gita*, which has been translated a great many times with an astonishing variation in results.

The story of the *Mahabharata* is almost buried under accretions of philosophy, theology and moral lessons, but in brief it goes as follows:

In the ancient kingdom of the Kurus along the upper Ganges river there lived two brothers, Pandu and Dhritarashtra. Pandu died young, leaving five sons, and Dhritarashtra became king of the Kurus and brought up Pandu's five sons (the Pandavas) along with his own hundred sons. The five Pandavas were, of course, god-born, like the heroes of Homer, each from a different nature-deity of the Vedic age. The eldest, Yudhishthir, was pious; the second, Bhima, was a great fighter, and the third, Arjuna, was a hero distinguished above all others in archery and feats of arms; the two youngest were twins, Nakula and Sahadeva. An unknown rival, Karna, appears in the tournament and fights Arjuna to a draw, for the first time throwing some doubt on the hitherto unrivaled prowess of the hero. This was welcome to the cousins of the Pandavas—Dhritarashtra's own

[1] Macdonell: *A History of Sanskrit Literature*, p. 284.

sons—who were jealous and coveted the throne to which the eldest Pandava had been declared heir. All the princes are suitors for the hand of the princess Draupadi, but she—by a polyandrous anomaly unique in Hindu literature—chooses to marry all five of the Pandava brothers. The jealous cousins continued to conspire against the five, and consequently the kingdom had to be divided, the Pandavas taking the part on the Jumna near modern Delhi. Yudhishthir's weakness (in the midst of his piety) was gambling; his jealous cousins, being aware of this, arranged for an expert gambler to play at dice with Yudhishthir until he had lost his wealth, the treasures of his kingdom, his elephants and slaves, his empire, his brothers, himself and, finally, his wife Draupadi.

The blind old king Dhritarashtra, their uncle, released the Pandavas from the actual bond slavery to which this condemned them, and they retired to the forest to live as fugitives, Draupadi accompanying them. They remained for twelve years in the forest.

When the term of banishment was up, the Pandavas (Yudhishthir being king) demanded the restoration of their kingdom. The Kauravas, their jealous cousins, of course refused, against the counsel of their aged father, Dhritarashtra, and the only recourse was the arbitrament of war. Pandavas and Kauravas then made preparation for the bloodiest conflict ancient India had ever seen, and the details of the preparation (with the councils of war and the speeches made there) are exhaustively given. Then, on the eve of the battle on the field of Kurukshetra, the hero Arjuna, the most skilful warrior of the Pandavas, falls into despondency at the thought of the coming struggle against his own kindred, and is admonished by the Lord Shri Krishna, his divine charioteer, in the great poem known as the *Bhagavad Gita*.

After the eighteen chapters, songs or cantos of the Gita (which has so much the air of an interpolation that earlier scholars were sure it must be one), the battle begins and lasts eighteen days. The Pandavas win after a dreadful destruction, and at the high point of the battle the hero Arjuna meets and vanquishes his old opponent Karna, the one foeman worthy of his steel. In the concluding books, all a sort of epilogue, there are lamentations and funeral descriptions followed by a prolonged moral and philosophical discourse from the dying Kaurava prince, Bhishma; this in turn is followed by the successive deaths of all the characters and the ascent to heaven for the final meeting with the Lord Shri Krishna in all his glory.

This "didactic compendium," as Macdonell calls it, imposed upon a primitive epic by many unknown artists over many ages, had come to be recognized as possessing sacred authority by the fifth century A.D., and thus was *dharma-shastra*, or scripture for the teaching of man's duty and religion. By the time of Shankara (circa 800 A.D.) it was as worthy of commentary and citation as any of the Vedic texts themselves. What all these philosophers and scholars do not say, however, is that it had also become a source of joy to the whole of the Indian people, who in its almost endless store of poetic legend have found food for the imagination of young and old through many centuries. The incidental stories piled up upon the basic narrative of the Pandavas and Kauravas are almost without number, and in spite of a strong didactic element, they are full of persuasive charm and suggestive humanity, so that the *Mahabharata* as a source of tales known to all the people is like a combination of Bible, Mother Goose, Homeric mythology and Grimm's fairy tales. The millions of Indians who cannot read learn these from their parents and hear them from wandering minstrels in song and story; simplified versions are innumerable; in recent years the technological instruments of the day (radio, films) have given them a new form of interest. The epic everywhere else has died: Homer, Virgil and their kindred are known to scholars only; even Dante and Goethe, their European descendants in less mythopoeic form, tend more and more to be the poets of literary folk; but in India the *Mahabharata* and the *Ramayana* live for the whole people.

But in straight English, unaccompanied by Sanskrit chanting, one is at a loss what to recommend. There are many translations; some of those into German and French may be better than those into English; some day I should like to hear it read aloud in Italian or Spanish, which seems to me a little nearer to Sanskrit vocally than our northern tongues. Mr. Gandhi himself always preferred the metrical English version of Sir Edwin Arnold—published under the title of "The Song Celestial" in 1865—and I have suspected that it might be because this was the first he ever knew; he read the Gita for many years in that version. For myself I always prefer eloquent prose to indifferent verse, and the Arnold translation does not appeal to me (even though I see it is very remarkable that he was able to put such an accurate version into English meters). I have tended to rely upon an extremely westernized and "literary" version in rhythmical prose by W. B. Yeats' friend who called himself "Shree Purohit Swami"—his own spelling—which is dedicated to Yeats on his seventieth birthday (1935) and betrays in some of its phrasing a tinge of the Celtic Twilight. Yeats later worked with Purohit on another translation published as *The Ten Principal Upanishads* in 1937, not long before his death; to this work he wrote an introduction which expresses what we all feel about the "scholarly" but unreadable versions of the great Indic poems.

"For some years," says Yeats, "my friend George Russell (A.E.) has quoted me passages from some Upanishad, and for those forty years I have said to myself—some day I will find out if he knows what he is talking about. Between us existed from the beginning the antagonism that unites dear friends. More than once I asked him the name of some translator and even bought the book, but the most eminent scholars left me incredulous. Could latinised words, hyphenated words, could polyglot phrases, sedentary distortions of unnatural English:—'However many Gods in Thee, All-Knower, adversely slay desires of a person'—could muddles, muddled by 'Lo! Verily' and 'Forsooth', represent what grass farmers sang thousands of years ago, what their descendants sing today? So when I met Shree Purohit Swami I proposed that we should go to India and make a translation that would read as though the original had been written in common English: 'To write well,' said Aristotle, 'express yourself like the common people, but think like a wise man,' a favourite quotation of Lady Gregory's—I quote her diary from memory. Then when lack of health and money made India impossible we chose Majorca to escape telephones and foul weather, and there the work was done, not, as I had planned, in ease and leisure, but in the interstices left me by a long illness. Yet I am satisfied; I have escaped that polyglot, hyphenated, latinised, muddied muddle of distortion that froze belief. Can we believe or disbelieve until we have put our thought into a language wherein we are accustomed to express love and hate and all shades between? When belief comes we stand up, walk up and down, laugh or swing an arm; a mathematician gets drunk; finding that which is the prerogative of men of action." And then, later, after a digression to show that English literature after 1922-1925 had cast off its preoccupation with social problems to create myths and ask the most profound questions, he says:

"Shree Purohit Swami and I offer to some young man seeking, like Shakespeare, Dante, Milton, vast sentiments and generalizations, the oldest philosophical compositions of the world, compositions, not writings, for they were sung long before they were written down. . . . Whatever the date, those forest Sages began everything; no fundamental problem of philosophy, nothing that has disturbed the schools to controversy, escaped their notice.

"It pleases me to fancy that when we turn towards the East, in or out of church, we are turning not less to the ancient west and north; the one fragment of pagan Irish philosophy come down, 'the Song of Amergin', seems Asiatic; that a system of thought like that of these books, though perhaps less perfectly organised, once overspread the world, as ours today; that our genuflections discover in that East something ancestral in ourselves, something we must bring into the light before we can appease a religious instinct that for the first time in our civilisation demands the satisfaction of the whole man."

For accuracy of rendering there is a praiseworthy version by Bhagavan Das and Annie Besant: it contains the Sanskrit text, a literal translation by Bhagavan Das and a flowing one by Mrs. Besant. And for the Gandhi interpretation there is, of course, the *Gospel of Selfless Action* with Sanskrit text and English rendering, preceded by Mahadev Desai's exposition of the Gandhi view ("My Submission") and followed by a detailed analysis. One of the great translations is apparently that made into Latin by August Wilhelm von Schlegel, the author of the German Shakespeare, with a Sanskrit text included—an early landmark in Sanskrit scholarship. Quite recently in America a new English translation, done in a collaboration like that of Yeats and Purohit (in which only one partner knows Sanskrit), has been published by Christopher Isherwood and Swami Prabhavananda. Another, with the Sanskrit words transliterated, has been published by Professor Radhakrishnan.

With all the defects of modern rhythmical prose, I still prefer the translation of Swami Purohit. Perhaps this is for no other reason than that it was the one I used in listening to the Sanskrit chants, which may give it in my mind's ear some touch of the ancient sonority: when I quote the Gita, it is from this that I shall quote. However, since Purohit spells his long i's phonetically—"Bheema" and "Bheeshma" instead of the more usual Bhima and Bhishma—I shall take the liberty of bringing his orthography into line with that adopted elsewhere in this book.

The poem begins with the question by the aged blind king, Dhritarashtra:

"The King Dhritarashtra asked: O Sanjaya! What happened on the sacred battlefield of Kurukshetra, when my people gathered against the Pandavas?"

The rest of the poem is supposed to be narrated by Sanjaya, who is endowed with supernatural vision for the purpose of telling the blind old king what happens in the battle. Sanjaya thus overhears and narrates the dialogue between the Lord Shri Krishna and the despondent hero Arjuna.

"Our army seems the weaker, though commanded by Bhishma," the narrator says, "their army seems the stronger, though commanded by Bhima."

The generals and warriors blew their conches, their horns made of shells, and "violently shook heaven and earth." At this point Arjuna, whose flag bore the Hanuman (the monkey-god) and whose charioteer was the Lord Shri Krishna himself in human form, asked to have his chariot drawn up between the two armies in battle array so that he could see them. The Lord Shri Krishna listens to the request and Arjuna beholds his kinsmen on the two sides.

"And his heart melted with pity and sadly he spoke: O my Lord! When I see all these, my own people, thirsting for battle,

"My limbs fail me and my throat is parched, my body trembles and my hair stands on end,

"The bow Gandiva slips from my hand, and my skin burns. I cannot keep quiet, for my mind is in a tumult.

"Ah, my Lord! I crave not for victory, nor for kingdom, nor

*for any pleasure. What were a kingdom or happiness or life to
me,*

"*When those for whose sake I desire these things stand here
about to sacrifice their property and their lives:*

"*Teachers, fathers, and grandfathers, sons and grandsons, un-
cles, fathers-in-law, brothers-in-law and other relatives.*

"*I would not kill them, even for the three worlds; why then
for this poor earth? It matters not, if I myself am killed.*"

The human pity and indecision of Arjuna on the eve of the
battle are instantly familiar to all men and establish a universal
familiarity of reference for the discourse of the Lord Shri
Krishna in reply. The theme is anything but novel; from ancient
and modern literature parallels could be brought, but it is perhaps
enough to say (as Mahadev Desai does) that Shakespeare found
it fruitful. Lady Blanch in *King John* is almost as sad as Arjuna:

> "*Which is the side that I must go withal?*
> *I am with both: each army has a hand;*
> *And in their rage, I having hold of both,*
> *They whirl asunder and dismember me.*
> *Husband, I cannot pray that thou mayst win;*
> *Uncle, I needs must pray that thou must lose;*
> *Father, I may not wish the fortune thine;*
> *Whoever wins, on that side shall I lose;*
> *Assured loss before the match be played.*"

Macbeth and Hamlet are similarly riven in the earlier parts of
those plays; Brutus in *Julius Caesar* cannot bring himself to
bloodshed "for the general good." The heroic hesitation and despondency on the brink of violence reflect a feeling deep in all
humanity, whatever its time or place, the revulsion against taking
the life of one's own kind, or more broadly, any life at all. As a
matter of fact, even Dante, the product of an age of incessant
bloodshed, put the violent in the *Inferno* (misunderstanding
Aristotle, who did not), in accordance with whether their deeds
of violence were against their neighbors, against themselves or
against God. The dilemma of Arjuna is perennial and more ancient than any written word: it exists today as in all other days.
What gives the Gita its appeal to the heart of man is the comprehensive nature of Krishna's reply, which in almost any in-

terpretation—and above all in Gandhi's—provides a key to the meaning of life in this universe.

Krishna calls upon Arjuna to overcome his faintheartedness and arise. Arjuna protests that it would be better to live on alms in this world than to slay the venerable elders, Bhishma and Drona; nor can we tell, says he, whether it is better to conquer or be conquered in this case; with his senses beset by anguish the hero says, "I will not fight," and falls silent.

"The wise grieve neither for the dead nor for the living," Krishna tells him. External relations are impermanent; the Spirit pervades all things and alone survives; it discards worn-out bodies and takes on fresh ones; death is as sure for that which is born as birth is for that which dies.

"The end and the beginning of beings are unknown. We see only the intervening formations. Then what cause is there for grief?"

(This beautiful couplet becomes, in the Gandhi-Desai version: *"The state of all beings before birth is unmanifest; their middle state manifest; their state after death is again unmanifest. What occasion is there for lament, O Bharata?"*)

Krishna then admonishes the warrior about his fame and the disgrace or dishonor he brings upon it by refusing to fight, and passes on to the highest peak of his discourse: the "philosophy" (according to Purohit) or the "attitude" (according to Gandhi) of Action.

Renouncing the fruits of action, looking on pleasure and pain, success and failure, with an equal eye, and thus rising above all worldly bypaths, including Vedic scriptures and philosophy, the intellect contemplates the Infinite and thus attains spirituality. In this resounding passage Krishna enjoins upon Arjuna to act and act rightly, but with no view to reward (no motive of what Gandhi called "selfish purpose"); there is also a warning against "being enamored of inaction." (Some have chosen to see in this a criticism of the Buddhists, who are otherwise unmentioned in the Gita.)

There follow then the famous nineteen *shlokas* which conclude the second song, discourse or chapter. They are the ones Gandhiji had chanted at every prayer-meeting, morning and evening, for many long years. They begin with Arjuna's question, how can one recognize the man who has reached understanding and concentration, pure intellect, and who is steady? How does such a man talk, live and act?

When a man has put aside all the cravings of the senses and finds his comfort or satisfaction in the Self (the soul—*Atman*) he is called the man of secure understanding. He is free from passion, fear and wrath, has no attachment anywhere, feels neither joy nor resentment at what comes his way; he holds all the senses in check and contemplates the Lord; if he does all this he attains to rest in God (Brahman) and thus oneness with Brahman.

Many may see at once that this is a definition which has parallels in the New Testament, Plotinus, St. Augustine, the Islamic mystics (Jalaluddin Rumi, the Sufi, is particularly to be quoted) and St. John of the Cross, to name a few. Passages from other literatures which in whole or in part give the same view of the "man of secure understanding" and the path to union are often (or usually) quoted in editions of the Gita, and their range is great. The Gandhi-Desai version quotes all that I have quoted and many more, ranging from Epictetus to Spinoza and Tolstoy. The celebrated *shlokas* 54-72, containing Arjuna's question and Krishna's definition in reply, thus touch in many of their elements upon a whole body of contemplative writing through the centuries. The enormous merit of the passage to Hindus, of course, is that it comes from the great age of the Indic past, is phrased with power and beauty in the Sanskrit language at its highest moment, and compresses into a brief chant all that a whole philosophical system had to teach about the perfectability of man. (The second song is in fact called *Sankhya-yoga*, or the path of discrimination.)

The third song, in Gandhi's view, considered as a whole, was the key to the Gita. In it Arjuna, more perplexed than ever, asks Krishna why, if detachment is superior to action, the Lord wishes him to engage in this dreadful battle. Krishna replies that there are in fact two attitudes in the world, that of the path through knowledge (or discrimination), and that of the path through action: *karma-yoga*. Freedom from action is not to be enjoyed by not undertaking action nor yet by renunciation of action; for nobody is ever inactive in this creation for one moment. Man excels when he engages his body in *karma-yoga*,

without attachment, with his senses under the full control of his
mind: he must do his allotted task as a form of sacrifice to the
gods (or powers of nature), without a thought of reward. Action
by the best men is also an example to others; and as for Krishna,
if he were not always in action these worlds would perish. The
interplay of the qualities of nature cause the act (or the form of
the act), with which, therefore, the wise man feels no attachment (and for which he will consequently claim no credit).

*"Therefore, surrendering thy actions unto Me, thy thoughts
concentrated on the Absolute, free from selfishness and without
anticipation of reward, with mind devoid of excitement, begin
thou to fight."*

When Arjuna asks what drives man to sin against his will, the
Lord Shri Krishna replies that it is lust, wrath, passion, which ob-
scures knowledge and envelopes this universe; Arjuna's first task
then is to overcome the passions. Thus ends the third song, the
karma-yoga or path of action.

In IV, when Krishna says he has taught this great secret to
sages and lawgivers of old, Arjuna objects that they lived before
Krishna did; thus he brings on himself a great poetic outburst on
the cycle of births and deaths. Krishna has been born many times
and knows his births and deaths, as Arjuna does not; for Krishna
is Lord of all beings, and yet comes to birth from age to age
whenever the right declines and the wrong prevails. He comes
on earth to save the righteous and destroy the wicked; one who
knows this secret of Krishna is set free at death to join him.
Krishna is not affected by action, nor is he concerned with the
fruits of action, burnt pure by knowledge. There are various
sacrifices pithily described, but Krishna tells Arjuna that knowledge is superior to them all. The greatest of sinners can cross the
ocean of sin by the boat of knowledge: let the Bharata then renounce and choose his path and arise! (*Jnana-yoga* or the path of
wisdom.)

The next two songs, V and VI, teach renunciation and self-
control. In the fifth chant Arjuna complains that Krishna has
praised both renunciation of action and right performance of
action; Krishna replies that both lead to salvation but that of the
two, *karma-yoga* (performance of action) is better than *sann-*

yasa (renunciation). The right action performed without regard
for its fruits is as pure as renunciation: both lead to the ruler of
all worlds and friend of all beings. In the sixth song Arjuna is
told some of the ways in which he can discipline his senses and
obtain self-control.

From Discourse VII to XIII we have the exposition of the
nature of reality and of devotion, in which Krishna develops the
theme of the universality of God in many forms and the salvation of the human soul by love, sacrifice, offerings of all kinds
and contemplation directed toward the Supreme. Discourse XII
(as Gandhi said—or Song XII or Canto XII) is one of the shortest of all, and Gandhiji used to recommend that it be committed
to memory: it defines the devotees who are dear to Krishna. Its
twelfth *shloka* puts renunciation of the fruits of all action at the
very top of the devotee's scale: it is better than practice (i.e.,
devotional exercises).

The thirteenth canto embarks upon a Hindu philosophical
lesson which is continued in the fourteenth, employing the terms
(mature and soul, the not-self and the Self, *prakriti* and *purusha*)
familiar in almost every ancient text. In the fourteenth we have
an account of the three-fold qualities of nature (the *gunas*—this
word is constantly used in Hinduism and is said to be familiar to
every Indian) and of how to transcend them. The fifteenth, in
logical progression, describes the perfection which is the Supreme Being (Purushottama), whom to know is to know all.
In the sixteenth and seventeenth, Arjuna is admonished about the
divine and devilish heritages, and in reply to a question about
those who act in faith (although without this particular revelation), Krishna answers in verses on the necessity of faith and
single-minded renunciation of the desire for fruits. Acts performed in any other spirit count for nothing in the hereafter as
here. (This seventeenth canto contains a condemnation of excessive austerities, ostentatious asceticism and the like.)

Returning to his main theme, the Lord Shri Krishna in the
eighteenth and final canto differentiates again between the renunciation of actions springing from selfish desire and the abandonment of the fruits of all action: an allotted task must be
performed, without attachment or desire of fruit, ignoring pain
and pleasure. There are various kinds of wrong action, among

which the clinging (with attachment) to righteousness is named as one because it, too, is desirous of fruit. Man wins to perfection by devotion to duty.

"If thou in thy vanity thinkest of avoiding this fight, thy will shall not be fulfilled, for Nature herself will compel thee.

"O Arjuna! Thy duty binds thee. From thine own nature has it arisen, and that which in thy delusion thou desirest not to do, that very thing thou shalt do. Thou art helpless.

"God dwells in the hearts of all beings, O Arjuna! He causes them to revolve as it were on a wheel by His mystic power.

"With all thy strength, fly unto Him, and surrender thyself, and by His grace shalt thou attain supreme peace and reach the eternal home.

"Thus have I revealed to thee the truth, the mystery of mysteries. Having thought over it, thou art free to act as thou wilt.

"Only listen once more to My last word, the deepest secret of all; thou art My beloved, thou art My friend, and I speak for thy welfare.

"Dedicate thyself to Me, worship Me, sacrifice all for Me, prostrate thyself before Me, and to Me thou shalt surely come. Truly do I pledge thee; thou art My own beloved.

"Give up then thy earthly duties, surrender thyself to Me only. Do not be anxious; I will absolve thee from all thy sin."

In the end Arjuna has no questions left. *"My delusion has fled,"* he tells the Lord.

"By Thy grace, O changeless One, the light has dawned. My doubts are gone, and I stand before Thee ready to do Thy will."

2

Mr. Gandhi said, "My interpretation of the Gita has been criticized by orthodox scholars as being unduly influenced by the Sermon on the Mount."

This was inevitable, since Gandhi himself at various periods in his life came under orthodox Hindu criticism as being too close to Christianity. It was inevitable in any case because the Gita has to be guarded by the orthodox at all times: long ago a Christian influence upon it had been suspected, and the nineteenth century European scholars tended to claim it in a way which gave offense to Indians. That aspect of the matter need not concern us—in fact, if we went off into such speculations it would be equally easy to detect a Hindu influence upon Christianity, especially in those texts in which Jesus tells men they can become sons of God like himself, "the eldest in a vast family of brothers." This idea is indeed Hindu, and antedates Christianity by many centuries: the Upanishads in which it is expressed are five hundred to a thousand years earlier than the New Testament. But the interweaving of such influences is beyond us. We are here concerned rather with the question of whether Gandhi's interpretation of the Gita—and hence his supreme law of truth and life—owes much or little or nothing to the Sermon on the Mount.

First we must ask if Christ taught non-violence, and the answer can hardly be anything but yes. "Resist not evil" is quite explicit: "whosoever shall smite thee on thy right cheek, turn to him the other also." [2] The verse immediately following this injunction is the one which most particularly struck Mr. Gandhi in his youth when—at the age of twenty—he made his first acquaintance with the great Christian document. It is: "And if any man will sue thee at the law, and take away thy coat, let him have thy cloke also." He was so penetrated with the truth and beauty he felt in these verses—in the whole Sermon—that through years of effort he actually became something like a summation of the Beatitudes, the meek, the merciful, the pure in heart, the peacemaker. It would be senseless to deny that a life so long and saintly owed something of its formulable essence to the lesson he took to heart when he was twenty. Of course it did. His reverence for Jesus and for the Sermon on the Mount illumined his long struggle and gave him strength for it.

But from this to an assumption that his was a Christian interpretation of the Gita is, it seems to me, an unjustifiable step. If you grant him the initial bold leap, in which Kurukshetra becomes the heart of man, all the rest of his interpretation is well within the framework of the Upanishads and the text of the Gita. His reasons for making that bold leap, which he formulates as we have already seen, were all based upon his perception of

2 Matthew 5, 39.

self-evident truth (i.e., self-evident to him) as shown by long study of the Gita itself. He brought to this study an array of special characteristics which may have determined his views more than he realized, but whatever their origins, these views were the sincere expression of a powerful spirit. I do not think it is necessary to seek an exclusive or predominant Christian influence in them, any more than it is necessary to attribute them to Buddha or any other teacher. As a matter of fact, Socrates comes as near to the Gandhian statement of non-violence as does Jesus himself. And in the New Testament there are contradictions, not only between the four Gospels and the earlier Epistles but within a single Gospel, so that in reality only one great Christian passage, the Sermon on the Mount as given in Matthew (and in Matthew alone), is a bold and clear declaration of non-violence as supreme law.

It has been said that Confucius taught non-violence, but I am unable to find it so. Moderation, social decorum, the golden mean and the good life as Confucius saw them provided as a matter of course for coercion and military power. He took such things, it would appear, for granted, although he did say in the *Analects* that the army would be the first factor in government that he would give up. In the *Shiki* of Szema Ch'ien there is a famous passage in which Confucius is threatened by a military officer named Huan Tuei. His disciples said, "We had better hurry away." Confucius said, "Heaven has endowed me with a moral destiny. What can Huan Tuei do to me?"

In these and similar passages there is a touch of the indomitable non-violence of Gandhi, but I have not been able to discover any passage in which Confucius explicitly teaches non-violence as a weapon against violence. Indeed there are passages (such as the one in which he says, "If we are to return kindness for evil, then what are we to return for evil?") which seem to indicate a contrary teaching. His most explicit direction in the *Analects* is the celebrated rule of "reciprocity" (*shu*), which is translated: "Do not do unto others what you do not want others to do unto you."

More precisely than this, so far as I know, Confucius did not state or impose any rule of non-violence. It was a rule for himself, of course, because violence would have been unbecoming in a sage—contrary to *li*, the propriety of conduct in social relations, the *pietas* of the Romans. But in his intercourse with the governing powers of his own age one cannot see that Confucius ever had a notion of abandoning the ordinary powers of coercion. Again and again he even advises this or that feudatory to attack another for practical reasons. And indeed, in the centuries when Buddha, Socrates and Confucius were alive, any attempt to introduce non-violence as a rule in the relations of states would have been chimerical indeed.

Absolute non-violence was, of course, Buddha's rule for himself and the members of his monastic order. This included non-violence toward all sentient beings, whatever they might be. It is clear that the chief reason why Buddha immured himself during the rainy season was that in that period, then as now, it was almost impossible to stir anywhere out of doors in India without inadvertently stepping upon some form of the sudden, lush and extravagant insect life. Compassion for all creatures was fundamental in Buddhism from the very beginning. But aside from that, which was something he found as an element in Hinduism before him, where is the non-violent teaching of Buddha? I do not find it. Primitive Buddhism appears [3] to consist entirely of the Four Sacred Truths and the Eightfold Path, which are metaphysical concepts without social application in ethics and politics. The "deliverance" of the self (instead of its "realization" as in Hinduism) was Buddha's aim, and he appears to have made no endeavor to carry the *ahinsa* of his own teaching into the social realm. Perhaps it was implied from his metaphysics, but the fact is that one sees today, in Southeastern Asia, whole generations of young men doing a term of service as Buddhist monks and thereafter quite cheerfully going on to serve in the army; so I am unable to perceive a clear doctrine of social non-violence in Buddhism, either primitive or modern. The philosophical belief does not appear to have any great influence on the social and political action.

And this, of course, is true also of Christianity. Two thousand years of violent war have constituted the history of all those na-

[3] Oldenberg: *Buddha*, Part II.

tions which profess belief in Jesus Christ. Popes and saints have been warriors in the Christian centuries; no idea of "turning the other cheek" seems to have prevailed except in the case of isolated mystics and, at the very beginning, in the early Christian martyrs. Until the ageing, bewildered and indignant Tolstoy wrote *The Kingdom of God Is Within You*, early in the present century, I doubt if anybody had ever plainly said in so many words that the Sermon on the Mount should be taken as a guide to the relations of men in society. Tolstoy's horror at conscription in czarist Russia, his dislike for the police and the courts, his rebellion against all forms of social coercion, as poured out in that ill-organized but passionate book, reached a young man in South Africa, Mohandas Karamchand Gandhi; and from this communication between older and younger genius the concept of non-violence as a social force slowly evolved.

When I say "evolved" I do not mean to suggest that Tolstoy alone was responsible for the central Gandhian idea and its deployment in history. The Tolstoy influence operated as a spur, but the elements were already there. They came from the depths of Hinduism, where *ahinsa* (literally "non-violence") has been, in various degrees of radiance, a force of light since the dawn of time. *Ahinsa* is one of those innumerable Sanskrit negatives for which one wishes the English language had some more positive equivalent. (*Advaita*, non-dualism, is another.) It is not really a negative idea but it reaches us in a negative form with the obstreperous prefix "non." As Gandhi interpreted it, it very often came close to being the same thing as the early Christian concept of "love." ("Faith, hope, love, these three; but the greatest of these is love.") There was a celebrated episode in the 1920's when the Mahatma permitted the veterinaries to anaesthetize a calf which was incurably ill and suffering. Orthodox Hinduism was outraged; the Mahatma courageously defended his course and faced the logical corollary that under some circumstances it might be equally advisable to remove a human life.[4] In other words *ahinsa* was, or became, in Gandhi's eyes, not negative at all but positive: not non-violence, but love.

By the time he had finished his translation of the Gita into

[4] Griswold: *Insights into Modern Hinduism*, p. 258.

Gujarati, with the notes in which he gives—very simply and plainly—his interpretation of it, the year was already 1929. He had lived a great life in the struggle for his people, both in South Africa and in India, and much of his practical technique had been fully developed and put into practice on a huge scale for twenty years. Some of the aspects of non-violence as a technique he owed to Henry Thoreau in the form of "civil disobedience." Other aspects had been developed by experiment in South Africa and had received the name of *satyagraha*. These were, objectively considered, political techniques in the Indian struggle. It is for the psychologists to decide whether such techniques can turn back upon the mind which gave them birth and influence its highest view of pure truth; I think not. My own view is that Gandhi's native genius, rooted in Hinduism, predisposed him to the aspiration toward *ahinsa* as the final flower of truth; that the Sermon on the Mount helped to strengthen this natural disposition when he was young; that the practical applications of the belief in intervening years were the product of events, necessities, and his own practical talent on the plane of external relations; but that his pure doctrine, as expressed in his interpretation of the Gita, was the expression of his soul's self at its highest level. I believe this because he asserted it to me at an hour when I felt him to be near his death and believed that he did also; I could have no doubt in the matter then or now. I return to his own words: "Ultimately one is guided not by the intellect but by the heart."

3

If I have made the progression of ideas plain, the reader will now see that no real comprehension either of India in the present century or of Mr. Gandhi's essential doctrine is possible without the Gita: the Gita is the key. His own astonishing career in public life derived its unique quality from the inner resources he never failed to consult for a great part of every day over about fifty years; his morning and evening prayers, his hours of daily meditation, his weekly day of silence, were disciplines and fortifications. At the center of this meditative and devotional citadel was the Gita. In India such sources

of strength are instinctively understood and reverenced even
by those who do not possess them. Mr. Gandhi was Mahatma
by spontaneous appellation of the people; his darshan was the
most valued in all India because the people felt in him some form
of realization of (or communion with) God; and when it became generally known, as it did long ago, that the Gita was his
highest source of spiritual language, then the Gita, too, returned
to an even greater familiarity among the people.

His Gujarati translation, made for the simple and poor, was
put into Hindi, Bengali and Marathi soon after. Thousands of
people who had little or no acquaintance with it before memorized the passages he wished them to memorize. Among his immediate followers and in larger circles of Hindu nationalism
some acquaintance with the great poem in Sanskrit became quite
common. Although saints and scholars had talked of the Gita
for centuries, and it was chanted regularly in schools or temples
—and although the *Mahabharata* as a whole, particularly its innumerable secondary myths and legends, had been folklore for
a millenium or two—I think it is quite fair to say that a general
acquaintance with the Gita among unscholarly and even unlettered people, among the general mass of Indians, awaited the
mission of Gandhi. Thus the poem which gave him such strength
was by him more widely disseminated than ever, so that the interaction enhanced the power of the Gita itself in the Indian consciousness.

No Western parallel exists: but if we could imagine a national
leader, social reformer and political genius with the personal
habits of Francis of Assisi existing in a Christian country, and
could further imagine that this unique personage insisted daily
for forty or fifty years on a textual knowledge of the New Testament in the original Greek as well as in modern languages, succeeding in some measure, then we might have a notion of what
Gandhi in relation to the Gita has meant in India. If the scholars
would have none of his Gita, no matter: it was for the people.

In the same way general notions of *karma-yoga* (the way of
action) came to be widely diffused. A professor at the Hindu
University of Benares spoke to me with scorn on this subject.
"Every other policeman you run into nowadays," he said, "calls
himself a *karma-yogin* and says that his work is *karma-yoga*."

No doubt this is quite true. The distinctive teaching of the Gita—not to be found elsewhere in the great Hindu scriptures—is that action in the world is in itself righteous if pursued selflessly. For a people which for some thousands of years has been taught that the world is a delusion, that holiness consists in withdrawing from the world and that the "householder" (i.e., the ordinary adult living an ordinary life) has little chance of realizing the ultimate truth of God, the Gita has unique value. Gandhi's emphasis upon it and his wish to bring it to masses of ordinary people made many Indians perceive for the first time that action in their own lives, in their own world, might be as good in the end (if selflessly pursued) as the most extreme austerity in an anchorite's cave. The social value of this teaching in a country so religious as India is self-evident.

There is discernible to this day a slight resentment on the part of academic scholars against such a generalization (or vulgarization, if you like) of the Gita's teaching. In the same way Gandhi himself in all the aspects connected with darshan, religious teaching and the Gita, is looked upon with some reserve. I have heard him called a "political leader" in rather disparaging terms by an academic philosopher in Benares, and I have been told on high authority that until Gandhi's time only "withdrawn" spiritual lights (hermit saints) were supposed to give vitality or grace by darshan. Under the traditional limitations no man who worked in the world, however good his work, could achieve the "spirituality" which it is assumed those who live in caves have reached. This is why one can say that Gandhi not only transcended the categories and transvaluated the values of the West, but quite literally those of India also. No man ever lived or worked more constantly in the world, and yet the instinct of the Indian people declared him to be the great soul of their common soul, valued his darshan more than any other and attributed to him a "spirituality" beyond any other. This broke down some age-old habits of mind, but I cannot see that the phenomenon is in any respect contrary to the meaning of the Gita.

The reverse is, in fact, true: in Gandhi's own life and personality, I perceive, or think I perceive, an embodiment and enactment of the Gita's teaching. It does not appear to me that any other has existed throughout Indian history. (According to the Gita itself, a King Janaka, who was of course a Kshatriya and therefore lived and worked in the world, had achieved spirituality and could confound the Brahmins; but Janaka remains in prehistory.) If we are to consider the Gita under the aspect of prophecy, which should be legitimate for any religious scripture, then the selfless warrior created by its burning words, the hero of the righteous battle and fulfillment of the Lord Shri Krishna's injunctions was Mahatma Gandhi. It could not possibly be said that the Lord Buddha, in his contempt for the external world, was the Gita's warrior in any sense. Still less could any of the secular rulers of India, or its hermit saints or scholarly philosophers, fulfill the inspired words. These seem to me to refer more precisely to Gandhi than to any other figure I can discern in the whole long pageant of Indian history. His interpretation of it, therefore, in terms of non-violence, acquires the value of life rather than the value of literature: he lived the Gita in non-violent terms. That was his interpretation and he proved it by his hero's death. Just as life transcends letters, so the Gandhi-Gita triumphs over the unanimous dissent of the scholars by the dramatic perfection of the life given to it.

Does this mean, then, that self-realization in the sense of the Vedanta came to Gandhi in the end, and that he was assumed into, or united with, Brahman? To such a question each observer will reply in accordance with his own most intimate beliefs. As a small exegetical detail, it is literally true that the definition given in the Gita of the conditions under which the mystic (or spiritual sage) leaves life never to return—i.e., to achieve union with the Supreme—were fulfilled at Gandhi's death in every respect except one.

"*If, knowing the Supreme Spirit,*" says the Lord Krishna in Song VII, "*the sage goes forth with fire and light, in the daytime, in the fortnight of the waxing moon, and in the six months before the Northern summer solstice, he will attain the Supreme.*"

It so happens that the moon was waning, not waxing, when Gandhi died; but all the other conditions were fulfilled. According to the Gita, if the mystic departs under these conditions he need not be born again, but if he departs by the "dark path" (i.e., in gloom, at night, during the opposing conditions of moon and solstice) he must be born again. Considering that it was Gandhi's expressed wish to be born again as an untouchable, the orthodox may find in the waning moon some support for belief that his prayer was granted.

To a Western mind there would seem little need to explore these possibilities. We all prefer to answer, as Confucius so often did, "I do not know." Certainly in Hinduism there must be solid ground for supposing that the karma passed on by Gandhi was immeasurably great, if any man is born to inherit it, just as in primitive Christianity his martyrdom would have seemed in itself the seal of union with God. However that may be, my own view is that his interpretation of the Gita was thereby proved— that at his death he actually became the Gandhi-Gita.

FORERUNNERS OF GANDHI

"For a century in the new India," Romain Rolland wrote in 1928, "unity has been the target for the arrows of all archers." These words in the introduction to his *Life of Ramakrishna*, a work of rare comprehension for Indian mysticism, are not strictly true; it would be easy to compile a list of very stout archers in the India of the past hundred years or so whose target was anything but unity. The divisive influences are great; they are perhaps greater today than ever. But what Rolland means is that the leaders thrown up by the spirit of India since 1928 have all made efforts toward unity, and that a singular family resemblance in compassion for humanity and aspiration toward Godhead runs through them. If Mahatma Gandhi was, as I believe, the most formidable historical phenomenon of the whole series, the one of which consequences on the largest scale have already been observed and of which others are yet to be seen, it is because the combination of his gifts touched the Indian consciousness in all its main areas. In no one of these areas was he without a precursor, and in some of them he had many; it was the combination and its harmonization with destiny in the sense of historical time that made Gandhi's genius so powerful. He was always ready to acknowledge his masters, who were indeed, each in his field, more highly developed than he: there was Gokhale in politics, Lokamanya Tilak in scriptural knowledge, others in other fields of work; there were in sanctity of personal life a large number of Hindu exemplars; and, above all, in sheer mysticism, that is, in the quality Indians call "spirituality," the Mahatma very humbly recognized himself to be a follower. There is no record of trance or trancelike conditions with Gandhi, no matter how severely he taxed his body by fasts or privations, and if he ever had a vision (as he must have had at some time or other) he never confessed it. He made the most rigorous effort throughout his life to keep to the level of sanity and concrete labor upon which he felt that he could be of most use to his people. Thus he would show a livelier interest in some new method of fertilizing the soil, some new use for homespun cloth, some innovation in diet or possible improvement in housing, than in the tales of wonder which abound in India.

And yet he was the product of all that went before him, including the extremest forms of mysticism. One reason why he disliked the Kumbh Mela—the religious fair at Allahabad which takes place every twelve years—when he saw it in 1918 was that all the excesses of religiosity among ascetics and *sadhus* were to be seen there; some of these things (I believe) seemed to him like a parody of what he most deeply felt. But certainly his reverence for Ramakrishna was strong and unfeigned, and a more extreme mystical phenomenon than Ramakrishna has yet to be observed on earth. Gandhi's reserve on the subject of religious "realizations" was seldom broken—never with respect to himself—but he wrote a foreword to the official *Life of Ramakrishna* (the biography prepared by the Ramakrishna disciples) in 1924 which is worth quoting in its brief entirety:

The story of Ramakrishna Paramahansa's life is a story of religion in practice. His life enables us to see God face to face. No one can read the story of his life without being

convinced that God alone is real and that all else is an illusion. Ramakrishna was a living embodiment of godliness.
His sayings are not those of a mere learned man but they are
pages from the Book of Life. They are revelations of his
own experiences. They therefore leave on the reader an impression which he cannot resist. In this age of skepticism
Ramakrishna presents an example of a bright and living faith
which gives solace to thousands of men and women who
would otherwise have remained without spiritual light.
Ramakrishna's life was an object-lesson in *ahinsa*. His love
knew no limits geographical or otherwise. May his divine
love be an inspiration to all who read the following pages.

M. K. GANDHI

Sabarmati,
Margheersh, Krishna 1,
Vikram Samvat 1981.

The short paragraph with its stubby, willing but embarrassed
sentences, ending with a date in the Hindu era (corresponding
to November 12, 1924) reveals more than it says. Gandhi was
unable to resist his own feeling that the hand of God had somehow fallen upon Ramakrishna, but at the same time he was even
more unable to go to the lengths of the true disciples to whom
Ramakrishna was not only "an embodiment of godliness" but
was, in simple fact, an incarnation of all the gods and goddesses
of all the religions. The very book which Gandhi thus intro-
duces starts out with the dreams, visions and supernatural omens
which preceded the birth of Ramakrishna and is hardly well
embarked upon its narrative before it is calling him "the divine
child." Such was not Gandhi's language. He may have felt that
these words referred to something which was in essence true—
indeed he must have felt so or he would not have written a foreword to the book—but it was not his way of speech. He preferred (like Rolland) to see "the divine spark" in all men and a
god only in God: consequently Ramakrishna in these sentences
of Gandhi's emerges as a human being of rare gifts. In a country
which, like India, has been all too inclined to excessive deification, the aseptic value of Gandhi's sanity could not be more
clearly shown.

And yet the fact remains that India possesses a special faculty of throwing up leaders whose significance is first understood or expressed in mystical religious terms: Ramakrishna (1836-1886) is the latest and from the point of view of Western psychology the most extreme, but the phenomenon has existed through millennia and exists to this moment. (There are a number of great contemporary examples, of whom their disciples speak in terms which the West reserves for God alone.) Gandhi could not disown a tendency so deep in Hinduism: it is nothing more than the thesis embedded in the Vedanta, that by realizing the Self the mystic is united with God. Thus Ramakrishna, the illiterate Bengali temple priest, cataleptic in youth and at all times a casebook of psychoanalysis, becomes one of the most formidable instruments in the revival of Hinduism, founder—through his great disciple Vivekananda—of a monastic order which has worked indefatigably for the regeneration of India, and represents to millions of devotees a divine incarnation no less revered than those of ancient times. The phenomenon could not have occurred outside of India.

But Hinduism was burgeoning with movements of reform and revival even before Ramakrishna. Indeed the whole nineteenth century in India provided a record of such movements on a scale unknown either in the West or in preceding Indian experience. The impact of British sovereignty, with its good and bad influences, had something to do with this: certainly a willingness to learn from the West was characteristic of many Indian movements, even in the strict sphere of religion. The British were aware, from the earliest days, that Hinduism was a world in itself which they might well study if they wished to rule India: translations from Hindu scriptures began in the eighteenth century and an impetus to systematic study of the Indian past was given by the early British rulers. (The first English translation of the Gita was made under the encouragement of Warren Hastings.) The crumbling Moghul empire had been Moslem, the British Raj was by definition Christian, and Hinduism had been for some centuries—thanks to unscientific methods of study, an astonishing indifference to accurate chronology, and a decline in scholarship under the petrified Brahminism of the day—without the power of renewal. The opening up of India, the acquisition of new wealth in certain privileged classes, an awakening of the national pride in its two important respects, the desire for reform and the desire for self-expression, helped to create the climate in which a dozen vigorous movements of revival could take place. At the outset of the nineteenth century, Hinduism was not only caste-ridden, but had such age-old abuses as *sati*—the burning of widows on their husbands' funeral pyres—and the marriage of children fastened upon it with Brahminical fanaticism. Educated and patriotic Hindus were bound to see these things with new eyes after the revolutionary change produced by the coming of the British. There would be—and there was—a desire to put the best foot forward, coupled with some sense of shame over abuses which shocked the Westerners so greatly; but there was also a genuine stir of conscience at the lethargy with which ancient errors had been allowed to dominate Hindu society. Calcutta, the commercial capital of the new India, growing rapidly and enriching certain classes of the Hindu community as it enriched England, was the natural center for such new currents of thought in the dawning century.

Most observers have agreed that the regeneration of Hinduism —or, to be cautious, the beginning of movements in that direction —can be dated from the activity of Ram Mohan Roy (1774-1833) who founded the religious society called the Brahmo Samaj in 1828. A Brahmin of great wealth and culture, with a hereditary position at the Moghul court in Delhi, Roy became familiar with Islamic culture in Persian and Arabic before he studied the Hindu scriptures. He began his life as a rebel when he was barely sixteen by attacking idolatry and orthodox Hinduism, for which his irate father disowned him; he then had four years of wandering through the country, during which time he studied Buddhism. When his family welcomed him back to Calcutta he was twenty years old, but he was not destined to remain in their good graces for long. The custom of *sati*, the burning of widows, horrified him and aroused his reforming zeal to such a degree that in 1799 his family ceremonially expelled him. This subject continued to be one of Roy's great crusades until the time of his death, and he did as much as any one Hindu to bring about a change of heart among the orthodox.

Roy's studies in English, Greek and Hebrew began in 1798

and continued throughout his life. The Christian influence upon the development of his mind was strong, and in 1820 he published a work called *The Precepts of Jesus, a Guide to Peace and Happiness*. He also briefly (about 1826) belonged to a Unitarian society, but Hinduism itself, in the Vedas and Upanishads, as it existed before it acquired the characteristics of later Brahminism, was the central influence of his life and his most persistent field of study. By the 1820's Roy's position in his native Calcutta was very great. Wealth had come to him at his father's death, and after some years of hard struggle his ideas for the reform of Hinduism had been increasingly considered among the more thoughtful of his own people. Among British civil servants and missionaries he found encouragement even from his most difficult days. Finally, in 1828, he was able with a group of associates to found the Brahmo Samaj, the House of God.

This universalist association was open to all comers, without distinction of color, caste or nationality. It was dedicated to the worship of "the Eternal, Unsearchable and Immutable Being, who is the Author and Preserver of the Universe." Roy wished its members to encourage "charity, morality, piety, benevolence, virtue and the strengthening of the bonds of union between men of all religious persuasions and creeds." The service consisted of recitations from the Vedas, readings from the Upanishads, sermons on Vedic texts and the singing of hymns which were, for the most part, composed by Roy himself. At this period no forms of prayer were used and the Brahmo Samaj could hardly have been defined as a "church." Its most distinctive characteristic, aside from the universalism which put all religions on more or less the same basis (barring, of course, idolatry), was the uncompromising simplicity with which it swept away all the dead lumber of Hinduism, the rites and ceremonies, the whole immense machinery of caste with its manifold abuses and the customs of *sati* and child marriage.

From the Brahmo Samaj were to come, as the nineteenth century unfolded, some of the most powerful influences upon the modern spirit of India. The Tagore family for three generations was at the center of the movement, although the poet Rabindranath abandoned it in his maturity to return to orthodox Hinduism. Ram Mohan Roy himself, the founder of the Brahmo Samaj, was a man of such commanding personality that he did not fail in an effect on everybody who came near him, and the broadest lines of his teaching were to give the direction for all who followed him in India for a century. That is, his universalism—his aim at the target of unity—and his energetic devotion to social reform were imprinted, as primary characteristics although in varying proportions, upon all the great teachers of the next hundred years down to and including Gandhi. The Brahmo Samaj itself as an organization never did reach the masses; it remained a society of middle-class intellectuals; its professed doctrine changed several times during the century and its veering from deism to theism and back again caused successive internal quarrels; but at all times from 1828 to the recent past its influence upon Indian thought has been far greater than its numbers would indicate. Hardly a leader in the late nineteenth century failed to come under its spell at some time or other—even Dayananda, the stern and uncompromising Vedic fundamentalist—and the conclusion is obvious that it must have expressed a deep need, a widespread and urgently experienced aspiration, on the part of all thoughtful Indians.

The first of those needs, the most insistent of those aspirations, was certainly the demand for unity. Any Hindu given to reflection must have perceived during those decades that the easy subjugation of India to Western sovereignty, the humiliating conditions under which life had to be pursued thereafter by even the most privileged of native sons, and the sense of hopeless decline and decay which permeated the whole of Hinduism for half a century, were due most of all to the multiplicity of forms in the primary aspect of Indian life, its religion. The very thing which enabled Hinduism to survive into modern times, its hospitality to every formulation of truth, was also the element which encouraged cruel abuses and permitted the growth of unlimited variation as well as degrading excess in polytheism and idolatry. To go back to the Vedas and Upanishads and find therein a counsel of lofty purity for the spiritual life, an assertion of Godhead beyond and above all such forms, seems to have been the most acute necessity for every questing spirit, every active mind and original personality, during the period between Ram Mohan Roy and Gandhi. It seems to be implied in the teaching of all the leaders for those seventy or eighty years that if Hinduism can accomplish a social reform of its own free will, and can rise to a pure unity of concept in the idea of God, its external destiny will take care of itself. Something very like this lies at the origin of Gandhi's mission, although he added to it those forms of external action which his peculiar genius found or invented as the need arose.

Ram Mohan Roy must have been one of the most startling, as he was one of the most original, of the Indian leaders here to be considered. He was lavish in entertainment, opulent in his way of life, as unlike an Indian mystic as may be imagined; he was at all times a friend of the English, whose coming to India he regarded as the beginning of a new era for his own people; he was friendly to Islam throughout his life; and into the Calcutta of those days he must—with his seven languages and his European culture, his wealth and variety of acquaintance—have introduced a note of cosmopolitanism never known before. We can see now that the originality of his idea was too great for his followers. The Brahmo Samaj after his death was repeatedly subjected to doctrinal changes and shifts which left the system of Ram Mohan Roy, so rationalistic and universalist, almost buried under accretions. He was perhaps too much ahead of his time, but without some such indomitable personality—quite willing to use his advantages, worldly or other-worldly—it is not easy to see how a great movement of reform and revival could have been started in the petrified Hinduism of those days. Whatever was flamboyant or eccentric in Roy served his purpose too, along with his austerity of philosophic method and his sound scholarship. When the Emperor at Delhi sent him on an embassy to England he made a deep impression, and ended his life in that characteristic enterprise, dying at Bristol on September 27, 1833. He is buried at Bristol and a portrait of him is preserved in the museum there.

2

The Tagore family was associated with Roy and the Brahmo Samaj from the beginning. Dvarakanath Tagore, grandfather of the poet Rabindranath, was Roy's friend and supporter. Debendranath Tagore, the poet's father, was head of the Brahmo Samaj as the second successor to Roy, and most of its mature formation was his work. Debendranath received one of those appellations arising from the people which are so common in modern India, and was known as "Maharshi" (the Great Seer) all through the later part of his life. He was, like Roy, a Brahmin and wealthy, with the charm, wit and good looks which seem to have run through many generations of the Tagore family. The poet Rabindranath has left, in his *Recollections*, a few fleeting glimpses of the awe-inspiring but kindly father, the great man of the numerous Tagore clan and a figure of great consequence in Calcutta. Another glimpse comes in the memoirs of Swami Vivekananda, who as a youth went to see the Maharshi to ask, "Have you seen God?" (It was apparently young Vivekananda's embarrassing habit to produce this question for all whom he thought capable of answering it.) The Maharshi Tagore answered: "My boy, you have yogi's eyes."

The Tagores were a gifted breed. Poets, singers, reciters of verses, preachers in the Brahmo Samaj, they were all active and sociable, fond of talk and of gatherings in which everything from political argument to amateur theatricals took place. The poet's *Recollections* enshrine a number of the cousins and other relatives in the imprecise nostalgic glow of a house whose rooms and verandas were forever full of people coming and going, remembered as being all amiability, poetry and flowers. The word used for these unceasing assemblies was *mujlis*, which in Bengali meant any kind of uninvited informal gathering. Life in the Tagore household appears to have been one long *mujlis*, and we derive an impression both of Debendranath's popularity and of his wealth from the accounts of its cheerful hubbub.

Debendranath's influence spread not only over all Bengal, but to a considerable extent over all India. The Brahmo Samaj under his administration reached what was probably its peak of prestige in the middle of the century (1859-1865), to be followed by a series of doctrinal quarrels and divisions brought on by the revolt of Keshab Chander Sen, a brilliant preacher and religious innovator who did not happen to be a Brahmin. Before he was twenty-five Keshab had already split the Brahmo congregation in Calcutta. The poet Tagore tells us in his *Recollections* that his father had no objection to a non-Brahmin conducting church services for the Brahmo Samaj; but certainly Debendranath's conservatism on a number of points was the chief reason for the revolt of the non-Brahmin Keshab. Debendranath, for example, did not like intercaste marriage or the remarriage of widows, two reforms which Keshab and the young men were insisting upon. Keshab and his followers left the Tagores in 1867 to found the Brahmo Samaj of India, a more advanced universalist cult than the distinctly Hindu organization (called Adi, or Original, Brahmo Samaj) of Debendranath. This in turn went through more doctrinal shifts and schisms, until Keshab ended his life with a "New Dispensation" church which accepted all religions as true, borrowed baptism and the Lord's Supper from Christianity, and relied on ideas from other non-Hindu sources as well as from Ramakrishna for its body of belief. A great, restless and ebullient spirit, Keshab appears in all this activity to have split and weakened the universalist movement in India beyond repair. Statistically its branches grew smaller as they grew more numerous, and toward the end of the nineteenth century the minds which were still obstinately attracted to the idea of unity tended to find or seek it in Hinduism itself. Eight or ten thousand members of the various branches of Brahmo Samaj were still active, but the vital impulse for which Ram Mohan Roy had spoken was now turned in upon its own origin and sought for the regenerative power of unity in those ancient philosophic concepts which had been phrased anew by Ramakrishna.

It was Ramakrishna, therefore, and not the Calcutta intellectuals of the Brahmo Samaj, who gave the most living current, direction and experiential reality to the Hindu revival. But the Brahmo Samaj, Roy and the Tagores and Keshab, all had their seminal effect through the nineteenth century and after, perhaps in ways which are not easily traced. The poet Tagore, even after his return to Hinduism, showed in the formation of his intellect all that the Brahmo Samaj had done to his earliest experience, and his own universalism as shown in his late work, *The Religion of Man*, is its legitimate child. Tagore in the early novel called *Gora*, which stands apart from all his other work in many qualities, treats of the old Brahmo society of Calcutta in a mood of affectionate reminiscence. We feel in the leisurely, pleasing pages of that book some family resemblance to the French Protestant society described by André Gide, or to the Boston intellectuals of Emerson's day as treated in a hundred books. The Brahmo society of Tagore's youth was high-minded, abstemious, animated by all sorts of projects for social reform, full of intellectual curiosity darting about in all directions, and filled with the sort of patriotism which felt that India could be revived only by its own spirit from its own resources. Gora was a young man of a Brahmin family who believed in strengthening Hinduism by fanatical insistence on the old rites and the caste system, only to discover, in the end, that he was no Brahmin in fact, but the foundling child of an English-Irish couple killed in the great Indian mutiny. Gora's family life, his wonderful Hindu mother (foster-mother) and the Brahmo family into which he finally married, all become real to us in Tagore's sorrowing, almost painful, narration; and his gravitation to the Brahmo Samaj, through a beautiful young Brahmo girl with whom he falls in love, is given inevitability by the poet's sense of the wrongs of Hindu society.

The rational universalism of the Brahmos was not, however, with all its charm and its appeal to intellectuals, dynamic enough to do much to India as a whole. The *mystique* of the Hindu revival, its emotional force and authority over the masses, came from quite another source: from the Bengali saint Ramakrishna and his impassioned monastic disciples. Here again, as has also happened in the West, reason and unreason appeared to move in the same direction, were in fact extremes of the same general statement, but it was unreason which gave the power, created the tide, set in motion the sun, moon and stars for generations of men.

3

Ramakrishna was born February 18, 1836, in the village of Kamarpukur in Bengal. His name was Gadadhar (a Shiva name) and his parents were simple, devout and very poor Brahmins. The child's birth had been preceded by visions, omens and signs which need hardly cause surprise, since the pious, illiterate villagers who were his parents were well past the ordinary age for having children. (His father was sixty, his mother probably in her late forties.) Khudiram, the father, was on a pilgrimage to Gaya in the year before the child's birth and had a vision in which the Lord Buddha announced to him the coming event as an Incarnation of himself. Chandra, the mother, had similar dreams and visitations. When the child was born it did not take long for him to acquire the family habit of communication with the invisible. It was in the air he breathed; he must have heard of such things as soon as he heard anything; his older brother, the priest Ramkumar, was much given to prophetic visions, and their mother, Chandra Devi, never ceased to be troubled by the spirits from the time her pregnancy began. The child Gadadhar therefore was predisposed, by heredity and early experience, toward unrestrained mysticism. His father had always been convinced, ever since the vision of Buddha, that this was a child of divine gifts, and never stopped saying so even in the earliest years. The tranquil simplicity with which Ramakrishna in later times used to speak of himself as a divine incarnation troubled even his most devoted disciples (such as Vivekananda), but no doubt, since he had heard this stated ever since he could remember, it did not seem so strange to him.

The first trance recorded for this extraordinary being took place when he was six years old and was occasioned by seeing a flight of white cranes fly across a thundercloud. The beauty of the spectacle threw the boy into an ecstasy of happiness in which he lost consciousness; some neighbors found him lying in the field and carried him home to his terrified parents. He was destined to spend a great part of his life—Romain Rolland says about half of it—in these supernormal states, trance or ecstasy, and all through the early part of his life they were accompanied by definite physical symptoms. One was an afflux of blood to the skin, which is fairly common among Indian mystics: in later years Ramakrishna used to look at the skin of visiting *sadhus* to see whether they had the purplish tinge which comes of such experience, and if they did he knew that their claim to ecstasy was real.

Up to the age of twenty Gadadhar, as he was still called, had the ecstatic experience frequently but without being able to give it much explicable meaning. At one time when he was playing

Shiva in some amateur theatricals, he became Shiva; at other times he became one of the other gods or goddesses; his losses of consciousness and his astonishing behavior might have landed him in a lunatic asylum, even in India, if his family had not kept their belief in his divine mission. His brother Ramkumar tried to get him through school but failed: the boy refused to learn and preferred his semi-imaginary life in the native village to any study in Calcutta.

A rich woman of low caste wished to found a temple there and had difficulty obtaining a Brahmin to officiate as a priest; she offered the place to Ramkumar, Gadadhar's older brother, who was able to serve only for one year and then died (1856). The rich benefactress, Rani Rasmani, thereupon accepted the younger brother in his stead, and Gadadhar—whom we may as well call Ramakrishna henceforth—entered upon his lifework.

His evolution in the next thirty years was remarkable. If he had continued as a mere visionary, a cataleptic with religious mania, he would have been one of the innumerable poor *sadhus* of India without effect upon the mind of his time. But, as it happened, this strange and sexless creature, who was both male and female in his own visions, whose trances lasted for days or (on one occasion) for weeks, who subjected himself to ferocious austerities and had the most fantastic conversations with the unknown, was also a genius, with a mind which was able to struggle through and eventually to surmount every extravagance of his own temperament. As for the origins of that temperament, the explanations both pathological and psychological, some are so obvious that they need not be mentioned. Ramakrishna, a child of nature, had certainly never heard of them and would not have cared if he had. We may agree with William James when he says, in *The Varieties of Religious Experience*, that we must "be ready now to judge the religious life by its results exclusively," so that "the bugaboo of morbid origin" need not disturb us. As he also suggests: "If there were such a thing as inspiration from a higher realm, it might well be that the neurotic temperament would furnish the chief condition of the requisite receptivity."

Ramakrishna went through ten years of intense ritual devotion as priest of the goddess Kali. This goddess, to whom he always referred as "The Mother," is identified with Parvati and other wives (*shakti*—energies) of Shiva, and at the highest level of the Hindu pantheon is worshipped throughout India. She does appear, however, to be a survival from pre-Aryan antiquity, absorbed into Hinduism by the method of identification, but presenting a good many Dravidian characteristics. Under an enormous variety of names she is worshipped all over South India, where the village goddesses usually have some vague resemblance or approximation to Kali, even when the identification is not clear. God as Mother is a familiar concept in all centuries of Hinduism. Kali, however, has many terrible aspects, is a destroyer as well as a preserver, and is usually represented in the aspects of menace and vengeance. Her skin is black and her appearance anything but kindly. It is all the more remarkable, therefore, that the gentle, pure and ecstatic young priest Ramakrishna saw her practically always as beneficent, in all the tenderness and forgiving grace of the mother-concept.

He was not given these visions to begin with. He was so consumed with love for Kali that he engaged in every excess of fasting, sleeplessness and incessant devotion. All this is described to us by himself and his disciples: how he stripped himself of all clothing, even of the sacred thread which no Brahmin should ever remove, and prostrated himself before her. His losses of consciousness, his trances and cataleptic fits, became a matter of public scandal and he was in danger of losing his place as priest of the temple. For a time he was unable to perform his duties because of the frequency of these seizures. His benefactress, Rani Rasmani and her family kept him on in spite of his condition and in spite of the widespread belief that he was insane. (The seizures in which he became rigid sound like what is called in sanatoria "catatonic schizophrenia," while some of the others appear to have been cataleptic.) At length, after some years of this intense suffering, the devotee received his reward in the form of a vision of the goddess, who never left him thereafter; even in his latest and sanest years he used to consult her regularly and report her commands to his disciples.

At various times during his *sadhana*—religious apprenticeship or training—Ramakrishna's madness for God took other forms. He became Radha, the mistress of the Lord Krishna, for six months at one time; he became the monkey-god Hanuman at another. In these as in other cases (as later when he went through months of preparation for the visions of the Lord Jesus and the Prophet Mohammed) his method was that which is called "dramatic imitation." When he was about to become Radha he dressed and lived as a woman, associated only with women and hypnotized himself into thinking he was a woman until the vision of Krishna arrived. In short, all the morbid phenomena were there. It seems beyond doubt that this extraordinary being possessed a histrionic instinct of the most advanced type, which, combined with his capacity for browbeating his own consciousness into almost any belief, ended by a form of possession in which he actually *became* that upon which he had fixed his desire.

But all this hallucinatory life of the religious craving, although real enough to him, might still have ended in ordinary insanity if he had not received external help when it was most needed. The first of his *gurus* was, characteristically for him, a woman: she came up the temple steps one day from the Ganges and told him she had been sent to him by the spirit of God. This woman is known in the literature of the subject as "the Brahmin Nun," or *Bhairavi Brahmani*, and her real name has not transpired. (Ramakrishna would never have asked her.) She stayed at Dakshineswar for six years and played a great part in bringing the ecstatic and ignorant neophyte up to a clearer level of consciousness. When she arrived he had been through the worst of his sufferings, his body was a wreck and his mind unhinged; he had been told, and apparently believed, that he was insane. The Bhairavi consoled him and said that he was not insane but had been blessed by a state of religious ecstasy which it took others many years to achieve. The nun, who appears to have read a great deal in devotional literature, was a *Bhakta*, a devotee of the *Bhakti-yoga*, and as Ramakrishna confessed to her all his extraordinary inner experiences she told him that he had lived through, by his own nature and instinct, all the stages through which the *Bhakta* is supposed to go in his search for God. Ramakrishna and the nun established the relation of mother and son, and she remained to instruct him in what he already knew indeed, but knew without realizing that any human being except himself had ever experienced. She conducted this instruction systematically, according to all the "nineteen attitudes," or ways of the soul in devotion, and ended by declaring that Ramakrishna had achieved them all and was an incarnation of the divinity.

In 1864 another momentous visitor arrived at Dakshineswar. This was an ascetic known as the Naked Man (*Tota Puri*), who, like the Brahmin Nun, has no other name. Ramakrishna had achieved a knowledge of the Personal God and was much calmer in mind; what remained, in the higher reaches of Hinduism, was the Impersonal God, and this Tota Puri proceeded to teach him. This knowledge—the Vedanta—requires of the devotee a renunciation so complete that all forms or names must be surrendered, including those of divinity. It was a struggle even for Ramakrishna, who was no novice at ecstasy, to achieve the concentration necessary for *nirvikalpa samadhi*, the abstraction of the spirit from the body in union with Brahman; but this, too, he reached at last.

The cataleptic trance which followed the departure of the Naked Man lasted six months. A devoted nephew managed to keep the body of Ramakrishna alive while his consciousness was roaming the infinite. The mystic was rigid for a great part of this time and how he survived at all is a puzzle to Western minds. On his return to normal consciousness he was wasted and ill, suffered a violent attack of dysentery, and had learned never again to lose himself so far. He developed disciplines—described to us by his disciples who witnessed them later—by which his last conscious thought before going into *samadhi* would be something very simple and terrestrial, such as the autohypnotic iteration: "I will have a smoke. I will have a smoke." This apparently remained somewhere in his consciousness and was able to drag him back after relatively brief periods of trance. He also repeatedly warned his disciples in later years against extreme forms of religious ecstasy and declared to them (especially to Vivekananda) that service to mankind was far more important.

For an extraordinary transformation had taken place in Ramakrishna as a result of all these fearful experiences. When he came back to earth, so to speak, in 1866, having explored every form of mystical adventure on all the planes known to Hinduism, he came to the conclusion that both versions of reality (the Personal and Impersonal God: body and spirit: Bhakta and the

Vedanta) were aspects of the same. His exacerbated sensibility had been worn so raw that for months after his return to normal consciousness he could not bear to hear sounds of violence: he would howl with grief when he heard two boatmen on the Ganges in a quarrel. In his senses and essence he felt himself to be both of them. The differentiation between human beings was difficult for him to resume: he maintained to the end of his days that all persons and things were forms of the same spirit. But he did not yield to the idea that Maya was illusion, that the appearances of the universe were unreal or that the life of men on earth had no meaning. He felt, on the contrary, that God was everywhere and in everything, and that if there were a difference between the personal and impersonal, it was as between milk and its whiteness or the diamond and its luster. Thus he was able (years later) to produce with conviction his famous formula, "Jiva is Shiva"—that is to say, all souls are god—which Vivekananda as a boy heard and adopted as his "living truth."

Ramakrishna had by this time (1866) become curiously famous, at least in Bengal, as a mystic whom some derided, many thought insane, and many others had begun to think gifted beyond the ordinary run even of saints. The process by which he reconciled both the personal and impersonal aspirations in his own case—that is, the illusory world, or Maya, including his personal devotion to Kali—with the great unthinkable Supreme which he had touched in ecstasy, was one which led him, step by step, toward the further conclusion that all the great religions were true. He had his own way of reaching this conclusion: nothing less than the vision of the Prophet Mohammed, followed by the vision of the Lord Jesus Christ, would settle the matter, and each of these visions had to be reached by the long, hard way of prayer, privation and self-hypnosis. To see Mohammed, for example, he went through months of living as a devout Moslem, reciting Moslem prayers and eating Moslem food. When at last he had brought himself to the pitch of believing fully in the Islamic God with attributes, the vision of Mohammed appeared, and, as was usual with Ramakrishna, entered into his own body and became one with him. From this state of consciousness, which was a very high form of ecstasy, he passed into the highest (*nirvikalpa samadhi*) in which again he realized the Brahman without attributes and had, after an interval, to descend painfully to his own body and life again.

The process was not dissimilar some years later (toward 1874) when he had his vision of Jesus Christ. It was brought on by having the New Testament read to him by a Moslem friend and by seeing a picture of the Madonna and Child in the house of another friend. For Ramakrishna, who worshipped God as Mother throughout his life more than in any other aspect, the picture became a vision which dwelt in him for many days and was followed by the vision of Christ himself. The Christian phase enveloped him much more powerfully and completely than the Islamic phase had done some years earlier, and it was only after another ascent to *nirvikalpa samadhi* that he was able to return again to himself. He always believed thereafter that Jesus of Nazareth was an incarnation of God—the incarnation of God as love—but of course not the only one. Buddha, Krishna and Chaitanya, the poet of the love of God, were others. From the time of his vision Ramakrishna kept a picture of Christ in his room and burned incense to it twice a day, morning and evening; his references to the subject as collected by his disciples in *The Gospel of Sri Ramakrishna* are those of a believer. With all this he knew little of doctrine and nothing of theology, and his way into Islam and into Christianity was that of the *Bhakti-yoga*, the way of love.

But by the late 1860's and early 1870's he was rapidly developing a prose style of his own in conversation—along with improvised songs and poetry—which were to revitalize Hinduism as nothing had done for centuries. The *Bhakti-yoga* into all religions, Hinduism included, was all he ever claimed for himself, and in spite of the prodigious memory which enabled him to quote sacred texts at will, he was not lettered enough to use the language of the learned. What he used was his native Bengali, comprehensible to any peasant, salty and earthy and full of metaphors from the farm, field and road. In that language he began to expound the most abstruse doctrines of the Vedanta, and the extraordinary thing is that the philosophical content seldom went astray. Great scholars, pundits and sages were drawn to Dakshineswar to talk with the ignorant little temple priest and went away wondering. It seemed to many of them that an astonishing genius had come to earth in the most unexpected form, and that the ancient truths of Hinduism had never been more simply and plainly expounded. From the Brahmo Samaj —the rationalist camp at the other pole from Ramakrishna's ecstatic mysticism—famous preachers and teachers began to come, including (1874) Keshab Chander Sen, who had himself moved into a final mystic phase and was pushed further into it by Ramakrishna. Keshab was half a Christian already, and Ramakrishna did nothing to discourage his new ardors.

But it was the young boys who gathered around him at the end of his life who were destined to carry Ramakrishna's teaching throughout the world. These, his "children," for whom he had prayed, began to frequent the temple of Dakshineswar from 1879 on, but most of them came in 1883. They were nearly all Brahmin boys in their teens, students of the various colleges in Calcutta and sons of prosperous families. The fame of Ramakrishna as one who had "seen God" was by this time widely disseminated in Bengal, his conversations with such great men as Debendranath Tagore, Swami Dayananda Sarasvati and Keshab Chander Sen had been noised about in the city, and the growing order and serenity of Ramakrishna's own doctrine and his mastery of its exposition had been appreciated by numerous visitors from all parts of India.

The Master, as he was henceforth called, was a small man with a gentle, hesitant voice and soft, burning eyes which obviously must have had some hypnosis in them (they are invariably mentioned in all accounts). He was forty-seven in 1883 and had weathered all the storms of his psychosomatic ordeal without great effect upon his body except in one respect: incessant talking, singing and praying had aggravated a throat condition which was rapidly to become cancer of the throat, from which he died three years later. He was invariably dressed in a loin-cloth— having abandoned the *sannyasin's* yellow robe years before— even in the city of Calcutta, which was one reason why the Tagores were unable to receive him in their house. (Debendranath asked him to lunch one day on condition that he "cover himself up a little," but the Master said he had no clothes and Tagore wrote him a polite little note telling him not to bother about lunch.)

Prolonged trances, cataleptic fits and wild behavior were a thing of the past; so also were the unbridled excesses of *Bhakti-yoga*, sheer love of God (or of the gods and goddesses) carried to the pitch of mania; the Master who attracted the questing youth in 1883-1886 was a gentle, philosophic creature with a genius for the pithy phrase, the precise dialect word and the illuminating parable from ordinary life. Ramakrishna had in fact developed a doctrine which, for all its mystic base, had a rational universalism which could be expounded without embarrassment before the learned brethren of the Brahmo Samaj. To the young men of Calcutta he offered a pure and exalted form of Hinduism which reached out to and embraced (or attempted to embrace) the other world religions as well. What is perhaps more surprising, in view of the Master's own rapturous experimentation with all the varieties of religious supraconsciousness for so many years, was the common sense with which he held the young men within limits and advised them against the amateur ecstasies to which they were all somewhat inclined. Undue austerities, too, although he had practised them himself almost to suicide, were forbidden by his precepts. He was himself likely to go into a trance at any moment, but by now these trances had the character of complete absorption or contemplation rather than of any definitely pathological condition; moreover, they did not last long any more—hours instead of days—and were taken to be a normal aspect of his religious personality.

During the late 1860's and the 1870's Ramakrishna had traveled a certain amount, had been to Benares and some other holy places, and had witnessed a little of the boundless poverty and suffering of India's masses. His hypersensitivity made the suffering of others unendurable to him, and the stories told of his few journeys abound in such details. He now burned with the desire to be of use to the poor and the unhappy, and yet realized that his own life was too near its end to afford him any opportunity. In this way the coming of the young disciples for whom he had prayed was the climax of his life, because he felt sure—and was indeed not mistaken—that they would take up the work which he could not do himself in the world.

By this time, too, a considerable number of "householders," as devout Hindus call them—that is, ordinary, normal men with

jobs and families—had formed the habit of journeying out from
Calcutta to Dakshineswar to see Ramakrishna on Sundays. A
Sunday afternoon in the temple garden was, Swami Nikhilananda
tells us,[1] a sort of festival. "Refreshments were often served. Professional musicians now and then sang devotional songs. The
Master and the devotees sang and danced, Sri Ramakrishna frequently going into ecstatic moods. The happy memory of such
a Sunday would linger long in the minds of the devotees. Those
whom the Master wanted for special instruction he would ask to
visit him on Tuesdays and Saturdays. These days were particularly auspicious for the worship of Kali."

The young disciples—those who afterward became monks—
went to Dakshineswar on weekdays when the householders
were not present. Their course of instruction was quite different
from that of the householders. "M.," the author of *The Gospel
of Sri Ramakrishna*, was Mahendranath Gupta, a householder,
and consequently his book—published in five volumes in Bengali
from 1897 to 1932—recording a very large number of conversations between Ramakrishna and his visitors or devotees, deals
only with the week-end talks and does not give much space to
the "youngsters," the future monks who were Ramakrishna's
lifework. For this we rely upon the memoirs of the various
disciples and above all upon the works of Vivekananda, the greatest of them.

One simple rule appears to have dominated the Master's specific ethical teaching both for the "youngsters" and for the
householders. It was to free themselves from the bondage of "lust
and gold" (or "woman and gold"—the phrase, which recurs constantly in the Ramakrishna literature, is variously translated).
Ramakrishna himself had, apparently instinctively, thought of all
women as mother from his earliest childhood, had adored the
mother-concept in Kali all his life, and regarded any other relation or attitude as a form of slavery. With the householders, most
of whom had wives and children, he could not enforce the full
austerity of his own attitude, but toward the boys he was extremely severe and taught them to regard women in any aspect
except as mother with distrust. (The Christian saints who taught
the same are innumerable.) For gold, that is, for the metal itself

[1] *The Gospel of Sri Ramakrishna*, Introduction, p. 65.

and for the currency based upon it, as for all considerations arising out of them, Ramakrishna had contempt and loathing which
by the end of his life had produced, on his preternaturally sensitive organism, effects of a psychophysical nature never before
recorded. Swami Vivekananda, as a youthful skeptic, once hid a
piece of gold in the Master's bed under the mattress and then
lurked in the neighborhood—half-scientist and half-mischievous
urchin—to see what would happen. The Master came in, sat on
the bed and moaned with pain, starting away in horror. He had
been burned by the invisible piece of gold.[2] Stories of his violent
antipathy to money of all kinds, its effect on his digestion, skin
and general condition, are told by many who knew him.

Ramakrishna's attitude toward women, governed by the goddess Kali, was reverential in the extreme. He did obeisance even
to a prostitute, we are told, seeing in her, as in all women, "the
Mother." He was forever counselling his disciples to think of
women only in that way and to drive any other thought from
their minds. If his beloved disciple, Naren—he who was to be
Vivekananda afterward—had had even the shadow of an impure
thought the Master could detect it at once and would refuse to
talk with the boy. The rule of *brahmacharya*, absolute chastity
even in thought, is common in India for students of religion, for
monks, for *sannyasin* (those who have renounced the world) and
in general for all who wish to pursue a contemplative life. Ramakrishna not only made it a rule for his disciples but actually, by
the use of those telepathic or communicative powers which
were generally acknowledged, made himself a sort of detective
for finding out when one of the youngsters had had a fleeting
thought verging on impurity.

His own wife, Sarada Devi, who was five years old when they
were ceremonially wedded, had returned to him at the age of
fourteen as a devotee. Vivekananda has told us that Ramakrishna
on that occasion, after searching his heart and praying to the
Mother, said to her that if she wished him to give up his religious mission he would abandon it and live with her as husband.
She refused; he initiated her into the worship of Kali and performed rites, finally, with her on the throne of the goddess in
the temple hall at midnight; both fell into the trance of ecstasy.

[2] *Life of Swami Vivekananda*, Vol. 1.

From then on Sarada Devi was as consecrated a personage as Ramakrishna himself, and was known by the devout, as she is still, under the name of "the Holy Mother."

The coming of Narendranath Dutt, the boy who was years later to become Swami Vivekananda, was the climax of Ramakrishna's work. Intuitive, compassionate and morbidly sympathetic as he was, Ramakrishna had felt for some years that work in the world—work for the suffering, the impoverished, for those adrift in doubt and illusion—was what he longed to do, so as to pass on some of the power he believed he had acquired in the upper reaches of the religious consciousness. For this some other instrument was required; his own life was not enough, would soon be over, and had almost all been spent in visions and trances in a temple garden. The youthful spirits who found their way to Dakshineswar were all good in their way, but none had the quality Ramakrishna felt to be necessary. He had dreams (or extrasensory perceptions) in which he was made aware that some such great instrument was to be put at his disposal while there was still time. On one occasion he saw a great streak of light flash across the whole sky of North India from Benares to Calcutta. Then was when he cried out: "My prayer has been granted and my man must come to me one day."

His "man" was then eighteen years old.

4

Narendranath Dutt was a Kayasth youth, son of a well-to-do family belonging to the Brahmo Samaj. He had been a natural leader from childhood, high-spirited, active, well-grown and remarkably intelligent. His leaning toward philosophy was marked from an early age, and his aptitude for learning was strong in almost every branch of study. He had studied singing and instrumental music for several years from two teachers, had a naturally good voice and had acquired a considerable repertoire of songs, mostly devotional, in Bengali, Hindi, Urdu and Persian. Aided by a memory which could absorb whole pages of a book, word for word, these natural gifts had made him a precocious scholar, so that when he entered the Presidency College at the age of sixteen (1879) he was treated as a phenomenon. Professor William Hastie, the scholar-principal of the Scottish Churches' College (a Presbyterian institution) to which he went next, declared in so many words: "Narendranath is really a genius. I have traveled far and wide, but I have never yet come across a lad of his talents and possibilities, even in German universities, amongst philosophical students. He is bound to make his mark in life."

Narendranath—Naren, they called him for years—had become a member of the reformed Brahmo Samaj at the age of fifteen, and at about the same time joined an organization for the education of the Indian masses without regard for caste, creed or color. He was an enthusiastic Brahmo, repudiating the Hindu notions of caste, polytheism, idolatry, divine incarnations and the necessity of a *guru*. In English, as in Indian languages, his capacity for disputation, exposition and persuasion had developed early and made him a welcome recruit to the reforming groups of young Bengal. But a vein of mystic aspiration—the desire to "see God"—had been present in him from early childhood and was not quenched by the rationalism of the Brahmo Samaj. It was at about this time, toward his eighteenth year, that he walked out along the Ganges to the garden of the venerable Maharshi Debendranath Tagore and asked him point blank: "Sir, have you seen God?" Debendranath said kindly: "My boy, you have yogi's eyes." Naren was cruelly disappointed and thought then of the "madman of God," out at Dakshineswar.

In November, 1881, Naren was asked to go to the house of a friend, Surendranath Mittra, to sing. He found himself in a company grouped about Sri Ramakrishna, the Master. The Master had liked his singing and invited him to come to Dakshineswar. (We may imagine that this was all done far more emotionally than the bald record relates: Ramakrishna was always carried away by the mere sight of Naren.)

At last Naren went to Dakshineswar, in a carriage with some fellow-students. The probability is that he had no remote idea of what he was getting into: some attraction for the madman, perhaps, coupled with a disturbing notion that such as he were more likely to have seen God than most of the gentry of Calcutta. Ramakrishna's own account of this meeting (usually called "the first meeting," although they had actually exchanged words before) is given in the *Life of Swami Vivekananda*—the official *Life*, prepared by disciples and published by the Advaita Ashrama —as follows:

"Narendra entered this room by the western door. He seemed careless about his body and dress, and unlike other people, unmindful of the external world. His eyes bespoke an introspective mind, as if some part of it were always concentrated upon something within. I was surprised to find such a spiritual soul coming from the material atmosphere of Calcutta. A mat was spread on the floor. He sat on it just near the place where you now see the big jar containing the water of the Ganges. The friends with whom he had come appeared to be ordinary young men with the usual tendencies toward enjoyment. He sang a few Bengali songs at my request. One of them was a common song of the Brahmo Samaj, which begins:

> *O my mind, go to your own abode.*
> *In the foreign land of this world*
> *Why roam uselessly like a stranger?*

"He sang the song with his whole heart and put such pathos into it that I could no longer control myself but fell into an ecstatic mood.

"Then he took leave. But after that I felt such a constant agonizing desire to see him! At times the pain would be so excruciating that I felt as if my heart were being squeezed like a wet towel. Then I could no longer check myself. I ran to the northern quarter of the garden, a rather unfrequented place, and there cried at the top of my voice, 'O my darling, come to me! I cannot live without seeing you!' After some time I felt better. This state of things continued for six months. There were other boys who came here; I felt greatly drawn toward some of them, but nothing like the way I was attracted toward Narendra."

Naren's account of the same meeting is this:

"Well, I sang the song, but shortly after he suddenly rose and taking me by the hand led me to the northern verandah, shutting the door behind him. It was locked from the outside; so we were alone. I thought that he would give me some private instructions. But to my utter surprise he began to shed profuse tears of joy as he held my hand, and addressing me most tenderly as one long familiar to him, said, 'Ah, you come so late! How could you be so unkind as to keep me waiting so long! My ears are well-nigh burnt in listening to the profane talk of worldly people. Oh, how I yearn to unburden my mind to one who can appreciate my innermost experience!' Thus he went on amid sobs. The next moment he stood before me with folded hands and began to address me, 'Lord, I know you are that ancient sage, Nara—the Incarnation of Narayana—born on earth to remove the miseries of mankind,' and so on!

"I was altogether taken aback by his conduct. 'Who is this man whom I have come to see?' I thought. 'He must be stark mad! Why, I am but the son of Viswanath Dutt, and yet he dares to address me thus!' But I kept quiet, allowing him to go on. Presently he went back to his room, and bringing me some sweets, sugar-candy and butter, began to feed me with his own hands. In vain did I say again and again, 'Please give the sweets to me, I shall share them with my friends.' He simply said, 'They may have some afterwards,' and desisted only after I had eaten all. Then he seized me by the hand and said, 'Promise that you will come alone to me at an early date.' At his importunity I had to say 'Yes,' and returned with him to my friends." [3]

Once they had returned to the other room Sri Ramakrishna said to the others (devotees all) sitting there: "Behold, how Naren beams with the light of Sarasvati, the goddess of learning!" The others, some of whom had been coming to Dakshineswar for years, were startled indeed to hear the newcomer praised in such terms. Ramakrishna then asked Naren: "Do you see a light before falling asleep?" Naren said, "Yes, sir." Ramakrishna said: "Ah, it is true! This one is a Dhyana-Siddha—an adept at meditation even from his very birth."

Naren's further account of the strange encounter follows:

"I sat and watched him. There was nothing wrong in his words, movements or behavior toward others. Rather, from his spiritual words and ecstatic states he seemed to be a man of genuine renunciation, and there was a marked consistency between his words and life. He used the most simple language, and I thought, 'Can this man be a great teacher?' I crept near to him and asked him the question which I had asked so often: 'Have you seen

[3] *Life of Swami Vivekananda*, Vol. 1, p. 56.

God, sir?' 'Yes, I see him just as I see you here, only in a much intenser sense. God can be realized,' he went on. 'One can see and talk to Him as I am doing with you. But who cares to do so? People shed torrents of tears for their wife and children, for wealth or property, but who does so for the sake of God? If one weeps sincerely for Him, He surely manifests Himself.' That impressed me at once. For the first time I found a man who dared to say that he had seen God, that religion was a reality to be felt, to be sensed in an infinitely more intense way than we can sense the world. As I heard these things from his lips, I could not but believe that he was saying them not like an ordinary preacher but from the depths of his own realizations. But I could not reconcile his words with his strange conduct with me. So I concluded that he must be a monomaniac. Yet I could not help acknowledging the magnitude of his renunciation. 'He may be a madman,' I thought, 'but only the fortunate few can have such renunciation. Even if insane, this man is the holiest of the holy, a true saint, and for that alone he deserves the reverential homage of mankind!' With such conflicting thoughts I bowed before him and begged his leave to return to Calcutta." [4]

The second visit of the bewildered and rather shocked young man took place almost a month later and again deserves narration in his own words, since the experience it describes is so far from usual and so easy to disbelieve or misinterpret. He told his fellow-disciples in later years:

"I did not realize then that the temple-garden of Dakshineswar was so far from Calcutta, as on the previous occasion I had gone there in a carriage. The road seemed to me so long as to be almost endless. However, I reached the garden somehow and went straight to Sri Ramakrishna's room. I found him sitting alone on the small bedstead. He was glad to see me and calling me to his side, made me sit beside him on his bed. But the next moment I found him overcome with a sort of emotion. Muttering something to himself, with his eyes fixed on me, he slowly drew near me. I thought he might do something queer as on the previous occasion. But in the twinkling of an eye he placed his right foot on my body. The touch at once gave rise to a novel experience within me. With my eyes open I saw that the walls

[4] *Life of Swami Vivekananda*, Vol. 1, p. 57.

and everything in the room whirled rapidly and vanished into naught, and the whole universe together with my own individuality was about to merge in an all-encompassing mysterious Void! I was terribly frightened and thought that I was facing death, for the loss of individuality meant nothing short of that. Unable to control myself I cried out, 'What is it that you are doing to me? I have my parents at home!' He laughed aloud at this and stroking my chest said, 'All right, let it rest now. Everything will come in time!' The wonder of it was that no sooner had he said this than that strange experience of mine vanished. I was myself again and found everything within and without the room as it had been before.

"All this happened in less time than it takes me to narrate it, but it revolutionized my mind. Amazed, I thought, what could it possibly be? It came and went at the mere wish of this wonderful man! I began to question if it were mesmerism or hypnotism. But that was not likely, for these acted only on weak minds, and I prided myself on being just the reverse. I had not as yet surrendered myself to the stronger personality of the man. Rather I had taken him to be a monomaniac. So to what might this sudden transformation of mine be due? I could not come to any conclusion. It was an enigma, I thought, which I had better not attempt to solve. I was determined, however, to be on my guard and not to give him another chance to exert a similar influence over me.

"The next moment I thought, how can a man who shatters to pieces a resolute and strong mind like mine be dismissed as a lunatic? Yet that was just the conclusion at which one would arrive from his effusiveness on our first meeting—unless he was an Incarnation of God, which was a far cry. So I was in a dilemma about the real nature of my experience as well as the truth about this remarkable man, who was obviously pure and simple as a child. My rationalistic mind received an unpleasant rebuff at this failure in judging the true state of things. But I was determined to fathom the mystery somehow.

"Thoughts like these occupied my mind during the whole of that day. But he became quite another man after that incident and, as on the previous occasion, treated me with great kindness and cordiality. His behavior toward me was like that of a man who meets an old friend or relative after a long separation. He seemed not to be satisfied with entertaining and taking all possible care of me. This remarkably loving treatment drew me all the more to him. At last, finding that the day was coming to a close, I asked his leave to go. He seemed very much dejected at this and gave me his permission only after I had promised to come again at my earliest convenience."

On the third visit, which occurred a few days later, Ramakrishna went into a trance and touched Narendranath on the chest; the boy lost all consciousness for a while, and when he recovered he found the Master stroking his chest. Naren himself had no idea of what had occurred during his loss of consciousness, but Ramakrishna himself afterwards narrated to the disciples that he had questioned the youth closely about his own antecedents, his mission in this world and the duration of his mortal life. This interrogation under what we can only call hypnosis (for lack of a better word) confirmed Ramakrishna in his belief that the boy Naren was or would be the instrument for the fulfillment of his own work in life, and that this was in fact the man his visions had always foretold—the man who would come some day to "save the world."

Thus began the long, slow process by which Naren came to regard Ramakrishna not as a madman, but as the only really sane man in a world of lunatics. It took years. The boy was bright as a new-minted coin and not to be deceived by any form of pretense—as he showed in his relations to the other youths in the circle. He was constantly laying traps for the Master himself, trying to catch him up in contradictions or logical impossibilities, testing his claims and statements in every way. Ramakrishna, who would not have troubled with any other skeptic by this time, took infinite pains with Naren and permitted him to say whatever he pleased. Every proof of Naren's doubts was to him a proof of intellectual strength: he even wanted these doubts to exist so that they could be overcome. He felt, it seems, that his own terrible "tempests of the soul" were being reproduced as tempests of the mind in Naren's case, and that this, too, was necessary, since the world-mission which he felt to be necessary needed a powerful weapon of externalization.

Ramakrishna's personal love for Naren is all too easy to explain in the catch-phrases of Western psychology. The impersonal element—arising perhaps from that—is one which goes into the depths of Hinduism. In the very beginning the Master hailed Naren as Shiva, with himself as *Shakti*. (Shakti or energy is the feminine principle: the wives of Shiva, goddesses or aspects of God under various names, Kali being one, are his Shakti.) His words were: "Behold, in you is Shiva! And in me is Shakti! And these two are One!" The childlike and innocent Ramakrishna felt himself throughout life to be at least part feminine and at times all feminine, as when he was possessed by the Mother Kali. He recognized the Shiva-principle of masculinity in Naren and declared in explicit terms a continuity of being between them. When he saw Naren he would sometimes chant a Vedic hymn and go into a trance, particularly after the boy had not visited the temple for a week or two. During the longer absences—which occurred later when the Dutt family lost its fortune and Naren was obliged to look for a job in Calcutta—the Master was desolate, and on one occasion actually went into the city to look for the beloved disciple at the evening services of the Brahmo Samaj. Ramakrishna was on this occasion only about half-conscious and, of course, hardly clothed at all. He advanced up the aisle of the church in that state, reached the pulpit and there went into a trance. The bewilderment and confusion of the congregation were extreme; somebody turned off the lights and Naren, in the darkness found his way from the choir loft to the pulpit, rescued the unconscious Master and got him back to Dakshineswar. When he regained consciousness Ramakrishna showed no regret for what he had done, and the puzzled, exasperated boy was faced again with the dilemma which he has well described for us.

Calcutta seethed with disapproval of Ramakrishna's influence over the young. It was bad enough to have a mystic who went into trances in the most inopportune times and places, who exercised an inexplicable influence over learned and pious men, and to whom hundreds of serious persons, maharajahs, prime ministers and professional men, the lords of trade and industry, occasionally made pilgrimage. But when this weird apparition suddenly (1881-1883) acquired a whole school of awestricken boys, twenty or thirty of them, drawn from the best middle- and upper-class families of Calcutta, all in various degrees athirst for

God, the families were distinctly annoyed. The last years of Ramakrishna were beclouded by the efforts of parents and guardians to take his disciples away from him—an effort in which they were circumvented often by the ingenuity of the boys themselves, but in which they succeeded to such an extent that on his deathbed he had only twelve of them around him.

The objection of the families is easy to understand: they did not want their sons to become monks. Ramakrishna's constant preaching against "lust and gold" was not at all suited to the commercial aristocracy of the city. The boys all should have married young and would not do so; Ramakrishna was inevitably blamed. The struggle in Naren's family was particularly acute, because he, as a brilliant student and a highly personable young man, had opportunities for marriages which would have brought large dowries; he would not hear of them.

But the "old man," as they called him (he was now approaching fifty), acquired an ascendancy over these youths which was to last out their entire lives, long indeed after his own death. They recognized in him, first of all, a childlike innocence which made him different from any other adult they had ever known, and which enabled them to speak to him as they could not to anybody else beyond their own age. Like St. Louis Gonzaga and dozens of other Catholic mystics, Ramakrishna had never had a sexual experience in his life, unless it be maintained that his religious temperament, visions and ecstasies were themselves sexual. His preaching of purity was accompanied by an extra-sensory acuteness for its opposite, so that he could detect even the occasional transgression and never failed to inveigh against it. But above his purity were his intense "realizations," to which every Indian mind looks with awe; he had "realized" all the gods and goddesses of all the religions, had communicated with, and thus become a part of their being; his life itself was holy, innocent and yet compassionate; he spoke a language which (it seems) combined the simplicity of a child or a peasant with the most exalted concepts known to Hindu philosophy. These qualities subjugated all who came within his sphere. There is no record, so far as I have been able to find, of any person who saw or heard Ramakrishna who did not feel that he was an extreme example of religious genius. For the very young men who were to be-

come his missionaries after his death, these were the ruling characteristics of their Master. What they did not know—or what,
according to the psychoanalytic jargon, they felt only in their
"subconscious"—was the way in which human love colored the
whole phenomenon. There can be no doubt that Ramakrishna,
the little brown man with the gentle voice, stammering as he
tried to say what he meant, exercised a personal charm which
transcended every other consideration and made those who came
to him his servants forever. He recurred in visions to all his
disciples over and over again, long after his death, because his
own personality had so enveloped them in its magic in their very
first youth, before they were twenty. One can feel this even
now, in reading the conversations which were recorded by some
of them every day while they were fresh. The little man sat on
the floor and gossiped about this or that: who had come to Calcutta lately? Was it true that a Mr. Cook was giving public
lectures on philosophy? What had happened to This-one-or-
that-one, whose sister had married a Mohammedan? And then,
suddenly: how do you believe in God? In what way? In a formless God or in a personal God? Have you even thought about it?
In the running ordinary course of his talk he dealt with everything that happens or can happen. Did the bird nest in that tree
or in this one? Where was the boy when his mother found out
that he was the one who ate all the honey? This kind of question, with comments upon all the possible answers, sprinkled
through his discourse, gave the gatherings in Ramakrishna's room
at the temple of Kali an earthiness, an ordinariness, into which his
sudden disquisitions upon the Divine Mother, upon the relative
and absolute, differentiated and undifferentiated, came with the
effect of sunlight on the home farm. The Vedanta itself was by
no means unknown; every form of Bhakta, devotional approach
to God, was familiar to the Bengali devout; the life of the peasantry, the language of children, the habits of ordinary people,
were equally known; but the combination and admixture provided an aliment which had the rarity not to be found in any of
its parts. There can be no question that Ramakrishna in the last
six or eight years of his life had mastered the secret of commanding the attention of men and exciting their wonder. He did it
without trying, by giving free rein to his own childlike but

ecstatic sense of reality and abhorrence of the workaday world, the world of illusion, of "lust and gold," from which he wished to save the "unsullied" youths who came to him.

Narendranath Dutt's progress from skepticism to belief and something approaching adoration took about three years. It is clear that during the last year of the Master's life and for the better part of the year before Naren had been a firm believer. He accepted not only the "realizations" of Ramakrishna, his communication with the Divine Mother and with all other aspects of the divine, but the further possibility that any human being might do likewise. This concept of the Vedanta—realization of the Self, any Self, by union with Brahman—had previously seemed to him the last word in sacrilegious nonsense. At first he railed against Ramakrishna, the boy of eighteen against the aureoled mystic of forty-five or forty-six, for putting forward any such doctrine. With the passage of the five years they spent together, all of Naren's rationalism and skepticism vanished, to give way to an ardent desire to share Ramakrishna's supraconscious experiences, to renounce the world and "realize," to see God.

Ramakrishna was in these closing years of his life extremely censorious of any unauthorized excursions into the realms of the unknown. He had himself suffered so much, had been so often on the very brink of insanity and physical dissolution, that he tried now to save his young followers from the same excesses. Tears, trances and ecstasies in imitation of his own, produced by boys of sixteen and eighteen, aroused the robust common sense that was somewhere concealed beneath his ultramundane exterior. He forbade such things and encouraged Naren to find out their origins and expose them. (Naren discovered that some of the boys were actually rehearsing their trances and ecstasies at home before exhibiting them before the Master.) One of the disciples was a spiritualist, or had been until Ramakrishna took him in hand; the Master admonished him sternly. "Think of ghosts all the time and you will become a ghost," he said. "Think of God and you will become God. Take your choice."

The essential doctrine of Ramakrishna as taught during his last four years of life to the young disciples followed three main lines:

1. All religions are true and all religious belief is true. (We are reminded of Krishna's teaching in the Gita, which accepts every offering, every prayer and sacrifice, if it is made with sincerity.)

2. The divisions of Hindu philosophy between Dualism (*Dvaita*), "qualified" non-dualism or "qualified" monism (the *Vishishtadvaita* of Ramanuja), and absolute non-dualism or monism (*Advaita*) correspond to stages in the soul's progress. Dualism explains and systematizes the world for the ordinary human being in the duties of life: it makes life easier for the impoverished and illiterate masses, who must have polytheism and idolatry to help them through their task of living. By the mind's effort an advance is made toward Ramanuja's view, in which Brahman is both immanent and transcendent; but the soul's realization in union with Brahman makes all else seem illusory and thus rises to absolute monism. Such realization and union are rare; hence the necessity for the more earthly views of life.

3. Men have their duties in accordance with this progression: patiently and modestly, without desire for selfish advantage, they can work in the world and win through. Ramakrishna hoped for his young men, and above all for Naren, a worldly mission which would aim not only at religious enlightenment but at the relief of suffering. Political nationalism was remote from his nature, and yet there can be no doubt that what he felt—as it took form afterward in the work of Vivekananda—was primarily for the Indian masses in this respect. His contact with the world even in India was slight, but it was enough to give him a passionate sympathy for the abjectly poor and their suffering.

Ramakrishna's sense of the possibility of helping mankind was quickened to a certainty by Naren. In that extraordinarily gifted youth, with all his wit, learning, independence and desire for truth, the Master knew that he had found the exponent without whom everything he had learned through his own ordeal would be lost. Ramakrishna did not want to create a "cult," nor did he regard anything in his own system of belief as being original. (He cautioned the disciples repeatedly against anything savoring of sect, or of "Ramakrishnaism.") What he did want was to bring into life, into the life of the world, all the ancient truths and cause men to live by them. For this reason he tried to keep the ardent Naren from going too far in mysticism, which, as he felt or knew, would in the end result (as it had resulted in his own case) in an isolation from the contemporary life of mankind.

His throat condition, caused by the circulatory disorders incident to his many trances, turned into cancer in 1885. The disciples moved him to a more comfortable house in Calcutta and later to another in the suburb of Cossipore, where he spent his last months instructing them. The "Holy Mother," Sarada Devi, came and took charge of the cooking for the little monastery. The *Mahasamadhi* (great ecstasy), as his disciples call it, came to him on Sunday, August 15th, 1886. Some days before the end he had gone into a trance with Naren present; Naren had lost consciousness soon afterward. When he recovered, the Master was weeping and said, "Today I have given you my all and I am now only a poor fakir, possessing nothing. By this power you will do immense good in the world, and not until it is accomplished will you return." According to the belief of the disciples, the Master henceforth lived—that is, through his most rarefied powers—in Narendranath, and what expired a few days later was only the earthly shell of a great spirit.

5

These wonders of mysticism are, it may be freely confessed, incomprehensible and surrounded by clouds of doubt for any Western mind nurtured, as all are, upon materialist empiricism. If we have not ourselves had such experiences we doubt them because our whole civilization is based upon concepts of measurement—weight, mass, velocity, temperature and the like. If modern physics and the most ancient Upanishads happen to agree that the material universe is an illusion of which the formulable essence is energy, our tendency is to regard that as a remarkable coincidence and no more. But it is beginning to be explicitly admitted among scientists that the human consciousness is a mystery, that the pulsations of the brain—which have been measured by machines as they leave the head, varying considerably in energy as shown by the mechanical graph—cannot begin to be explained electronically, and that our knowledge of ourselves, in spite of three generations of psychologists, is infantile. It is not for me, therefore, to doubt the extrasensory experiences or powers of Shri Ramakrishna. On the contrary, whatever their nature, whatever scientific rule-of-thumb might be applied to them, it is beyond any question, I think, that they were real to him, real to his disciples, and therefore real in the only sense with which reality can be given meaning by human creatures.

Narendranath, the future Vivekananda, wavered for a long time and perhaps throughout his life upon some of the essential problems about his Master. We find him in letters using phrases like "this wonderful saint, or Avatara (Incarnation), or whatever you may wish to call him" [5] in reference to Ramakrishna. He did not dogmatize, although the temptation to do so must have been great. And his own feeling of weakness, imperfection, inability to fulfill his task, kept him from believing fully (as the other disciples did) that the Master's spiritual power had been transferred to him. He felt a responsibility for them, he was their natural leader and he never could divest himself wholly (even in his struggle to "renounce" everything, even his *Gurubhai*, or brothers under the same Master) of a concern for their welfare; but he did not claim to be any more advanced than they on the road.

There were twelve of the boys in the Cossipore garden house during Ramakrishna's last days. He invested them with the yellow robe (or ochre robe) of the *sannyasin*, and thus was himself the founder of the Ramakrishna Order of monks, although he had no organizational preoccupations whatever and gave them no practical advice. Eleven of the twelve became known in after years under their monastic names, the Swamis Brahmananda (first Abbot of the Order), Advaitananda, Vivekananda (Naren), Shivananda (second Abbot), Yogananda, Ramakrishnananda, Saradananda (secretary of the Ramakrishna Mission for many years, biographer of the Master), Abhedananda, Niranjananda, Premananda, Adbhutananda. The twelfth, Gopal Junior, did not become a monk but returned to the world (he was the younger brother of Gopal Senior, who became Advaitananda). There were other youngsters who were in reality disciples and

5 *Life of Swami Vivekananda*, Vol. 1, p. 226.

afterward became monks, but whose parents succeeded in keeping them from joining Ramakrishna at Cossipore. One of them—indulging in mystic frenzies against Ramakrishna's wish and Naren's discipline—became insane and went home; four others came when they could get away from their families.

This was the group which remained together after the Master's death and formed the Ramakrishna Brotherhood at Baranagore, near the place of cremation on the Ganges. A "householder" friend paid the lease of an abandoned country house which possessed every inconvenience; there the young men practised the most extreme austerities, with almost no food or sleep, praying, singing or arguing philosophical questions at all hours. Naren was then twenty-one and the master of them all at logical disputation as in learning, and of course then, as at all other times, his singing voice was a gift of superabundance.

Hindu monasticism, a very ancient growth, has two characteristic aspects, of which the first, represented by the wandering and begging friar, traditionally dominates over the institutional mission. The Ramakrishna Brotherhood was deliberately institutional to begin with—inspired by a desire to perpetuate Ramakrishna's teaching—but the impulse toward pilgrimage and wandering is very deep in the Hindu after he has renounced the world. For thousands of years it has been taught that the *sannyasin* (he who has renounced) should have no ties of any kind to family or place, but should wander in his search for God and accept only such food as is necessary for life—accepting it, what is more, from anybody without regard for caste or other conditions. This tradition was further reinforced by Ramakrishna's incessant preaching against "lust and gold." There was indeed little probability that either lust or gold would come the way of the lean and hungry young ascetics of Baranagore, but through fear of temptation they undoubtedly felt drawn to the poverty and humiliation of the mendicant's lot. Consequently some of them went off on pilgrimage almost as soon as Ramakrishna's body had been cremated; others drifted away afterward; and it is one of the most remarkable proofs of Ramakrishna's power over them all that they never failed to come back.

Naren, after a pilgrimage to Benares and return, spent only a

few months at Baranagore and then took up his wandering. At
first he visited the holy places (Benares, Ayodhya, Vrindavan
and the like, taking in the sights of Lucknow and Agra on the
way), with the Himalayas as his aim; but toward the end of 1888
he returned to the monastery at Baranagore and remained a year,
teaching his *Gurubhai* (brother-monks, brothers-in-the-same-
Guru) the essence of the mission they were to fulfill. Much of
this time was spent upon the ancient Hindu scriptures, which
Naren felt to be insufficiently known in Bengal or in India as a
whole. Then, at the end of 1889, he started out again as a wandering beggar, but (after a period of retreat at Benares) was forced
to return to the monastery. It was only in July, 1890, that he was
able to begin his real wanderings, which were to take him all
over India and were to end only in May, 1893, with his departure
for America under the new name of Swami Vivekananda. In
these wanderings, from his twenty-fifth to his twenty-eighth
year, he came of age in India's beauty and sorrow. Many times
the lowliest of people aided him with food when he was almost
at the end of his endurance; at other times ruling princes found
him out, brought him to their courts and sat at his feet to ask
questions. He led the life of the true *sannyasin*, the itinerant monk
who accepts whatever comes. His adventures were many, and
he found that even among his fellow-mendicants there were elements not at all to his liking, but by and large he came to know
India and to feel that from the Himalayas to the southernmost tip
of Cape Comorin—"the last bit of Indian rock," he called it—
there was a people waiting to be awakened.

"We are so many *sannyasins*," he wrote a few months later,
"wandering about and teaching the people metaphysics—it is all
madness. Did not our Gurudeva used to say, 'An empty stomach
is no good for religion'? That those poor people are leading the
life of brutes is simply due to ignorance. We have for all ages
been sucking their blood and trampling them under foot."

His great idea was to combine renunciation, the age-old ideal
of India, that which created the *sannyasins*, with a life of service.

"Suppose," he says, "some disinterested *sannyasins*, bent on
doing good to others, go from village to village, disseminating
education and seeking in various ways to better the conditions
of all down to the Chandala, through oral teachings, and by

means of maps, cameras, globes and such other accessories—will not that bring forth good in time? All these plans I cannot write out in this letter. The long and the short of it is—if the mountain does not come to Mohammed, Mohammed must go to the mountain. The poor are too poor to come to schools and Pathsalas; they will gain nothing by reading poetry and all that sort of thing. We as a nation have lost our individuality, and that is the cause of all mischief in India. We have to give back to the nation its lost individuality and *raise the masses*. The Hindu, the Mohammedan, the Christian all have trampled them under foot. Again the force to raise them must come from inside, that is, from the orthodox Hindus. In every country evil exists not with, but against religion. Religion, therefore, is not to blame, but men."

He had heard of the Parliament of Religions, a gathering planned as part of the World's Fair at Chicago in 1893. From all over the world there were delegations; the Indian press had spoken of them; various devout Hindus during the Swami's wanderings had suggested that he might go. In his meditation on "the last bit of Indian rock," he thought of America: there he could get help for the Indian masses and could speak out for what he believed India might tell the West. It was no less that the Swami—learned indeed in many ways, but knowing nothing of the world outside of India—took upon himself in those last days of his wandering.

At Pondichéry and Madras, where he went next (end of 1892), he engaged in debates with pundits and found himself famous. Young men thronged to see him in Madras, although he was not himself much older than they. His idea of going to America was eagerly supported there and funds were raised to pay for the journey. It was here (1893) that one of his most famous answers was made. A modern young man, imbued with Western ideas or perhaps with philosophic curiosity, asked, "Swamiji, why is it that the Hindus, in spite of their Vedantic thought, are idolaters?" Vivekananda turned on him with flashing eyes and said, "Because we have the Himalaya!" Perhaps it is necessary to have seen the Himalaya to see how precise this answer was, and how it explains the instinct of the Hindu to adore.

The Maharajah of Khetri, the Maharajah of Jaipur and the

Maharajah of Mysore were among those who defrayed the cost
of the Swami's mission to the United. States. It was at Jaipur's
court that Naren finally assumed the name he was to carry henceforth, Vivekananda—hitherto he had changed his monastic pseu-
donym from time to time so as to avoid notoriety. He embarked
at Bombay on May 31, 1893, in first-class passage, dressed in a
robe of ochre silk and a turban of the same material—all things
upon which his friends had insisted. He had traveled for three
years throughout India with no luggage but a pocket copy of
the Gita and a begging-bowl for alms: now he was to invade
the unknown West in fine raiment, paying for everything like
a tourist, and laden down with unfamiliar belongings. The
Swami, naturally quick to learn even the least important things,
watched his fellow-travelers to see what the customs and ordinary
courtesies of Europeans were. He did not have the dietary trouble
many Indian *sadhus* would have faced, because he had schooled
himself for years to eat anything that was offered him—even fish
or meat. Ramakrishna, himself so careful about diet, unwilling to
eat any but "innocent" food (as Gandhi called it), had always
said Naren could eat anything. His view was that some inner
purity or supreme mission had so treated Naren's character that
any food he took was thereby purified—a matter in which the
Master had been most severe with all others. Vivekananda was
also without caste prejudice by now, having forced himself to
overcome all those notions of "pollution" which so afflicted the
Hindu society of his time. He was thus able to associate quite
freely with foreigners, to eat with them and take food from their
hands. No shadow could degrade or pollute him—of all those
shadows which, in his day (and to a considerable extent even
in ours), were thought to bring impurity upon a high-caste
Hindu.

The ship stopped at Colombo, Hongkong and Nagasaki-Kobe-
Yokohama—giving the Swami a chance to describe in vivid letters
his impressions of other Asiatic peoples—then Vancouver and
Chicago. He had no warm clothing for the Canadian journey
and was extremely unfamiliar with the uses of money, as well as
of currency values. In his ochre robe and turban he was the
object of great curiosity, and was, of course, cheated on a grand
scale by everybody with whom he came into contact. One day

in Chicago left him bewildered and heartsick. He knew nobody at all, was followed by jeering children, was overwhelmed by the crowds, noise and general confusion, and realized after one visit to the World's Fair how little, indeed, he had ever known about the West. After a few days spent in a courageous effort to get used to his surroundings and to see all the exhibits at the Fair, he went to the Information Bureau to find out about his Parliament of Religions, and discovered that no delegates were received there without credentials. Neither Vivekananda nor his numerous Hindu friends (maharajahs and prime ministers among them) had thought of credentials: the "act of presence," as the French say, had seemed to them enough. What was just as bad was the fact that the Parliament opened only after the first week in September. It was now mid-July and the Swami could quite easily see that the money he had brought from India would not last much longer. His English disciple, Sister Nivedita, afterward wrote: "Nothing could have been more typical of the unorganizedness of Hinduism itself than this going forth of its representative unannounced, and without formal credentials, to enter the strongly guarded doors of the world's wealth and power."

Somebody told him that Boston was cheaper than Chicago and in his unhappiness he decided to try it. On the train to Boston an elderly lady fell into talk with him, asked him to stay in her house near Boston, and when he did so she introduced him to a number of her friends. The rudeness (most of it probably unconscious) and ignorance shown by their questions occasioned him great suffering, but he bore it in the hope that something good for his mission would come of it. At this time he prayed to Jesus Christ, because he felt that since (as he said) he was among "the sons of Mary," the Nazarene face of God would shine upon him. He was then advised (a great crisis) to buy American clothes and thus avoid the street scenes which caused him such embarrassment; the unfamiliar clothes were torture and their cost was more than he could afford; but help was at hand. Among the visitors who came to see him were some from Harvard University, and finally J. H. Wright, professor of Greek there, who was able to talk to him in philosophical language. Wright, after four hours with Vivekananda, insisted that he should represent Hinduism at the Parliament of Religions and volunteered to see that the credentials were put in order. Wright gave him his ticket to Chicago and a letter to the committee which took care of Oriental delegates in such matters as housing and arrangements. The Swami was so overjoyed at his good fortune—and so grateful to what he called a literal manifestation of Divine Providence—that he lost the piece of paper with the addresses on it, and wandered helplessly in Chicago on his arrival there. On that first night he reverted to his *sannyasin* habits and slept in a box in the railroad freight-yards. In the morning, after his prayers, he "smelt fresh water" and, pursuing the smell, found himself eventually on the Lake Shore Drive beside Lake Michigan. He then began begging from house to house but—never having begged in America before—probably used a wrong technique. He asked at each house for food and for the address of the committee on the Parliament of Religions. He was turned away very rudely and insulted by the domestic servants of the rich merchants who lived along the street. At that time Vivekananda had never used a telephone and had never heard of a city directory; he was no better off than Socrates or Jesus would have been in the same position. As he sat, exhausted and resigned, beside the road, awaiting the will of God, a door before him opened and a lady appeared who asked him if he was a delegate to the Parliament of Religions. He told her at once what his situation was; she led him into her house and said that after he had breakfasted and rested she would take him to the offices of the Parliament of Religions. This was Mrs. George W. Hale, who with her husband and children were to be among Vivekananda's devoted American friends.

From then on all his more elementary difficulties were over. What remained was the great task of representing Hinduism worthily before the delegates of the world's religions. Vivekananda went into a period of prayer and meditation during which, as he afterward related, he felt no personal anxiety, fear or even confidence, but an awareness that he was about to carry out the mission entrusted to him by Ramakrishna, which is to say, in his system of belief, by God's will as expressed through the dead Master.

What happened is, even now, not quite forgotten, and in those far-off days of our parents or grandparents it was one of the most remarkable events of the age. There were an enormous number of delegates to the Parliament from almost every country on earth, and among them great church dignitaries, philosophers of international fame, scientists and writers who took an interest in the world's religions. Besides all the Christian churches, the delegates represented Islam, Judaism, Zoroastrianism (Mazda), Shinto, Confucianism, Buddhism, and Jainism. The Brahmo Samaj had sent official representatives, but Vivekananda was the only representative of the traditional and all-embracing Hinduism of India. The public every session numbered between seven and ten thousand.

On Monday morning, September 11th, the Parliament was opened with prayers by John Cardinal Gibbons, Archbishop of Baltimore, then the only American cardinal. There was music and a welcoming address, after which the visiting delegates were called upon to reply. Vivekananda, taken aback by the size of the assembly and all the pomp and ceremony which attended it, took refuge in deep meditation and prayer addressed chiefly to Sarasvati, the goddess of learning, and under the circumstances it is doubtful if he even heard most of the speeches. (He had never spoken in public in his life except twice in Madras and Hyderabad.) Repeatedly the chairman called on him and he said, "Not yet." At last, toward the end of the long afternoon, he accepted his call and got up for a brief speech.

That speech alone sealed a great many fates. It made Vivekananda a world figure and consequently enhanced his prestige in India beyond measure; it ensured the continuance and development of the Ramakrishna Mission; it made the modern Western world aware of Hinduism as it had never been before. It had undoubtedly been preceded by a good deal of the sectarian claim and counterclaim which disfigure the religious life of the West. When Vivekananda, an imposing personage, rose from his meditation and said that he spoke for "the Mother of Religions, a religion which has taught the world both tolerance and universal acceptance," he probably brought a healing breeze of relief into the crowded, hot and long-suffering assembly. His beautiful voice and his hitherto unsuspected gift for public speaking no doubt had a great deal to do with it, but essentially what con-

stituted his amazing victory over all the religious nabobs of the
hour was the calm universalism of what he had to say. He had
found in his capacious memory two texts from the Hindu *shastras*
which won the vast audience. The first was a Vedic hymn:

"As the different streams having their sources in different
places all mingle their water in the sea, so, O Lord, the different
paths which men take through different tendencies, various
though they appear, crooked or straight, all lead to Thee."

The second, from the Gita, was:

"Whosoever comes to Me, through whatsoever form, I reach
him; all men are struggling through paths which in the end lead
to Me."

The brevity of this first address, read now in black on white
after so many years, evidently gives no idea of the luminous
novelty it possessed for that huge international audience in
Chicago. It was followed by an ovation and Vivekananda was
henceforth an immense celebrity wherever he went. Life-size
posters showing "the Monk Vivekananda" were put up in the
streets of the World's Fair, and it is related that a good many
of the throng paused to bow before it. The press of the world—
India of course most avidly—reported this unexpected happening
in full, and persons who had never previously known that India
possessed either a full-grown religious system or a philosophy
of its own interested themselves in the Vedanta overnight. Vivekananda was the dominant figure of the whole Parliament of
Religions. In the remaining sessions, where he spoke often, he
was kept to the last so that the crowds would stay, and since
the sessions lasted from ten in the morning until ten at night, the
amount of sectarian literature they had to listen to before they
got "the Monk Vivekananda" must have been vast. On September 15th the Swami spoke on "Why we disagree," and on
September 19th he read his famous paper on Hinduism, which
remains to this day a persuasive document. At that time, when
all he had to say was unknown to his audience, when he was
himself at the superb height of powers which, in voice, speech,
appearance and personal electricity must have been rare indeed,
the effect was unlike any other. When the Parliament closed
after seventeen days, during which Vivekananda had repeatedly

spoken, there was little in the way of an American "success" that was not his for the asking.

Vivekananda was miserable at the excitement which now surrounded him, because he saw quite plainly that his old anonymous life as a wandering beggar-monk was over. He could not again, in India or anywhere else, live as a *sannyasin*, and, according to his beliefs, his own realization would thus be indefinitely delayed. But above all the contrast between the material standards of America and those of his poor, unhappy India oppressed him. He had been taken to visit a prison for women near Boston some weeks before, while he was still unknown, and wrote home, "It is the grandest thing I have seen in America. How the inmates are benevolently treated; how they are reformed, and sent back as useful members of society; how grand, how beautiful, you must see to believe it! And Oh, my heart ached to think of what we think of the poor, the low, in India. They have no chance, no escape, no way to climb up." Now he was beset by the invitations of the rich, lived in the house of a rich man in Chicago, was "lionized" by hostesses, and was deeply unhappy. His too-comfortable bed seemed to him filled with thorns. He has recorded that in his sorrow he prayed to the Divine Mother on the first night in this vein: "O Mother, what do I care for name and fame when my motherland remains sunk in utmost poverty! To what a sad pass have we poor Indians come when millions of us die for want of a handful of rice, and here they spend millions of rupees on their personal comfort! Who will raise the masses in India? Who will give them bread? Show, O Mother, how I can help them."

Among the offers he received for lecture tours he chose one and embarked upon a tour which was one of the most bizarre in the history of that strange American institution. He had two wishes: to explain Hinduism and the Vedanta to the West, and to obtain enough money to start philanthropic centers throughout India (the Ramakrishna Mission). He did not wish to proselytize or to preach Ramakrishna. His lectures, all extemporaneous, were of a philosophical nature and it seems doubtful if more than a very small fraction of any audience understood what he said. The audiences, huge and enthusiastic, came for the beauty of his voice and person, the "magnetism" which is mentioned in all contemporary accounts, and out of curiosity to see "the Monk" who had taken the country by storm. Vivekananda was paid enormous fees and drew enormous audiences, but his ignorance of the world was still so great that it was easy to cheat him in money matters. On one occasion he discovered that his manager had been paid $2500 for a lecture and had given him only $200 of it. A quarrel about such things was repugnant to Vivekananda, but he broke with the manager (at considerable loss) out of sheer indignation. He had some painful experiences also with Christian missionaries and backers of missionary societies, whose anxiety for their enterprises in India made them oppose the Swami as a danger to their future collections of money. Vivekananda fought back from the platform in a manner which the newspapers of the day seem to have admired highly. On his tour of the United States, one of his principal occupations, in the midst of much bewilderment and discomfort, was the sightseeing: the museums, the achievements in engineering and architecture, the universities and great industrial establishments all aroused his keenest interest, with the perpetual undertone of questioning as to how he could make use of all this for India and in India.

He was lecturing twelve or fourteen times a week, meeting thousands of new people, answering questions for many hours every day. Among his new friends was the agnostic Robert Ingersoll—"Bob" Ingersoll—who said to him: "Forty years ago you would have been hanged if you had come to preach in this country, or you would have been burned alive." His progress through the United States was all reported in full in India, where, by 1894, he had become a figure of national importance *in absentia*. Public meetings in Calcutta, Madras, and elsewhere sent him messages; the English-language and vernacular press gave much space to his triumphs; what he had done and was still doing was of a nature to revive India's pride in her ancient glories, and thus many elements in Indian society rejoiced in it. It has often been said that the nineteenth century gave India as a whole an "inferiority complex." Whatever that shopworn phrase may really mean, there could be little doubt that India passed the greater part of the century under a cloud of doubt, depression, self-abasement and gloom, which kept pace with the economic development—spotty but vigorous—in certain areas and the unification of the country under foreign rule. To the awakening which took place in the 1890's and at the beginning of the twentieth century Vivekananda contributed an element which Western writers have too often ignored in their concentration upon politics: politics alone could not have accounted for the phenomenon in such a country. Hinduism itself had to revive before there could be a political movement of any genuine strength among the masses. In the *Cambridge History of India*, Vol. VI (1858-1918) Vivekananda is mentioned only once, Ramakrishna not at all, and yet it is quite easy to see now that they had a more permanent importance for the modern development of India than most of those public figures who are treated at great length.

The Swami tired of his lecturing forays, not only because of the physical and nervous exhaustion they brought upon him, but because his whole being rebelled at constant publicity and uncomprehending adulation. He took quarters of his own in New York and started to teach a small number of Americans in whom he found aptitude for learning Hindu ways of meditation and concentration. His regular classes started in February, 1895. At the same time he was writing a stream of letters to India, giving advice to friends and disciples, sending money for various purposes and keeping in touch with the Ramakrishna monastery at Baranagore. The periodical called *Brahmavadin* was founded in Madras in that year, with money supplied by Vivekananda, for the purpose of teaching the Vedanta.

Much calumny came his way in New York, and above all in connection with the so-called "psychic powers" which have always been a pet mania of the lunatic fringe. Vivekananda taught meditation and frequently lost himself in it, but he was a vigorous opponent of any trifling with "psychic powers" or other traps of the pseudo-occult. He regarded such experimentation—with all its temptation to fraud and self-deception—as a positive danger to the development of mind and soul, and repeatedly said so; but this did not prevent popular legend from surrounding him with the stories always told of a "yogi." Among those who came to him were a few whom he desired to initiate as *sannyasin*, and after a long course of instruction he did so; but most of those who frequented his classes remained students and disciples. He received the visits of many psychologists and philosophical pundits (among them William James) and was championed by, among others, the electrician Nikola Tesla; Sarah Bernhardt—no doubt out of curiosity more than anything else—took her turn; Emma Calvé, the opera singer, became a real devotee. In the summer of 1895 he took his classes to Thousand Island Park, in the St. Lawrence River, where they lived as in an Indian *ashrama*, each doing his share of the community work.

It was at Thousand Island Park that Vivekananda first began to speak of Ramakrishna. It is a little remarkable that during this whole period (1893-1895) he does not seem to have mentioned his Master either in public or in private. In all probability he felt that the general ignorance of Hinduism which surrounded him required, above all, some enlightenment on fundamental principles before he could go on to anything so startling as the personality of Ramakrishna. It is also probable that he felt some embarrassment at the task of presenting a phenomenon so alien—dear to him, indeed, but very nearly incomprehensible to Western minds. When he felt that his American friends had a basis of acquaintance with the Vedanta, he was ready to talk to them about his own extraordinary *guru* and the enlightenment which had come to him from that source.

The life at Thousand Island Park—of which numerous descriptions exist by the American disciples—was made up of work, teaching and conversation interspersed with long walks in the woods. As has been customary in India for many centuries, the *guru* talked to his disciples on all subjects and answered all questions, keeping to a steady course of instruction in the Vedanta through it all, but mixing the elements so that a funny story or a reminiscence might come in at any moment. This system of instruction is the merest commonplace in India today as always, but nothing of the kind had been seen in America before. He taught from June 19th to August 6th, and some part of what he said was published afterward by the American disciples under the title of *Inspired Talks*. As the students were all Christians, he began with the Gospel of St. John as his text, progressing to the ideas of Maya and self-realization from a Christian base. It was Vivekananda's effort to form a few disciples who could carry on such teaching after his departure, but not in the externally organized form familiar to the West; he had some difficulty making this clear. "Organization" in the Western sense was not in his mind and was alien to Hindu thought: it was an inner organization that he wished to perpetuate by the age-old means of individual instruction in an endless chain. To this end he initiated a few *sannaysin* who seemed to him ready to renounce the world, and then left Thousand Island Park (August 6th) for Paris and London.

He remained in London one month and, allowing for the modulation from one country to the other, repeated his American successes as a public speaker and a private personality. By December he was ready to return to New York for (he thought) the last time, to complete the work he had undertaken there. In this final winter he established the Vedanta Society for the purpose of publishing texts and commentaries on Hindu philosophy. He also delivered three lectures on the ways toward union (*Bhakti-yoga*, *Raja-yoga* and *Karma-yoga*) which aroused wide attention and were put into print immediately, remaining among the best of his published work. He spoke to the graduate philosophy school at Harvard, was offered a professorship in Eastern philosophy there, formed friendships in all directions and appears to have acquired some influence over William James, who in one extant letter addresses him as "Master." The usual clouds of rumor surrounded him, and at home in India the Christian missionaries—whose collections of funds had declined sharply since his arrival in America—spread reports that his diet in the United States was highly unorthodox. Vivekananda's reply does not deny the charge, but asserts that "if the missionaries tell you that I have ever broken the two great vows of the *sannyasin*, chastity and poverty, tell them that they are *big liars*."

The mission of Vivekananda to the West was not, as his fieriest disciples thought at the time, an event bound to change the world's course: it did, however, build a bridge. As Romain Rolland said, "He was the St. Paul of the Messiah of Bengal. He founded his Church and his doctrine. He traveled throughout the world and was the aqueduct, akin to those red arches which span the Roman Campagna, along which the waters of the spirit have flowed from India to the Europes and from the Europes back to India, joining scientific reason to Vedantic faith and the past to the future." All this is true, but on a somewhat more limited scale than the enthusiasts of fifty years ago believed. There is a Vedanta Society in New York today and there are twelve Ramakrishna-Vivekananda Centers in the United States (with a predominantly Christian public), but the influence of the Ramakrishna-Vivekananda revival upon the mind of the West has passed chiefly through individual minds—of which Rolland's was one—without a clearly measurable result upon the general consciousness. It is to India that we must look for the widest and deepest effect of this movement upon men and history.

6

From April to December, 1896, Vivekananda was in London and on the continent of Europe. His London lectures and private lessons on this visit had a more resounding success than before, and he acquired some English disciples who were to follow him to the very end. Among these was Miss Margaret Noble, who became the first nun of the Ramakrishna order under the name of Sister Nivedita, did important work in India—particularly in education for girls—and wrote a number of books on the Hindu revival.

The Swami by this time was so famous that all the Orientalists, even the most academic, were anxious to talk to him, and he became particularly friendly with Professor Max Muller of Oxford, then coming to the end of his long, busy life. (Paul Deussen, professor of philosophy at Kiel, after meeting Vivekananda in Germany, followed him to London and spent some weeks with him.) A visit to Switzerland aroused Vivekananda's nostalgia for the Himalaya and made it certain that his return to India would not be long delayed.

He landed at Ceylon on January 15, 1897, to find himself a national hero of the Hindus. Mobs in the streets, triumphal arches, addresses of welcome—all the apparatus which was to become familiar later with the leaders of the national movement—were his fare, and his progress across India from Ceylon to Madras was one long parade. In Madras itself the preparations were even more elaborate (there were seventeen triumphal arches) and immense multitudes had gathered for darshan. Vive-kananda, who had not expected all this, rose to the occasion, but by the time he had gone through some days of the Madras welcome he could stand no more, and took a boat for Calcutta to avoid the overland parade. At Calcutta the reception was the greatest of all, for along with the national and religious pride there was local Bengali feeling astir. Thousands of people had been waiting around the railroad station for hours before his train came in, and the Swami was overwhelmed with flowers and garlands thrown at him; the horses of his carriage were un-hitched before he had gone far, and a group of Bengali boys pulled him through the beflagged streets and cheering crowds. In his very first public speech in Calcutta, in response to the official welcome of the city, Vivekananda sounded the keynote of his whole movement—a rejuvenation of Hinduism through the Vedanta, abandonment of fanaticism, superstition and hy-pocrisy, and a life of service.

It was this combination ("renunciation and service") which he had now to present to his fellow-monks of the Ramakrishna Order, to whose monastery he went as soon as he could escape the public ceremonies. He had to propose to them some ideas which were not easy to assimilate all at once. They were ac-customed to spending their time in prayer and meditation, con-centrating upon the welfare of their own souls, and he now called upon them to work for their fellow-men, in areas of famine or disease and among the masses. To many of them it seemed that these notions came from the West, and that in Hinduism "self-realization" was the only duty of the *sannyasin*. Vivekananda railed at them: then and later he was to say that his own "realization" or "liberation" mattered little, that the wel-fare of the Indian masses was more important than any individual salvation, and that he was willing to go to hell if he could by doing so be of service to his fellow-men.

His plans for the Ramakrishna Order were unfolded then and during the five remaining years of his life; a considerable groundwork had been laid, and all the main lines of the work well begun, before his death on July 4, 1902. He had to win over his fellow-monks and then, with the aid of the European and American disciples who had followed him to India (some of them wealthy), he had to build the home monastery at Belur on the Ganges and another at Mayavati in the Himalaya. The monastery in the Himalaya was for pure study and contemplation of the Vedanta, with worship of the nameless and formless supreme (no images, rites or ceremonies): the home center at Belur, although disregarding caste and a good many other usages of orthodox Hinduism, was a center of work, employed Hindu forms of worship and meditation and study not unlike the monasteries of the Benedictines in the Middle Ages. Along with this, Vivekananda wanted the monks to engage in work among the poor, the diseased and the sufferers from famine. Two of the monks had already been sent to England and America; others now went to other parts of India to start the philanthropic work of the Ramakrishna Mission. Vivekananda also was bent upon using the Order as a means for promoting the education of the poor and of women, and set about the task as soon as funds permitted.

All this was a great deal for a man who was already exhausted by overwork and religious austerities. Vivekananda was only forty-four when he returned to India in 1897, but he had lived a great deal, both externally and internally. After seeing his work well on its way, he yielded to repeated petitions from the disciples he had left in the West and returned for a final tour of America (1899-1900) and a visit to the Paris Exposition of 1900, where he represented Hinduism at a congress of the history of religions. On his return to India this time he had well-defined symptoms of asthma, diabetes and dropsy, which did not keep him from a schedule of work and travel that held his companions in awe.

During his last months, from March to July, 1902, Vivekananda did not leave the home monastery at Belur. He spoke a number of times to his disciples and to Sister Nivedita of his approaching death, which none of them believed to be so near. He had been busy drawing up rules of discipline, study and work for the Ramakrishna Order, incessantly preaching that "service" was as important as "renunciation" (a new idea to Hindu monasticism), and making spirited attacks upon the various abuses and inadequacies he found in the orthodox. One of his passages with a devout orthodox Hindu who asked him to

give money for the protection of cows became famous. Vivekananda railed at the man; there was then a great famine in the
South. Like Gandhi after him, he accepted Hinduism but did
not allow it to obliterate relative values, and the idea of spending large sums of money to save cows from the butcher while
men died by thousands enraged him. His views on caste, "pollution" and the like were also very similar to Gandhi's, and of
course (like Gandhi) he was himself technically "outcaste"
because he had been across the seas, which, under the old dispensation, no orthodox Hindu could do. Moreover, Vivekananda
had European disciples, both male and female, in his immediate
following, and this again gave offense to the orthodox. The
known sanctity and austerity of his own life, the work begun
and rapidly developed by the Ramakrishna Mission under his
direction, and perhaps most of all the encouragement he had
given the pride and hope of the whole country by his triumphs
in the West, protected Vivekananda against any serious attack
by fanatics, but they could make their disapproval felt.

Some parts of his experience in these last years is difficult for
a Western mind to understand. One was the conviction that he
could name the time of his own death—a conviction shared by
his disciples. (Others, such as his mystical seizure in the cave of
Amarnath in the Himalaya, fall into a category familiar enough,
and comprehensible in such a character as Ramakrishna, for instance, but sound oddly uncharacteristic for Vivekananda.) On
the last day of his life, the Swami meditated for three hours (from
eight to eleven in the morning), taught a Sanskrit grammar
class in the monastery for two and a half hours, enjoyed his
food more than was usual, and took a long walk with a disciple.
That evening at nine o'clock, lying down in his room, he asked
a disciple to fan him and seemed to go into meditation. At 9:10
he was dead. The disciples believed then, and believe today,
that he chose the hour of his departure, just as Sri Ramakrishna
had predicted he would some seventeen years before.

7

The legacy of the great Swami was an organization which has
made an enormous contribution to the awakening of India, to

the revival of Hindu culture, the welfare of the masses and the creation of a national spirit. Vivekananda himself was overwhelmingly, painfully patriotic. From the time he first went to the West, India merged with "the Mother" in his mind as an object of adoration, and his most urgent admonitions to his fellow-monks and the novices during his last years were for service to India. When one of his European followers asked him once what was most necessary to be done, he replied: "Love India!" He believed, and repeatedly said, that India's national religious genius was for renunciation, and his distinctive contribution was to utilize this age-old phenomenon for the service of the masses. His monks had to learn that work for others was a form of devotion to God: that was his lesson repeated in a thousand different ways. He wanted every monastery to have a hostel for the poor and a refectory for all who came; he wanted every monk to realize that working in the garden, cooking, baking, sweeping floors, preparing food for the poorest wayfarer—all of which he did himself—were aspects of worship. The monks were to work among the diseased, in epidemics and famines, among the poorest of the poor, and they were also to be able to teach modern science and Hindu scripture alike. "Don't-touchism"—as he called it—was Vivekananda's enemy in Hindu society as it was Gandhi's afterwards. The caste system, so long as it referred to duties, was right, was part of the Hindu religion, but when it began to inflict penalties and sufferings (as on the pariahs) it was wrong.

The exact codification of Vivekananda's religious belief in any Western sense would be impossible. He was himself an *Advaitin*, a monist, believing that all things were a manifestation of God but that the supreme was unknowable and unnameable; yet he took part in all the rituals of Hindu worship at various times, including simple image-worship. He also would have done the same to Christian forms if he had not been afraid of giving offense. Once in the Alps he was saved by a hair's breadth from falling over a precipice; on the way down the mountain he asked one of his English disciples, Mrs. Sevier, to stop at a wayside shrine and put some wild flowers before the image of the Virgin Mary for him. He did not want to do it himself because there were some Swiss worshippers present. It appears from his voluminous writings that he did not make much distinction between the aspects of divinity worshipped in the great world religions, and a harmony between them was—as it was with his master, Ramakrishna—the highest hope he could entertain for society.

The results of his work were not great in the West, in spite of the excitement that constantly attended him there: in India itself they were invaluable to the nation. There are today some sixty-six monasteries and sixty-six missions of the Ramakrishna Order in India, along with colleges, secondary schools, vocational, agricultural, industrial and primary schools throughout India. The outdoor dispensaries (one of Vivekananda's favorite projects) treated 1,572,019 patients in 1945. There are nine indoor hospitals, a number of *sevashramas* for the feeding and housing of the poor, and a considerable number of institutions for work among women (free clinics for expectant mothers, homes for widows, etc.). Relief work has been undertaken on an emergency basis in every one of the great cataclysms which periodically devastate India. The Ramakrishna Mission's Institute of Culture (Calcutta) conducts lecture courses on everything from the Upanishads to modern American town-planning, and the publishing houses of the organization, both in the Himalaya (at Mayavati) and in Calcutta, Madras and Nagpur have continued to put forth literature in Hindi, Sanskrit and English. There are free libraries and reading rooms attached to a great many of the Mission's institutions throughout the country.

All this is open to everybody, without distinction of caste, religion or nationality. In that respect alone the Ramakrishna Mission was a landmark in the rebirth of India.

The Ramakrishna-Vivekananda centers in the Western world (of which twelve are in the United States) tend to attract forlorn and puzzled Christians more than any others. These centers have regular classes in the Gita and the Upanishads as well as lectures on the harmony between religions. Their effect is difficult to estimate. Even in Vivekananda's lifetime his audiences included a great many devotees of "New Thought," members of the Theosophical Society, and others whose intellectual soundness might be open to doubt. The great Swami had an easy way of dealing with such. Once he was asked (by a member of some "New Thought" society) if he had ever seen an "elemental." Vivekananda replied: "Oh, yes, of course, in India we eat them for breakfast."

Departing entirely from the realm of religion or of mysticism —and forgetting the effects upon philosophy or culture in general—it must be seen that the Ramakrishna-Vivekananda movement stirred Hinduism as it had never been stirred in modern times. There were other movements afoot; nationalism was just getting its breath at the beginning of the twentieth century; Annie Besant was touring India from one end to the other, lecturing the young men (in English) on the splendors of their own heritage; the railroads, the telegraph and the popular press were playing their vital parts in the general drama of awakening; but the most profoundly Hindu element in the Hindu revival will eventually be seen to be (I believe) the monastic mission which bears Ramakrishna's name. It reached into the masses, and wherever its influence was felt the ancient beliefs were seen to be higher and truer than the imprisoning restrictions of modern caste. It preached duty to India in the form of "service" (that word most often on Mahatma Gandhi's lips) and although it was never political, and indeed upon the evidence Ramakrishna was himself unaware of politics, it had vast political effects not included in its conscious program. The call to reform, restore and revive India, to help India in every way possible for human effort, was essentially Vivekananda's call, and of all the makers of modern India, his was the most classless and purely patriotic voice. Until Mahatma Gandhi came home from Africa, twelve years after Vivekananda's death, there was no element in the whole complex of forces which had that one thing without which India could never have awakened—that is, a national appeal from a religious source. Vivekananda knew very well that the Indian masses could be aroused, if ever, only through their religious consciousness, and that any progress made would have to start from the fundamental principle (and perhaps the only principle) of unity in the land. It would not be so in other lands; it was so in India.

8

That is why the student of these matters in mid-century, consulting volumes written only a few decades ago, is taken aback by the distortion of values in them. I have already remarked that the *Cambridge History of India*, Vol. VI, which treats the period 1858-1918 under the title "Indian Empire," mentions Vivekananda only once and Ramakrishna not at all. Neither of them is treated in the *Encyclopaedia Britannica*, either separately or under any of the numerous headings into which that work divides its information on India. The history of India given in that *Encyclopaedia* has room for whole sections on such matters as "The Visit of the Prince of Wales, 1921," but no consideration worthy the name is given to the formidable revival of the Hindu consciousness at the end of the nineteenth century and the beginning of the twentieth.

When this is the case with such solid works of reference, it is to be expected that other books on India would be even more eccentric; and such is the case. Except in the very special class of works written by Indians who are themselves involved and therefore lacking in perspective, there is little notice given the historic importance of what happened to the Hindu mind. We have a mountain of works on ancient Hindu philosophy and religion, a fair amount on anthropology and languages, but practically nothing of serious value about the phenomenon—call it renascence, call it *risorgimento*—which created the conditions of readiness for the genius of Gandhi.

And of course this in its turn is a symptom of the same underlying cause, that which gave India its century of gloom and its decades of struggle, the rule of the foreigner. The British were, on the whole, just rulers or tried to be; but they were foreigners, and to the end of their tenure in India they never seem to have known it. One goes through dozens and dozens of their books without discovering the slightest awareness of the Hindu consciousness as such. Their main interest was administrative—the collection of revenue coming always first, as their books say with refreshing candor—and whole chapters of the British history in India consisted, so far as one can tell from the books, in arguments between themselves on how the "natives" were to be governed, but without so much as a paragraph or even a line of print about what these same "natives" were thinking, feeling or developing within themselves. An immense part of the British literature on India (and it is itself immense) consists of detailed narrative of the long tussle between the Secretary of State for India, in London, and the Viceroy at Calcutta (or later Delhi), on executive power. The Indian Civil Service (originally all British) is good for another great section in the historical treatment. These were no doubt of interest once; but where are the snows of yesteryear? What we should like to know now, and are forced to piece together from whatever we can, is how the miracle of renascence occurred in India like new buds springing under the snow.

The British rule, as is well known, was a fairly accidental and haphazard enterprise in the eighteenth and early nineteenth centuries, with the private profit of the East India Company as its chief objective. The participation of the British Government, increasing after 1833, made it clear to everybody that sooner or later the whole of India would come under the British Crown, but on the whole the conquest, annexation and general subjugation (some of it quite peaceful, by "alliance" with native princes) of the sub-continent was an unplanned, year-to-year, and mainly commercial undertaking. No two provinces were governed alike in those far-off days; local customs were preserved along with British law and new regulations; the local British officials had almost absolute powers in some provinces and were subject to higher law in others; the revenue was collected direct in some and through "farmers" (*zamindari*) in others; there were many different kinds of military establishment in the hodge-podge. In those days not much attention was given to education or other services of welfare to the population, and as there were no telegraphs or railways, the heterogeneous empire was governed more or less at the will of local (British) officials.

A dividing point in the history of British India comes with the Great Mutiny of 1857, when the Sepoys of the Bengal army revolted and set off a fire of national rebellion through Northern and Central India. Like most great events in India, the Mutiny had a religious origin, too: the new Enfield rifles introduced that year had a cartridge with a heavily greased patch at the end. The grease used, by some incredible error on the part of the British supply services, was made of cows' and pigs' fat, thus giving deep offense to Hindus and Muslims both. There might have been some such rebellion in any case: the haphazard, patchwork government of the East India Company had long passed its historical usefulness, the whole of India was now under its sway and the situation demanded some radical change. The Mutiny, as we can see in perspective, was the necessary explosion without which the unification and (relative) modernization of India might have been still longer delayed. After much carnage, the British—commanding Sikhs, Gurkhas and Punjabis, among others—overcame the dethroned princes, their widows, heirs and hangers-on, who had joined with the mutineers, and on August 2, 1858, Queen Victoria signed the act which transferred the Indian subcontinent to the British Crown.

The constitutional situation altered from 1858 to 1910 fundamentally, although not on paper: what occurred was, of course, the revolution in systems of communication. At the time of the Mutiny there were telegraph wires only from Calcutta to Bombay and from Bombay to Madras; there were only a few miles of railway; there was no reliable means of swift communication with London. Within a few decades all that had changed. By 1880 there were 20,000 miles of railway in India, all the main cities and towns were linked by telegraph, and the submarine cable laid through the Red Sea in 1870 had entirely changed the relation of the distant empire and the home government. From that period onward, the government of India was still conducted by the Viceroy with almost unlimited powers, it is true, but he was under the constant check of the India Office, and it all depended very much on personalities, political influence and other elements which have no place in written constitutions. There were some viceroys who acted more or less as messengers of the London government—Lord Elgin, who was Viceroy for a year and a half (1862-1863) used to ask for instructions twice a day. There were others who insisted, like Lord Curzon, on their full autocratic authority and were scarcely to be controlled by any London government. On the whole, it can be said that after the enormous alteration in the conditions of life brought about during the great years of development (1860-1900), when trade boomed, wealth piled high and there was a sudden tightening and acceleration of all lines of communication, the government of India was conducted from London, the Anglo-Indian officials were more and more disregarded (even the British, that is), and India really became, in every respect, a colonial empire.

What the spectator of these vast changes must see, at even so little distance in time, is how brief it all was. The books written in the early part of the present century all speak of the British Empire as if it had endured for long ages and was to last forever. There must have been times in India, around the turn of the century and during the next decade or so, when this seemed to be the fact. But in truth the sprawling, straggling, accidental empire which had grown up in the eighteenth century, produced by the enterprise, greed, bravery and governing genius of certain British soldiers and sailors, only became a real empire, actually knit together and governed from an imperial center, after 1870-1880. The profitable heart of this empire—the only part of it that historically has yielded wealth to the imperial center—was India. If we take the laying of the Red Sea cable (1870) or the proclamation of Queen Victoria as Empress of India (1877) as convenient dates for its beginning and 1947 as the fixed date of its end, it may be seen that it lasted some seventy-odd years, which is less than a moment in the history of a country like India.

True, this integrally imperial period had been preceded by the hodge-podge exploitation of the East India Company, the golden age of the *condottieri* in the eighteenth century, and a general rather discreditable praeludium in which Englishmen, by and large, went to India to get all the money they could squeeze from it; but much of that occurred without the control, approval or even full knowledge of the home government, and falls rather into the category of an irresistible natural development. India was in feudal chaos under the dying Mogul Empire when the vigorous newcomers came, and it was in the nature of the British adventurer, bold, brave and also greedy, to seize what he could get. Pearls by the handful, gold in bars, diamonds and rubies and emeralds in jugs—these are the stories of the wealth

Englishmen brought home from India; the English novels of the early nineteenth century are full of it; but this was still not an empire. The Empire (1877-1947) became self-conscious, aware that it was an empire and determined to be one, only after its own sun had gone past the zenith.

However, these are the thoughts of an observer in retrospect. To an Indian, Hindu or Muslim, the rule of the mighty foreigner must have seemed, around 1900, to be almost as solidly established as the rotation of the seasons. We discern something of that acceptance in the stories of Rudyard Kipling, which deal with Anglo-Indian life from the point of view of the army. Into this view of life there penetrates no concept of the deep seriousness of Indian religious consciousness, that secret union and common pool of the voiceless millions. Even today India is 87% illiterate, which means that out of four hundred million people some 348,000,000 can neither read nor write. Hindu religion is mentioned in Anglo-Indian literature chiefly as a source of humor—as on religious festivals when the "natives" have "quaint" customs—or in the light of pseudo-occult revelations of one sort or another. There were British scholars of the first rank who studied the Hindu scriptures and wrote works of quality upon them, but little of this penetrated into the life of the "Empire." The "Empire" expressed itself most characteristically—and also with most life, color and humanity—in Kipling, whose knowledge of the physical existence of India has seldom been equaled. Not even among Indian writers does such a sense of the vast country, its violent extremes and its innumerable varying peoples, seem to inhabit the printed page; and yet in Kipling, who knew India so well, is there to be found any suggestion of what constitutes the basis of the Hindu consciousness.

This "imperial" period at the end of the nineteenth century is the one in which Ramakrishna, Vivekananda, Gandhi, Tagore, Aurobindo Ghose, Bhagavan Das and the Maharshi all grew us; its ideas and prejudices, its limitations and opportunities, established the external environment, the social geography, for every aspiring youth, directing his steps into courses of study, thought and habit alien to those of his ancestors because only through the English system, with the English language and law, could

any effort be made amongst his fellow-men on the higher levels
(the surface of life) from which the destinies of the submerged
millions were ostensibly controlled.

Thus we are to imagine the sensitive and gifted Hindu youths
of sixty or seventy years ago divided, psychologically, between
an inner life which reached back through the ages to the Vedic
forest and dreamed of God, and an outer life which had to con-
form to the customs introduced by an imperial stranger with
strictly practical notions of social relations. The British came
into India with pledges to respect the religions of the inhabitants
("Shaster and Coran," as they put it), and the pledges were, on
the whole, kept even to excess, even to honoring the abuses of
those religions; but respect did not always go hand-in-hand with
understanding. The Hindu youth came up against incomprehension from the moment (at the age of fourteen or so) when
he began to study the foreign master's ways. The hurt and puzzled responses of the heart do not even have to be imagined:
we have records of them in numerous books, including Gandhi's
autobiography. Generations were wounded in their most intimate feeling, their reverence for their own families and ancestors, their awe of the Vedic gods, by the rude hands and voices
of the conqueror. Christian missionaries came to India to convert the "heathen," and the gentlest of men, Gandhi himself,
felt in his boyhood the depth of this insult to his religious consciousness. Wherever administration made contact with the people, whenever a railway ticket was bought or a tax paid, and
even in the most casual encounters in the city streets or country
roads, the Indian (Hindu or Muslim) was made aware of his
subsidiary status to the "sahib," the white master. All were alike
subjects of the Queen-Empress, true; but there were different
classes of subjects and the Indian was, he must often have felt,
the lowest.

Along with this constant humiliation—a humiliation which was
a condition of life, never lessened or altered or mitigated by any
circumstance—there went, of course, a realization of what England had brought to India. Sometimes this realization was reluctant, sometimes it was not admitted; at the height of the
national struggle it was often even denied. I have yet to meet an
Indian, however, who does not, in ordinary informal conversa-

tion, recognize the benefits of the British interlude. It is clearly understood that most of what the British did—roads, railways, telegraphs and administrative uniformity leading to unity—was done for the advantage of Britain; it is also frequently stated that none of these things was done well enough or on a large enough scale; it is also obvious that the profit to England—dwindling in the present century, but colossal throughout the nineteenth—was financially much greater than the benefit to India. Even so, one has only to review, however briefly, the course of the British in India to see that without them India's development would have been vastly retarded: there might not have occurred an Indian renaissance even yet.

The young Hindu toward the end of the nineteenth century had, in his heart of hearts, to be grateful to the British for the powerful aid they had brought to social reform in India. He had also to recognize that without the British the fragmentation of India into warring feudal states, the exploitation by conscienceless princes, the general medievalism of techniques and economic life, the cruelty of rich toward poor and the illiteracy of the masses might have continued unrelieved for another hundred years or so. The British could have done much more, certainly; but the little that they did was more than would have come to pass without them. This, too, helped to create among educated Hindus of seventy or eighty years ago a feeling that India was doomed, that there was some decay of a vital principle at work, that the foreigner was indeed naturally superior and would always remain so, and that there was small hope for the masses in a land where even the princes were slaves. This is what is called the "inferiority complex" of the nineteenth century in India, brought into being not only by the worst aspects of foreign rule, but also—and perhaps even more—by the best.

We have seen two quite different but complementary responses to this social and historical situation. In the first, Ramakrishna took refuge in the trances and visions of a religious ascetic in a temple garden; in the second, Vivekananda, drawing his strength from that same religious pool common to all Hindus, tried to revive the sense of ancient splendor in the Hindu truth and a national pride of religious origin (the only kind possible to evoke at that stage of development). It was his contribution to Indian nationhood—whether he got it from the West, from his own temperament and spirit, or from the ancient scriptures he knew so well—to interpret social and patriotic service as a religious duty, and to impress that view upon millions of Indians who had had only the most rudimentary notions of patriotism before.

Ramakrishna and Vivekananda represented tendencies that had always been present in Hindu life, and indeed Ramakrishna's retirement—if it had not been haunted in his last five years by a sense of mission to be passed on to others—might have gone as unperceived as those of thousands of other *sadhus* who through the centuries have withdrawn from the brutal world. In his case, metempsychosis justified itself on a highly practical plane, for although he himself renounced the world and withdrew from it for good, he returned to it after his own death in the work of his powerful disciple. There were others—such as Tilak in Bombay—who at the end of the nineteenth century transmuted the national feeling of humiliation into a sort of militant nationalism which was to provide another strain in the coming revolution. There were some foreigners who contributed to the Hindu awakening by coming to India to learn something: Madame Blavatsky, the founder of the Theosophical Society, although she may herself have been the most unmitigated quack, played just such a part because she made many Hindus turn back to their own ancestral sources for strength. If a foreign lady of importance (so we can imagine the young Hindu intellectual of Bombay or Calcutta thinking), who no doubt has access to all the treasures of the world, comes to our poor India to seek the truth, then perhaps we have something of our own to contribute: perhaps we are not merely slaves and providers of wealth for the British Empire, but heirs to a special knowledge which it is erroneous to forget or neglect. (Annie Besant, later on, still more powerfully contributed to this reminder by her many long lecture tours in all parts of India.)

The buds were, then, astir with life. The British contributed to the renaissance more than they knew and more than the Indians even now are eager to admit. But as the nineteenth century came to an end there was a harmony of opinion among those who felt most deeply the coming of the dawn—in the

Brahmo Samaj, with the Tagores, with Vivekananda's monks and Tilak's scholars, even among the enlightened businessmen such as Tata—which held that every force of progress in India tended toward unity. That this might be national in form was the aim of many, but that it would be religious in origin was the conviction of all. India's philosophical difference from all other countries, producing its millennial isolation between the seas and the Himalaya, now came to life again in the realization that one source of strength for the countless millions of the oppressed, perhaps their only real source of strength, the secret of their being, was the religious consciousness in which they were— beyond and above the multitudinous diversity of forms—more united than other peoples, more essentially one. Thus a psychological readiness for the mission of Mahatma Gandhi came into existence just as he was about to fulfill it.

GANDHI'S HYMNS

The two Christian hymns which Gandhi loved above all others are associated with his name in India. They have become familiar far beyond the bounds of the Christian churches, because the Mahatma caused them to be sung and played so often. Their texts are given in full because his choice of these particular hymns sheds much light upon his own religious personality.

Lead, Kindly Light

Lead, kindly Light, amid th' encircling gloom,
 Lead Thou me on:
The night is dark, and I am far from home,
 Lead Thou me on!
Keep Thou my feet! I do not ask to see
The distant scene; one step enough for me.

I was not ever thus, nor prayed that Thou
 Shouldst lead me on;
I loved to choose and see my path; but now
 Lead Thou me on!
I loved the garish day; and spite of fears,
Pride ruled my will: remember not past years.

So long Thy power hath blest me, sure it still
 Will lead me on
O'er moor and fen, o'er crag and torrent, till
 The night is gone;
And with the morn those angel faces smile,
Which I have loved long since, and lost awhile.

J. H. Newman

When I Survey the Wondrous Cross

When I survey the wondrous cross
 On which the Prince of glory died,
My richest gain I count but loss,
 And pour contempt on all my pride.

Forbid it, Lord, that I should boast,
 Save in the Cross of Christ, my God:
All the vain things that charm me most,
 I sacrifice them to His blood.

See, from His head, His hands, His feet,
 Sorrow and love flow mingled down!
Did e'er such love and sorrow meet?
 Or thorns compose so rich a crown?

Were the whole realm of nature mine,
 That were a tribute far too small;
Love so amazing, so divine,
 Demands my soul, my life, my all.

Isaac Watts

Altekar, Dr. A. S.: *Benares and Sarnath: Past and Present,* Culture Publication House, Benares Hindu University, 1947.

Aurobindo, Shri: *Essays on the Gita,* 2 vols., Arya Publishing House, Calcutta, 1928.

——— *Evolution,* Arya Publishing House, Calcutta, 1944.

——— *Heraclitus,* Arya Publishing House, Calcutta, 1941.

——— *The Life Divine,* 2 vols., Arya Publishing House, Calcutta, 1944.

Besant, Annie: *How India Wrought for Freedom* (The Story of the National Congress told from Official Records), Theosophical Publishing House, London, 1915.

Bevan, Edwyn: *Indian Nationalism,* Macmillan and Co., Ltd., London, 1914.

Bloomfield, Maurice: *The Religion of the Veda,* G. P. Putnam's Sons, New York, 1908.

Burnet, John: *Early Greek Philosophy,* A. and C. Black, London, 1920.

Cambridge History of India, 6 vols., ed. by H. H. Dodwell, Cambridge University Press, 1932.

Cave, Sydney: *Redemption, Hindu and Christian,* Oxford University Press, 1919.

Chakravarti, Sures Chandra: *The Philosophy of the Upanishads,* University of Calcutta, 1935.

Crooke, W.: *The Popular Religion and Folk-Lore of Northern India,* 2 vols., Archibald Constable & Co., London, 1896.

Cumming, Sir John (Editor): *Political India 1832-1932*, Oxford University Press, 1932.

Das, Bhagavan: *The Fundamental Psychological Principles of World-wide Social Reconstruction and "A British-Indian Commonwealth" as a Beginning*, Benares, 1944.

―― *Mystic Experiences*, Theosophical Society, Benares, 1944.

―― *The Science of the Self*, The Indian Bookshop, Benares, 1938.

Deussen, Paul: *The Vedanta System of Philosophy*, trans. by J. H. Woods and C. B. Runkle, Harvard University Press, Cambridge, 1906.

Dutt, R. Palme: *India To-Day*, Victor Gollancz Ltd., London, 1940.

Eddington, A. S.: *The Nature of the Physical World*, The Macmillan Co., New York, 1944.

Eliot, Sir Charles: *Hinduism and Buddhism*, 3 vols., Edward Arnold and Co., London, 1921.

Farquhar, J. N.: *An Outline of the Religious Literature of India*, Oxford University Press, 1920.

Gandhi, M. K.: *An Autobiography or the Story of My Experiments with Truth*, Navajivan Publishing House, Ahmedabad, 1945.

―― *Mahatma Gandhi: His Own Story*, ed. by C. F. Andrews, George Allen and Unwin Ltd., London, 1930.

―― *Gandhiji's Correspondence with the Government 1942-44*, Navajivan Publishing House, Ahmedabad, 1945.

Gita, The Bhagavad (*The Song of the Good Lord*): *The Gita . . . The Gospel of the Lord Shri Krishna*, trans. by Shri Purohit Swami, Faber and Faber, Ltd., London, 1935.

―― *The Gospel of Selfless Action, or the Gita According to Gandhi*, ed. by Mahadev Desai. (Gandhi's Gujarati translation, and notes, with an additional introduction and commentary.) Navajivan Press, Ahmedabad, 1946.

―― Other editions of the *Gita*, in translation with or without the original Sanskrit, by Bhagavan Das and Annie Besant, Benares, 1905; by Professor Radhakrishnan, New York, 1948; by Christopher Isherwood, Los Angeles, 1948.

Griswold, H. D.: *The Religion of the Rigveda* (in "The Religious Quest of India" series), Oxford University Press, 1923.

Havell, E. B.: *The Ideals of Indian Art*, John Murray, London, 1920.

Jaini, Jagmanderlal: *Outlines of Jainism*, ed. by F. W. Thomas, Cambridge University Press, 1940.

James, William: *The Varieties of Religious Experience, 1901-1902*. (Invaluable for this subject; obtainable in Modern Library. V.S.)

Kalidasa: *Shakuntala and Other Works*, trans. by Arthur W. Ryder, J. M. Dent and Sons, London, 1920.

Keith, A. Berriedale: *Buddhist Philosophy in India and Ceylon*, Clarendon Press, Oxford, 1923.

—— *A History of Sanskrit Literature*, Clarendon Press, Oxford, 1928.

—— *The Religion and Philosophy of the Veda and Upanishads*, vol. 31, Harvard Oriental Series, Harvard University Press, 1925.

Kulkarni, V. B.: *The Future of Indian States*, Thacker and Co., Bombay, 1944.

Lyall, Sir Aifred: *Asiatic Studies, Religious and Social*, John Murray, London, 1899.

MacDonell, Arthur A.: *A History of Sanskrit Literature*, D. Appleton and Co., New York, 1900.

Mac Munn, Sir George: *Turmoil and Tragedy in India, 1914 and After*, Jarrolds, Ltd., London, 1935.

Maha-Bharata, The: Condensed into English Verse by Romesh C. Dutt, Kitabistan, Allahabad, 1944.

Majumdar, R. C. and Raychaudhuri, H. C. and Datta, Kalinkar: *An Advanced History of India*, Macmillan and Co., Ltd., London, 1946.

Moreland, W. H. and Chatterjee, Atul C.: *A Short History of India*, Longmans, Green and Co., New York, 1936.

Murray, Gilbert: *Five Stages of Greek Religion*, Columbia University Press, 1925.

Muzumdar, Haridas T.: *Gandhi Triumphant! The Inside Story of the Historic Fast*, Universal Publishing Co., New York, 1939.

Oldenberg, Dr. Hermann: *Buddha: His Life, His Doctrine, His Order*, trans. by William Hoey, Luzac and Co., London, 1928.

Oman, John Campbell: *Cults, Customs and Superstitions of India*, George W. Jacobs and Co., Philadelphia, 1908.

—— *The Great Indian Epics—The Stories of the Ramayana and the Mahabharata*, George Routledge and Sons, Ltd., London, 1895.

Otto, Rudolf: *India's Religion of Grace and Christianity Compared and Contrasted*, trans. by Frank Hugh Foster, Macmillan Co., New York, 1930.

—— *Mysticism East and West*, trans. by Bertha L. Bracey and Richenda C. Payne, The Macmillan Co., New York, 1932.

Radhakrishnan, S.: *An Idealist View of Life*, Hibbert Lectures for 1929, London, 1932.

—— *Gautama the Buddha*, Bombay, 1945.

—— *Indian Philosophy*, 2 vols., George Allen and Unwin, Ltd., London, 1931. (Most important. V.S.)

—— *Religion and Society*, George Allen and Unwin, Ltd., London, 1947.

Rai, Lajpat: *The Political Future of India*, B. W. Huebsch, Inc., New York, 1921.

Rajagopalachari, C.: *Vedanta, the Basic Culture of India*, The Hindustan Times, New Delhi, 1946.

Rajput, A. B.: *Maulana Abul Kalam Azad*, A Lion Publication.

Ramakrishna, Sri: *The Gospel of Ramakrishna*, trans. into English with an introduction, by Swami Nikhilananda, Ramakrishna-Vivekananda Center, New York, 1942.

—— *The Teachings of Ramakrishna*, Mayavati, Almora, Himalayas, 1944.

Raman, T. A.: *What Does Gandhi Want?*, Oxford University Press, New York, 1942.

Ramayana, The: Condensed into English Verse by Romesh C. Dutt, Kitabistan, Allahabad, 1944.

Ravoof, A. A.: *Meet Mr. Jinnah*, Muhammad Ashraf, Kashmiri Bazar, Lahore, 1947.

Rolland, Romain: *The Life of Ramakrishna,* Mayavati, Almora, Himalayas, 1944.

Saunders, Kenneth: *Buddhism,* Robert McBride and Co., New York (after 1927).

Sen, Gertrude Emerson: *Voiceless India*, Indian Publishers, Benares, 1946.

Singh, Anup: *Nehru, The Rising Star of India*, John Day Co., New York, 1939.

Smith, Wilfred Cantwell: *Modern Islam in India*, Victor Gollancz, London, 1946.

Smith, William Roy: *Nationalism and Reform in India,* Yale University Press, New Haven, 1938.

Socialist Party Policy Statement, Socialist Party Central Office, Bombay, September, 1947.

Socialist Party Programme, Socialist Party Central Office, Bombay, October, 1947.

Stevenson, Mrs. Sinclair: *The Rites of the Twice-Born*, Oxford University Press, 1920.

Smith, Vincent: *The Oxford History of India,* Oxford Press, 1921.

Tagore, Rabindranath: *Collected Poems and Plays*, The Macmillan Co., New York, 1941.

—— *The Gardener*, Macmillan and Co., Ltd., London, 1943.

—— *Gora*, London, 1924.

—— *The Home and the World*, trans. by Surendranath Tagore, The Macmillan Co., New York, 1915.

—— *Hungry Stones and Other Stories*, Macmillan and Co., Ltd., London, 1943.

—— *The Religion of Man*, The Macmillan Co., New York, 1931.

—— *Reminiscences*, Macmillan and Co., Ltd., London, 1944.

—— *Sadhana, the Realization of Life* (The Harvard Lectures), The Macmillan Co., New York, 1913.

Thomas, Wendell: *Hinduism Invades America*, The Beacon Press, New York, 1930.

Thompson, Edward: *Rabindranath Tagore, Poet and Dramatist*, Oxford University Press, London, 1926.

Thoreau, Henry David: *Cape Cod and Miscellanies*, Houghton Mifflin & Co., Boston, 1906.

Upanishads, The Ten Principal: Put into English by Shree Purohit Swami and W. B. Yeats, Faber and Faber, Ltd., London, 1937 and The Macmillan Co., New York, 1937.

Urquhart, W. S.: *The Vedanta and Modern Thought*, Oxford University Press, 1928.

Whitehead, A. N.: *Science and the Modern World* (The Lowell Lectures, 1925), The Macmillan Co., New York, 1944.

Whitehead, Henry: *The Village Gods of South India*, Oxford University Press, 1921.

Woolacott, J. E.: *India on Trial, A Study of Present Conditions*, Macmillan and Co., Ltd., London, 1929.

Zeller, Dr. E.: *A History of Greek Philosophy*, trans. by S. F. Alleyne, Longmans. Green and Co., London, 1881.

M